Indigenous Rights and United Nations Standards

Self-Determination, Culture and Land

Alexandra Xanthaki

CAMBRIDGE
UNIVERSITY PRESS

CAMBRIDGE UNIVERSITY PRESS
Cambridge, New York, Melbourne, Madrid, Cape Town, Singapore, São Paulo, Delhi

Cambridge University Press
The Edinburgh Building, Cambridge CB2 8RU, UK

Published in the United States of America by Cambridge University Press, New York

www.cambridge.org
Information on this title: www.cambridge.org/9780521835749

First published 2007
Reprinted 2008

A catalogue record for this publication is available from the British Library

ISBN 978-0-521-83574-9 hardback

Transferred to digital printing 2009

Indigenous Rights and United Nations Standards

The debate on indigenous rights has revealed some serious difficulties for current international law, posed mainly by different understandings of important concepts. This book explores the extent to which indigenous claims, as recorded in the United Nations fora, can be accommodated by current international law. By doing so, it also highlights how the indigenous debate has stretched the contours and ultimately evolved international human rights standards. The book first reflects on the international law responses to the theoretical arguments on cultural membership. After a comprehensive analysis of the existing instruments on indigenous rights, the discussion turns to self-determination. Different views are assessed and a fresh perspective on the right to self-determination is outlined. Ultimately, the author refuses to shy away from difficult questions and challenging issues and offers a comprehensive discussion of indigenous rights and their contribution to international law.

ALEXANDRA XANTHAKI is a lecturer in International Human Rights at Brunel University. After graduating from Athens Law Faculty, Alexandra completed an LLM in Human Rights at Queens University, Belfast, and later a PhD at Keele University under the supervision of P. Thornberry. She has published on human rights, group rights and indigenous rights and has repeatedly acted as a consultant to the United Nations Special Rapporteur on Indigenous Issues. She has participated in several projects funded by the European Commission, DfID and international NGOs in the UK, Greece and Ukraine. She is a member of the Athens Bar.

Established in 1946, this series produces high quality scholarship in the fields of public and private international law and comparative law. Although these are distinct legal sub-disciplines, developments since 1946 confirm their interrelation.

Comparative law is increasingly used as a tool in the making of law at national, regional and international levels. Private international law is now often affected by international conventions, and the issues faced by classical conflicts rules are frequently dealt with by substantive harmonisation of law under international auspices. Mixed international arbitrations, especially those involving state economic activity, raise mixed questions of public and private international law, while in many fields (such as the protection of human rights and democratic standards, investment guarantees and international criminal law) international and national systems interact. National constitutional arrangements relating to 'foreign affairs', and to the implementation of international norms, are a focus of attention.

The Board welcomes works of a theoretical or interdisciplinary character, and those focusing on the new approaches to international or comparative law or conflicts of law. Studies of particular institutions or problems are equally welcome, as are translations of the best work published in other languages.

A list of books in the series can be found at the end of this volume.

Contents

Table of cases

International courts

League of Nations

Permanent Court of Justice

International Court of Justice

United Nations Human Rights Committee

Regional courts

African Commission on Human Rights

Inter-American Commission on Human Rights

European Court on Human Rights

National Courts

Australia

Canada

Norway

United States

Table of statutes

United Nations documents

Conventions and Treaties

Declarations

Commission Drafting Group/WGIP/other indigenous fora:
UN Doc. E/CN.4/Sub.2/404 179

UN Doc. E/CN.4/Sub.2/1982/33, Report of the WGIP on its First Session 176

UN Doc. E/CN.4/Sub.2/1985/22 121

UN Doc. E/CN.4/Sub.2/AC.4/1990/3 (Comments on the First Revised Text of the Draft declaration on Rights of Indigenous Peoples) 39, 167, 193

UN Doc. E/CN.4/Sub.2/1991/34 (Working Paper on the Ownership and Control of the Cultural Property of Indigenous Peoples, Erica-Irene Daes) 232

UN Doc. E/CN.4/Sub.2/1991/39,2 12

Statement of the Representative of the Four Directions Council during the 10th Session of the WGIP (1992) 193

UN Doc. E/CN.4/Sub.2/1992/31 (Technical Conference on Practical Experience in the Realisation of Sustainable and Environmentally Sound Self-Development of Indigenous Peoples, Santiago, Chile, 18–22 May 1992) 236

UN Doc. E/CN.4/1993/29 121

UN Doc. E/CN.4/Sub.2/1993/26/Add1 (Explanatory Note concerning the Draft Declaration on the Rights of Indigenous Peoples, Erica-Irene Daes) 187, 189

UN Doc. E/CN.4/Sub.2/1993/28 (Study on the Cultural and Intellectual Property of Indigenous Peoples, Erica-Irene Daes) 227

UN Doc. E/CN.4/Sub.2/AC.4/1993/10 (Future Role of the Working Group: Working Paper submitted by Mr Miguel Alfonso Martinez, Member of the Working Group) 10

UN Doc. E/CN.4/Sub.2/AC.4/1993/1 124

UN Doc. E/CN.4/Sub.2/AC.4/1993/8 11

UN Doc. E/CN.4/Sub.2/1994/2 (Technical Review of the Draft Declaration) 121, 125, 232

UN Doc. E/CN.4/Sub.2/1994/31, Preliminary Report of the Special Rapporteur Erica-Irene Daes submitted in conformity with Sub-Commission Resolution 1993/44 230

Other Anti-Discrimination Committees/Fora:

Committee of the Rights of the Child:

Economic, Social and Cultural Rights Committee:

Concluding Observations: Philippines, UN Doc. CCPR/CO/79/PHIL of 1 December 2003 229

Concluding Observations: Suriname, UN Doc. CCPR/C/82/SURI of 4 May 2004 228, 274

Concluding Observations: Colombia, UN Doc. CCPR/CO/80/COL of 26 May 2004 126, 274

Concluding Observations: Finland, UN Doc. CCPR/C/82/FIN of 2 December 2004 228, 275

Concluding Observations: Greece, UN Doc. CCPR/CO/83/GRC of 25 April 2005 45

Concluding Observations: Thailand, UN Doc. CCPR/CO/84/THA of 8 July 2005 228, 256, 274, 275

Concluding Observations: Uganda, UN Doc. CCPR/CO/80/UGA of 4 May 2005 45

Concluding Observations: Thailand, UN Doc. CCPR/CO/84/THA5 of 20 April 2006 124

Concluding Observations: Canada, UN Doc. CCPR/C/CAN/CO/5 of 20 April 2006 37, 46, 125, 271

Concluding Observations: Congo, UN Doc. CCPR/C/COD/CO/3 of 27 March 2006 124

List of Issues to be taken up in connection with the Consideration of the Second and Third Periodic Reports of the United States of America, UN Doc. CCPR/C/Q/3 of 30 March 2006 271–2

Sub-Commission on Minorities:

Study by the Special Rapporteur Francesco Capotorti on the Rights of Persons belonging to Ethnic, Religious and Linguistic Minorities for the Sub-Commission on the Prevention of Discrimination and Protection of Minorities, UN Doc. E/CN.4/Sub.2/384/Add. 1–7 229

UN Doc. E/CN.4/Sub.2/AC.5/1997/WP.7 (The Right of Persons belonging to Minorities to enjoy their own Culture, M. Schulte-Tenckhoff) 42

UNESCO:

Florence Agreement on the Importance of Educational, Scientific and Cultural Rights (1950) 234

International Labour Organisation documents

Conventions/Declarations

Requests, Observations and Reports

Other international instruments

Regional documents

Africa

Americas

Europe

Indigenous Organisations' documentation

National legislation/documentation

Australia

Cambodia

Canada

Guatemala

Norway

Pakistan

Philippines

Russian Federation

South Africa

United States

Venezuela

Vietnam

Acknowledgments

Several people have been instrumental in completing this book. First, I would like to thank the indigenous representatives in the United Nations fora who allowed me to obtain an insight into their struggle. I also owe a special debt to Patrick Thornberry who introduced me to indigenous rights, infected me with his enthusiasm and gave me invaluable guidance, initially as my supervisor for the doctoral dissertation out of which the book grew and later as a mentor and friend. Dominic McGoldrick also encouraged me and pushed me in ways that went beyond his original involvement as examiner of my dissertation. Gudmundur Alfredsson, the other examiner of the dissertation, provided me with helpful comments and the invaluable opportunity to work closely with the United Nations Special Rapporteur Rodolfo Stavenhagen. My involvement with the Special Rapporteur greatly strengthened my knowledge of national practice on indigenous rights and my confidence to write this book; I would like to thank him for both. I would also like to thank James Crawford, Finola O'Sullivan, Jane O'Regan, Wendy Gater and Laurence Marsh for their patience and practical help at all stages of the process and the anonymous assessors for their invaluable comments. Other people who have helped me and encouraged me in different ways include Stephen Allen, Erica-Irene Daes, Julian Burger, Everaldo Fernandez, Nazila Ghanea, Emmanuel Melissaris, George Pavlakos, Constantin Stefanou, Francesca Thornberry and Dawn Sedman. Special thanks to Panos Koutrakos for all his help and advice and to Evaggelia and Ioannis Premetis for being close to me in this journey. My parents, Efthimia and Alexander Xanthakis, provided a constant flow of love and support; their patience and great sense of humour were seriously challenged at times. Finally, without the funny and sometimes serious chats with Helen Xanthaki and the unconditional love, support and at times amazing optimism of Richard Race this book would not have been completed.

Introduction

Indigenous rights are currently at the forefront of the international human rights agenda. It is widely recognised that indigenous peoples are among the most marginalised and vulnerable around the world and their human rights situation is in need of urgent attention. International bodies have undertaken the challenge to help improve the situation of these communities. However, opinions differ about the relevant policies of states, the measures that must be taken and, ultimately, the rights that must be recognised as vested in these communities. Should they be given special protection? And to what extent? Should they have the right to decide on matters that affect them, even when such decisions affect the wider population of the state? This book will look at the responses that current international law offers to such questions.

These questions are already the focus of an ongoing international discussion, a discussion in which indigenous peoples have managed to secure a strong voice. Although dispersed around the world, their common characteristics and common history of oppression, discrimination and disrespect have led to shared claims at the international level. These communities would seem in the first instance unlikely protagonists of an international movement, because of their vulnerability, their scarce resources and the often limited modes of communicating with other communities due to different languages and poor transport.[1] Yet, since 1977 when over 150 indigenous representatives attended a United Nations conference on discrimination against their communities, indigenous peoples have been increasingly active at the international level. Through cooperation, they have succeeded to bring the claims of their communities to the forefront of the international agenda and to actively involve international organisations in their struggle. Anghie questions whether the post-colonial world can 'deploy for its own purposes the law which had enabled its suppression in the first place'.[2] This is exactly what indigenous peoples are trying to do. In their quest for justice, indigenous representatives have placed a lot of faith in the United Nations and its international law. Through tight cooperation, intense lobbying and deep knowledge of the system, they have used openings in the organisation and have created new opportunities for their participation and further influence of the decision-making processes. Grounding their demands on the existing applicable human rights principles, they have articulated a vision for their communities that is different from other actors; a vision they have firmly framed in the language of international law.[3] Although indigenous peoples have not been part of the creation of international law, they have refused to stand on its periphery and have been determined to become equal partners in its evolution. In a relatively short time they have managed to get their voices heard, have shifted attitudes and initiated a wave of intense international support for their claims.

This wave of support has been an important factor for the establishment of several United Nations fora on indigenous issues. The most enduring has been the Working Group on Indigenous Populations (WGIP), widely viewed as a great success of the United Nations system. Established by the Sub-Commission in 1982, just after the Cobo study reported that indigenous peoples are separate peoples who have been denied their rights, the WGIP has been the first body in the international arena entrusted to review developments pertaining to the human rights of indigenous peoples and to give attention to the evolution of standards concerning indigenous rights.[4] The discussions of the group have substantially contributed to the better understanding of past experiences and contemporary claims of these communities and have initiated meaningful exchange of opinions between indigenous representatives and states. Attendance has been monumental for a group of this kind; each session has been attracting up to 700 individuals. The WGIP has been the only United Nations working group where the interested party has shown such commitment and enthusiasm. The WGIP has become an institution and a 'training field' for indigenous peoples.[5] Their representatives have constantly been pushing the boundaries for greater participation in the deliberations of the group and with the help of very supportive chairpersons, not least Erica-Irene Daes, the WGIP Chairperson from mid-1980s until very recently, they have achieved almost equal rights to those of states. From 1985 to 1993, the group has been working towards a draft Declaration on the Rights of Indigenous Peoples (draft Declaration). After the text was adopted by the Sub-Commission, another working group of the then Commission on Human Rights was created to further elaborate the draft Declaration (Commission Drafting Group). Since the establishment of the Commission Drafting Group, the future of the WGIP has been questioned. Some commentators believe that it has a permanent role to play in securing recognition and protection of indigenous rights; others view it as a medium-term forum to be replaced gradually by the Permanent Forum on Indigenous Issues.[6] The future of the Group is further challenged by the recent changes in the UN structure. Still, the WGIP has been an essential platform on the international stage for indigenous peoples from all around the world to come together, articulate their claims and further a common vision about their status.[7]

The Commission Drafting Group has been meeting since 1995 to further elaborate the draft Declaration.[8] The polarisation of positions on important aspects of the text has had a disastrous effect on progress in adopting the draft Declaration. Agreement on the Declaration has not been reached in 2006; the process has taken much longer than originally anticipated by many and doubts about its eventual success have been expressed during the last few years. Yet, one must not forget the positives that have emerged from the process: international law's need to protect these communities has been widely accepted; indigenous active participation in the formation and setting up of such protection has also been agreed. Procedurally, indigenous peoples have strengthened their position: after endless pressure, indigenous representatives have been given the floor as frequently as states; they have been given access to informal consultations with governments; and their proposals have been included in the annual reports to the Commission. These are great steps both in general and in terms of the specific, given the high status of the Commission within the previous UN hierarchy, let alone its political nature. In assessing the work of the Commission Drafting Group, the unexpected changes in the opinions of states on controversial rights must also not be forgotten; such changes can be attributed to a degree to the understanding of indigenous peoples' positions reached after intense and lengthy discussions during the meetings of the Working Group. Such discussions have also exposed the lacunae in current international law concerning the protection of indigenous peoples and have even challenged the existing system of international human rights. Since its creation the basis of discussion was the text agreed by the

WGIP, but the text sent and adopted by the newly created Council of Human Rights in 2006 was diluted. The draft was not adopted by the General Assembly in November 2006. Indigenous suggestions for an alternative understanding of several principles of international law have caused profound discussions on issues concerning collective rights, special measures, land claims and restitution. At the core of the debate lies the right of self-determination and the question of whether indigenous peoples should enjoy it; its radical interpretation by indigenous groups has put into question the understanding of the right as well as its place in international law. These are the issues on which this book will focus, since they are the claims on which the transnational indigenous movement itself has chosen to focus.

Increasing awareness of indigenous issues strengthened the argument that a permanent platform for discussion and elaboration of indigenous issues was essential. The idea of a permanent forum, initiated by indigenous representatives, members of the WGIP and many member states of the United Nations, was put forward by the Vienna World Conference and was adopted by the United Nations General Assembly.[9] In April 2000, the Permanent Forum on Indigenous Issues (Permanent Forum) was established as a subsidiary body of the Economic and Social Council.[10] Contrary to both working groups, the Permanent Forum is a permanent body of the ECOSOC (thus very high in the United Nations hierarchy), whose mandate goes beyond human rights to include issues such as economic and social development, culture, the environment, education and health. The Forum has satisfied claims for sui generis status of indigenous peoples in the United Nations, claims justified on the basis of past injustices that such peoples have suffered[11] and the scale of their cultural differences measured against the populations living in the same states.[12] As indigenous peoples are not merely groups organised around particular issues, but long-standing communities with historically rooted cultures and distinct political and social institutions, it was argued that they should be entitled to have a presence in their own right in the international arena, rather than as representatives of a segment of the civil society.[13] The Permanent Forum consists of eight independent experts appointed by the governments and eight selected by indigenous peoples themselves;[14] this makes the Permanent Forum the first United Nations body whose membership extends beyond governments and independent experts. All these attributes create a valid argument for the Permanent Forum being the most significant step taken so far by the United

Nations to recognise indigenous peoples' real status.[15] Certainly, the Permanent Forum has made important recommendations on indigenous health; prior informed consent and participatory research guidelines; indigenous children and youth; collection of data; indigenous women; and matters related to poverty and development goals. However, it has been argued that the real difference this body could make would be in coordinating and evaluating all indigenous activities within the United Nations.[16] Such focus would address fears about duplication, conflicting programmes and waste of UN resources.[17]

The Permanent Forum works closely with the United Nations Special Rapporteur on the question of human rights and fundamental freedoms of indigenous peoples, Rodolfo Stavenhagen. Since the establishment of his post in 2001, the Special Rapporteur has reported on issues close to indigenous peoples' hearts. These include the impact of development projects; human rights issues in the administration of justice; education and language; and the implementation by member states of legislation related to indigenous peoples by the member states. Also, more so than in other fora, the Special Rapporteur has been able to address particular situations in countries, an opportunity linked to his several visits to member states.

The plethora of bodies on indigenous issues demonstrates the importance that the United Nations, and ultimately the international community, currently places on the protection of these communities. This is also reflected in the growing relevant academic literature that tackles indigenous issues in political theory,[18] specific regional indigenous situations and domestic indigenous cases.[19] In all such analyses, international law has been used to prove violations, to support arguments located in the realm of political theory, to analyse specific rights[20] and even to offer a radical vision of indigenous rights.[21] However, very few books engage in a comprehensive analysis of current international law standards relevant to indigenous claims.[22] This book contributes to this aspect of the debate. It evaluates the United Nations instruments that are devoted to the protection of indigenous peoples and assesses whether indigenous main claims, as recorded in the relevant United Nations fora, are consistent with current international standards. Several states and commentators argue that indigenous claims go beyond the existing standards and therefore cannot be accommodated. This book tests these views. It does not overlook that indigenous peoples have differing positions with respect to many issues; to claim otherwise would deny them their different cultures, histories and positions in the world. However, in their variety of positions, indigenous peoples have agreed on some minimum rights that the international community must recognize. This book has tried to stay true to indigenous claims by widely using indigenous statements made in the United Nations fora.

Essentially, this book attempts to find a balance between an understanding of international law that neglects its dynamic nature and a picture of international law in defiance of any set rules. Finding its way through these opposing approaches, it looks for an accurate and realistic picture of how indigenous claims fit or could fit into current international law. The analysis also hopes to highlight that the relationship between indigenous peoples and international law is a mutually beneficial one: international law can help indigenous peoples as much as they have helped the evolution of that law. As already mentioned, the indigenous debate has initiated a re-evaluation of human rights standards and has obliged the international community to take a closer look at other meanings and applications. Although it may be doubtful whether 'it is possible to create an international law that is not imperial',[23] the indigenous debate has through an analysis of current standards initiated a discussion on important questions that had been considered answered in international law. It has also strengthened the image and possibility of global civil society.[24] Indigenous peoples around the world have consciously decided to use the United Nations as the main forum for the improvement of their situation and to use international law for the accommodation of their claims, although it was not formulated with their participation. Indigenous belief in the United Nations and international law pushes hard for the restoration of the credibility of the United Nations and the use of international law.[25]

In its attempt to offer a comprehensive discussion of the main indigenous claims, the analysis is divided in two parts. The first part focuses on the foundations of the indigenous debate in international law. Chapter 1 discusses the normative foundations of the indigenous claims. The preservation of indigenous identity through their recognition as collectivities has met states' reluctance. The debate about non-state identities has its own place within wider debates on cultural membership and its importance in the post-national world. The chapter looks for the responses of international law to the arguments and fears in this discourse, placed mainly within the realm of political philosophy. I argue that the protection of the different loyalties of the individual is as important as the protection of the individual herself. The analysis demonstrates that, indeed, indigenous claims for collective rights have solid foundations in international norms and, contrary to some arguments, they can and should be accommodated. Conflicts with individual rights and other interests cannot be used as an argument for not recognising collective rights.

Chapter 2 discusses the legal foundations of indigenous rights. Indigenous rights can be deduced from general human rights instruments as well as minority instruments. Both have been analysed in general and with specific reference to indigenous peoples. Notably, Thornberry analysed extensively the general human rights instruments and their effectiveness in protecting indigenous rights.[26] Although these standards will be liberally used throughout this book, chapter 2 specifically examines the less analysed legal instruments that are devoted to the protection of indigenous peoples. Authors usually briefly refer to the ILO Convention concerning Indigenous and Tribal Peoples in Independent Countries, No. 169 and totally ignore the ILO Convention concerning the Protection and Integration of Indigenous and Other Tribal and Semi-Tribal Populations in Independent Countries, No. 107. Chapter 2 also pays particular attention to the monitoring bodies of these instruments, which offer interesting insight into the interpretation of the texts. Critics would query the value of a detailed dissection of ILO Convention No. 107; however, one must not neglect the fact that Convention No. 107 is in some states with large indigenous communities (including Bangladesh, Cuba, El Salvador, Ghana, India, Mexico, Paraguay and Tunisia) the only binding instrument that sets out specific obligations with respect to their indigenous communities. Also, a quick look at the work of the monitoring bodies reveals that the Convention is interpreted very much in accordance with the spirit of ILO Convention No. 169. Some critics would suggest that the ILO conventions are not so important, as they have only been signed by a limited number of states. However, these texts show the actual standards that exist in current international law affecting indigenous peoples. Even if signed by a relatively small number of states, the conventions are for indigenous communities an important political weapon, when faced with the inactivity of the state towards the protection of their rights. Chapter 3 touches upon the emerging law: the draft Declaration on the Rights of Indigenous Peoples. The draft Declaration recognises controversial rights, such as prohibition of cultural genocide, reparation of indigenous cultural objects and control of natural resources, issues that current international law has not yet tackled. The chapter examines whether these and other provisions of the draft Declaration fall within the existing standards of international law. Such a lengthy analysis of the draft Declaration can become the object of criticism; after all, critics may suggest, it is a mere text, not an instrument as such. However, this would overlook the importance of the draft Declaration for indigenous peoples as well as its importance for the evolution of human rights standards in general.

Part 2 of the book focuses on important clusters of claims; and there is none more important for indigenous peoples than the right to self-determination. Self-determination has been the basis of the trans-national indigenous movement. Chapter 4 places the indigenous claims within the wider debate on the meaning and beneficiaries of self-determination. The chapter highlights the fact that since the inclusion of self-determination in the UN Charter its meaning has been evolving according to the needs of each period: initially, it was equated to decolonisation, then it included liberation from racist regimes, and lately it has incorporated democratic governance. The next stage of the right is not clear; the plethora of claims based on self-determination, the fear of secession and vague and inconsistent practice have complicated its application even further. International law does not give a precise answer as to whether indigenous peoples are the beneficiaries of the right. What would the recognition of an unqualified right of self-determination practically mean to indigenous peoples and sub-national groups in general? And how realistic is the expectation for such recognition? The chapter discusses such issues, drawing widely on the statements of states to show existing state practice.

Chapter 5 turns to the study of indigenous cultural rights; it first examines the existing protection of cultural rights in international law and then analyses issues that are of particular importance to indigenous peoples. Problems arise from the discrepancy between the indigenous understanding of culture as a way of life and the non-indigenous perception of culture as capital. Another challenge for international law poses the communal focus of indigenous claims for the protection of their culture and its clash with the individualistic approach of international law in protecting cultural objects. The chapter attempts to see whether there is some common ground and discusses the misappropriation and misuse of indigenous cultural heritage, the reparation of indigenous cultural objects and biodiversity rights.

In analysing indigenous land rights, chapter 6 draws from earlier chapters. As international human rights are very vague on property rights, indigenous land claims often use the right of self-determination, or their right to culture or prohibition of discrimination as the legal basis for land rights. The chapter discusses these directions and uses national case law to highlight relevant state practice. The rights of indigenous peoples to collectively own land, to participate in decisions about their lands, to manage and use lands they have been living in and their rights to natural resources are discussed in depth; national practice is particularly essential in this theme.

Before embarking on the analysis, the scope of this book has to be defined. The definition of indigenous peoples is a controversial matter. States deny the indigenousness of some groups, as a way to avoid fulfilling their obligations towards them. Even though definitions have been advanced by international organizations, among others the International Labour Organisation (ILO)[27] and the World Bank,[28] there is no universally accepted definition of indigenous peoples. In fact, it is questionable whether a formal definition would be desirable. Historically, indigenous peoples have been subjected to multiple definitions and classifications imposed by others; they stress that their right to define themselves, rather than be defined by others, must be respected.[29] Indeed, self-determination has always been the fundamental criterion of identifying minorities and indigenous peoples. Apart from undesirable, a formal definition would also be futile.[30] International law refrains from sharp and tight definitions that may limit the flexibility of applying instruments to different circumstances.[31] For practical reasons and with the consent of indigenous representatives, the United Nations have adopted a working definition put forward by Martinez Cobo.[32] According to it:

> Indigenous communities, peoples and nations are those which, having a historical continuity with pre-invasion and pre-colonial societies that developed on their territories, consider themselves distinct from other sectors of the societies now prevailing in those territories, or parts of them. They form at present non-dominant sectors of the society and are determined to preserve, develop and transmit to future generations their ancestral territories, and their ethnic identity, as the basis of their continued existence as peoples, in accordance with their own cultural patterns, social institutions and legal systems.[33]

The Cobo definition, which will be followed in this book, allows for some fluidity and lack of precision; indigenous peoples are recognised through a cluster of associated factors. Elements of indigenousness include: historical continuity with pre-invasion and pre-colonial societies; distinctiveness from the other sectors of the society;

non-dominance in the society; and determination to preserve, develop and transmit to future generations its ancestral territories and ethnic identity, in accordance with the group's cultural, social and legal systems. The historical continuity criterion requires: an extended period of occupation of ancestral lands reaching to the present; common ancestry with the original occupants of these lands; culture and/or specific manifestations, such as religion, history, oral traditions, customs; language; and other relevant factors.[34] Historical continuity is widely preferred to historical priority, as the latter would eliminate many groups in need of indigenous protection. This has been accepted by the United Nations which urges 'a broad geographical representation'[35] in indigenous activities 'in all the areas where indigenous peoples live ... Latin American countries, North America, Australia, Nordic countries, and Asian and Pacific countries'.[36] It is noteworthy that recent years have seen the participation of several African indigenous groups.

The recognition of indigenous rights is essential for the further survival and development of these communities. The subject is a large one that touches upon several disciplines and many different geographical areas. My hope is that this analysis contributes to the promotion of indigenous rights and the further evolution of international law away from its colonial and Eurocentric past towards a more inclusive and, ultimately, fairer international community.

Notes

1. A. Brysk, 'Turning Weakness into Strength: The Internationalization of Indian Rights' (1996) 32 *Latin American Perspectives* 38–57.
2. A. Anghie, *Imperialism, Sovereignty and the Making of International Law* (Cambridge: Cambridge University Press, 2004), p. 8.
3. R. Morgan, 'Advancing Indigenous Rights at the United Nations: Strategic Framing and its Impact on the Normative Development of International Law' (2004) 13 *Social and Legal Studies* 481–500.
4. ECOSOC Resolution 1982/34, 7 May 1982.
5. J. Scott, 'Indigenous Peoples and the Creation of an Inclusive International Legal System', Paper delivered at Carnegie Council on Ethics and International Affairs, New York, 14 April 2004.
6. See 'Future Role of the Working Group', Working paper submitted by Miguel Alfonso Martinez, Member of the Working Group, UN Doc. E/CN.4/Sub.2/AC.4/1993/10.
7. M. Dodson, 'Comment' in S. Pritchard, 'Working Group on Indigenous Populations: Mandate, Standard-Setting Activities and Future Perspectives'

in *Indigenous Peoples, the United Nations and Human Rights* (London: Zed Books, 1998), pp. 40–64 at 62.

8. 'Establishing a Working Group to Elaborate a Draft United Nations Declaration on the Rights of Indigenous Peoples' (March 1995), Commission on Human Rights, Report on the 51st Session, UN Doc. E/1995/23 and also UN Doc. E/CN.4/1995/L.11/Add.2 para.1 (1995). As quoted in R. L. Barsh, 'Indigenous Peoples and the UN Commission on Human Rights: A Case of the Immovable Object and Irresistible Force' (1996) 18 *Human Rights Quarterly* 782–813.
9. UNGA Resolution 48/163 of 21 December 1993. See 'A Permanent Forum in the United Nations for Indigenous People: Information Received from Governments and Indigenous Organisations', UN Doc. E/CN.4/Sub.2/AC.4/1993/8, para. 6.
10. HRC Resolution 2000/87, 27 April 2000. For the discussion on the establishment of the Permanent Forum, see E/CN.4/2000/L.68.
11. J. Anaya, 'The Influence of Indigenous Peoples on the Development of International Law' in S. Garkawe, L. Kelly and W. Fisher (eds.), *Indigenous Human Rights* (Sydney Institute of Criminology, 2001), pp. 109–17.
12. W. Kymlicka, 'Theorising Indigenous Rights' (1999) 49 *University of Toronto Law Journal* 281–93.
13. Anaya, 'Influence of Indigenous Peoples'.
14. J. Debeljak, 'Barriers to the Recognition of Indigenous Peoples' Human Rights at the United Nations' (2000) 26 *Monash University Law Review* 159–94 at 188.
15. S. Chakma, 'Permanent Forum on Indigenous Issues: Chasing the Mirage' in *The Indigenous World 1999–2000* (Copenhagen: IWGIA, 2000), pp. 402–19.
16. E.-I. Daes, 'A United Nations Permanent Forum for the World's Indigenous Peoples – A Global Imperative' in G. Alfredsson, J. Grimheden, B. G. Ramcharan and A. de Zayas (eds.), *International Human Rights Monitoring Mechanisms* (Dordrecht: Martinus Nijhoff, 2002), pp. 371–9.
17. *Ibid.*
18. P. Keal, *European Conquest and the Rights of Indigenous Peoples: The Moral Backwardness of International Society* (Cambridge: Cambridge University Press, 2003); D. Ivison, P. Patton and D. Saunders (eds.), *Political Theory and the Rights of Indigenous Peoples* (Cambridge: Cambridge University Press, 2001); R. Niezen, *The Origins of Indigenism, Human Rights and the Politics of Identity* (University of California Press, 2003).
19. P. Havemann, *Indigenous Peoples' Rights in Australia, Canada and N. Zealand* (Oxford: Oxford University Press, 1999); N. Patterson and W. Saunders (eds.), *Citizenship and Indigenous Australians: Changing Conceptions and Possibilities* (Reshaping Australian Institutions Series) (Cambridge: Cambridge University Press, 1998); R. Howitt with John Connell, Philip Hirsch, *Resources, Nations and Indigenous Peoples: Case studies from Australasia, Melanesia and Southeast Asia* (Oxford: Oxford University Press, 1996).
20. P. Aikio and M. Scheinin, *Operationalizing the Right of Indigenous Peoples to Self-Determination* (Turku/Abo: Abo Akademi University, 2002); T. Simpson,

Indigenous Heritage and Self-Determination (IWGIA, 1997); James Crawford, *The Rights of Peoples* (Oxford: Clarendon Press, 1988).

21. J. S. Anaya, *Indigenous Peoples in International Law* (Oxford: Oxford University Press, 1996). For a review of the book, see 47 (1998) *ICLQ*, 244–5.
22. The main exception is P. Thornberry, *Indigenous Peoples and Human Rights* (Melland Schill Studies in International Law) (Manchester: Manchester University Press, 2002).
23. Anghie, *Imperialism, Sovereignty*.
24. R. Falk, *On Humane Governance, Toward a New Global Politics* (Cambridge: Polity Press, 2005), pp. 199–200.
25. *Ibid.*
26. P. Thornberry, *Indigenous Peoples*.
27. See chapter 3.
28. The World Bank Operational Directive 4.20 states:

    > The terms 'indigenous peoples', 'indigenous ethnic minorities', 'tribal groups' and 'scheduled tribes' describe social groups with a social and cultural identity distinct from the dominant society that makes them vulnerable to being disadvantaged in the development process. For the purposes of this directive, 'indigenous peoples' is the term that will be used to refer to these groups.

29. 'Indigenous Peoples and Minorities: Reflections on Definitions and Description', Paper commissioned by Minority Rights Group from P. Thornberry, submitted to the 1996 session of the WGIP, 9.
30. See 'Comments by the Aboriginal and Torres Strait Islander Commission concerning a Definition of Indigenous Peoples in Information Received from Indigenous Peoples' Organisations', UN Doc. E/CN.4/Sub.2/AC.4/1996/2/Add.1, 1.
31. Thornberry, *Indigenous Peoples*, pp. 33–60.
32. This was discussed and adopted in the second session of the WGIP.
33. M. Cobo, *Study of the Problem of Discrimination Against Indigenous Populations* (Geneva: United Nations, 1981), paras. 362–82.
34. *Ibid.*, para. 380.
35. Sub-Commission Resolution 1984/35C, final operative paragraph (d).
36. UN Doc. E/CN.4/Sub.2/1991/39, 2.

1 Recognition of cultural membership and implications

Introduction

The recognition of collectivities and collective rights is one of the most contested issues in international law and politics. For some, group rights are in stark contrast with the traditional approach of liberal rights theory, which views human rights as individual rights. The extensive philosophising on cultural membership is generally perceived by international lawyers as very engaging and relevant to debates on collective rights; yet, sometimes it appears to be ignoring new developments in international law. If international law is defined as the system of rules and principles that govern international relations,[1] its normative directions on the issue cannot be ignored. Indigenous claims provide an excellent example of the importance of cultural membership and its challenges.

The importance of cultural membership

Although indigenous claims include individual rights, in their overwhelming majority they are famously of a collective nature. Indeed, the collective element is prominent in indigenous claims, from self-determination to cultural rights and land resources. Indigenous peoples view the recognition of their collective rights as a token of respect towards their identity and communities as well as the only way for their survival and development. As long ago as 1989 indigenous leaders agreed on the following statement:

> [T]he concept of indigenous peoples' collective rights is of paramount importance. It is the establishment of rights of peoples as groups, and not merely the recognition of individual rights, which is one of the most important purposes of

this Declaration [on the rights of indigenous peoples]. Without this, the Declaration cannot adequately protect our most basic interests. *This must not be compromised.*[2] (emphasis added)

Indigenous insistence that their collective identity must be recognised and protected by international law fits well with the communitarian approach that advocates for the importance of cultural membership. Communitarians have offered two main justifications for the respect of culture. The first one, based on the intrinsic value of culture, has been elaborated by Taylor. He views culture as one of the 'irreducibly social goods' where 'the nature of the good requires that it be sought in common'[3] and warns against the atomism of contemporary political thought that values good on the basis of what benefits individuals. Ironically, his anathema is at the core of the second justification of culture, which focuses on the bond between the individual and her culture.[4] Indigenous statements employ this second justification, as they often emphasise that indigenous individuals cannot see themselves separate from their cultures:

Our knowledge, our cultures and our languages belong to us, they are what makes us who we are.[5]

The bond between indigenous and their cultures was recognised by coloniser states: the destruction of indigenous cultures was viewed as an acceptable means of securing and maintaining control over them.[6]

Ultimately, respect for indigenous peoples presupposes respect for their culture. Kymlicka puts forward two specific kinds of respect for individuals: respect for them as members of a distinct community, in which case society must recognise the legitimacy of claims made by them for the protection of the culture; and respect for them as citizens of the common political community, in which case society should recognise the importance of being able to claim the rights of equal citizenship.[7] He explains:

If we respect Indians as Indians, that is to say, as members of a distinct cultural community, then we must recognise the importance to them of their cultural heritage, and we must recognise the legitimacy of claims made by them for the protection of their culture.[8]

McDonald maintains that we cannot perceive ourselves away from the allegiances we belong to, such as family, community, nation or people; we cannot see ourselves only as 'me' and not as 'us'.[9] According to him, the attachments we have to our culture are 'constitutive ends',

ends that constitute the persons we are. Living by these attachments is essential in understanding ourselves as the particular persons we are.[10] Communitarians believe that our attachment to a community is not necessarily a voluntary one and that the social attachments that determine the self are not necessarily chosen ones.[11] They believe that cultural allegiances go beyond values we happen to believe and hold; beyond the obligations we voluntarily incur and the 'natural duties' we owe to human beings as such; they are the core of who we are.

MacIntyre clarifies that one person's life can only be understood by looking at that person's actions within a story, but such a narrative meets the narratives of other people who also come to be a part of the individual's story. It is the community and its culture that sets up the form and shape as well as the circumstances and the background of these narratives.[12] Australian indigenous peoples have declared:

> The traditional knowledge of indigenous peoples provides the foundation of our personal identity and ancestral anchorage. It provides a distinctive world view that outsiders can rarely grasp.[13]

International law has tentatively accepted the importance of culture for the individual and humanity. The 1966 UNESCO Declaration of the Principles of International Cultural Cooperation has declared the respect that nations should have to 'the distinctive character of each culture', whereas the 2001 UNESCO Declaration on Cultural Diversity notes that culture is at the heart of contemporary debates on identity and social cohesion[14] and links the protection of culture to human rights. The 1989 UNESCO Recommendation on the Safeguarding of Traditional Culture and Folklore specifically protects the culture of sub-national groups. Also, human rights instruments protect the culture of the individual; for example, the Convention on the Rights of the Child states that education must develop respect for the child's 'own cultural identity, language and values' as well as for 'the national values of the country in which the child is living'.[15]

Autonomy and the neutral state

The tentative character that is evident in the recognition of cultural membership by international law is mainly based on the fear that such recognition strips away the individual from her own autonomy. In liberal thought, human beings are conceptualised as fundamentally autonomous agents; they must remain free to act in accordance with their own rationality and their independent notion of what is good and valuable without the influence of cultural frameworks. Free choice must not be compromised.[16] This entails a neutral state that enforces only basic individual rights. Therefore, only individual rights must be promoted by the state and they must prevail over any interest of the collectivity.[17] Collective rights are seen as inherently political,[18] that 'imply permissible inegalitarian ranking of members in the interests of preservation of "tradition".'[19] Mitnik argues that affirmative action sacrifices the individual constitutive autonomy, as individuals who fall within the group described by the law will be given affirmative action without a choice.[20] Thus, states must ignore group differences, because the recognition of collective rights would mean that the state would take a position and would create a hierarchy. In essence then, the traditional liberal approach suggests that individual rights must be promoted within an essentially neutral and non-virtue promoting state for two reasons: first, because individual rights have a positive effect on the persons' welfare or utility;[21] and second, because individual rights solely protect the autonomy[22] and self-authorship[23] of individuals.

The traditional liberal view has attracted severe criticism and has been accused of being 'strongly supportive of an abstract or acultural individualism' and of ignoring the realities of current societies.[24] Indeed, the neutral state approach promotes blindness to group differences and encourages a rather outdated outlook on societies as homogeneous.[25] It maintains the traditional distinction between the individual and the state; further it derives from a notion of 'monotheism of the state', recognising unlimited sovereignty of the state.

In actual truth, a state cannot be neutral:[26] in the face of unequal circumstances between the majority and minorities, unequal opportunities and unequal treatment, state neutrality is in effect an affirmation of the way of life, the choices and the ideas of the dominant group and an overlook of the other groups.[27] The neutral state does not promote justice; rather, it maintains the status quo. Members of cultural groups do not have the same opportunities to live and work in their own culture and make their own choices to the same degree as the members of majority cultures. The only way to rectify their disadvantage is by providing them with special rights. Then, they will be given a similar degree of opportunity as members of the majority culture. Thus, special rights are accepted in order to ensure equality of circumstances and redress the vulnerability of non-dominant groups. Within this framework, the question is shifted from *whether* the state must take a position by recognising collective rights to *which* position the state will take – the position of the dominant group by maintaining a seemingly neutral position or the position of the vulnerable groups by recognising collective rights in an attempt to redress the balance. Kymlicka has argued that collective rights are compatible with the Rawlsian and Dworkinian notion of justice, where justice removes or compensates for the undeserved or 'morally arbitrary' disadvantages, particularly if these are 'profound and pervasive and present from birth'.[28] Raikka highlights two further arguments in favour of group differentiated rights that are especially relevant for indigenous communities: first, many indigenous groups have signed historical agreements with the current states that entitle them to group-differentiated rights and are therefore morally justified in having them. Second, indigenous peoples are the rightful owners of the land and are therefore justified in having relevant group-differentiated rights, in particular territorial rights.[29]

Nevertheless, it must be acknowledged that affirmative action can have some negative consequences. For example, measures specifically for indigenous peoples focus on the indigenous element of the identity of the people concerned and separate them on the basis of this from the rest of the population; apart from ignoring the other elements of their identity, these measures can perpetuate the exclusion of indigenous.[30] For this reason, many indigenous individuals object to such measures. Also, positive measures lead in some cases to more hostile attitudes by the rest of the population, as such measures are perceived as unfair to them. For example, there is undoubtedly some bitterness among non-indigenous North Americans about the special tax benefits indigenous reservations enjoy. In Australia, the press has documented negative feelings about the special measures for Australian Aborigines related to their lands; as has the press in New Zealand. This can increase the tensions between the communities and the negative perceptions of indigenous peoples with of course negative consequences for their rights. Any affirmative action will need to take the costs into account; yet, these considerations should not result in the abandonment of positive measures for these communities. As Dworkin concludes in his discussion of affirmative action in American higher education, unless and until a large and sophisticated study proves otherwise, 'we have no reason to forbid affirmative action as a weapon against our deplorable racial stratification, except our indifference to that problem, or our petulant anger that it has not gone away on its own'.[31]

Notwithstanding the challenges, international law has accepted special measures as a legitimate way of reaching equality. The Permanent Court of Justice made in its Advisory Opinion the distinction between formal equality (ultimately, the neutral state thesis) and substantial equality (attempted by the recognition of collective rights) and advocated the latter.[32] International norms prescribe positive measures for racial groups, but also for children, immigrants, refugees, women and individuals of other vulnerable groups in order to push them to reach the standards set in general human rights. The various instruments on minorities, such as Article 27 of the International Covenant on Civil and Political Rights (ICCPR) and the United Nations Declaration on the Rights of Persons Belonging to National or Ethnic and Linguistic Minorities (Declaration on Minorities) protect members of groups, whereas the International Convention against All Forms of Discrimination encourages special measures 'to ensure the adequate development and protection of certain racial groups and individuals belonging to them'.[33] Of special interest is the comment of the Committee on the Elimination of All Forms of Discrimination about the opinion of the USA that special measures are permitted but not required; the Committee's response was as follows:

> With regard to affirmative action, the Committee notes with concern the position taken by the State party that the provisions of the Convention permit, but do not require States parties to adopt affirmative action measures to ensure the adequate development and protection of certain racial, ethnic or national groups. The Committee emphasizes that the adoption of special measures by States parties when the circumstances so warrant, such as in the case of persistent disparities, is an obligation stemming from article 2, paragraph 2, of the Convention.[34]

The Committee has recently asked, among others, Uruguay for 'information on special measures, such as affirmative action programmes' for indigenous peoples;[35] and urged Fiji to adopt such measures.[36] The Human Rights Committee has also repeatedly encouraged the establishment of such measures. In its General Comment, the Committee emphasised that equal treatment does not mean identical treatment in all cases[37] and has made clear that tolerance and non-discrimination are not adequate measures to fulfil Article 27 of the ICCPR. Among others, the Committee has recently urged Finland to give priority to positive measures for the elimination of discrimination,[38] has welcomed the positive measures that New Zealand has taken on Maoris[39] and has asked for more information on positive measures for indigenous peoples in the Philippines.[40] Other UN bodies have also referred to positive measures with respect to indigenous persons. Although states have traditionally been reluctant, lately special measures have been more easily accepted. Thornberry asserts that the non-discrimination legal formulation is becoming more sensitive to issues of culture and identity.[41]

International law also challenges the monotheism of the state by recognising various groups other than the state. The number of entities that enjoy legal personality - if only for some purposes - is being expanded. Currently, non-state entities such as inter-governmental organisations, regional organisations, non-self governing territories, liberation movements and insurgent communities, non-governmental organisations, corporations and autonomous local administrations can act to some extent as agents in the international arena.[42] Also, a different status is recognised to many sub-state communities in Cyprus, Bosnia, South Africa and the former USSR,[43] whereas states practice includes constitutional arrangements where autonomous regimes and wide collective rights are recognised to sub-national groups.[44]

The flaws of the neutral state thesis are not the only weaknesses of the liberal objections to the recognition of cultural membership. The idea of complete individual autonomy, a core argument against the recognition of cultural membership, also seems unrealistic. The individual does not live in her own glass bubble protected by any influence; every day, she comes in contact with various opinions, different views and approaches. In a globalised world, it is unrealistic to expect an uncompromised degree of autonomy.

It is also doubtful whether a system of individual rights can sufficiently protect the autonomy of individuals; Taylor and Kymlicka maintain that moral autonomy can only be developed through a self-understanding that must be sustained in interaction with others. According to Taylor, the autonomous, self-determining individual needs a social matrix that promotes in practice this exact idea of autonomy and gives opportunities for the individual to practice and develop her autonomy.[45] Kymlicka argues that each person needs the *security* of the cultural framework from which she makes her choices.[46] Cultural membership seems crucial to development and ultimately autonomy.

The need for multiplicity of cultural frameworks

Supporters of a cosmopolitan understanding of autonomy insist that the influence of a culture can lead to its blind devotion. Concerns about illiberal practices, especially oppression of women, and secularisation of groups have provided powerful and difficult arguments to shift. It is often argued that if the state recognises such groups, it legitimises these practices. The liberal's concern is often for the members of the minority who will suffer at the hands of majority, if collective rights are introduced. Howard insists that recognition of collective rights 'imply the risk of progressive exclusion of categories of individuals internal to a national society from membership in the community'.[47]

The difficult issue of conflicts between individual and collective rights will be examined later; suffice to say here that denial of cultural membership does not necessarily solve the problem: in many states, where cultural membership is not recognised, illiberal practices continue to thrive. At the same time, it is true that exposure to *a single culture* can run the danger of insularity. The idea of *a single* culture excludes the group from the ideas of other cultures and perpetuates the false perception that cultural membership is predetermined, firmly fixed and inflexible. Groups become clear-cut and pushed into mutually exclusive oppositions. The approach of 'otherness' generally denies the particularities of the various groups and overlooks variations among the individuals belonging to the same group. It leads to the fear of the other group (xenophobia), nationalism and incites discourses about the purity and virtue of a particular group and its culture.[48]

However, the danger of insularity is most commonly avoided by the realities of today's global interaction. Waldron explains:

> We are not the self-made atoms of liberal fantasy, certainly, but neither are we exclusively products or artefacts of single national or ethnic communities. We are made of our languages, our literature, our cultures, our science, our religions, our civilisation – and these are human entities that go far beyond national boundaries and exist, if they exist anywhere, simply in the world.[49]

Indeed, the individual is not usually a member of one homogenous cultural framework from which to extract her choices, but has access to *a variety* of cultural sources, *a variety* of stories and roles. Apart from the wider influences, she has specific loyalties beyond the state, in smaller groups such as families, local communities, ethnic, religious and cultural groups, as well as bigger ones, such as regional organisations (e.g. the European Union) or even the international society. Kymlicka stresses the need for a multiplicity of cultural frameworks to choose from:

> In deciding how to lead our lives, we do not start *de novo*, but rather we examine 'definite ideas and forms of life that have been developed and tested by innumerable individuals, sometimes by generations'. The decision about how to lead our

lives must ultimately be ours alone, but this decision is always a matter of selecting what we believe to be most valuable from the various options available, selecting from a context of choice which provides us with different ways of life.[50]

Sandel agrees with Kymlicka:

> As a self-interpreting being, I am able to reflect on my history and in this sense to distance myself from it, but the distance is always precarious and provisional, the point of reflection never finally secured outside the history itself.[51]

This concept of distance between the individual and her background when making a decision is an interesting one. Waldron has gone as far as talking of a 'manager' within each individual whose role is to manage her own various allegiances. The manager must be away from the self, so that she can keep a distance from all the cultures involved.[52] This vision of a cosmopolitan manager who decides which cultural allegiance provides the decisive element on each occasion has received strong criticism. MacIntyre finds the idea that we can put in question the merely contingent or synthetic social features of our existence problematic.[53] On the contrary, Sandel supports the idea of distance between the individual and her background, but argues that 'a manager' with no loyalties and allegiances entails a person with no values, commitments or projects of her own.[54]

More and more, international standards endorse the idea of multiple loyalties and encourage the diversity of cultures. The 2001 UNESCO Declaration on Cultural Diversity notes that culture is at the heart of contemporary debates on identity and social cohesion[55] and affirms that respect for the diversity of cultures is necessary for international peace.[56] The Declaration goes on to say that the diversity of cultures is as important as biodiversity for nature.[57] It views the defence of cultural diversity as 'an ethical imperative, inseparable from respect for human dignity. It implies a commitment to human rights and fundamental freedoms, in particular the rights of persons belonging to minorities and those of indigenous peoples'.[58] The text supports cultural pluralism[59] and links the protection of culture to human rights. However, it also makes clear that in case of conflict, individual rights prevail: 'No one may invoke cultural diversity to infringe upon human rights guaranteed by international law, nor to limit their scope'.[60] The 1989 UNESCO Recommendation on the Safeguarding of Traditional Culture and Folklore also protects the culture of sub-national groups, whereas the UNESCO Declaration on Race and Racial Prejudice establishes the responsibility of the state to protect human rights and fundamental freedoms on an equal footing for individuals and groups.[61]

Current human rights standards adopt a multicultural approach that recognises and celebrates the elements of different cultures. For example, the Convention on the Rights of the Child states that education must develop respect for the child's 'own cultural identity, language and values' as well as for 'the national values of the country in which the child is living'.[62] Other instruments protect the cultures of vulnerable groups. For example, articles 1 and 2 of the Convention on the Prevention and Punishment of the Crime of Genocide enumerate those acts that constitute genocide 'when intended to destroy, in whole or in part, a national, ethnical, racial and religious group'. Whereas toleration allows minorities to exercise their culture as long as they do not affect the majority, multicultural policies demand equal respect for all minority cultures and can so require the distribution of political and economic resources in such a way as to sustain and ensure the future of minority cultural communities.[63]

Interaction of cultures

Multiculturalism does not entail the coexistence of various cultures as separate entities that happen to exist and develop independently within the state; neither does international law. More and more international norms encourage the interaction of the various groups within the state. The 1966 UNESCO Declaration of the Principles of International Cultural Cooperation declares that 'in their rich variety and diversity, and in the reciprocal influences they exert on one another, all cultures form part of the common heritage belonging to all mankind'.[64] The Declaration makes clear that cultural cooperation, aiming at the mutual benefit of the nations practising it, is a right and a duty for all peoples and nations and should be exercised in a spirit of broad reciprocity. All nations must respect the distinctive character of each culture, while promoting their enrichment in an atmosphere of friendship and peace.[65] The UN Declaration on Minorities also stresses the need for mutual knowledge and understanding between minorities and the majority within the state (article 4.4). Both the Framework Convention on National Minorities by the Council of Europe and the OSCE Copenhagen Document reassert the spirit of tolerance and intercultural dialogue, mutual respect and understanding that should exist among the minorities and the majority.[66] The idea of reciprocity among cultures is also emphasised in the comment of the Committee on Human Rights in relation to the protection of cultural rights:

The protection of these rights is directed to ensure the survival and continued development of the cultural, religious and social identity of the minorities concerned, *thus enriching the fabric of society as a whole.* [emphasis added][67]

It appears that international provisions envisage groups forming concentric circles around the individual. Apart from her own attributes and choices as an independent agent, the person is also influenced by her immediate group (such as her family), peer group (such as the local group), ethnic, religious and cultural group, her nation (peoples), state, continent/region and, finally, loosely by the main culture we all share as citizens of a common world. The closer the circle to the person, the more influence it has on her. In order to protect the individual, all the various 'circles' – loyalties – around her need to be protected. Thus, international law includes a different set of protection for the individual (by establishing individual rights), but also for her family, ethnic, cultural or religious group, the society she lives in, and finally the culture of her continent and the culture of the world itself (by establishing collective rights). All these groups represent a series of multiple loyalties held by the individual and consequently incorporate various cultures that influence the individual. For example, a Sami that lives in Finland has been exposed to the specific culture of his family, the culture of his village (which sometimes has a different linguistic dialect), the Sami culture, the Finnish culture as well as the European culture. The Indian Crees share the culture of their reservation, the culture of the overlapping American Indian community and they also share characteristics of the Canadian culture; they are also part of the North American culture, subjects of the human rights system of the Americas as well as members of the international community. Their lives and choices represent a mixture of characteristics of the above communities.

The existence of regional human rights instruments recognises that continents have specific cultures. For example, article 1(a) of the Statute of the Council of Europe proclaims that the aim of the organisation is 'to achieve greater unity between its Members for the purpose of safeguarding and realising *the ideals and principles which are their common heritage*' [emphasis added]. Although the human rights system gives the central role to the individual, protection is also given to the person as a member of groups, such as the family,[68] ethnic, national, religious and linguistic groups,[69] nations (peoples)[70] and even the continent and the world. Even though most of these provisions establish individual rights or individual rights in a collective capacity, 'it is hard to see how one could avoid the collective dimension to some of them'.[71] In this way, international law recognises the importance of groups for the individual and prescribes that these groups should be protected.

This approach echoes the teachings of personalism. Personalists have viewed the individualistic tradition and the communitarian approach as complementary rather than contrasting. According to the *Encyclopaedia of Philosophy*, personalism is a 'philosophical perspective or system for which person is the ontological ultimate and for which personality is thus the fundamental explanatory principle.' Personalists regard the 'person' as an essential part of the community, and distinguish it from the 'individual' that is regarded as an isolated entity.[72] Thus, they use the term 'person' or 'personality' to emphasise relationships with others in the community and a corresponding link with the community and the relations between the latter and society.[73] They believe that a person is inseparable from the context of the world around him and that he lives in community with others and not as an isolated individual; thus, they support the establishment of community rights, particularly for communities smaller than the state. This definition of a person agrees with Garet's theory about the three equally important components of every human being: (a) personhood, namely the individual good; (b) communality, namely the group good; and (c) sociality, the common good.[74] Although personalism recognises collective rights, it does not ignore the negative consequences of group membership; thus, rights exist to counteract the tyranny of the state as well as the tyranny of groups and they can be claimed against the state as well as groups.[75]

This understanding of loyalties is consistent with the image of loyalties forming concentric circles around the individual. This model minimises the danger of a monolithic attachment to one cultural framework by the existence of some common values as expressed in international decisions, including treaties, customary law, general principles and soft law; a kind of 'international public reason'.[76] In other words, the international community operates as a society of societies with its own public culture and conception of public reason.[77] The conditions of international public reason serve as a constraint on acceptable conceptions of domestic justice, as well as on the conduct of societies toward one another.

Also, this model emphasises the contribution of groups to the common society. Young has emphasised that difference is not to be perceived as exclusion. Although primarily interested in social groups, her approach is very helpful to cultural groups. She views different groups as:

overlapping, as constituted in relation to one another and thus, as shifting their attributes and needs in accordance with what relations are salient. In my view, this relational conception of difference as conceptual helps make more apparent both the necessity and possibility of political togetherness in difference.[78]

In Young's model, difference does not mean otherness, or exclusive opposition, but rather specificity, variation, heterogeneity. Different groups potentially share some attributes, experiences or goals. Their differences will be more or less salient depending on the groups compared and the purposes of the comparison. The characteristics that make one group specific and the borders that distinguish it from other groups are always *undecidable*. Yet, all groups understand themselves as participants in the same society, subjects to interaction, exchange and interdependency.[79] The interaction causes, sometimes, friction and conflicts that are resolved through institutions and procedures of discussion that all participants have accepted as legitimately binding. It is important that the groups are not pushed towards a largely manufactured cultural consensus or a symbolic order;[80] although not opposing the groups are heterogeneous and have a differentiated place in public life. Young calls this model 'the heterogeneous public' and encourages this model of multiculturalism.

It has been argued that multiculturalism is bad for indigenous groups: Idleman makes the distinction between the consequences of multicultural policies for minorities and its consequences for indigenous peoples. According to him, indigenous peoples ask for separatist policies; yet, multiculturalism means the end of separation policies for indigenous peoples and consequently the end of their semi-sovereign status, autonomy and separate rights.[81] Waldron seems to give an appropriate answer:

> Just as the allegedly self-made individual needs to be brought to a proper awareness of her dependence on social, communal and cultural structures, so too in the modern world particular cultures and national communities have an obligation to recognise their dependence on the wider social, political, international and civilisational structures that sustain them.[82]

It must be recognised that the protection of indigenous identity is not the sole reason why indigenous rights must be recognised. Justifying indigenous claims solely on the need to preserve indigenous identity reduces aboriginality to one of the many cultural identities, dehistoricises it and strips away its powerful rights arguments.[83] It must be acknowledged that the current situation of indigenous peoples is the result of a history of oppression initiated by the state and maintained by the current non-indigenous communities and embedded in state instruments.[84] Therefore, indigenous rights must also be recognised as a means to end the era of indigenous oppression and disrespect. Against this past, pluralism and inclusion become even more fundamental imperatives.

Still, the main answer to Idleman's argument relates to the interactive element of multiculturalism. It is true that indigenous peoples have not been stressing the needed interaction among indigenous and non-indigenous groups, but this is mainly due to the use of such arguments to justify assimilationist policies, i.e. when the state would require the conformity of indigenous peoples to the non-indigenous modes of life. This model fits what Addis calls 'paternalistic pluralism', where minorities are seen as 'others' in need for protection but rely on an enlightened majority to 'save them'.[85] An obvious example of such model is the (1957) ILO Convention 107 on Indigenous, Tribal and Semi-tribal Populations whose aim has been the integration of indigenous peoples who are 'at a less advanced stage than the stage reached by the other sections of the national community'.[86] In contrast, 'critical pluralism' views minorities as partners in the creation or recreation of the society. The state actively engages in a dialogue with minorities in order to find the best way and resources to make minority cultures flourish. In addition, the state creates institutions that enable the rest of the population to open itself up to all groups by accepting them all as dialogue partners.[87] Walzer endorses this model by applying it to indigenous educational policies. He maintains that commitment to the tolerance of difference prescribes the recognition of indigenous control over their educational systems, but citizenship claims also prescribe that indigenous pupils are taught to some extent the history and values of the state.[88]

The recent UNESCO World Commission Report emphasises the importance of cultural pluralism and political democracy. The Report states that 'the challenge today ... is to develop a setting that ensures that development is integrative and that there are best practice institutions built on genuine commitment to being inclusive'.[89] The idea of critical pluralism is realised through the various provisions on participation of minority groups in the decision-making process of the society they live in.[90] The UN Declaration on Minorities proclaims that members of minorities have the right to participate effectively in decisions at the national and, where appropriate, regional level.[91] Especially the ILO Convention No. 169 concerning Indigenous and Tribal Peoples in Independent Countries adopts a broad concept of participation in relation to indigenous peoples: states should not only consult indigenous peoples on matters which affect them directly; the consultations must be undertaken with the objective of achieving agreement or consent to the proposed measures.[92] As Falk notes:

> One role of the robust society is to overcome both normative and cultural blindness to human suffering. The raising of awareness requires deliberate efforts to counterpart the vulnerability of previously excluded groups; lessening vulnerability in turn depends on developing decentralised participatory democracy ... Democratisation is both a vital precondition and a crucial ingredient of human rights protection.[93]

Contrary to many states' fears, pluralism and diversity contribute to the protection of national sovereignty. The dissolution of the former Yugoslavia and the former Soviet Union indicate that pluralism may be essential in maintaining the state's sovereignty. If the state denies its multicultural character, its citizens will inevitably feel dissatisfied and oppressed and will be more likely to revolt and try to undermine the state's sovereignty. In contrast, if pluralism and sovereignty are viewed as supplementing principles, collective rights of cultural groups are recognised (pluralism) and the state can maintain its role as a decision maker and manager of its various activities (sovereignty).

Preservation of cultures

The interaction between cultures within the state also addresses another criticism concerning the protection of cultural membership, namely that it leads to the artificial preservation of cultures. The argument has a core of truth: preservation results in inauthentic cultures. Cultures do not stay the same; they change, adapt to different circumstances, amalgamate with other cultures and sometimes they gradually disappear. To preserve a culture could mean to choose a specific version of the culture at a temporal point and insist that this version must persist, irrespective of any changes in the surrounding environment or the circumstances. According to Waldron, preservation may succeed in preserving the culture, 'but not what many would regard as its most fascinating feature: its ability to generate a *history*.'[94] The need to eradicate all parochial perceptions of their cultures is a great concern for indigenous peoples; they often express their discontent with the use of the word 'folklore' as an expression of their cultures; they consider the term 'inappropriate to denote indigenous cultures as it diminishes the importance of indigenous cultures as a living heritage'.[95]

Similarly to their cultures, cultural groups are not fixed and unchanging entities, but are constantly forming and dissolving in response to political and institutional circumstances. Kukathas uses this argument to reject the importance of culture, even for the constitution of group identity.[96] He claims:

> it is not acceptable to evaluate or choose political institutions or to establish legal rights on the basis of the claims or interests of cultural communities because those very institutions or rights will profoundly affect the kinds of cultural communities individual decide to perpetuate or to form.[97]

However, the model of pluralism and interaction among the cultures living within the state protects cultures, while encouraging their natural evolution through dialogue. Dialogue leads to revisibility and re-evaluation of the group cultures which, according to Kymlicka,[98] are important processes that can lead to mutually corrective engagements. Through this process, groups are reconceptualised and recast and their differences are adjusted and reconstituted in a process of constant and genuine dialogue. Through dialogue group practices are challenged to accommodate in their own world the objective reality of the other. They interact, exchange ideas and benefit from the cultures of all the groups rather than just from their own culture. Waldron cautions that there is a contradiction between the evaluations that Kymlicka's revisibility condition leads to and the secure cultural framework Kymlicka aspires to. He maintains that genuine evaluations can only take place when the individual and the culture are vulnerable to challenges and comparisons from outside and are therefore not secure; otherwise, the evaluations have no practical effect, as there is no basis for an informed and sensible choice.[99] I cannot see the contradiction between feeling secure in a cultural framework and being open. Security does not mean isolation, neither does it mean stagnation. On the contrary, it seems to me that if cultures feel respected and celebrated, they become more open and more willing to re-evaluate practices and values.

Further, some communitarians reject the desirability of the revisibility condition, on the ground that constant revising of the values and beliefs can undermine the culture and its authenticity. It is argued that constant re-evaluation of cultural practices can be individually and socially destabilising, not to mention time-consuming. Some individual re-evaluations concerning the character of the culture and membership will put the individual outside the culture and some collective re-evaluations can destroy the culture. According to these critics, there must at least be a limit to the principles that an individual can re-evaluate. McDonald concludes that: 'there is no single, uniform, cross-culturally valid, prudential rationale for taking revisibility as a premier desideratum for personal and political life'.[100] Notwithstanding these difficulties, I believe that the re-evaluation of the culture is undoubtedly important, as it contributes to the evolution of the culture, avoids its stagnation and makes it more relevant to the needs and realities of today's society. Within this framework, the model of concentric circles allows the individual to be open to influences by several groups and enables her to transfer these outside values, criticisms and objections back to the cultural group, where they will be discussed and taken into account.

Especially on collective rights

So far, we have established that cultural membership is important for the individual and should be protected. For indigenous peoples and many commentators, the obvious way to protect the group is through collective rights. In the indigenous debate, this translates into recognising that indigenous peoples have the right to control matters that affect them and to manage, as a group, aspects of their lives, such as their education, language and lands.

Yet, not all states agree to this. France has repeatedly stated that 'collective rights did not exist in international human rights law, and therefore [France] had reservations with regard to those articles that aimed to establish collective rights'.[101] This is not an accurate representation of current international law. Even though the human rights system is essentially focused on individual rights, collective rights are tentatively recognised. Earlier texts such as the Genocide Convention, the UN Charter and the (1970) ECOSOC Resolution 1503 on gross violations of human rights[102] include collective elements. In subsequent texts the collective element becomes more prominent. For example, the 1969 International Convention on the Elimination of All Forms of Racial Discrimination contains significant recognition of rights of groups in provisions about special measures for the advancement of 'ethnic groups' and individuals and in obligations upon states and public institutions not to racially discriminate against 'groups of persons'. The African Charter on Human and Peoples' Rights stands out amongst regional human rights conventions in its substantive recognition of peoples and collective rights and the recognition of duties of the individual towards her family, national community and African cultural values.[103] The United Nations Declaration on Rights Belonging to National or Ethnic, Religious and Linguistic Minorities aims at protecting the identity and existence of minorities.[104] More recently, the Rio Declaration recognised the role 'of indigenous people and their communities and other local communities' in environmental management and development and the obligation on states to recognise and support their 'identity, culture and interests'. Also, both ILO conventions on indigenous rights protect collective rights. The ILO Convention No. 107 was unique in 1957 in recognizing the collective rights of indigenous peoples,[105] whereas the ILO Convention No. 169 expressly recognises a wide range of collective rights for indigenous groups, including non-discrimination, consultation and decision making, recognition of customary laws and institutions, land ownership and use of natural resources. Although the ratification of this convention has been limited, its clear recognition of collective rights combined with its binding force represents a significant development in the debate on collective rights. It is also noteworthy that the monitoring mechanisms of all the above texts have over the years greatly advanced the idea of collective rights.[106] Finally, the third generation rights signify the unconditional recognition of collective rights, including the right to self-determination, development, peace, co-ownership of the common heritage of mankind, a healthy environment and the culture of mankind.[107]

One of the arguments against collective rights focuses on the moral standing of the group; according to it, groups cannot be right-holders because they have no morally significant interests. The current chapter has highlighted two counter-arguments in this debate: some theorists believe that groups can have rights because they can be valuable in and of themselves; others believe that groups can have rights, because they are valuable to the individual. Jones notes that 'it is simple nonsense – nonsense upon stilts – to suppose that, if we treat individual persons as the ultimate units of moral concern, that must prevent us from taking full account of the communal dimensions of their lives'.[108] Wellman takes a completely different approach: he argues that such a discussion is only relevant if the defining feature of human rights is to recognise and protect the rights of the right-holder. If on the other hand, the essential feature of human rights is agreed to be the occupation 'of a position of dominion in some adversarial context', then the problem is sidestepped.[109] This rings a bell for indigenous communities, whose claims are essentially for more control within an environment of conflict about their values. If rights are essentially a method of conflict adjudication, this conflict provides a compelling case for ascribing rights to indigenous peoples.[110]

Another argument against collective rights relates to their necessity. Even if the importance of culture is accepted either as a valuable good or because of its benefits to individuals, it is still not clear that collective rights are necessary to protect it. It has been suggested that most collective rights are essentially reducible to rights of the members of the group; therefore they have no real practical value, as the same result can be achieved through individual rights.[111] Liberals suggest that rights to culture can be adequately protected,[112] for example through the individual right to association.[113]

However, at least in some cases, protecting the vulnerable by individual rights is just not possible. Providing indigenous peoples with a system of individual rights fails to protect them from the main violations of their human rights, because these include violations of a collective nature, towards indigenous communities as a group. Land rights, for example, have a value as individual rights that is different from their value as community rights. This became obvious in the United States when the General Allotment Act (1887) allowed reservation land to be divided into parcels owned by individual tribal members, which they could then sell. By the time the Act was repealed by the Indian Reorganisation Act of 1934, the size of reservations in the USA was reduced to less than a third of what had been almost fifty years before.[114] This demonstrates the assimilationist results that individual rights can have on vulnerable groups. The liberal would argue that it was the free choice of any individual to sell her land; however, those rights were given to the individual, because of her membership of the indigenous group and would not be given to her otherwise. Indeed, even leading opponents of the idea of collective rights have come to agree that indigenous rights are 'an emerging exception' to their polemic against collective rights and that indigenous peoples are in need of collective rights because their way of life is fragile, under attack, and fundamentally incompatible with mainstream legal and social institutions.[115]

Indeed, I would go further to argue that minority rights, rather than just indigenous rights, must also be established as collective rights. Jones notes that not all group claims must be grounded in collective rights, but highlights two cases where collective rights are the imperative: first, when the title to a good has a collective form that cannot be divided into a number of rights held individually by the members of the group; and second when the claim of the individual is not adequate to substantiate a right.[116] In order to highlight his argument, he refers to the individuals' freedom to worship. This, he claims, can be realised individually in community with others. However, the right of minorities not to have their sacred sites desecrated cannot be perceived as an individual right, as the sacred site is a special property of the faithful as a group and the desecreation violates a right possessed by this group. In other words, the good in this case cannot be divided. Also, he continues, although individuals can have the right to use their language, an individual's claim to have official documents in the minority language, including administrative documents, court proceedings, tax forms and road signs, would not substantiate such a right, as the cost for the realisation of such right would exceed the benefit for the individual. However, a group's claim to such right could be substantiated, as the benefits for the group would justify the cost for the realisation of the right.[117] I agree with Jones, but can see a wider application in the second case he refers to. For example, this category also includes the freedom of religious worship, and in particular the establishment of religious buildings: individuals cannot ask for the establishment of a religious building, but a group can, because the benefits would substantiate the cost. The same goes for establishing educational minority establishments and many other aspects of minority rights, currently viewed in international law as individual rights under collective capacity. It is not the numerical difference that substantiates the cost; it is the importance of the religious or other buildings for the group, rather than each individual separately.

Arguably the most powerful argument against collective rights relates to the conflicts that arise between collective and individual rights. Several states have expressed their fears that collective rights restrict individual rights. The USA explained its rejection of indigenous collective rights on this precise basis:

> characterising a right as belonging to a community, or collective, rather than an individual, can be and often is construed to limit the exercise of that right (since only a group can invoke it), and thus may open the door to the denial of the right to the individual. This approach is consistent with the general view of the United States, as developed by its domestic experience, that the rights of all people are best assured when the rights of each person are effectively protected.[118]

Indeed, not all cultures perceive autonomy as important. Often the individual's choices are put below the group's well-being and in some occasions, the individual has to accept uncritically the choices of the group. Clitoridectomy; polygamy; forced marriages; domestic violence;

insensitive treatment of victims of rape; these have all been justified in the name of tradition and culture.[119] Should such practices be allowed within a liberal state? Which right will prevail in cases of conflict? Are communities permitted to discriminate in terms of gender or disability?[120] The debate has particularly focused on conflicts between women's rights and group rights. Some insist that the recognition of collective rights to groups that violate rights of individuals would perpetuate these illiberal practices.

While international law tries to facilitate groups in protecting their rights, it stresses that minorities must perform these rights in an orderly and peaceful manner within the rule of law and democracy and with respect to the existing system of international law.[121] Principle 4 of the 1991 CSCE Geneva Meeting of Experts on National Minorities affirms that persons belonging to a national minority will enjoy the same duties of citizenship as the rest of the population; thus, their communities must respect their individual rights. The text urges members of minorities to claim rights through the parliamentary and legal systems and to use peaceful methods; they should be guided by the principles of dialogue and consultation in pursuing their rights. Article 3(2) of the UN Declaration on the Rights of Minorities protects the individual from the group. It establishes that 'no disadvantage shall result for any person belonging to a minority as the consequence of the exercise or non-exercise of the rights set forth in this Declaration'. This could be interpreted as an attempt to find a balance between individual and collective rights.[122]

In general, perceiving cultural frameworks as concentric circles around the individual, as explained earlier, provides ways to prevent possible conflicts between collective and individual rights. If groups are not seen as antagonistic, but as equal partners within the same society that respects and celebrates their differences and if interaction among them is encouraged, then changes could be instigated. If the individual is open to influences by several cultural frameworks, then conflicts will be resolved through the process of re-evaluation of the cultural practices by the group itself. For example, Nasieku Tarayia, a member of the Maasai people, argues in favour of reforms in the Maasai treatment of women, but within Maasai control of their overall cultural integrity and existence as a distinct people.[123]

The problem occurs when the group is not open to other influences, the individual is not open to other cultural frameworks and thus, the revisibility process is not initiated. Then, some commentators argue that *prima facie* individual rights prevail.[124] Even Kymlicka reluctantly agrees that when a choice has to be made, the choice must be to protect individual rights. He also puts forward criteria to determine the prevalence of the individual right, including:

> the severity of discrimination within the community, the extent of division within the community, the existence of any treaty obligations, the nature of the proposed interference, and so forth. For example, there is a large difference between coercively imposing liberalism and offering various incentives for liberal reforms.[125]

It appears to me, however, that the current debate on illiberal practices is too focused on minority groups and a choice of individual rights over collective rights is too easily made. First, illiberal practices do not take place only in minority cultures; they also do so in majority cultures. Honig cautions that 'we must all resist the all too familiar and dangerous temptation to mark foreignness itself as fundamentally threatening to women'.[126] Second, conflicts between rights is a common phenomenon in human rights; apart from the general distinction between derogatory and non-derogatory rights, no predetermined hierarchy exists. Any such conflicts between rights, principles and norms are generally solved on an ad hoc basis, after taking into account various considerations. The same process must be used in conflicts between individual and collective rights.

Garet believes that any hierarchical framework would violate the principle of non-derivation among the three elements of a human being, namely personhood, communality and sociality.[127] Pertney also explicitly rejects any hierarchy between collective and individual rights, although his general interpretative principles to facilitate their coexistence imply a prevalence of individual rights: firstly, 'the particular collectivity must not be impaired in its capacity to continue either by the state or by claims on behalf of individuals'; and secondly, 'a particular collectivity must respect the maximum individual rights consonant with the preservation of the group'.[128] Johnston also notes that 'in light of the potential diversity of group claims, it might be premature to attempt to construct a generalised framework for their adjudication'.[129]

Also, an untroubled prevalence of individual rights over collective rights indicates the treatment of culture 'as a theoretical construct'[130] and a failure to grasp the meaning and daily existential experience of culture for some groups. Human rights decisions have to be taken in accordance with the traditions, beliefs and histories of the groups or persons concerned, *all* individuals concerned, rather than solely Anglo-American culture, history and practices.[131] Even though Western liberal cultures are focused on the individual, other cultures prioritise collectivities and this is something that needs to be taken into account, when making such decisions. Also, framing conflicts in terms of a dilemma where the one or the other should be chosen is a poor tactic.[132] Minorities and indigenous peoples whose historical and cultural circumstances are partly shaped by colonialism and/or oppression are invited to choose between the practices of their culture or the liberal model of the states that have oppressed them; they feel their culture is under threat by the state and it is not surprising if they side with their culture. For example, in Canada leading Aboriginal activists argue that liberal equality is simply not the central organising political principle of indigenous communities and that liberal rights are inconsistent with Aboriginal culture and traditions.[133] If the discrepancies between non-indigenous and indigenous values had not been presented in black or white terms, maybe these leaders would not have taken such absolute positions.

If the criticism of the Eurocentric nature of human rights is seriously taken into account; if one agrees with Anghie's position that international law is still influenced by its 'civilizing mission';[134] and if we consider that voices for the recognition of collective rights come from the peoples who have been oppressed by the colonial past of international law; then, the starting question to the current debate should not be 'why collective rights *should be* established'; rather, 'why collective rights *should not* be established'. On this question the liberals have no decisive general case against collective rights.[135] A system of human rights that ignores the widespread voices for collective rights because of its perceived inconsistency with western liberal theories strikes me as cultural imperialism. Such a direction justifies the complaints of vulnerable societies, including indigenous, that international law has done nothing to salvage them and much to damage them; it is law that promises liberation, but in truth oppresses.[136] The major challenge of current human rights is not to implement the priority of individual rights over the claims of communities; but rather, to devise a fair way of preserving the core values of both sides.[137]

Is this possible? International law seems to suggest so. The model of concentric circles highlights the existence of 'a wider circle', common values that are more or less common to the whole humanity; otherwise called 'international public reason' as discussed earlier in this chapter. These values include – but are not restricted to – non-derogable rights, such as the right to life and prohibition of torture. No cultural practices can violate these rights. However, other practices do not violate the core of individual rights and could prevail. This approach seems to be shared by the Human Rights Committee. On the one hand, the Committee strongly condemned polygamy and genital mutilation as practices that contravene women's rights and asked Uganda to take strong measures against them;[138] on the other, the Committee refrained taking a clear position on the possible violations that Muslim women face in Greece as a result of the non-application of Greek law to the Muslim minority on issues of marriage and inheritance.[139] In the former case, the Committee felt that the cultural practices violated the core of the right to marry and the prohibition of torture; in the second case, the Committee did not feel confident that this was the case. Similarly, in the case of wearing headscarves, many argue that the cultural practice prevails over the liberal application of women's rights. For these reasons any decision about possible violations of individual rights by the group must be taken on an ad hoc basis.

In making these ad hoc decisions, several principles must apply. In *Lovelace*,[140] *Kitok*[141] and *Länsman*,[142] the Human Rights Committee asked for the existence of a reasonable and objective justification for the prevalence of one right over the other; consistency with human rights instruments; the necessity of the restriction; and proportionality. It is argued that the complete neglect of one right – be it collective or individual – for the safe realisation of the conflicting right would in most cases violate the principle of necessity.[143]

A strong argument has also been made that any restriction of the individual's rights must take into account the opinion of the individual in question.[144] It is important though that the individual reaches this decision without inappropriate interference. It is equally important to respect the individual's decision, rather than label her as a victim of culturally generated false consciousness in need of liberation.[145] Friedman sets a three steps test to determine whether the individual has made the decision freely: (a) she must be 'able to choose among a significant and morally acceptable array of alternatives'; (b) she must be 'able to make their own choices relatively free of coercion, manipulation and deception'; and (c) she must have been 'able to develop, earlier in life, the capacities needed to reflect on their situations and make decisions about them'.[146] If these criteria are applied to the current controversy surrounding headscarves, the adult woman who has reached the decision to wear her scarf after careful reflection because of her deep beliefs and without any coercion or manipulation by others must be free to do so.

The Human Rights Committee has adopted the same approach: as mentioned earlier, in its 2005 conclusions on the Greek report, the Committee discussed the non-application of the general legislation of Greece to the Muslim minority on issues of marriage and inheritance and its consequences for Muslim women. Rather than allowing the state to restrict the group's authority and expressing its own opinion on which right should prevail, the Committee asked for increased awareness by Muslim women of their rights and the availability of remedies.[147] Anaya stresses that any assessment about a cultural practice must allow a certain deference to the group's own interpretive and decision-making processes in the application of universal human rights norms, just as states are accorded such deference.[148] So, when educated Muslim women suggest that headscarves and even veiling is an empowering practice, because it allows professional women to move from the familiar settings of their rural homes and 'emerge socially into a sexually integrated' urban world that is 'still an alien, uncomfortable social reality for both women and men',[149] the state and ultimately the international community must take these views into account. The same goes for indigenous women.

The issue of representation in the decision-making process does not focus only on women. All voices must be heard, particularly the voices of vulnerable members of the group.[150] In the concluding observations on Canada, the Human Rights Committee expressed its concern in 2006 about the discriminatory effects of the Indian Act against Aboriginal women and their children in matters of reserve membership and matrimonial property on reserve lands. The Committee urged the state to seek solutions with the informed consent of indigenous peoples, but also stressed that 'balancing collective and individual interests on reserves to the sole detriment of women is not compatible with the Covenant.'[151] Kukathas points out the differences and various conflicts of interests that could exist within the group. He notes that when elites are confronted with modernisation, they often develop interests distinct from the masses and in some cases they abuse the masses for personal ends.[152] If a decision about an illiberal practice is made by the elite, it may not reflect all sections of the group and thus could lead to further illiberal results.

The right to exit is a further condition to take into account when making a decision about restricting a collective right. If the individual has the right to exit the group and, through her choice, she stays and accepts the illiberal practices, as long as these practices do not violate the core of any individual human right, there is no reason, I believe, to restrict the collective right. Kukathas places a lot of weight on the right of exit of individuals provided that they have an open-market society into which they can enter.[153] However, the right to exit is not always adequate for the protection of individuals against oppressive methods used by groups. If someone has been denied education, literacy and the right to learn about the world outside the group, she does not really have a substantial freedom to leave because she lacks the preconditions (knowledge and experience) to make a meaningful choice.[154] For this reason Halev sets some minimal standards that are needed to ensure that exit is really an option. These standards include freedom from physical abuse, decent health care and nutrition, the ability to socialise with others, a minimal education and a mainstream liberal society.[155] Unfortunately, some indigenous peoples, belonging to the poorest nations in the world, will not satisfy these criteria.

Concluding comments

Cultural membership can be an inherent part of any individual; therefore, it must be protected. Its protection via collective rights is compatible with normative possibilities opened up by international law and human rights. Although the list of collective rights universally recognised as such is rather short, international law is moving towards accepting more rights for cultural groups. This is because international norms recognise that the individual has several group loyalties and attempt to accommodate them. Also, cultural groups are not perceived anymore as a threat to national sovereignty; they can coexist and influence each other and the state's predominant culture and can thus mutually develop and evolve. This can be done through equal dialogue and genuine cooperation. Within this framework, dangers related to the diminishment of the freedom and autonomy of the individual, his lack of choice and the practice of illiberal customs can be eliminated. Conflicts will arise between collective and individual rights, in the same way that conflicts arise between individual rights. The cases will have to be solved on an individual, ad hoc basis; the tests of reasonableness, objectiveness and necessity will help this process.

If participatory democracy is the important phrase for the twenty-first century, international law must continue to look at the genuine claims of groups and seriously try to accommodate them. Indigenous peoples' claims concerning the recognition of collective rights can be accommodated.[156] Current international law and its conceptual foundations allow for this recognition. Recognition of indigenous collective rights does not necessarily mean that in every case indigenous collective rights will prevail over individual rights of members of indigenous communities; but it does mean that indigenous communities and their cultures will be better protected from violations of their rights.

Notes

1. M. Dixon, *Textbook on International Law* (London: Blackstone Press Ltd, 3rd edn 1996), p. 2.
2. United Nations Sub-Commission, 'Indigenous Peoples Preparatory Meeting: Comments on the First Revised Text of the Draft Declaration on Rights of Indigenous Peoples', July 1989, UN Doc. E/CN.4/Sub.2/AC.4/1990/3/Add.2.
3. C. Taylor, *Philosophical Arguments* (Harvard: Harvard University Press, 1995), pp. 127–45.
4. J. Johnson, 'Why Respect Culture?' (2000) 44 *American Journal of Political Science* 405–18 at 407.
5. Statement of the Federation of Independent Aboriginal Education Providers in 'Review of Developments pertaining to the Promotion and Protection of Human Rights and Fundamental Freedoms of Indigenous People: Indigenous Peoples' Education and Language', Note by the Secretariat on Information Received from Intergovernmental Organisations and Indigenous Peoples, UN Doc. E/CN.4/Sub.2/AC.4/1998/2 of 3 June 1998, p. 8, para. 2.
6. W. W. Borah, *Justice by Insurance: The General Indian Court of Colonial Mexico and the Legal Aides of the Half Real* (Berkeley: University of California Press, 1983), pp. 6–24.
7. W. Kymlicka, *Liberalism, Community and Culture* (Oxford: Oxford University Press, 1991), pp. 151–2.
8. *Ibid.*, p. 124.
9. M. McDonald, 'Should Communities have Rights? Reflections on Liberal Individualism' (1991) 4 *Canadian Journal of Law and Jurisprudence* 217–37 at 219.
10. M. Sandel, 'The Procedural Republic and the Unencumbered Self' in S. Avineri and A. de-Shalit (eds.), *Communitarianism and Individualism* (Oxford: Oxford University Press, 1992), pp. 12–28 at p. 23.
11. *Ibid.*, p. 3.
12. A. MacIntyre, *After Virtue: A Study in Moral Theory* (London: Duckworth, 1981), p. 221. Nevertheless, MacIntyre limits these narratives to the family, the tribe and the neighbourhood, rather than to the state, the nation or the class. See A. MacIntyre, 'Justice as a Virtue: Changing Concepts' in Avineri and de-Shalit, *Communitarianism*, pp. 51–64.
13. 'Protecting the Rights of Aboriginal and Torres Strait Islander Traditional Knowledge', Background paper submitted by the Aboriginal and Torres Strait Islander Commission (Australia) in 'Substantive Issues Arising in the

Implementation of the International Covenant on Economic, Social and Cultural Rights', UN Doc. E/C.12/2000/17 of 27 October 2000, para. 32.
14. Preamble, para. 6.
15. Article 29.1.c of the Convention on the Rights of the Child.
16. See J. S. Mill, *On Liberty* (1857).
17. W. Kymlicka, 'Liberal Individualism and Liberal Neutrality' (1989) 99 *Ethics* 883–905 at 899. Raz maintains that civil and political rights are not the only determining factors of political action and that in some cases other factors may prevail. Joseph Raz, *The Morality of Freedom* (Oxford: Clarendon Press, 1986), pp. 193–216.
18. McDonald, 'Should Communities', p. 228.
19. R. Howard, 'Dignity, Community, and Human Rights' in A. An-Na'im (ed.), *Human Rights in Cross-Cultural Perspectives* (Philadelphia: University of Pennsylvania Press, 1992), pp. 81–102 at p. 83.
20. E. J. Mitnick, 'Three Models of Group Differentiated Rights' 35 (2004) *Columbia Human Rights Law Review* 215–58 at 246.
21. Utility is individualistic because it is considered to be the utility of individual members of the society, but also because the primary goods that are considered as the sources of utility and welfare have always been considered to be culturally neutral, transculturally valued goods. McDonald, 'Should Communities', p. 223.
22. J. Rawls, *The Theory of Justice* (Cambridge, Mass.: Harvard University Press, 1971), pp. 139–42.
23. See Raz, *Morality of Freedom*, p. 369.
24. McDonald, 'Should Communities', p. 224.
25. V. Van Dyke, 'The Individual, the State and Ethnic Communities in Political Theory', (1977) 29 *World Politics* 343–69 at 363.
26. See also C. Taylor, 'The Politics of Recognition' in A. Gudmann, *Multiculturalism* (Princeton: Princeton University Press, 1994), pp. 25–74 at p. 58.
27. A. Addis, 'Individualism, Communitarianism, and the Rights of Ethnic Minorities' (1992) 62 *Notre Dame Law Review* 615–76 at 644.
28. W. Kymlicka, 'Reply to Kukathas' (1992) 20 *Political Theory* 140–6.
29. J. Raikka, 'Autonomy and Cultural Rights' in Z. Skurbaty (ed.) *Beyond a One-Dimensional State: An Emerging Right to Autonomy?* (Leiden: Martinus Nijhoff Publishers, 2005), pp. 211–75.
30. K. Fierlbeck, 'The Ambivalent Potential of Cultural Identity' (1996) 29 *Canadian Journal of Political Science* 3–22 at 21.
31. R. Dworkin, *Sovereign Virtue: The Theory and Practice of Equality* (Cambridge, Mass.: Harvard University Press, 2000), p. 408.
32. See SPCIJ, Series A/B, No. 64, 1935.
33. Articles 1.2 and 2.2 of the Convention.
34. 'Concluding Observations of the Committee on the Elimination of All Forms of Discrimination: United States of America', 14 August 2001, UN Doc. A/56/18, paras. 380–407 at para. 399.

35. 'Concluding Observations of the Committee on the Elimination of All Forms of Racial Discrimination: Uruguay', 12 April 2001, UN Doc. CERD/C/304/Add.78, para. 13.
36. 'Concluding Observations of the Committee on the Elimination of All Forms of Racial Discrimination: Fiji', 12A/, UN Doc. CERD/C/62/CO/3 of 2 June 2003, para. 15.
37. General Comment 18(37), *Human Rights Committee Report* A/45/40 (1990), Volume I, 173–5.
38. 'Concluding Observations of the Human Rights Committee: Finland', UN Doc. CCPR/C/79/Add. 91, para. 10.
39. 'Concluding Observations of the Human Rights Committee: New Zealand', 7 August 2002, UN Doc. CCPR/C/75/NZL, para. 14.
40. Summary Record of the first part (public) of the 2140th meeting: Philippines, 23 October 2003, UN Doc. CCPR/C/SR.2140, paras. 7 and 20.
41. P. Thornberry, 'Ethnic Dimensions of International Human Rights' in A. Hegarty and S. Leonard (eds.), *Human Rights, An Agenda for the 21st Century* (London: Cavendish Publishers, 1999), pp. 355–77 at p. 367.
42. Dixon, *Textbook on International Law*, pp. 109–10; also I. Brownlie, *Principles of Public International Law* (Oxford: Clarendon Press, 4th edn 1992), pp. 58–70.
43. For a discussion on these cases, see B. G. Ramcharan, 'Individual, Collective and Group Rights: History, Theory, Practice and Contemporary Evolution' (1993) 1 *International Journal of Group Rights* 27–43.
44. V. van Dyke, 'Human Rights and Rights of Groups' (1994) 18 *American Journal of Political Science* 725–41; also V. van Dyke, 'Justice as Fairness: For Groups?' (1975) 69 *American Political Science Review* 607–14.
45. C. Taylor, 'Atomism' in Avineri and de-Shalit, *Communitarianism*, pp. 29–50 at p. 49.
46. Kymlicka, *Liberalism, Community and Culture*, p. 169.
47. Howard, 'Dignity, Community and Human Rights', p. 97.
48. I. M. Young, 'Together in Difference: Transforming the Logic of Group Political Conflict' in Will Kymlicka (ed.), *The Rights of Minority Cultures*, (Oxford: Oxford University Press, 1995), pp. 155–78.
49. J. Waldron, 'Minority Cultures and the Cosmopolitan Alternative' in Kymlicka, *The Rights of Minority Cultures*, pp. 93–119 at p. 103.
50. *Ibid.*, p. 164, quoting Rawles, *A Theory of Justice*, (1971), pp. 563–4.
51. Sandel, 'The Procedural Republic and the Unencumbered Self', p. 24.
52. Waldron, 'Minority Cultures and the Cosmopolitan Alternative', p. 111.
53. MacIntyre, *After Virtue*, p. 220.
54. As quoted in Waldron, 'Minority Cultures and the Cosmopolitan Alternative', p. 111.
55. Preamble, para. 6.
56. Preamble, para. 7.
57. Article 1.
58. Article 4 of the Declaration.

59. Article 2.
60. Article 4 of the Declaration.
61. Article 6, para. 1 of the Declaration.
62. Article 29.1.c of the Convention on the Rights of the Child.
63. Johnson, 'Why Respect Culture?', p. 406.
64. Article 1.2 of the Declaration.
65. Articles 5–8 of the Declaration.
66. Article 6.1 of the 1994 Council of Europe Framework Convention for the Protection of National Minorities and para. 36 of the *Copenhagen Meeting of the Conference on the Human Dimension of the OSCE* (1990).
67. General Comment no. 23 (50) on Article 27, UN Doc. CCPR/C/21/Rev.1/Add.5, 26 April 1994.
68. Article 16.3 of the Universal Declaration and Article 23 of the International Covenant on Civil and Political Rights proclaim that 'the family is the natural and fundamental group unit of society and is entitled to protection by Society and the State'.
69. Such as Article 27 of the International Covenant on Civil and Political Rights and the United Nations Declaration on Ethnic, National, Religious or Linguistic Minorities.
70. Such as the right to self-determination, see Article 1 of the International Covenant on Civil and Political Rights and Article 1 of the International Covenant on Economic, Social and Cultural Rights; the right of peoples to peace, see United Nations Declaration on the Right of Peoples to Peace; the right to economic, social, cultural and political development, see United Nations Declaration on the Right to Development.
71. Ramcharan, 'Individual, collective and group rights', p. 30.
72. V.A. Leary, 'Postliberal strands in Western Human Rights Theory' in An-Na'im, *Human Rights in Cross-Cultural Perspectives*, pp. 105–132 at p. 108.
73. *Ibid.*, p. 106.
74. See R. Garet, 'Communality and Existence: The Rights of Groups' (1993) 56 *South California Law Review* 1001–50.
75. Leary, 'Postliberal strands in Western Human Rights Theory', p. 118.
76. E. Kelly, 'Justice and Communitarian Identity Politics' (2001) 35 *The Journal of Value Enquiry* 71–93.
77. *Ibid.*
78. Young, 'Together in Difference', p. 157.
79. M. Schulte-Tenckhoff, 'The Right of Persons Belonging to Minorities to Enjoy their own Culture', Working paper submitted to the 1997 working group on minorities, UN Doc. E/CN.4/Sub.2/ AC.5/1997/WP.7, paras. 28–30.
80. G. Delanty, 'Re-inventing Community and Citizenship in the Global Era: A Critique of the Communitarian Concept of Community' in E. Christodoulidis (ed.), *Communitarianism and Citizenship* (Aldershot: Ashgate, 1998), pp. 33–52 at p. 39.
81. S. Idleman, 'Multiculturalism and the Future of Tribal Sovereignty' (2004) 35 *Columbia Human Rights Law Review* 589–660.

82. Waldron, 'Minority Rights and the Cosmopolitan Alternative', p. 103.
83. J.A. Green 'The Difference Debate: Reducing Rights to Cultural Flavours' (2000) 33 *Canadian Journal of Political Science* 133–44 at 138.
84. *Ibid.*
85. Addis, 'Individualism, Communitarianism'.
86. Article 1 of the Convention.
87. Addis, 'Individualism, Communitarianism', p. 621.
88. M.F. Shaughnessy and M. Sardoc, 'An Interview with Michael Walzer' 21 (2002) *Studies in Philosophy and Education* 65–75 at 69.
89. World Commission on Culture and Development, *Report: Our Creative Diversity* (Paris: UNESCO, 1995), Chapter II, p. 70. UNESCO organised in January 1999 the colloquium 'Towards a Constructive Pluralism' where the idea of pluralism was discussed in depth.
    See http://www.unesco.org/culture/culturalpluralism/html_eng/overview.ht.
90. See for example, Article 15 of the 1994 Council of Europe Framework Convention for the Protection of National Minorities; also para. 35 of the Copenhagen Meeting of the Conference on the Human Dimension of the OSCE (1990).
91. Article 2.3 of the UN Declaration on Minorities.
92. Article 6.2 of ILO Convention No. 169. For an analysis of this Convention, see next chapter.
93. Richard Falk, 'Cultural Foundations for the International Protection of Human Rights' in An-Na'im, *Human Rights in Cross-Cultural Perspectives*, pp. 43–64 at p. 48.
94. *Ibid.*, 110.
95. 'Protecting the Rights of Aboriginal and Torres Strait Islander Traditional Knowledge', Background paper submitted by the Aboriginal and Torres Strait Islander Commission (Australia) in 'Substantive issues arising in the Implementation of the International Covenant on Economic, Social and Cultural Rights', UN Doc. E/C.12/2000/17 of 27 October 2000, para. 4.
96. C. Kukathas, 'Are there any Cultural Rights?' (1992) 20 *Political Theory* 105–39 at 111.
97. *Ibid.*, 112.
98. Kymlicka, *Liberalism, Community, Culture*, p. 61.
99. Waldron, 'Minority Cultures and the Cosmopolitan Alternative', p. 109.
100. M. McDonald, 'Liberalism, Community and Culture' (1992) 42 *University of Toronto Law Journal* 113–31 at 117 and 129.
101. See Commission on Human Rights, Report of the Working Group established in accordance with Commission on Human Rights Resolution 1995/32, UN Doc. E/CN.4/1997/102, para. 108.
102. Resolution 1503 (XLVIII) of the Economic and Social Council on 'Procedure for dealing with communications relating to violations of human rights and fundamental freedoms'.
103. Articles 20, 22 and 24 for collective rights and Article 29 for the duties of the individual towards her group.

104. Article 1 of the Declaration.
105. Article 11.
106. H. Ketley, 'Exclusion by Definition: Access to International Tribunals for the Enforcement of the Collective Rights of Indigenous peoples' (2001) 8 *International Journal on Minority and Group Rights* 331–68.
107. Article 1 of the UNESCO Declaration on Race and Racial Prejudice proclaims that 'all individuals and groups have the right to be different, to consider themselves as different and to be regarded as such'; Article 2 states that 'all individuals and groups have the right to be different'.
108. P. Jones, 'Individuals, Communities and Human Rights' (2000) 26 *Review of International Studies* 199–215 at 215.
109. C. H. Wellman 'Liberalism, Communitarianism and Group Rights' (1999) 18 *Law and Philosophy* 13–40.
110. *Ibid.*, 25.
111. J. Donnelly, 'Human Rights' in J. Dryzek, B. Honig and A. Phillips (eds.), *Oxford Handbook of Political Theory* (Oxford University Press, 2006) forthcoming, published at http://www.du.edu/~jdonnell/papers/oxford_handbook.pdf (accessed on 20 July 2005).
112. Y. Tamir, *Liberal Nationalism* (Princeton: Princeton University Press, 1993), pp. 45 and 53; also, Y. Tamir, 'Who do you Trust?' (1997) 22 *Boston Review* at http://www.bostonreview.net/BR22.5/toc.html (accessed on 19 July 2005).
113. Kukathas, 'Are there any Cultural Rights?'.
114. S. Hutt, 'If Geronimo was Jewish: Equal Protection and the Cultural Property Rights of Native Americans' (2003) 24 *Northern Illinois University Law Review* 527–62.
115. Donnelly, 'Human Rights'.
116. Jones, 'Individuals, Communities and Human Rights', pp. 211–14.
117. *Ibid.*
118. See US Delegation comments on section 1 of the draft Declaration in the 1995 working group on indigenous peoples (on file with the author). Similar comments are included in Commission on Human Rights, Consideration of a Draft United Nations Declaration on the Rights of Indigenous peoples, Information received from Governments, United States of America, UN Doc. E/CN.4/1995/WG.15/2/Add.1, paras. 10–12. Similar views were expressed in the 1998 working group on indigenous peoples: see Commission on Human Rights, Draft report of the working group established in accordance with Commission on Human Rights Resolution 1995/32, E/CN.4/1998/WG.15/CPR.1, para. 40. In the same meeting, Japan and Sweden were also very negative concerning the establishment of collective rights.
119. S. Okin, 'Is Multiculturalism Bad for Women' (1997) 22 *Boston Review* at http://www.bostonreview.net/BR22.5/toc.html accessed on 25 July 2005.
120. Thornberry, 'Ethnic Dimensions of International Human Rights', p. 367.
121. Ramcharan, 'Individual, Collective and Group Rights', p. 41.
122. M. M. M. Estebanez, *International Organisations and Minority Protection in Europe* (Turku/Abo: Abo Akademi, 1996), p. 40.

123. G. N. Tarayia, 'The Legal Perspectives of the Maasai Culture, Customs, and Traditions' (2004) 21 *Arizona Journal of International and Comparative Law* 183–222.
124. R. Alexy, 'Individual Rights and Collective Goods' in C. Nino, *The Ethics of Human Rights* (Oxford: Oxford University Press, 1991), pp. 163–81.
125. Kymlicka, 'Reply to Kukathas', p. 144.
126. B. Honig, 'Complicating Culture' (1997) 22 *Boston Review* at http://boston review.net/BR22.5/honig.html accessed on 25 July 2005.
127. Garet, 'Communality and Existence'.
128. W. F. Pertney, *The Aboriginal Rights Provisions in the Constitution Act* (Saskatoon: Native Law Centre, 1987), p. 52 as quoted by Darlene Johnston in Kymlicka, *Rights of Minority Cultures*, p. 189.
129. *Ibid.*
130. C. I. Nyamu, 'How Should Human Rights and Development Respond to Cultural Legitimization of Gender Hierarchy in Developing Countries' (2000) 41 *Harvard International Law Journal* 381–418 at 394.
131. A. Eisenberg, 'Context, Cultural Difference, Sex and Social Justice' (2002) 35 *Canadian Journal of Political Science* 613–28 at 624.
132. *Ibid.*, p. 625.
133. *Ibid.*, p. 624.
134. A. Anghie, *Imperialism, Sovereignty and the Making of International Law* (Cambridge: Cambridge University Press, 2004).
135. Wellman, 'Liberalism, Communitarianism, and Group Rights'.
136. P. Thornberry, *Indigenous Peoples and Human Rights* (Manchester: Manchester University Press, 2002), p. 63.
137. Eisenberg, 'Context, Cultural Difference', p. 624.
138. 'Concluding Observations of the Human Rights Committee: Uganda', 4 May 2004, UN Doc. CCPR/CO/80/UGA, paras. 9 and 10.
139. 'Concluding Observations of the Human Rights Committee: Greece', 25 April 2005, UN Doc. CCPR/CO/83/GRC, para. 8.
140. Communication No. 24/1977; views in UN Doc. A/36/40 (1981).
141. Communication No. 195/1985; views in UN Doc. A/43/40 (1988).
142. Communication No. 511/1992; views in UN Doc. A/50/40 (1995).
143. For more discussion on these cases, see Thornberry, *Indigenous Peoples*, pp. 154–60.
144. S. M. Okin, 'Multiculturalism and Feminism: No Simple Question, No Simple Answers' in A. Eisenberg and J. Spinner-Halev (eds.), *Minorities Within Minorities, Equality, Rights and Diversity* (Cambridge: Cambridge University Press, 2005), pp. 67–89.
145. B. Parekh, 'A Varied Moral World' (1997) 22 *Boston Review* at http://boston review.net/BR22.5/parekh.html accessed on 25 July 2005.
146. M. Friedman, *Autonomy, Gender, Politics* (Oxford: Oxford University Press, 2003), pp. 188 and 201.
147. 'Concluding Observations of the Human Rights Committee: Greece', 25 April 2005, UN Doc. CCPR/CO/83/GRC, para. 8.

148. J. Anaya, 'International Human Rights and Indigenous Peoples: The Move towards the Multicultural State' 21 (2004) *Arizona Journal of International and Comparative Law* 13–61 at 26.
149. L. Ahmed, *Women and Gender in Islam: Historical Roots of a Modern Debate* (New Haven: Yale University Press, 1992) pp. 223–4.
150. See J. T. Levy, 'Sexual Orientation, Exit and Refuge' in Eisenberg, Spinner-Halev, *Minorities Within Minorities*, pp. 172–88.
151. 'Concluding Observations of the Human Rights Committee: Canada', UN Doc. CCPR/C/CAN/CO/5 of 20 April 2006, para. 22.
152. Kukathas, 'Are there any Cultural Rights?', p. 113.
153. *Ibid.*, pp. 133–4.
154. Kymlicka, 'Reply to Kukathas', p. 143.
155. J. Spinner-Halev, 'Autonomy, Association and Pluralism' in Eisenberg, Spinner-Halev, *Minorities Within Minorities*, pp. 157–71.
156. For contra, see J. E. Oestreich, 'Liberal Theory and Minority Group Rights' (1999) 21 *Human Rights Quarterly* 108–33, where he reaches the conclusion that indigenous claims as included in the draft Declaration of indigenous peoples are contrary to liberal theory.

PART I

United Nations instruments on indigenous peoples

2 The ILO Conventions

Convention No. 107

The ILO and indigenous peoples

The International Labour Organisation (ILO) showed its interest in the situation of indigenous and tribal peoples early on, shortly after its creation in 1919. In 1921, the organisation undertook studies on the situation of indigenous workers and subsequently in 1926 the Committee of Experts on Native Labour was established to set up standards for the protection of indigenous workers. The work of this committee formed the basis of several conventions.[1] In 1953, the ILO published an important study concerning the living and working conditions of indigenous and tribal populations in all the parts of the world.[2] During the same year, the United Nations launched the Andean Indian Programme, in which the ILO had an active part.[3] In 1957, during the 39th session of the International Labour Conference, the Committee on Indigenous Populations (Conference Committee) discussed the draft text of a convention and a recommendation relating to indigenous populations in independent countries. After receiving the replies of governments to a questionnaire, the International Labour Conference adopted at its 40th session the Convention concerning the Protection and Integration of Indigenous and Other Tribal and Semi-Tribal Populations in Independent Countries, No. 107 (Convention No. 107) and its accompanying Indigenous and Tribal Populations Recommendation (Recommendation No. 104). Convention No. 107 was the first international convention that focused specifically on the rights of indigenous peoples.

Convention No. 107 has been ratified by twenty-seven countries, fourteen of which are in Latin America; six in Africa and the Middle

East and two in Europe. Each state has to provide regular reports on the situation of indigenous populations and the legal protection available in the country.[4] These reports are examined by the ILO Committee of Experts on the Application of Conventions and Recommendations (CEACR), a body consisting of twenty independent experts on labour law and social problems who are named by the Governing Body of the ILO on the recommendations of the Director-General. Any problems concerning the application of the Convention are included either in the CEACR 'direct requests' or, in more serious cases, in their 'observations'. In addition, the ILO Constitution establishes the possibility of 'representations', i.e. claims of failure to implement the Convention submitted by a workers' or an employer's organisation. A special committee of the Governing Body (Tripartite Committee) examines the substance of the representation and makes recommendations to the Governing Body. The Governing Body can either close the case by publishing its finding or refer the case to the 'complaints procedure' set out in Articles 26–34 of the Constitution. A Commission of Enquiry can be set up to investigate the complaint and make recommendations to the parties. Their reports are transmitted to the Governing Body and the parties concerned. The Constitution also allows for the possibility to refer the decision to the International Court of Justice. Convention No. 107 is now closed for ratification, but remains valid for those countries, eighteen in total, which have ratified this Convention rather than Convention No. 169. In contrast to ILO Convention No. 107, Recommendation No. 104 is not subject to ratification and provides more specific guidelines for the protection of indigenous peoples.

One of the main positive aspects of Convention No. 107 is its binding nature: its provisions established for the first time in international law specific state obligations towards indigenous peoples. Numerous states were opposed to its establishment; for example, during the *travaux préparatoires* Canada insisted that the proposed instrument was too detailed for general application and suggested:

> The countries concerned with the problem could more usefully ask the United Nations or its specialised agencies to set up study groups with a view to the exchange of information and experience.[5]

Similarly, the USA noted:

> The problems to be faced in each country differ so greatly and the means at the disposal of each country vary so much that it would appear necessary to have

flexibility in planning and executing measures to accomplish the protection and integration of these populations.[6]

Several states suggested the establishment of a non-binding instrument instead of the Convention. However, during the plenary sitting, the overwhelming majority decided that a new convention should be established.[7]

The content of the Convention was a matter of contention. The text was quite radical for its time and includes a wide range of rights, such as the right to life, education, social security, health and participation; this expanded the scope of previous ILO initiatives restricted to issues of labour, land-tenure and forms of slavery. Several states maintained that some provisions of the Convention fell outside the constitutional or traditional field of competence of the ILO[8] and argued that the organisation would surpass its competence by adopting an instrument not focused only on the living and working conditions of indigenous populations. This was a rather weak argument as the field of competence of the ILO – as determined in the Declaration of Philadelphia – is wide enough to encompass issues of social justice and human rights. In any case, the ILO had already been dealing with the indigenous question for quite some time and had experience on the topic; this was recognised by the United Nations, UNESCO and other international organisations who all agreed to collaborate in the creation of this Convention, without expressing any complaint about possible lack of competence by the ILO.[9] UNESCO noted that the 'problem' of indigenous populations was 'a comprehensive one; its educational and anthropological aspects could not be artificially separated from the general scope of the instrument'.[10]

Convention No. 107 attempted to redress the isolation and marginalisation of indigenous peoples and to ensure that indigenous peoples benefited from development programmes. Unfortunately, at the time development was viewed in a very state-oriented way and the understanding was that it was the role of professionals, technocrats and economic planners to determine the interests of the state.[11] This approach disregarded views of the peoples affected by the development projects. Also, the view at the time did not acknowledge that the interests of indigenous peoples were different from those of the state in which they were living. In actual fact, indigenous customs and systems were viewed as an obstacle to economic and social progress. All these views infiltrated the Convention and compromised its protection to indigenous peoples.

During the years after its adoption, the ILO has recognised the limitations of Convention No. 107. For example, in a 1984 report focusing on land issues, the International Labour Office noted that since the adoption of Convention No. 107, 'there have been significant changes in the situation of indigenous and tribal peoples, with regard to government measures, to pressure on the land and to action by representative organisations of the indigenous peoples themselves'.[12] Aiming at redressing the shortcomings of the Convention, the CEACR interprets the provisions in a flexible manner, taking into account current understandings concerning indigenous populations, development and the state.

Provisions of ILO Convention No. 107

Definition

Article 1 of the convention defines two kinds of 'populations' that benefit from its protection. The first category refers to:

> members of tribal and semi-tribal populations in independent countries, whose social and economic conditions are at a less advanced stage than the stage reached by the other sections of the national community and whose status is regulated wholly or partially by their own customs and traditions or by special laws or regulations.[13]

This category refers to shifting cultivators and nomadic tribes who may not have a historical association with a particular area of land, for example, an immigrant tribal or semi-tribal group or a nomadic tribal or semi-tribal one with no historical presence in the state.[14] The phrase 'at a less advanced stage' reflects a negative approach on indigenous lifestyles: it is assumed that the majority of the society is at a more 'advanced stage' than indigenous peoples. According to the Convention, the 'backwardness of these communities prevent them from 'sharing fully in the progress of the national community of which they form part'.[15] Notions of inferiority and superiority serve as a basis for the continuation of oppression of indigenous identities; it is particularly unfortunate when such notions are included in human rights instruments. Still, the language reflects the views of the time the Convention was adopted.

The second category refers to:

> members of tribal and semi-tribal populations in independent countries which are regarded as indigenous on account of their descent from the populations which inhabited the country, or a geographical region to which the country belongs, at the time of conquest of colonisation and which, irrespective of their legal status, live more in conformity with the social, economic and

cultural institutions of that time than with the institutions of the nation to which they belong.[16]

This definition seems to be applicable to groups characterised as indigenous because of their association with a particular territory. It is interesting to note that only this category uses the term 'indigenous'. Again, the language reflects the perceptions of the time: indigenous peoples 'live more in conformity with the social, economic and cultural institutions of that time than with the institutions of the nation to which they belong'.

During the deliberations about the Convention, several states objected to the proposed definition of indigenous populations. For example, the Indonesian representative:

> informed the Committee that the policy of his country was to abolish all differentiation between the various elements of the population. Moreover, all the national laws of the country applied to all sectors of the population. In these conditions, it was not appropriate to consider that certain tribal or semi-tribal groups were indigenous . . .[17]

The Convention does not make mention of self-identification, the fundamental criterion in identifying indigenous peoples. However, the CEACR has evidently adopted it, as they have repeatedly raised issues related to indigenous groups who have not been recognised by the state. For example, in 2005, the Committee urged India to recognise all scheduled tribes;[18] more explicitly, the Committee has noted that 'no distinction . . . made in the national legislation between different population groups . . . is not a sufficient reason for deciding that the Convention is not applicable to a country'.[19] It is noteworthy that one of the major successes of the Committee has been the use of its position to highlight the concerns of indigenous communities whose plea has not attracted international attention. For example, the Committee has repeatedly raised issues related to Bedouins living within several states.[20]

Integration

Article 2 sets out the main thrust of the Convention, which has been the promotion of the eventual integration of indigenous populations into the national society and the parallel protection of their culture and institutions. Governments must 'develop co-ordinated and systematic action' to this end, including: measures that enable the indigenous population 'to benefit on an equal footing from the rights and opportunities which national laws or regulations grant to the other elements of the population'; measures that promote the development of indigenous populations and raise their standard of living; and measures that create 'possibilities of national integration to the exclusion of measures tending toward the artificial assimilation of these populations'.[21] Although the Convention attempted in this way to strike a balance between integration and protection of indigenous rights, this balance was finally not reached. The blurring between integration and assimilation, as is obvious from the *travaux préparatoires*, has been an important obstacle to the adequate protection of indigenous rights. Portugal suggested that the term 'integration' should be defined as:

> the progressive incorporation of indigenous populations into the national community through measures aimed at guaranteeing for them the same rights and obligations as are established by law for the whole of the community.[22]

At the same time, Portugal opposed the inclusion of a provision encouraging indigenous handcrafts and rural industries, on the ground that it runs counter to 'the objectives of an integration programme'.[23] The International Labour Office strongly replied:

> The observation made by the Government of Portugal appears to be based on a restrictive interpretation of the concept of integration which is not in accordance with that reflected in the provisions of the proposed instrument as a whole.[24]

Still, there was no discussion establishing the parameters of the policy of integration; neither was there a discussion about the difference between voluntary and involuntary incorporation of indigenous populations in the national society. Only the USSR raised the issue:

> Integration should not be forced; indigenous peoples should be given the opportunity to develop freely and to administer themselves ... The opinion of the indigenous peoples themselves in regard to the proposed instrument should be taken into account.[25]

The Conference Committee decided against defining 'integration', on the ground that 'any definition of integration would necessarily be restrictive and therefore might not cover all the many aspects of the problem.'[26] According to the *travaux*, several countries even found Article 2(3) that excludes 'recourse to force or coercion as a means of promoting the integration of these populations into the national community' difficult to accept. The Portuguese government suggested the qualification 'except in the case of practices repugnant to generally accepted moral principles',[27] whereas the United Kingdom stated that the government would be completely ineffective if it was unable to have recourse to compulsion in the last resort if that was clearly in the interest of the peoples concerned.[28]

Also, paragraph 2.2 (c) of the Convention protects indigenous populations from 'artificial assimilation'; the qualification implies that non-artificial assimilation could be tolerated. The confusion between integration and assimilation is increased by the language of several other articles in the Convention that point towards assimilation. For example, Article 5 establishes that governments should stimulate 'by all means' the development among indigenous populations of 'civil liberties and the establishment of participation in elective institutions'. It is not clear what the term 'by all means' entails. Article 7 prescribes that indigenous peoples will be able to retain their customs and institutions, only if they are compatible with the national legal systems or the objectives of the integration programme. The compatibility will, of course, be decided by the state rather than by the indigenous group in question. Thornberry notes that this provision 'constitutes a severe obstacle to the retention of indigenous institutions and is phrased in such a manner as to indicate that indigenous institutions are not valued in their own terms'.[29] Article 9 is also qualified: indigenous social control systems can be retained, only if they are 'consistent with the interests of the national community and with the national legal system'. Nevertheless, one cannot ignore that other provisions set limits to the process of integration: for example, Article 4 proclaims that state parties must take 'due account of the cultural and religious values and ... forms of social control' existing among the populations. The article stresses the 'danger in disrupting the values and institutions' of the populations, 'unless they can be replaced by appropriate substitutes which the groups concerned are willing to accept'.

The CEACR has repeatedly commented on state policies of assimilation and paternalism with respect to vulnerable indigenous groups, such as the Yanomami of Brazil or the Chittagong Hill Tracts of Bangladesh.[30] In the (1990) Direct Request on Iraq, the CEACR adopted a clear tone against assimilation:

The Committee wishes to refer to the policy of assimilation of the populations concerned to which the Government refers at various stages in its report. The Committee would be grateful if the Government would supply information on the measures that have been adopted or are envisaged to protect the institutions, religions and cultures of the populations concerned in accordance with Articles 3, 4 and 5 of the Convention.[31]

In a Direct Request on Brazil the Committee went further to indicate positive examples of integration:

The Committee also notes that Brazilian Indigenist Policy is intended gradually to integrate Indians into civil society through measures to preserve and strengthen their identity and culture, as well as respect for their customs and traditions.[32]

Hence, it appears that the assimilationist and paternalistic elements of the Convention have gradually been ironed out by the CEACR in a way that agrees with the spirit of Convention No. 169, even contrary to ILO No. 107 express language. Anaya confirms that the use of Convention No. 107 to promote the spirit of Convention No. 169 is appropriate, given the fact that the central commitment of both Conventions is the advancement of indigenous peoples' rights. He notes: 'It would be anomalous to apply the Convention without regard to contemporary standards regarding these rights and interests'.[33] This policy of the Committee dramatically increases the value of the convention and its relevance to indigenous needs.

Protection of indigenous rights

Notwithstanding its integrationist approach, Convention No. 107 proclaims the protection of many indigenous rights. The prohibition of discrimination is set out at the very beginning of the text. Article 2 refers to the negative aspect of the right, whereas Article 3 protects the positive aspect of discrimination. It provides indigenous peoples with special measures 'only so long as there is a need for special protection' and not as a means of 'creating or prolonging a state of segregation'. The special measures are viewed as temporary 'so long as the social, economic and cultural conditions of the populations concerned prevent them from enjoying the benefits of the general laws of the country to which they belong'. Although multiple qualifications weaken the provision considerably,[34] during the *travaux* several states had found even this level of protection difficult to accept; the United Kingdom, notably, opposed 'the singling out of specific sections of the community for special treatment'.[35] During the following years, the CEACR has repeatedly put pressure on states to offer special protection to indigenous communities. For instance, in an individual observation published in 1994, the Committee criticised Colombia for 'certain movement in the country away from a recognition of special rights for indigenous peoples, or from programmes specially adapted to their needs'.[36] In this respect, the Committee has interpreted the letter of Article 3 in conjunction with Article 2 and in a manner consistent with the existing trends of international law and especially the International Convention for the Elimination of All Forms of Racial Discrimination.

Particular emphasis is given in the Convention to rights related to life, liberty and the prohibition of slavery, partly because these were important problems indigenous populations faced during the drafting of the Convention, partly because they are related to the work of the ILO, and partly because they were the least controversial rights. Over the years, CEACR comments have highlighted how, unfortunately, these provisions are still relevant to indigenous realities. For example, in its 1998 observation to Bangladesh,[37] the Committee referred to reports of human rights violations against the inhabitants of the Chittagong Hill Tracts, including the abduction of the Organising Secretary of the Hill Women's Federation, and to measures that the government has taken to protect the life and property of the tribal peoples.

Article 9 prohibits compulsory service, whether paid or unpaid. This has been especially important in countries where the practice of 'bonded labour' or 'attached labour' is still in practice.[38] In 2005, the CEACR raised this issue with respect to Pakistan. The Committee asked for measures to apply the Bonded Labour System (Abolition) Act, No. III (1992) within the areas where tribal peoples live.[39] The issue was also recently raised in other United Nations bodies.[40] The prohibition of Article 9 is in accordance with international instruments on slavery,[41] including the 1930 ILO Forced Labour Convention. Confusing is the provision of Article 7(3) of the 1930 Convention which provides that 'chiefs who are duly recognised and who do not receive adequate remuneration in other forms may have the enjoyment of personal services, subject to due regulation and provided that all necessary measures are taken to prevent abuses'. This must be viewed in conjunction with Article 1 of the 1930 Convention, which establishes the obligation 'to suppress the use of forced or compulsory labour in all its forms within the shortest possible period', but allows for a 'transitional period' during which forced or compulsory labour may be resorted to 'for public purposes only and as an exceptional measure, subject to the conditions and guarantees hereinafter provided'. Today, it would be incomprehensible to use this provision to nullify the effect of Article 9 of the ILO Convention No. 107. Article 7(3) of the Forced Labour Convention can only be seen as a 'purely transitional clause'[42] that has no effect anymore.

Article 10 of Convention No. 107 encapsulates the advantages and weaknesses of the text. The article starts by proclaiming that indigenous peoples should not be unfairly detained and should be able to take legal proceedings. In the Conference Committee, it was pointed out that this article 'merely affirmed that the general principle should apply to them ... defending themselves against possible abusive practices by giving guarantees established by law'.[43] Although one could argue that the relevant provisions in general human rights instruments make Article 10 redundant, the article is particularly valuable. The 2004 Report of the UN Special Rapporteur identified a 'pervasive denial of justice' towards indigenous peoples that

> may be the result of historical processes such as the appropriation of indigenous land by colonizers and settlers on the basis of the now defunct doctrine of *terra nullius*, the imposition of land-titling schemes from which indigenous communities may be excluded, the non-recognition of their cultural identity, the unilateral abrogation of treaties and agreements with indigenous peoples by national Governments, the pillaging of the cultural heritage of native communities, the official rejection of the use of native languages, etc.[44]

The UN Report confirms that the state penalties are not always appropriate for indigenous peoples. Many indigenous cultures do not share the emphasis of state justice systems on punishment and imprisonment, but tend to emphasise restitution, compensation and the restoration of social and community harmony. Indigenous people would benefit from these kinds of penalties more. Paragraph 2 of Article 3 attempts to suggest positive measures with respect to penalties. However, it does so in a paternalistic manner that defies its aim: 'In imposing penalties ... account shall be taken of the degree of cultural development of the populations concerned.' It is now understood that when dealing with indigenous persons the positive effects on the individual determine differentiations in penalties. The next paragraph of Article 3 clarifies: 'preference shall be given to methods of rehabilitation rather than confinement in prison'. Again, the CEACR has interpreted the provision in the light of current trends. In 2005, the CEACR asked Panama to provide information about relevant court cases.[45] Still, if the paternalistic tone of Article 3 is put aside, one can easily see the rich benefits of this article. As indigenous representatives still struggle to retain such a provision in the UN draft Declaration, a non-binding document, ILO Convention No. 107, a binding instrument, already imposes such an obligation on the state parties. The Convention also urges states to take into account customary laws of indigenous peoples (Article 7) and to use the indigenous methods of social control and indigenous customs in penal matters (Article 8); however, all these are subject to their compliance with the national systems. This restriction, found also in many minority instruments, compromises the protection this convention offers to indigenous communities.

Control over indigenous affairs

According to Article 2 of Convention No. 107, governments have 'the primary responsibility' for the protection of indigenous peoples. Some interpret this provision as a limitation on the interference of charitable or missionary organisations, which have been detrimental to indigenous communities. As the Cobo report suggests:

> On the one hand ... missionary organisations have transcribed and preserved indigenous languages and have provided the resources for intercultural contact and the dissemination of traditional values and customs, which might otherwise have been beyond the powers of many states; on the other hand, they have also been found to have applied in the past clear policies of forced assimilation with intimidatory and outright punitive measures ... and of having opened these communities to all kinds of destabilisation and acculturation pressures.[46]

The CEACR has noted that the unsupervised work of non-governmental organisations, including religious missionary groups, in indigenous areas of Paraguay and the exercise of extraordinary authority would constitute violation of the Convention. In an observation published in 1991, the CEACR expressed its concern

> over whether the Government is in fact 'developing coordinated and systematic action for the protection of the populations concerned' (Article 2 of the Convention), whether it has met the requirement to 'create and develop agencies to administer the programmes involved' in applying the Convention (Article 27) and whether the 'improvement of the conditions of life and work and level of education of the populations concerned' are being 'given high priority in plans for the overall development of areas inhabited by these populations' (Article 6).[47]

In other cases, the CEACR has requested governments to provide details of the 'programmes of systematic and coordinated action' that exist for the protection of indigenous peoples.[48]

The lack of recognition of control to indigenous communities is an important flaw of the Convention. Still, Article 5 requires the collaboration of indigenous populations and their representatives. The CEARC has continuously interpreted this provision within the spirit of ILO Convention No. 169 and has insisted on the 'involvement of indigenous leadership before development projects affecting their situation have been undertaken'.[49] The CEACR has actually expanded the scope of Article 5(a): the Committee has indicated that consultation with indigenous peoples affected by a project should be carried out throughout the various phases of the project rather than 'only at its inception';[50] 'tribals should be made partners in the large development projects'.[51] The CEACR has also suggested the formal participation of indigenous representatives in decision-making bodies.[52] Participation in non-decision-making bodies was found not to satisfy Article 5 of Convention No. 107. In its Observations to Panama, the CEACR expressed its satisfaction at:

> the Government's attention to resolving problems which arise between the indigenous populations of the country and other citizens, in a spirit of dialogue and negotiation ... This does not mean that no problems arise, but it does indicate that they are approached in a spirit of cooperation.

The Committee has repeatedly noted the positive example of Panama.[53] Unfortunately, the consent of indigenous communities is not necessary; mere consultation with indigenous representatives satisfies the criteria of the Convention.

Land rights

The provisions of Part II of the ILO Convention No. 107 recognising land rights are in some respects very strong. The convention recognises the right to ownership, 'collective or individual, of the members of the populations concerned over the lands which these populations traditionally occupy' (Article 11). The recognition of individual and collective ownership to indigenous peoples caused great tension during the *travaux* between Eastern and Western states, as was only to be expected from their ideological differences. On the one hand, Western states emphasised the importance of individual ownership. The United Kingdom argued that:

> the rights of non-integrated sections of the community and the economic well-being of the community in general may not necessarily, or invariably, be best secured by the establishment or perpetuation of communal land reservations such as those which appear to be envisaged in Articles 11 and 14(a) of the proposed Convention. The inevitability of the emergence of individualisation of land tenure has repeatedly been recognised ... and the East Africa Royal Commission, when reporting to Her Majesty's Government in 1955, advanced

the argument that 'the traditional policy of "land reservation" and of safeguarding sectional interests (in land) must be abandoned in the interests of the community as a whole'.[54]

On the other hand, Eastern European states pushed for recognition of collective ownership. The USSR stated:

the Convention should guarantee for indigenous persons the right to acquire or lease land in all parts of the country; that in regions inhabited by indigenous peoples where there is a dearth of land as result of seizure or colonisation, there should be a distribution of land in favour of the indigenous population; and that all provisions of a segregationist nature aimed at prohibiting the sale or leasing of land to indigenous peoples, etc., should be abolished.[55]

The final language refers to – but does not stress – the importance of collective ownership. This compromise has caused major criticism by indigenous peoples and their advocates.[56] They have to a large degree turned their back on Convention ILO No. 107 partly because of its reluctance to go all the distance with collective rights. The response of the ILO has been that at the time the International Labour Conference

felt it would be inappropriate to lay down rules that would be too detailed when it adopted Convention No. 107, because of the varied circumstances under which indigenous and tribal populations live, making it impossible to formulate a general rule.[57]

Nevertheless, it must be kept in mind that in 1957 the Convention recognised collective land rights, while in 2006 several states are still not willing to accept inclusion of such rights to a non-binding instrument, namely the draft Declaration. The International Labour Office explained the other main strengths of the article:

The right of ownership grants full proprietary status which is superior to the present situation of many indigenous peoples in both ratifying and non-ratifying countries. The Article also uses the term 'recognised' rather than the term 'grant'. It thus implicitly accepts that the rights of ownership already accrue to indigenous populations, and are not ceded to them through the action of nation States.[58]

According to the provision, as long as the land is 'traditional', occupation must turn into ownership. The CEACR has observed that occupation does not have to be authorised by the government; in its 1990 report on India, the Committee noted:

traditional occupation, whether or not it has been recognised as authorised, does create rights under [Convention No. 107]. In addition, use of forests or waste lands, title of which is held by the Government, or hunting and gathering – again, whether or not this has been authorised – satisfies the use of the term 'occupation', and if it is traditional it meets the requirement of [Article 11 of the Convention 107]. The term 'traditional occupation' is imprecise, but it clearly conveys that the lands over which these groups' land rights should be recognised are those whose use has become part of their way of life.[59]

The test to qualify a land as 'traditional' has been elaborated further in national cases; this will be explored further in the chapter concerning land rights. Suffice to mention here that the indigenous communities must still occupy the lands in question; past occupation is not adequate according to the Convention. Irrespective of its weaknesses, the provision has according to Thornberry 'bite'[60] and 'a certain clarity compared to the more ambiguous "rights" in 169'.[61]

The right of indigenous persons to acquire or lease land is not explicitly guaranteed in the Convention. This right is arguably implied in the language of Article 3(3), which provides that any indigenous person benefiting from special measures shall also enjoy the general rights of citizenship without discrimination. Article 14 also protects the right of indigenous individuals not to be discriminated against in the acquisition of more lands for their immediate or future needs as well as more means to develop these lands. Paragraph 2 of ILO Recommendation No. 104 urges the states to adopt legislative or administrative measures for the conditions in which indigenous peoples use the land, while paragraph 3 urges states to ensure that indigenous peoples have 'a land reserve adequate for the needs of shifting cultivation so long as no better system of cultivation can be introduced' and recommends zones within which the animals of indigenous peoples can be fed 'pending their attainment of the objectives of a settlement policy for semi-nomadic groups'.

The issue of sub-surface resources is touched upon in Article 4 of Recommendation 104: members of indigenous populations should receive the same treatment as the rest of the populations 'in relation to the ownership of underground wealth or to preference rights in the development of such wealth'. The right established is an individual right, since it is recognised to *members* of indigenous populations. Despite the recommendation of both International NGO Conferences and the ILO's Committee on Indigenous Labour that indigenous peoples should receive a fair share of the benefits of the exploitation of resources within their lands, the provision did not find its way into the final text. Cases where indigenous peoples enjoy a share of the benefits of sub-surface resources have always been the exception rather than the rule. In 1985, Swepston and Plant recognised the difficulty and urged 'the adoption of guidelines at the international level for the exploitation of subsoil rights in indigenous-held land, pending the inclusion of provisions at international level'.[62]

Article 12 protects indigenous populations against their removal from their lands without their free consent, but its effectiveness is compromised by serious exceptions in the interests of national security, national economic development or indigenous health. These are exactly the excuses states often use to remove indigenous persons from their lands.[63] Still, the provision requires that any removal will take place in accordance with national laws and regulations 'rather than through administrative fiat'.[64] Also, the provision establishes compensation for displaced indigenous individuals with lands 'of quality at least equal to those of the lands previously occupied by them, suitable to provide for their present needs and future development' or other lands or money, if they prefer. The CEACR has clarified that the above language 'would create a presumption that displaced tribals should receive agricultural lands for lost agricultural lands, and forest lands for lost forest lands'.[65] The CEACR has also repeatedly stressed the negative effects of various development projects, referring to the damage of indigenous cultures, the loss of indigenous lands and the dispersion of indigenous communities and has asked for measures to rectify these situations.[66] In line with Convention No. 169, the Committee has insisted that peoples concerned must be consulted before the transfer takes place.[67]

The Convention also requires respect for indigenous customs in the transmission of ownership in so far as such customs 'satisfy the needs of these populations and do not hinder their economic and social development' (Article 13). Unfortunately, the decision on whether indigenous customs hinder the economic and social development of indigenous peoples belongs to the state. The Article also attempts to protect indigenous peoples from selling their lands for a fraction of their true value by asking states to make arrangements to prevent such situations. However, the provision has an intensely paternalistic tone, which has lead to equally paternalistic action by states: in light of this provision, several states have prohibited the sale or lease of any indigenous lands or regulated such sales or leases. Still, even in its present form, the provision has been used by the CEACR to highlight abuses of indigenous land rights.[68]

The above analysis demonstrates that the ILO Convention No. 107 contains some strong and relevant principles and guidelines concerning indigenous land rights; at the same time, it also demonstrates how these rights are compromised by a number of exceptions that states can put forward when indigenous rights conflict with other state priorities. Also, the text has no follow-up mechanisms; inadequate emphasis is given to the right of indigenous peoples to decide how to use their lands; inadequate measures are prescribed for the protection of indigenous peoples affected by development projects; and important components for indigenous livelihoods, such as hunting, fishing and rights to natural resources, are ignored.[69] The analysis also highlights how important the role of the Committee has been in keeping the Convention alive. This is something that has received insufficient attention.

Recruitment and conditions of employment

Indigenous peoples have traditionally been the lowest economic group and have been repeatedly exploited. Parts III, IV and V of Convention No. 107 recognise the situation and attempt to redress it. Part III deals with matters of recruitment and employment.

The text transfers the principle of non-discrimination against indigenous populations specifically to the area of employment and asks for protection and special measures for indigenous populations with regard to recruitment and conditions of employment (Article 15). Special measures, provided they are of a temporary nature, are encouraged 'so long as indigenous populations are not in a position to enjoy the protection granted by law to workers in general'. The explicit reference to special measures is an important step in the Convention, especially for the time it was adopted.

ILO Recommendation No. 104 deals with more specific rules concerning indigenous labour rights. The standards set in the Recommendation are similar to Articles 14 and 15 in the (1947) Social Policy (Non-Metropolitan Territories) Convention. During the *travaux*, the USSR asked for more protection contained in the Recommendation, such as provisions for written contracts of employment, specifying the duration of the contract, the date of expiry, the rate of remuneration and any other matters connected with employment,[70] but these suggestions were not adopted.

Article 15 has been widely used by the CEACR. So far, the Committee has highlighted coercive recruitment, non-payment of wages, denial of the right to organise for indigenous workers, lack of labour inspection,[71] slave-like conditions of workers including children[72] with no payment of lawful benefits and appalling conditions of work.[73] Also, the

CEACR has repeatedly highlighted cases of forced labour and has asked for more information on specific measures to tackle this problem.[74] These practices also constitute violations of other ILO Conventions, including the (1930) Forced Labour Convention, No. 29 and the (1957) Abolition of Forced Labour Convention, No. 105. The Committee has also 'named and shamed' specific states that systematically violate indigenous rights related to employment: for example, in June 1999, Brazil was invited to the International Labour Conference to discuss violations of indigenous workers' rights.[75]

It is true that the current language of the provision is too general and fails to oblige governments to set up concrete special measures, including on site inspections and follow-up procedures, in order to prevent labour exploitation.

Education and languages

Part VI of the Convention deals with the preservation of education and other cultural aspects of indigenous identities. The text establishes that indigenous peoples must 'have the opportunity to acquire education at all levels on an equal footing with the rest of the national community' (Article 21). This provision represents the general formula of the right to education as well as the right to equal access to education. Unfortunately, loyal to its integrationist drive, the Convention fails to establish the teaching of indigenous cultures as one of the aims of education for indigenous populations; on the contrary, according to Article 22(1) the primary aim is 'the process of social, economic and cultural integration into the national community'. Article 23 gives some basic recognition of indigenous cultures, noting that 'appropriate measures shall, as far as possible, be taken to preserve the mother tongue or the vernacular language'. Children belonging to indigenous populations 'shall be taught to read and write in their mother tongue or, where this is not practicable, in the language most commonly used by the group to which they belong'. However, states had difficulties accepting even such a basic formula; during the *travaux*, Portugal stated that the provision ran counter to the objectives of an integration programme, whereas the United Kingdom asked for the substitution of the words 'by the group to which they belong' with 'in the society'. If this latter suggestion had been adopted, states would only be obliged to teach indigenous children the language of the majority; thus, the provision would have been deprived of any ability to maintain and protect indigenous languages. Although this suggestion was not adopted, the provision has nevertheless been weakened by the addition of paragraph 2, which states:

Provision shall be made for the progressive transition from the mother tongue or the vernacular language to the national language or one of the official languages of the country.

It is noteworthy that in this section, the Conference Committee had considered introducing a section dealing with tribal groups in frontier zones. However, after the intervention of the United Kingdom, this section was deleted.[76]

Concluding comments

Analyses of instruments dedicated to the protection of indigenous populations often include little or no mention of ILO Convention No. 107;[77] however, this Convention is still binding on eighteen states, many of which have large numbers of indigenous individuals. The Convention is the only binding instrument that these peoples have which specifically addresses some important issues for them. The states' obligations are surprisingly wide, including land rights, development, displacement, employment issues – issues that are still present in indigenous realities.

Convention No. 107 and its accompanying Recommendation No. 104 attempted to achieve a balance between the protection of indigenous rights and the integration of indigenous populations into the national society. Unfortunately, the text often compromises the cultural survival of indigenous for the sake of what is called 'integration', a very vague notion that can be used in several cases to nullify the protection provided by the Convention. Barsh rightly maintains that 'the Convention assumes that it is more feasible to moderate the advance of imperialism, than to halt it'.[78] The paternalistic approach of the Convention fails to include indigenous populations in the decisions about their futures and matters that affect them. Although cooperation with them is established, this remains at a pretty basic level.

Still, the restrictive aspects of Convention No. 107 have been greatly minimised by the progressive interpretation by the CEACR, which disregards discredited elements of the Convention and interprets its language within the spirit of current discussions and developments in indigenous rights and in accordance with ILO Convention No. 169. The Committee has demonstrated an intense interest in the participation of indigenous peoples in the decisions that affect them, an interest that goes far beyond the reluctant language of ILO No. 107 and is very similar to the emphasis that the ILO No. 169 has adopted.

Convention No. 169

In the years following the adoption of Convention No. 107, more and more voices were raised supporting its revision.[79] Martinez Cobo, one of the pioneers of the revision stated in his study:

> More suitable and precise substantive provisions and more practical and effective procedural principles are needed. Particularly in substantive terms, stress must be placed on ethno-development and independence or self-determination, instead of on 'integration and protection'.[80]

Cobo supported the policies of pluralism, self-sufficiency and self-management for indigenous peoples. These policies and the revision of the Convention were also widely supported in the United Nations Working Group of Indigenous Populations as well as in a number of conferences concerning indigenous rights. The NGO Conference on Discrimination against Indigenous Populations in the Americas concluded in 1977 that:

> international instruments, particularly ILO Convention 107, [should] be revised to remove the emphasis on integration as the main approach to indigenous problems and to reinforce the provisions in the Convention for special measures in favour of indigenous peoples . . .[81]

On 26th June 1989, the International Labour Conference adopted the Convention concerning Indigenous and Tribal peoples in Independent Countries (Convention No. 169), which came into force on 5th September 1991.[82] The Convention, so far ratified by seventeen states,[83] represents a partial revision of Convention No. 107 and incorporates the major changes in perceptions on indigenous issues that have gained international support.

Procedure of the revision

After consultation at the 1986 Meeting of Experts, the ILO Governing Body decided in November 1986 to include in the agenda of the 75th Session (1988) of the Conference the first discussion of the revision of Convention No. 107. Before then, the Office had to prepare a report on different countries and a questionnaire that would be submitted to governments and should be returned at least eighteen months before the discussion.[84] The ILO advised the governments to consult indigenous and tribal populations in their countries, when preparing replies to the questionnaire. Although this was not a formal requirement of the procedure, it was considered 'desirable', since 'one of the major objectives of the proposed revision of the Convention was to promote consultation with these populations in all activities affecting them'.[85] The ILO also invited indigenous representatives to participate as observers in the Meetings of Experts as well as in the revision of the Convention at the 1988 General Conference. A second report based on the replies received by the governments, was submitted to the 1988 session of the Conference together with the proposed conclusions for the first discussion of the revision of Convention No. 107. A committee was established by the Conference to discuss the revisions and to produce a preliminary set of conclusions. Based on the first Conference discussion and the replies received, a convention was drafted and circulated to governments. Comments by governments, in consultation with indigenous organisations, were then summarised and submitted to the 1989 session of the Conference, along with a further draft of the revised Convention. At this second discussion, a final draft was concluded and adopted by 328 votes in favour, 1 against and 49 abstentions.[86]

Concerns were raised about a lack of effective participation of indigenous peoples in the General Conference.[87] Only international NGOs were allowed to attend during the discussions of the revision, with national and community indigenous organisations excluded. Moreover, indigenous participation was not formal, but was restricted to indigenous expressions of views without an active role in the formulation of the document.[88] Indigenous peoples were not happy; during the 1987 session of the UN Working Group on Indigenous Populations a consensus resolution by indigenous representatives was presented that expressed 'grave concern' about the content of the questionnaire that would form the basis of a draft revision.[89] The lack of indigenous participation has been one of the main reasons why indigenous peoples have not taken advantage of ILO Convention No. 169 as much as they could in view of its positive language.

Basic orientation of Convention No. 169

In the 1986 Meeting of Experts to discuss the revision of Convention No. 107, the International Labour Office noted the main reason of its revision:

> in the light of developments since the adoption of the Convention in 1957 – most particularly, the views which are frequently expressed by organisations

of indigenous peoples themselves at the national and international levels, the basic orientation towards integration should be removed from the Convention. Recognition should be given to indigenous and tribal populations to determine the extent and pace of the economic development affecting them, to maintain lifestyles different from those prevailing for the remainder of national populations, and to retain and develop their own institutions, languages and cultures independently of the dominant societal groups.[90]

The Meeting unanimously concluded that the integrationist language of Convention No. 107 was outdated and that the application of this principle was 'destructive in the modern world':[91]

In practice, [integration] had become a concept which meant the extinction of ways of life which are different from that of the dominant society. The inclusion of this idea in the text of the Convention has also impeded indigenous and tribal peoples from taking full advantage of the strong protections offered in some parts of the Convention, because of the distrust its use has created amongst them.[92]

Accordingly, the word 'integration' was deleted from the Preamble. Instead, paragraph 4 of Convention No. 169 reads:

Considering that the developments which have taken place in international law since 1957, as well as developments in the situation of indigenous and tribal peoples in all regions of the world, have made it appropriate to adopt new international standards on the subject with a view to removing the assimilationist orientation of earlier standards ...

The specific 'developments in the situation of indigenous peoples' seems largely to refer to the rise since the 1970s of the international indigenous movement that has crystallised common indigenous aspirations and claims[93] and has internationalised indigenous affairs.[94] A second principle that was agreed to run through the revised Convention concerned economic development. The Meeting of Experts agreed that the top-down approach, where 'the national government decided what was best for all inhabitants of the country, including indigenous populations, and imposed its own concepts without discussion or consultation'[95] could not be maintained. Since the adoption of Convention No. 107, there had been increasing recognition that development had to involve the persons affected at all levels of decision making and implementation. The Preamble of Convention No. 169 recognises the aspirations of indigenous peoples 'to exercise control over their institutions, ways of life and economic development and to maintain and develop their identities, languages and religions, within the framework of the States in which they live.[96]

A third general principle referred to indigenous cultures. The Meeting of Experts agreed that there should be:

> a recognition of the right of indigenous peoples to be different from the dominant society in the countries in which they live. This implies a rejection of the notion of cultural superiority by the dominant societal groups ...[97]

Equality of treatment combined with recognition of the right to be different was a major factor that the Meeting identified as a basic orientation of the Convention.[98] This principle was also included at the Preamble. Paragraph 7 calls attention to the 'distinctive contributions of indigenous and tribal peoples to the cultural diversity and social and ecological harmony of humankind ...'

The avoidance of an integrationist language, the broad recognition of indigenous control over their affairs and the deep respect for indigenous distinctiveness are obvious in the provisions of Convention No. 169 and go further than any other instrument available to indigenous peoples.

Provisions of Convention No. 169

Identification of the beneficiaries

Departing from Convention No. 107, Convention No. 169 was the first international instrument that referred to indigenous as 'peoples'. Article 1 of the Convention reads:

> This Convention applies to:
>
> (a) tribal peoples in independent countries whose social, cultural and economic conditions distinguish them from other sections of the national community, and whose status is regulated wholly or partially by their own customs and traditions or by special laws or regulations;
> (b) peoples in independent countries who are regarded as indigenous on account of their descent from the populations who inhabited the country, or the geographical region to which the country belongs, at the time of conquest or colonisation or the establishment of present state boundaries and who, irrespective of their legal status, retain some or all of their own social, economic, cultural and political institutions.
>
> Self-identification as indigenous and tribal shall be regarded as a fundamental criterion for determining the groups to which the provisions of this Convention apply.

In order to avoid the rigidity of a definition, the Secretariat of the ILO has repeatedly insisted that the provision is a statement of coverage rather than a definition of indigenous peoples.[99] The suggestion to use the terms 'peoples' was put forward by the International Labour Office and was supported by twenty-six states prior to the meeting[100] and by several experts and all indigenous and tribal representatives in the discussions of the Committee of Experts.[101] During the discussions the term 'peoples' was one of the most controversial aspects of the revision and was strongly opposed by a number of states led by Canada, and the employer caucus. Canada and Sweden suggested two amendments: the first one sought to replace 'peoples' with 'populations'; the second suggested that if 'peoples' were adopted, a clarification should be added that 'the use of the term "peoples" in this Convention does not imply the right to self-determination as that term is understood in international law'.[102] After vigorous attempts to reach consensus, the parties favoured the second option and agreed on the following formulation of Article 1.3 of the Convention:

> The use of the term 'peoples' in this Convention shall not be construed as having any implications as regards the rights which may attach to the term under international law.[103]

This provision represents a compromise between states' concerns and indigenous peoples' claims. Still, the language used represents tremendous progress from the previous Convention, because, as Thornberry suggests, it signifies a 'move from the vertical and hierarchical narratives of 1957 towards horizontal recognition of an equality-with-difference approach'.[104] In addition, the language implies recognition of the right to self-determination, even though the qualification excludes important aspects of it. In general, although self-determination is not established in the Convention, there are several provisions which protect aspects of the right, not least indigenous participation and control over matters that concern them. In its official commentary and several consequent statements, the ILO Office has explained that the recognition of self-determination for indigenous peoples is not within the mandate of the ILO, but of the United Nations. However, the Office also noted that since the concept of self-determination is in the process of evolving, it is important that the Office does not adopt a limiting terminology that would be against new trends in international law. Therefore, they concluded, the qualification in Article 1(3) does not refer to self-determination, 'because this might present an obstacle to further evolution of the concept with regard to these peoples'.[105]

The ILO Convention No. 169 statement of coverage modifies the descriptions of indigenous peoples contained in the earlier Convention. The term 'semi-tribal populations' is abandoned, as several states noted in their replies to the ILO questionnaires that it had a negative connotation and other states noted that it was irrelevant to their situation.[106] On the contrary, the terms 'indigenous' and 'tribal' are both used in an attempt to sidestep the arguments of some Asian governments that any discussions on indigenous rights did not concern them as they did not have any indigenous peoples within their territories, only tribal groups.[107] Similar arguments had been put forward with respect to areas in the Sub-African continent, where many peoples have tribal links and historical continuity, but were not the only victims of colonialism. During the 1986 Meeting of Experts to discuss the revision, the experts on Africa agreed that the Convention was applicable in Africa.[108] The distinction between who is an indigenous group and who is a tribal group is now mainly of theoretical importance, since both categories have the same rights in the Convention. Moreover, the demeaning reference in ILO Convention No. 107 to tribal peoples as being 'at the less advantaged stage' than the rest of the populations has been replaced in ILO Convention No. 169 by the criterion of distinctiveness.[109]

In the case of the second category in ILO Convention No. 169, that of 'indigenous peoples', their distinctiveness is outlined in a different manner, namely as peoples that retain their institutions, rather than just their customs and traditions. This distinction draws analogies with the distinction made by Kymlicka between 'national minorities' which includes indigenous peoples and where cultures are 'more or less institutionally complete' as opposed to 'ethnic groups', which are not.[110] Similarly, the Convention characterises tribal peoples by their own customs and traditions (less institutionally complete) as opposed to indigenous peoples who are characterised by their own institutions (institutionally complete).[111]

As with minorities, indigenous peoples are such irrespective of their legal status within the state. The use of the term 'independent countries' remains in the new Convention. As independent states represent virtually the whole globe, this reference has no real impact.[112]

Also, as with Convention No. 107, 'indigenous peoples' are linked to colonisation: their ancestors inhabited the country at the time of colonisation or conquest. However, this link is not mandatory: the ancestors of indigenous peoples could also have inhabited during 'the establishment of state boundaries'. The intention of the Convention is to cover a social situation, rather than to establish a priority based on whose ancestors had arrived in a particular area first.[113] This would be welcomed by Waldron, who believes the historical priority argument of indigenous peoples to be inherently flawed and exclusive.[114] Knop notes that the addition of this phrase also dilutes the historical injustice argument that has been put forward for indigenous special protection,[115] whereas Thornberry reminds us that reference to the descent of the individuals is unusual in human rights law, although not unique. For example, descent is referred to in article 1.1 of the International Convention on the Elimination of All Forms of Racial Discrimination. In any case, the Convention clarifies that ancestors of indigenous peoples may also have existed in countries that did not go through the process of colonisation. Thornberry also notes the use of the term 'populations' for the ancestors but 'peoples' for current indigenous communities. He argues that this could indicate

> a legal intervention of some kind to provoke the qualitative move from a mere 'population' to a 'people'. It is as if the peoples were 'established' by colonisation or analogous processes.[116]

Self-identification is a major novelty in ILO No. 169. The inclusion of this principle caused concern to several states; the ILO therefore reassured them that 'self-identification would not appear to be the sole criterion applied to coverage of the Convention';[117] still, it is explicitly a 'fundamental criterion'.

Collective rights

Convention No. 107 widely referred to rights recognised to members of indigenous populations, which implied the recognition of individual rights. The 1986 Meeting of Experts proceeded to a substantial discussion on the question of individual and collective rights.[118] A number of participants representing indigenous and tribal peoples explained the importance of collective rights, even though the employers' experts stressed the importance of protecting individual indigenous rights.[119] The Report on the Meeting concluded that 'the present concentration on individual rights [in Convention No. 107] was therefore misplaced because it ignored the fact that indigenous and tribal peoples were struggling for their rights as collectivities.'[120]

The text of the revised Convention attempts to strike a balance between collective and individual rights. On the one hand, the adoption of the term 'peoples' used continuously in the Convention is an important step in recognising the collective nature of indigenous rights; on the other hand, the qualification of Article 1(3) on the use of the term 'peoples' does not carry the recognition of indigenous as groups and limits the positive effects. Nevertheless, irrespective of the term 'peoples', several provisions in the Convention explicitly recognise the collective element in indigenous rights: Article 3 refers to the need to take into account the problems indigenous face as individuals and groups; Article 12 refers to the right of indigenous peoples to take legal proceedings 'either individually or through their representative bodies' for the protection of their rights; whereas Article 13 refers to the collective element of the relationship of indigenous peoples with their lands. Overall, the Convention is a fine example of how international law can evolve to respond to collective rights. The collective nature of the language goes far beyond other human rights instruments on groups, including the United Nations Declaration on the Rights of Minorities. This can only be seen as a major success of the Convention.

Protection of indigenous rights and cultures

The Convention specifically includes the general principle of non-discrimination in Article 3, but the principle also runs through the whole text; for example, Article 8(3) establishes that indigenous and tribal peoples shall enjoy the same rights as all other national citizens and shall assume corresponding duties. Under Article 12, they shall be able to take legal proceedings to protect their rights and shall be safeguarded against the abuse of their rights. Measures enabling them to understand and be understood in these proceedings shall be taken by the state. The CEACR has interpreted these articles to include positive state obligations: in an observation published in 1999, the CEACR argued that the fundamental rights of indigenous peoples of Mexico were violated because 'they were given no chance to mount an adequate defence and were kept in ignorance of the offences of which they were accused by being denied access to an interpreter or public defender'.[121] The Committee also noted that the objective of Article 12 is 'to compensate for the disadvantages they may be under, in that they may not possess the linguistic or legal knowledge required to assert or protect their rights'.[122] The Convention also requires that specific economic, social and cultural characteristics be taken into account, when applying general criminal penalties to indigenous individuals (Article 10). Article 11 prohibits any compulsory personal services in any form, either paid or unpaid, unless authorised by law for all citizens; the provision requires punishment of any type of bonded or forced labour, into which indigenous peoples are often trapped. The CEACR has condemned

> an extensive practice of forced labour for the repayment of debts contracted in ranch shops in the purchase of basic foodstuffs and other products of primary necessity at exaggerated prices. This circumstance, combined with the allegation that wages are not paid or are paid at the end of the contract, would signify that in order to survive the workers would have to become indebted and are obliged to work to repay their debt.[123]

The Convention also contains a provision that explicitly refers to positive measures: special measures shall be established to safeguard the 'persons, institutions, property, labour, cultures and environment' of indigenous peoples. Whereas the earlier Convention emphasised the temporary nature of the measures, Convention No. 169 emphasises the control of indigenous peoples over which special measures will be established. References to special measures are widely found in other provisions of the Convention: on collective ownership and possession of indigenous lands, language rights, and customary ways of solving internal disputes. It is currently widely accepted that provisions establishing positive measures recognise indigenous distinctiveness. The recognition of indigenous distinctiveness is also endorsed in Article 5, which recognises and protects the social, cultural, religious and spiritual values and practices of indigenous peoples. The CEACR often encourages special measures in connection with indigenous problems, for example problems with alcohol and suicide in Argentina;[124] measures for women and in particular for obtaining legal documents in Guatemala;[125] and to address indigenous poverty and discrimination in employment in Ecuador.[126]

Indeed, some of the Convention's most positive contribution is to be found in cultural provisions. According to Article 32, states are obliged to 'facilitate contacts and cooperation between indigenous and tribal peoples across borders, including activities in the economic, social, cultural, spiritual and environmental fields'.[127] This goes beyond the right of persons belonging to minorities 'to establish and maintain contacts' across borders included in the United Nations Declaration on the Rights of Persons belonging to Ethnic, National, Religious and Linguistic Minorities, adopted four years after the adoption of Convention No. 169. Keeping in mind the non-binding force of the Declaration on the Rights of Minorities and the binding nature of the

Convention No. 169, the establishment of such a state obligation is a major success of the Convention.[128] It is interesting that the CEACR was not satisfied with the mere establishment of contacts among the indigenous peoples of Paraguay, Brazil and Argentina, but asked for the special measures the state has adopted to facilitate such contacts.[129]

After pressure by indigenous representatives, Article 28 establishes the right of indigenous children 'wherever practicable' to be taught to read and write in their own indigenous language or the language most commonly used by the indigenous group. States must take measures to promote the development and use of indigenous languages. At the same time, states must provide opportunities to indigenous peoples to acquire 'fluency' in national or official languages. Barsh suggests that the provision implies a fiscal responsibility of states for language education.[130] Indigenous peoples must also be bi-cultural according to Article 29. Of paramount importance is the obligation of states, established in Article 31 to take positive measures to eliminate prejudices in respect of indigenous peoples and to ensure that indigenous societies and cultures are portrayed in history and other educational materials in a fair, accurate and informative manner. These provisions encapsulate the concept of true multiculturalism, where dominant and non-dominant groups interact, learn about and respect each other's culture; this reflects similar provisions in other human rights instruments, including General Comment 23(50) of the Human Rights Committee, the UN Declaration on Minorities, the Framework Convention and the OSCE Copenhagen Document.

Participation, co-management and self-government

The International Labour Office noted, in 1986, that there was

> a general recognition within the UN system that top-down development models must be replaced by more participatory models, with the poorest sectors of the society deciding on the basic approach to be taken to the solution of their own problems.[131]

The International Labour Organisation strongly believed that the new Convention should establish the solid procedural requirements of indigenous consultation and participation in programmes affecting them. During the meeting of the Committee of Experts, indigenous consultation and participation was the subject of vigorous debate. In the Working Document, the ILO Office made the distinction between development projects aimed at the benefit of the country as a whole and development projects that aimed to improve the conditions of life and work at the local level, advanced vocational training and created income-generating activities. Not only should the Convention encourage the latter, the Office maintained, it should also allow indigenous peoples to have an input into the decision-making process of the former and, further, promote indigenous projects of direct benefit to them.[132] This was not received by the Committee of Experts with much enthusiasm and several arguments were expressed against it; even the terms of consultation and participation were challenged by worker member of the committee as 'supplicant concepts' that gave the impression of revision, but in fact failed to recognise substantial rights. No consensus emerged from that meeting.[133]

Eventually though the Convention included the approach of the ILO Office as its main thrust: repeated throughout the whole text is the condition of 'cooperation with the peoples concerned'. Action to protect indigenous rights is not 'the primary responsibility' of governments, as stated in Convention No. 107, but 'a responsibility' which should be exercised with 'the cooperation of the peoples concerned' (Article 2). Any action must be in accordance with the principles of (a) recognition and protection of indigenous social, cultural, religious and spiritual values; (b) respect for the integrity of their values, practices and institutions; and (c) adoption of measures to mitigate the difficulties experienced by indigenous peoples facing new conditions of life and work, with their participation and cooperation (Article 5). This is a far cry from the text of ILO 107, especially since these principles are complemented by the principle of participation and consultation stated in Article 6.

Article 6 is indeed, the heart of the Convention, the 'key Article in the whole Convention'.[134] It requires consultation and participation 'whenever consideration is being given to legislative and administrative measures which affect [indigenous and tribal peoples] directly'.[135] Consultation is understood as:

> the process by which a government consults its citizens about policy or proposed actions. It is not consultation unless those consulted have a chance to make their views known, and to influence the decision.[136]

Although the requirement of consultation is weaker than the originally suggested requirement of consent, paragraph 2 ensures that consultation will be substantial: it 'shall be undertaken in good faith and in a form appropriate to the circumstances, with the objective of achieving agreement or consent to the agreed measures'. In other words, indigenous peoples must be provided with complete information that can be fully understood by them through their truly representative bodies that can make decisions on behalf of the people. The inclusion of the term consent, which was achieved after lengthy discussions, opens the way for more pressure on reaching consensus. Indeed, recent attempts have been taken by several United Nations bodies to push the boundaries of international law and accept consent of indigenous peoples rather than mere participation.[137] Another important element is that the provision explicitly specifies that consultation should occur though 'appropriate procedures' and indigenous 'representative institutions'; this is the first time that such a level of group authority is recognised in an international instrument. The representatives of the Mexican National Institute of Anthropology and History have maintained that:

> at the risk of distorting the right of indigenous peoples to consultation, a conceptual distinction must be made between an act of consultation which conforms to the Convention and any act of nominal consultation, information or public hearing carried out by the public authorities.[138]

Indeed, the tripartite committee set up to decide on a series of representations against Mexico has argued that consultations where the brevity of the hearing process hinders the objective of reaching consent is not the model envisaged in Article 6.[139] Also, the committee noted the difference in language between the government's statement that they had selected the 'most representative organisations of the indigenous movement' as opposed to the requirement in ILO No. 169 for the 'representative institutions of indigenous peoples'; the committee emphasised that such selection must be made only by indigenous themselves.[140] Therefore, indigenous groups have a powerful tool in their hands.[141]

Paragraph 6.1(b) provides that 'governments should establish means by which these peoples can participate to at least the same extent as other sectors of the population, at all levels of decision-making'. The language allows a possible opening for special treatment,[142] but at the same time, it encourages the empowerment of indigenous peoples to fend for themselves. The next paragraph goes even further and asks governments to help the establishment of indigenous institutions and initiatives, and to provide the necessary resources when appropriate.

Article 7 matches the right to participate actively in national decision making with the potential of autonomy in certain areas. The main thrust of the right is laid down in paragraph 1: it recognises the right of indigenous peoples 'to decide their own priorities for the process of development'; the right 'to exercise control, to the extent possible, over their own economic, social and cultural development' (but falls short of allowing them to stop or divert development); and the right to 'participate in the formulation, implementation and evaluation of plans and programmes' that affect them. The Article accepts that indigenous peoples will decide on their priorities according to their beliefs, institutions and spiritual well-being and stresses that plans for economic development will prioritise the improvement of indigenous conditions of life and work, levels of health and education and will take place with the cooperation of indigenous peoples. The cooperation of indigenous peoples is also needed in studies to assess the impact of development projects and in action to protect the environment of the territories where indigenous peoples live.

Article 8 recognises control of indigenous peoples in criminal matters. Whereas ILO Convention No. 107 had rather weak provisions aimed at the accommodation of indigenous customs in the judicial sphere, ILO No. 169 uses stronger language to protect indigenous customs *as well as their institutions* in the same sphere. Also, whereas ILO No. 107 made the indigenous input conditional on the national system, ILO No. 169 adds the condition of international human rights standards and provides for procedures aiming towards reaching an agreement in case of conflict. However, the right of indigenous peoples in criminal matters still only exists when their customs and institutions are not incompatible with the national system. Also, the text obviously implies that indigenous customs may be against international standards. The same formula is repeated in Article 9: indigenous customs concerning penal matters shall be taken into consideration by the authorities and courts; also, indigenous methods dealing with offences committed by indigenous persons shall be respected, as long as they are not contrary to 'the national legal system and internationally recognised human rights'. The CEACR has used this article to praise Costa Rica for the significant recognition, both in its statutory law and in its judicial system, of the customary laws of indigenous peoples and has urged the implementation of such laws.[143]

The Convention insists on indigenous consultation in other areas too: compulsory consultations with indigenous peoples must have occurred prior to any decisions on exploration or exploitation of mineral and/or other natural resources within indigenous lands; prior to removal and relocation of indigenous peoples; and to the design and launching of vocational training programmes. Health services shall be planned and administered in cooperation with indigenous peoples and shall take into account their special conditions as well as their traditional preventive care, healing practices and medicines (Article 25). In educational matters, governments shall ensure that members of indigenous peoples are trained and that they are involved in the formulation and implementation of education programmes, with a view to a progressive transfer of responsibility for these programmes to them (Article 27). This does not mean that the government can renounce its responsibilities; indigenous peoples have to be ready to accept these responsibilities and able to carry them out effectively. Government responsibilities may also include the financing of these activities.[144]

Land rights

Indigenous land rights were one of the main reasons for the revision of Convention No. 107. It had been widely suggested that the provisions of Convention No. 107 were not adequate to protect indigenous land rights; since 1977 the final report of the Legal Commission had recommended that:

> The right of indigenous peoples to own their land communally and to manage it in accordance with their own traditions and culture should be recognised internationally and nationally, and fully protected by law.[145]

The discussions on land rights were expected to be difficult; indeed, more than 100 amendments were submitted.[146] A special working group was entrusted to discuss the articles, but agreement was not possible. As Swepston acknowledges:

> Discussions were so tense that at one point certain members of the Conference Committee went away with this whole section and came back with a 'take-it-or-leave-it' text. No records were kept of the discussion in that special working group. So the legislative history here is almost a blank.[147]

Indeed, adoption of the land articles was only made possible after the Chairman suggested that they should be dealt as a 'package' text.[148] It is interesting to note that the draft Declaration on the rights of indigenous peoples has followed the same tactic.

The text of Convention No. 169 includes stronger guarantees on land rights than any other existing human rights instrument. Procedural requirements ensure the safeguarding of land rights and allow the provisions to be more effective. In line with the thrust of the Convention, the principles of participation, consultation, free and informed consent and compensation are emphasised; and several new issues, not least subsurface resources, are mentioned. Nevertheless, the provisions continue to allow the displacement of indigenous peoples from their territories in certain circumstances and to allow state authority over the exploration for and extraction of subsoil resources within indigenous territories.

The part on land rights starts with an affirmation of the 'special importance ... of [indigenous peoples'] relationship with the lands or territories' which they occupy or otherwise use. Both this recognition and the emphasis that states must respect it 'and in particular the collective aspects of this relationship' are additions from ILO No. 107, but in line with the case law of the Human Rights Committee.[149] Although 'general in import, [it] is nevertheless couched in mandatory language and must be given some meaning'.[150] The Governing Body used this provision to decide on a 1998 representation against Peru. A new Act allowed indigenous individuals to sell their lands, even though it was claimed that the lands belonged to the community as a whole; the Body noted that when lands held collectively by indigenous and tribal peoples are divided and assigned to individuals, the exercise of indigenous rights tends to be weakened and, in general, they ultimately lose all or most of their lands as well.[151]

During the drafting process, several states proposed replacing the term 'territories' with 'lands', even though Convention No. 107 used both terms interchangeably. Several governments feared that the use of the term 'territories' would imply sovereign rights in conflict with those of the state.[152]

The International Labour Office stated on the matter:

> It appears that the issues ... may be resolved if the word 'lands' were used in connection with the establishment of legal rights, while 'territories' could be used when describing a physical space, when discussing the environment as a whole or when discussing the relationship of these peoples to the territories they occupy.[153]

Paragraph 2 of Article 13 states that the term 'lands' includes the 'concept of territories, which covers the total environment of the areas which the peoples concerned occupy or otherwise use'. This widens the concept considerably and, consequently, widens the protection of Articles 16 and 17 – both referring to indigenous 'lands' – to include water resources and other elements.

Article 14 is arguably the most controversial but also the most fundamental Article of this part. It prescribes that 'the rights of ownership and possession of the peoples concerned over the lands which they traditionally occupy shall be recognised'. The provision refers to the rights of 'peoples', rather than 'members of populations' recognising the collective aspect of indigenous land rights. It also uses the term 'shall', rather than any weaker format. The ILO Guide on the Convention tried to bridge the gap between two extreme interpretations of the term 'traditionally', one that lead to the recognition of rights over land whenever occupied and one that recognised only rights of lands presently occupied. The Guide notes that the term 'traditionally' does not require present occupation,[154] but requires some connection with the present, maybe a relatively recent expulsion or a recent loss of title.[155] Certainly, the provision does not recognise any historical claim[156] and in this respect does not satisfy the current claims of indigenous peoples. Swepston has argued that, on the one hand, recognition of land rights based on prior sovereignty would not be accepted by the governments and, on the other, would disadvantage groups who do not enjoy such an element.[157] This is a weak argument. According to the definition included in the Convention as well as all other working definitions, all indigenous peoples enjoy historical continuity, even if they do not fulfil the element of priority in the lands they live in. Therefore, I cannot see how the recognition would act as a disadvantage to some indigenous groups. Hannikainen seems to believe that current occupation is necessary to benefit from Article 14. He concludes that Saami must currently occupy the lands in order to be the beneficiaries of Article 14.[158] This is a rather restrictive interpretation; if it is accepted, groups who have been forcefully expelled from their lands would have no remedy.[159] What is certain is that 'traditionally' does not mean in the traditional way; thus, indigenous peoples can have developed and changed their ways of life.[160]

Another vague point of the provision relates to the phrase '*rights* of ownership and possession'. Contrary to Convention No. 169, Convention No. 107 did not include both terms, but only gave rights to 'ownership'. It has been suggested that the inclusion of 'possession' weakens the provision, as it allows governments to recognise only rights to possession (restricted title) and not to full ownership (title). The problems that the vagueness of the provision causes are evident in the Sámi case. Sámi living in Finland argue that according to the provision, occupation for a long time creates the expectation of ownership; Finland disagrees, suggesting that according to the provision Sámi occupation only leads to occupation rights. This disagreement has been the main reason why Finland has not yet signed Convention No. 169.

It has been argued that 'possession' was added in the Convention to incorporate the belief of some indigenous groups that land cannot be owned, just entrusted from generation to generation.[161] Swepston maintains that the plural form of the term 'rights' when referring to ownership and possession indicates that the Conference intended that either possession or ownership would meet the requirements of the Convention. In this way, the Convention did not require immediate recognition of a right to title as the

> concept [is] meaningless and even dangerous in many cultures anyway. If it had, then it would have meant that, for instance no country with a system of reserved land could ever ratify the Convention (e.g. Brazil or the United States). Nor could a country which allowed restricted title for indigenous peoples, as in Australia where title is granted but indigenous communities must get permission to dispose of their lands.[162]

Also, the Committee of Experts concluded that:

> it was difficult to say precisely that what was called 'ownership' in one country had exactly the same implications in another country . . . While the Committee of Experts had not found an exact equivalence between 'possession' and 'ownership', it had not found the firm assurance of possession and use to be in violation of the requirement of ownership.[163]

The reference to both 'possession' and 'ownership' can indeed lead to restricted, rather than full title. States can use the language of the provision to get out of the obligation to recognise full ownership to indigenous communities. However, it must be recognised that states would not legally bind themselves to agree to indigenous ownership of all lands that indigenous communities occupied. The language represents a compromise between what indigenous peoples would want and what can realistically be expected. Although it does not go so far as to satisfy all indigenous land claims, the provision imposes important legal obligations on states. This coupled with paragraph 3, creating obligations for procedures to deal with disagreements between indigenous and states on land issues, is a welcome addition.

Article 14.1 also affirms that measures shall be taken 'in appropriate cases' to safeguard the right of indigenous peoples to use lands not exclusively occupied by them, but to which they have traditionally had access for their subsistence and traditional activities. This 'flexibility device'[164] ensures that governments are bound by the provision, but at the same time undoubtedly creates some leeway for them to compromise indigenous protection. The provision includes a particular mention of the rights of nomadic peoples and shifting cultivators. Article 14.2 encourages the identification of the lands that indigenous peoples traditionally occupy. This provision is an important argument in support of indigenous claims for demarcation, an important issue in some states, which has repeatedly been raised by the CEACR.[165] The term 'effective' is of particular importance as it ensures implementation, rather than mere regulation. This emphasis on implementation is also evident in the third paragraph of the provision: adequate procedures shall be established in the national system to deal with land claims. No time constraints have been set. This provision goes much further than ILO Convention No. 107 and addresses the issue of implementation of the convention; however, the text does not clarify whether procedures should be designed for all or only 'important' land claims.

The ILO Governing Body has clarified that Article 14.1 must be seen in the light of Article 2(1) of the Convention, which requires governments to develop, with the participation of the peoples concerned, 'coordinated and systematic action to protect the rights of these peoples and to guarantee respect for their integrity'.[166] At the same time, the Body has set some limits to the requirement of demarcation. In a 2000 representation against Denmark, the Body argued that demarcation of the land from which the Uummannaq community was removed fifty years earlier was not still required, since the group had been awarded compensation for lost hunting and trapping as well as for damage that occurred because of the relocation. The Committee believed that the demarcation of these lands would upset the lives of other indigenous groups currently living in that area.[167]

Article 15 is also a new addition to the revised Convention. The Article deals with the very sensitive issue of natural resources. Even the definition of the subject matter differs from state to state:

> Generally speaking, sub-surface resources are those not exposed on the ground, such as water, air and plants. They usually include minerals, gems and oil, but definitions vary. Some countries distinguish instead between renewable and non-renewable resources. In most countries, governments retain ownership of subsurface resources, whoever owns the land itself.[168]

Article 15 accepts that the majority of states retain exclusive ownership of natural resources, but safeguards other indigenous 'rights to the natural resources pertaining to their lands. These rights include the right of these peoples to participate in the use, management and conservation of these resources'. Again, the provision attempts to bridge the gap between what indigenous peoples claim and what is realistically possible. Also, whilst recognising the principle of state sovereignty over resources, the provision also recognises the need for prior consultation with and participation of indigenous peoples to the decision-making. In other words, the provision applies the general principles recognised in Articles 6, 7 and 11 of Convention No. 169 on land and environmental issues.[169] The provision also establishes the participation of indigenous communities 'in the benefits of such activities' and 'fair compensation for any damages which they may sustain'. The condition of participation in the benefits is left very vague, without precise commitments or safeguards and is also followed by the restriction 'wherever possible'. Still, the provision is quite far-reaching.

These rights have been deployed by the ILO monitoring mechanisms. In several instances, the CEACR has referred to projects that have had negative impacts on indigenous peoples and has asked governments to provide more information on the rights of indigenous peoples and the processes of consultation and participation.[170] In one such case against Bolivia, the ILO Governing Body decided in 1999 that the adoption of administrative decisions establishing forestry concessions in indigenous territories without any prior consultation with the indigenous communities was in violation of the Convention.[171] The tripartite Committee that was established to look at the case noted:

> in view of the fact that these measures to clear title to the land claimed and expropriations and concessions for mining and petroleum exploitation may directly affect the viability and interests of the indigenous peoples concerned, the Committee recalls that Article 15 of the Convention should be read in conjunction with Articles 6 and 7 of the Convention, and that by ratifying the Convention governments undertake to ensure that the indigenous communities concerned are consulted promptly and adequately on the extent and implications of exploration and exploitation activities, whether these are mining, petroleum or forestry activities.[172]

In adopting the Committee's report, the Governing Body requested Bolivia:

> to consider the possibility of establishing, in each particular case, especially in the case of large-scale exploitations such as those affecting large tracts of land, environmental, cultural, social and spiritual impact studies, jointly with the peoples concerned, before authorizing exploration and exploitation of natural resources in areas traditionally occupied by indigenous peoples.[173]

The Convention also includes a provision prohibiting the displacement of indigenous peoples. Article 16 follows the general principle introduced in Convention No. 107 that indigenous peoples 'shall not be removed from the lands which they occupy', other than in exceptional circumstances. However, in contrast to Convention No. 107, Convention No. 169 sets specific criteria to be fulfilled before any exception to the rule is allowed: the indigenous group in question must give their free and informed consent; if this is not possible, the state has to follow appropriate procedures established by national law, including public inquiries that would provide the opportunity for effective representation. Public inquiries reflect the accountability that the state should have when deciding on these matters; participation of indigenous peoples in these enquiries must be 'effective'. This reminds one of the UN Declaration on Minorities that also refers to effective participation. The language does not imply the right to veto, but indigenous peoples should be given a fair chance to put their case forward and to actually affect the decision. The provision refers to relocation, rather than mere removal, included in Convention No. 107. 'Relocation' incorporates the obligation of states to move the affected individuals to another location. This provision has been criticised for allowing displacement. Arguments for an optimum level of protection as opposed to realistic protection may be put forward. In addition, the provision includes a right to return: this is a great innovation not just in indigenous rights, but generally in international law. The right to return is part of the wider debate concerning restitution of past injustices and in this respect it represents an interesting analogy that supports other such claims. It comes as no surprise that the provision allows for other measures 'where return is not possible'. Still, this will not be decided by the state alone: whether return is possible must be determined 'by agreement or in the absence of such agreement, through appropriate procedures'. Even if this is the case, indigenous peoples shall be given 'in all possible cases' lands of 'at least equal' quality and status with their previous lands that are 'suitable to provide for their present needs and future development'. If they prefer, they can get compensation in money or in kind. Finally, they 'shall be compensated for any resulting loss or injury' deriving from the relocation.

The importance of agreement between the government and indigenous in cases of relocation has been once again stressed by the ILO Governing Body in its opinion on the 1998 representation against Mexico.[174] According to the representation, the rights of 5,000 indigenous Chinantec families were violated following the construction of a dam in the State of Oaxaca and relocation of the indigenous families from their traditional lands to Uxpanapa Valley. After a series of negotiations these families had accepted 260,000 hectares; however, they were only given 90,000 hectares. Also, the land disagreement was not resolved according to set procedures and several promised improvements in the Uxpanapa Valley had not taken place with dire results for the living and health conditions of the indigenous families. The tripartite Committee that considered the representation noted the negative consequences of the relocation that affected the indigenous group for a long time after the event and asked the government that:

> in the quest for solutions to the problems that still appear to affect the relocated Chinantec communities, it resume a dialogue to enable both parties to seek solutions to the situation facing these peoples in the Uxpanapa Valley.[175]

Article 17 recognises the indigenous procedures of land transfer and urges states to prevent non-indigenous peoples from 'taking advantage of [indigenous] customs or of lack of understanding of the laws on the part of [indigenous peoples] to secure the ownership possession or use of land belonging to them'. In the 1998 representation against Peru,[176] the International Labour Conference noted that, although the Government believed that individual titles were beneficial to the economic development, involving indigenous peoples in the decision as to whether this form of ownership should change was extremely important.

Article 18 deals with the problem of intrusion in lands either inhabited by indigenous peoples or designated as indigenous lands and urges Governments to take measures to prevent and punish such offences. The CEACR has repeatedly asked states for measures to ensure the implementation of this Article.[177]

Article 19 ensures that indigenous peoples are treated equally with the other sectors of the population with respect to national agrarian programmes to improve and expand their lands. A 1996 representation submitted by the Mexican National Trade Union of Education Workers (SNTE) alleged that the lack of recognition of the Huichol community of San Andrés Cohamiata in any agrarian census and the lack of any special measures to protect them constituted a violation of the ILO No. 169. The complainants specifically asked that the federal government return 22,000 hectares of lands, which had been given to agrarian units in 1960s, to the Huicholes. With respect to the restitution of lands, the tripartite Committee avoided taking sides:

> With regard to claims for the restitution of land, the Committee would like to point out that it does not claim to issue an opinion on the resolution of individual land disputes under the Convention or to make recommendations to the Governing Body for this purpose. The Committee considers that its essential task is rather to ensure that the appropriate means of resolving these disputes have been applied and that the principles of the Convention have been taken into account in dealing with the issues affecting indigenous and tribal peoples.[178]

Yet, the Committee recommended that measures, including positive ones, be taken to remedy the situation of the Huicholes and to protect them and their way of life. Also, measures should be taken to remedy the situation 'taking account of the possibility of assigning additional land to the Huichol people when they do not have the area necessary for providing the essentials of a normal existence, or for any possible increase in their numbers, as provided in Article 19'.[179] Later that year, the CEACR repeated the suggestion to the Government concerning the allocation of additional land.[180]

Recruitment, conditions of employment and vocational training

Part III of Convention No. 169 deals with recruitment and conditions of employment as well as vocational training. Article 20 extends the protection given in Article 15 of Convention No. 107 by covering a wide range of measures concerning rights such as equal employment and remuneration, the right to association, protection of women from sexual harassment, hazardous conditions and protection of seasonal and migrant workers. The Article sets from the beginning the main principles that should govern all matters relevant to recruitment and employment: cooperation of indigenous peoples in devising the policies and adoption of special measures to ensure recruitment and employment of indigenous peoples equally to other sectors of the population. Unfortunately, any policies will be adopted 'within the framework of national laws and regulations'. Still, the Convention urges the establishment of a national body to supervise the recruitment and conditions of employment of indigenous peoples.

The ILO has in the last ten years strengthened its efforts in combating child labour. The (1998) Declaration on Fundamental Rights and Principles at Work and its Follow-up urges the abolition of child labour, whereas the (1999) Convention on the Worst Forms of Child Labour, *No. 182* and the Worst Forms of Child Labour Recommendation, *No. 190* address a number of labour practices such as trafficking of children, debt bondage, child prostitution and forced labour. These instruments, together with the (1973) Minimum Age Convention, *No. 138* and the (1973) Minimum Age Recommendation, *No. 146* complement Article 20 of Convention No. 169 with their protection towards indigenous children.

Articles 21 to 23 protect vocational training and traditional economic activities and ensure that indigenous peoples have access to the training available to other citizens as well as continue to develop traditional activities.[181] Article 22 requires that measures should be taken to promote indigenous voluntary participation in vocational training programmes which are intended for the general population. It also requires that whenever existing programmes do not meet indigenous special needs, governments should provide special training and facilities with the participation of indigenous and tribal peoples. Article 23 provides that handicrafts, rural and community-based industries and subsistence economy and traditional activities shall be recognised as important factors in their lives.

Articles 24 to 31 continue to express the dual nature of protecting indigenous communities in health and education. Indigenous peoples should have the same rights as other members of the population, but should also have the right to apply, maintain and have their traditional medicinal practices, educational needs and languages protected. Indigenous peoples must be able to take control of their health and education services; however, this should not be used as a pretext for governments not to support these services whether financially or otherwise.[182] Convention No. 107 and Convention No. 169 have very different approaches in education: the relevant provisions in the 1957 Convention aimed at the gradual integration of indigenous peoples, whereas Convention No. 169 aims at the protection and development of indigenous systems and cultures. Thus, Convention No. 169 maintains that the educational programmes for indigenous peoples should address their special needs and incorporate their histories, knowledge, technologies, value systems and further aspirations; this is a big leap from Convention No. 107 that maintained that the programmes should take into account 'the stage these populations have reached in the process of social, economic and cultural integration into the national community'.[183] Also, Convention No. 169 ensures the involvement of indigenous peoples in the formulation and implementation of education programmes, aiming towards the gradual transfer of responsibility to these peoples; again, a big contrast to the requirement of 'ethnological studies' before formulating educational programmes in Convention No. 107.[184] This difference of approach is carried through to language provisions: although Convention No. 107 aimed at the progressive transition from the indigenous languages to the national language (Article 23 paragraph 3), Convention No. 169 stresses that children should learn and speak fluently both the mother tongue and the national language.

Concluding comments

In its 1999 Annual Report, the Committee of Experts rightly observed that Convention No. 169 represents 'the most comprehensive instrument of international law' for the protection of indigenous and tribal peoples.[185] The Convention establishes a wide range of rights to its beneficiaries, including guarantees for non-discrimination; protection of individual rights; political participation; the right to decide on their economic development; the right to the ownership and possession of their lands; rights to strengthen their social organisation, their educational and health services, their communication with the national society and their own legal personality.

Convention No. 169 makes a substantial advance on Convention No. 107 in several areas. Its most important contribution to indigenous rights, but also to international human rights, is arguably its multicultural outlook and its insistence on perceiving indigenous peoples as equal partners in the development and evolution of the national society. This is evident in the emphasis on collective rights that recognise indigenous identities but also in the principles of participation of and cooperation with indigenous peoples applied in all areas of indigenous activities and the emphasis on effective implementation of these principles. More specific successes of the text include the strengthening of land rights; the introduction of the issue of natural resources; the establishment of the principle of self-identification; and the many references to collective rights. Also important are the repeated references in the Convention to special measures, especially in view of the general cautiousness of other minority and human rights instruments. The Convention represents a minimum for the satisfaction of indigenous claims. Ten years since its adoption and while other international bodies discuss indigenous issues in the United Nations and elsewhere, standards are constantly evolving. The work of the Committee of Experts has surprisingly not been given attention. Yet, the Committee has applied the Convention in a constructive manner and has ensured that the interpretation of the text is in accordance with the evolving standards of international law.

According to the Committee of Experts, the application of the Convention is very complex and can have a profound impact on the state and its constitutional arrangements.[186] Indeed, on several occasions, its adoption and ratification has meant important changes in the domestic legal order and of course, the lives of indigenous peoples. For example, in the negotiations which lead to the adoption of the Agreement on Identity and the Rights of Indigenous Peoples in March 1995, the Government of Guatemala and the Guatemalan National Revolutionary Union (URNG) used the Convention, while considering its adoption, as part of the conceptual framework in order to reach agreement.[187]

Sixteen years after its adoption only seventeen states have ratified the Convention; this weakens the power of the standards that the Convention sets. However, the impact of the Convention cannot be understood only with reference to the ratifications as its text is widely being used as a point of reference in other countries. For example, in the Russian Federation, the Duma has been examining legislation and practical measures based on Convention No. 169 for the indigenous peoples of the North.[188] In the Philippines, the (1997) Indigenous Peoples Rights Act has been based on Convention No. 169. Moreover, the Convention can be used as guidance for a number of relevant decisions of Supreme Courts in national systems and has been used as an interpretative tool for domestic provisions touching on indigenous issues.[189] In addition to its legal functions, Convention No. 169 has also been used as a political tool: in countries where there is a political dialogue between indigenous peoples and the state Convention No. 169 can facilitate this dialogue by setting standards agreed by the international community.[190] Convention No. 169 has also been instrumental in the shaping of guidelines by other international bodies.[191] As it constitutes an instrument of international law, it represents evidence of new trends and further evolution of international human rights. This illustrates its capacity to influence the development of international instruments and national laws and to initiate discussions about further developments. Finally, the practical value of the Convention for the indigenous groups that can directly benefit from its provisions cannot be underestimated: since 1996, a number of representations have been submitted alleging failure to observe the provisions of the Convention in several countries.[192]

Notes

1. These include the (1930) Forced Labour Convention, the (1936) Recruiting of Indigenous Workers Convention, the (1939) Contracts of Employment (Indigenous Workers) Convention, the (1939) Penal Sanctions (Indigenous Workers) Convention. For the work of the Committee, see 'The Second Session of the ILO Committee of Experts on Indigenous Labour' (1954) 70 *International Labour Review* 418–41; see also International Labour Organisation, Technical Meeting on Problems of Nomadism in the Sahelian Region of Africa (Niamey, 9–20 September 1968), RTNS/E/R.2.
2. International Labour Office, 'Indigenous Peoples: Living and Working Conditions of Aboriginal Populations in Independent Countries', Geneva, 1953.
3. Aimed at integration and development, the Andean Indian Programme involved other international bodies, such as FAO, UNESCO, WHO and later, UNICEF, with the ILO being responsible for its general management. It began in Bolivia, Ecuador and Peru and later included Argentina, Chile, Colombia and Venezuela. During later stages, administration was transferred to national governments. See J. Rens, 'The Andean Indian Programme' (1961) 84 *International Labour Review* 423–61 and J. Rens, 'The development of the Andean Programme and its Future' (1963) 88 *International Labour Review* 547–63.
4. According to Article 22 of the ILO Constitution.
5. 'The Proceedings of the 39th Session of the Conference relating to Indigenous Populations in Independent Countries' in International Labour Office, Report VI(1). Protection and Integration of Indigenous and Other Tribal and Semi-Tribal Populations in Independent Countries, International Labour Conference, 40th Session (1957), p. 9; (herein 40th Session, Report VI(1)).
6. 'Replies from Governments' in International Labour Office, Report VI (2). Protection and Integration of Indigenous and Other Tribal and Semi-Tribal Populations in Independent Countries, International Labour Conference, 40th Session (1957), p. 7; (herein 40th Session, Report VI(2)).
7. The issue was decided with 125 votes to 1 with 32 abstentions. See 40th Session, Report VI (1), p. 43.
8. States that expressed this argument included Portugal, Australia and Canada. See 40th Session, Report VI (1), p. 5. The UK agreed with this opinion, see 40th Session, Report VI(2), p. 6. See Also G. I. Bennett, 'The ILO Convention on Indigenous and Tribal Populations – The Resolution of a Problem of *Vires*' (1972–73) 46 *British Yearbook of International Law* 382–92 at 384.
9. 40th Session, Report VI (1), pp. 6–7.
10. *Ibid.*, p. 6.
11. Note by the International Labour Office, Indigenous and Tribal Peoples and Land Rights, submitted to the United Nations Working Group on Indigenous Populations, 3rd Session (1986), 74.

12. *Ibid.*, p. 2.
13. Article 1 (1)(a).
14. The International Labour Office has stressed on several occasions the importance of including tribal populations in the scope of the Convention.
15. Preamble.
16. Article 1 (1)(b).
17. Similar comments were expressed by Egypt, Syria and Liberia. See 40th Session, Report VI (1), p. 8.
18. CEACR, Individual Direct Request concerning Convention No. 107, Indigenous and Tribal Populations, India, published 2005, para. 4.
19. CEACR, Individual Direct Request concerning Convention No. 107, Indigenous and Tribal Populations, Guinea-Bissau, published 1996, para. 3.
20. CEACR, Individual Direct Request concerning Convention No. 107, Indigenous and Tribal Populations, Egypt, published 2005; and *ibid.*, Syrian Arab Republic, published 2004.
21. Article 2.2(c).
22. ILO 40th session, Report VI (2), p. 15.
23. *Ibid.*, p. 25.
24. *Ibid.*, p. 26.
25. ILO 40th Session, Report VI (1), p. 4.
26. ILO 40th Session, Report VI (2), p. 15.
27. ILO 40th Session, Report VI(1), p. 13.
28. ILO 40th Session, Report VI (2), p. 12.
29. P. Thornberry, *International Law and the Rights of Minorities* (Oxford: Clarendon Press, 1991), p. 344.
30. See CEACR, Individual Observation concerning Convention No. 107, Indigenous and Tribal Populations, Bangladesh, published 1990, 1991, 1993, 1994, 1996, 1998 and 1999; also see CEACR, Individual Observations concerning Convention No. 107, Indigenous and Tribal Populations, Brazil, published 1990, 1991, 1993, 1994, 1995, 1996, 1997, 1998 and 1999.
31. CEACR, Individual Direct Request concerning Convention No. 107, Indigenous and Tribal Populations, Iraq, published 1990, para. 2.
32. CEACR, Individual Direct Request concerning Convention No. 107, Indigenous and Tribal Populations, Brazil, published 1990, para. 3.
33. S. J. Anaya, *Indigenous Peoples in International Law* (Oxford: Oxford University, 1996), p. 156.
34. Article 3.2 of ILO Convention No. 107.
35. ILO 40th Session, Report VI (2), 6.
36. CEACR, Individual Observation concerning Convention No. 107 Indigenous and Tribal Populations, Colombia, published 1994, para. 2.
37. CEACR, Individual Observation concerning Convention No. 107 Indigenous and Tribal Populations, Bangladesh, published 1999. On the same issue, see comments of the UN Special Rapporteur on Torture and other Cruel, Inhuman or Degrading Treatment or Punishment, UN Doc. E/CN.4/1997/7.

38. CEACR, Individual Direct Request concerning Convention No. 107, Indigenous and Tribal Populations, India, published 1990, para. 13.
39. CEACR, Individual Direct Request concerning Convention No. 107, Indigenous and Tribal Populations, Pakistan, published 2005, para. 6.
40. Report of the Working Group of Contemporary Forms of Slavery on its Thirtieth Session, UN Doc. E/CN.4/Sub.2/2005/34.
41. In particular, the Slavery Conventions of 1926; the Supplementary Convention on the Abolition of Slavery, the Slave Trade, and Institutions and Practices Similar to Slavery of 1956; the Convention on the Suppression of the Traffic in Persons and of the Exploitation of the Prostitution of Others of 1949; the Forced Labour Convention, 1930 (No. 29); the Abolition of Forced Labour Convention, 1957 (No. 105); and the Worst Forms of Child Labour Convention, 1999 (No. 182) of the International Labour Organization; the 2003 Protocol to Prevent, Suppress and Punish Trafficking in Persons, Especially Women and Children supplementing the 2003 United Nations Convention against Transnational Organized Crime; and the 2003 International Convention on the Protection of the Rights of All Migrant Workers and Members of their Families.
42. ILO 40th Session, Report VI (2), p. 15.
43. ILO 40th Session, Report VI (1), p. 17.
44. Report of the Special Rapporteur on the situation of human rights and fundamental freedoms of indigenous people, Rodolfo Stavenhagen, UN Doc. E/CN.4/2004/80, para. 12.
45. CEACR, Individual Direct Request concerning Convention No. 107, Indigenous and Tribal Populations, Panama, published 2005, para. 19.
46. Study of the problem of discrimination against indigenous populations, by Jose R. Martinez Cobo, Special Rapporteur of the Sub-Commission on the Prevention on Discrimination and Protection of Minorities, Geneva: United Nations, 1986, UN Doc. E/CN.4/Sub.2/1983/21, para. 41 (herein 'Cobo study').
47. CEACR, Individual Observation concerning Convention No. 107 Indigenous and Tribal Populations, Paraguay, published 1991, para. 4; and repeated *ibid.*, published 1993.
48. For example, CEACR, Individual Direct Request concerning Convention No. 107, Indigenous and Tribal Populations, Peru, published 1991, para. 18.
49. For example, CEACR, Individual Observation concerning Convention No. 107, Indigenous and Tribal Populations, Bangladesh, published 2005, para. 11; and also Individual Observation concerning Convention No. 107, Indigenous and Tribal Populations, Bangladesh, published 2002.
50. CEACR, Individual Direct Request concerning Convention No. 107, Indigenous and Tribal Populations, Brazil, published 1990, para. 13.
51. CEACR, Individual Observation concerning Convention No. 107, Indigenous and Tribal Populations, India, published 2003, para. 11.
52. CEACR, Individual Direct Request concerning Convention No. 107 Indigenous and Tribal Populations, Panama, published 1991, para. 7.

53. CEACR, Individual Observation concerning Convention No. 107 Indigenous and Tribal Populations, Panama, published 1992, para. 1; and repeated *ibid.*, published: 1995.
54. ILO 40th Session, Report VI (2), pp. 19–20.
55. *Ibid.*, p. 19.
56. L. Swepston and R. Plant, 'International Standards and the Protection of the Land Rights of Indigenous and Tribal Populations' (1985) 124 *International Labour Review* 91–106 at 97.
57. 1986 ILO Note to the working group on indigenous populations, p. 63.
58. 1986 ILO Note to the working group on indigenous populations, p. 62.
59. CEACR, Individual Observation concerning Convention No. 107 Indigenous and Tribal Populations, India, published 1990, para. 16. The Committee has repeated this comment in several consequent observations.
60. Thornberry, *Indigenous Peoples*, p. 334.
61. *Ibid.*
62. Swepston and Plant, 'International Standards' at 100.
63. Thornberry, *The Rights of Minorities*, pp. 360–1.
64. Swepston and Plant, 'International Standards' at 101.
65. CEACR, Individual Observation concerning Convention No. 107 Indigenous and Tribal Populations, India, published 1990, para. 23.
66. CEACR, Individual Direct Request concerning Convention No. 107 Indigenous and Tribal Populations, Brazil, published 1998; also CEACR, Individual Direct Request concerning Convention No. 107 Indigenous and Tribal Populations, Paraguay, published 1991, para. 17; also CEACR, Individual Direct Request concerning Convention No. 107, Indigenous and Tribal Populations, Peru, published 1991, para. 18; CEACR, Individual Observation concerning Convention No. 107, Indigenous and Tribal Populations, Bangladesh, published 2005, para. 9.
67. *Ibid.*, para. 18.
68. For example, CEACR, Individual Observation concerning Convention No. 107 Indigenous and Tribal Populations, Argentina, published 1998.
69. Working Document for the Meeting of Experts on the Revision of the Indigenous and Tribal Populations Convention, 1957 (No. 107), (Geneva, 1–10 September 1986), Geneva: ILO, 1986, 40 (herein 'ILO Working Document for 1986 Meeting of Experts').
70. ILO 40th Session, Report VI (2), p. 32.
71. CEACR, Individual Observation concerning Convention No. 107 Indigenous and Tribal Populations, published Mexico, 1995, paras. 4–5.
72. CEACR, Individual Observation concerning Convention No. 107 Indigenous and Tribal Populations, India, published 1996, paras. 2–4.
73. CEACR, Individual Observation concerning Convention No. 107 Indigenous and Tribal Populations, Brazil, published 1995, para. 5.
74. CEACR, Individual Observation Concerning Convention No. 107, Indigenous and Tribal Populations, Brazil, published 1993, para. 5.
75. ILCCR, Individual Observation concerning Convention No. 107, Indigenous and Tribal Populations, 1957 Brazil, published 1999.

76. 40th Session, Report VI (1), p. 27.
77. For example, S. J. Anaya, *Indigenous Peoples in International Law* (Oxford: Oxford University Press, 2nd edn 2004).
78. R. L. Barsh, 'Indigenous North America and Contemporary International Law' (1983) 62 *Oregon Law Review* 73–86 at 81.
79. ILO Working Document for 1986 Meeting of Experts, 33. Also see Swepston and Plant, 'International Standards'; L. Swepston, 'Indigenous and Tribal Populations: A Return to Centre Stage' (1987) 126 *International Labour Review* 447–55; N. Lerner 'The 1989 ILO Convention on Indigenous Populations: New Standards?' (1991) 20 *Israel Yearbook on Human Rights* 223–41 at 231–5.
80. Cobo Study, p. 44, paras. 336 and 337.
81. Report of the International NGO Conference on Discrimination against Indigenous Peoples in the Americas, Palais des Nations, Geneva, 1977, p. 22.
82. On 26th June 1989, the same day that the ILO Convention was adopted, the International Labour Conference also adopted a Resolution on ILO action concerning indigenous and tribal peoples urging for the implementation of the revised Convention. See 'Provisional Record No. 25: Report of the Committee on Convention No. 107', in International Labour Conference, Record of Proceedings, 76th session, 1989, Geneva, para. 167 ('Provisional Record No. 25 of 1989'). For an analysis of this Resolution, see Governing Body, 'Action on the Resolutions adopted by the Conference at its 76th (1989) Session', 244th Session, Geneva, 13–17 November 1989, GB.244/3/3 in Governing Body Minutes of Sessions 239–244, 1988–1989, II/7.
83. These are: Argentina, Bolivia, Brazil, Costa Rica, Dominica, Ecuador, Colombia, Denmark, Fiji, Guatemala, Honduras, Mexico, Netherlands, Norway, Paraguay, Peru and Venezuela.
84. Before the adoption of any ILO Convention, there is a 'double discussion procedure', which involves the reading of the text at successive sessions of the Conference. Part of this procedure involves the International Labour Office preparing a report on law and practice in different countries, together with a questionnaire. The report and the questionnaire requests governments to consult the most representative organisations of employers and workers for their answers, which must be transmitted at least 18 months before the relevant session of the Conference. See International Labour Office, *Handbook of Procedures relating to International Labour Conventions and Recommendations*, International Labour Standards Department, Geneva: 1995, section I, para. 3(a), p. 3.
85. 'International Action concerning Indigenous and Tribal Populations' in International Labour Office, Report VI(1). Partial Revision of the Indigenous and Tribal Populations Convention, 1957 (No. 107), International Labour Conference, 75th Session (1988), p. 2.
86. See International Labour Office, 'Provisional Record 32: Report of the Committee on Convention No. 107: Submission, Discussion and Adoption' in International Labour Conference, Record of Proceedings, 76th Session, 1989, Geneva, 32/6 ('Provisional Record No. 32 of 1989').

87. H.R. Berman, 'The International Labour Organization and Indigenous Peoples: Revision of ILO Convention No. 107 at the 75th Session of the International Labour Conference, 1988' (1988) 41 *The Review (International Commission of Jurists)* pp. 48–57 at p. 48.
88. *Ibid.*, p. 51.
89. *Ibid.*
90. ILO Working Document for 1986 Meeting of Experts, p. 1.
91. *Ibid.*, p. 10.
92. *Ibid.*
93. Ö. Ülgen, 'The Labour Exploitation of Indigenous Peoples: The Interface between Labour Law and Human Rights Law' (PhD Thesis, University of Nottingham, 1999), p. 154.
94. G. Alfredsson, 'International Law, International Organisations, and Indigenous Peoples, (1982) 36 *Journal of International Affairs* 113–24; also see C. Tennant, 'Indigenous Peoples, International Institutions, and the International Legal Literature from 1945 to 1993' (1996) 16 *Human Rights Quarterly* 1–57.
95. ILO Working Document for 1986 Meeting of Experts, p. 10.
96. Para. 6.
97. ILO Working Document for 1986 Meeting of Experts, p. 9.
98. *Ibid.*, p. 11.
99. L. Swepston, 'Economic, Social and Cultural Rights under the 1989 ILO Convention' in F. Horn (ed.), *Economic, Social and Cultural Rights of the Sámi, International and National Aspects* (Rovaniemi: Northern Institute for Environmental and Minority Law, 1988), pp. 38–46 at p. 38.
100. ILO, 75th session, Report VI(2). For a discussion on the replies of the states see K. Knop, *Diversity and Self-Determination in International Law* (Cambridge: Cambridge University Press, 2002), pp. 239–41.
101. ILO Working Document for 1986 Meeting of Experts, p. 7.
102. *Ibid.*
103. Article 1.3 of the ILO Convention No. 169.
104. P. Thornberry, 'Who is Indigenous?' in F. Horn (ed.), *Economic, Social and Cultural Rights of the Sami, International and National Aspects* (Rovaniemi: Northern Institute for Environmental and Minority Law, 1988), pp. 1–37 at p. 17.
105. 'Introduction', in International Labour Conference, Partial Revision of the Indigenous and Tribal Populations Convention, 1957 (No. 107), 76th Session, Report IV (2A), Geneva, 1989, pp. 8–9.
106. 'Replies received and Commentaries' in International Labour Conference, Partial Revision of the Indigenous and Tribal Peoples Convention, 1957 (No. 107), 75th Session, Report VI(2), Geneva, 1988, Question 9, 16–17.
107. ILO Working Document for 1986 Meeting of Experts, p. 15, n. 2.
108. *Ibid.*, p. 8.
109. Thornberry, 'Who is Indigenous?', p. 17.
110. W. Kymlicka, *Multicultural Citizenship: A Liberal Theory of Minority Rights* (Oxford: Clarendon Press, 1995), pp. 75–106.

111. Thornberry, 'Who is Indigenous?', pp. 17–18.
112. *Ibid.*
113. M. Tomei and L. Swepston, *Indigenous and Tribal Peoples: A Guide to ILO Convention No. 169* (Geneva: International Labour Organisation, 1996), p. 5.
114. J. Waldron, 'Indigeneity?: First Peoples and Last Occupancy' 2002 Quentin-Baxter Memorial Lecture, 5 December 2002. The lecture was published in (2003) 1 *New Zealand Journal of Public and International Law* 56–77.
115. Knop, *Diversity and Self-Determination*, p. 243.
116. Thornberry, 'Who is Indigenous?', pp. 18–19.
117. 76th Session, Report IV (2A), p. 13.
118. ILO Working Document for 1986 Meeting of Experts, p. 10.
119. *Ibid.*
120. *Ibid.*, p. 9.
121. CEACR, Individual Observation concerning Convention No. 169, Indigenous and Tribal Peoples, Mexico, published 1999, para. 6.
122. *Ibid.*
123. CEACR, Individual Observation concerning Convention No. 169 *Indigenous and Tribal Peoples*, Paraguay, 1999, para. 2. Similar comment has been made in the Individual Observation concerning Convention No. 169, Indigenous and Tribal Peoples, Peru, published 1999, para. 2.
124. Individual Direct Request concerning Convention No. 169, Indigenous and Tribal Peoples, Argentina, submitted 2005, para. 6.
125. Individual Direct Request concerning Convention No. 169, Indigenous and Tribal Peoples, Guatemala, submitted 2004, para. 3.
126. Individual Direct Request concerning Convention No. 169, Indigenous and Tribal Peoples, Ecuador, submitted 2004, para. 3.
127. Article 32 of the Convention.
128. R. L. Barsh, 'An Advocate's Guide to the Convention on Indigenous and Tribal Peoples' (1990) 15 *Oklahoma University Law Review* 209–36 at 230.
129. Individual Direct Request concerning Convention No. 169, Indigenous and Tribal Peoples, Paraguay, submitted 2003, para. 23.
130. Barsh, 'An Advocate's Guide', 230.
131. ILO Working Document for 1986 Meeting of Experts, p. 35.
132. *Ibid.*, p. 36.
133. See 'Extracts from the Report of the Meeting of Experts on the Revision of the Indigenous and Tribal Populations Convention, 1957 (No. 107)', International Labour Conference, Partial Revision of the Indigenous and Tribal Populations Convention, 1957 (No. 1957), Report VI (1), 75th Session, 1988, 100–18.
134. Swepston, 'Economic, Social and Cultural Rights', p. 42.
135. Article 6(a).
136. Tomei and Swepston, *Guide*, p. v.
137. Inter-Agency Support Group on Indigenous Issues, Report on Free, Prior and Informed Consent, Permanent Forum on Indigenous Issues, Third Session, New York 10–21 May 2004, UN Doc. E/C.19/2004/11.

138. Report of the Committee set up to examine the representation alleging non-observance by Mexico of the Indigenous and Tribal People's Convention, 1989 (No. 169), made under Article 24 of the ILO Constitution by the Union of Academics of the National Institute of Anthropology and History (SAINAH), submitted 2001, Doc. No. (ilolex): 162004MEX169B, para. 39.
139. *Ibid.*; also Report of the Committee set up to examine the representation alleging non-observance by Mexico of the Indigenous and Tribal People's Convention, 1989 (No. 169), made under Article 24 of the ILO Constitution by the Authentic Workers' Front (FAT), submitted 2001, Doc. No. (ilolex): 162004MEX169, para. 96; see also Report of the Committee set up to examine the representation alleging non-observance by Mexico of the Indigenous and Tribal People's Convention, 1989 (No. 169), made under Article 24 of the ILO Constitution by the Union of Workers of the Autonomous University of Mexico (STUNAM) and the Independent Union of Workers of the Jornada (SITRAJOR), submitted 2001, Doc. No. (ilolex): 162004MEX169A.
140. *Ibid.*, paras. 101–2.
141. R. L. Barsh, 'An Advocate's Guide to the Convention on Indigenous and Tribal Peoples' (1990) 15 *Oklahoma University Law Review* 209–36 at 220.
142. Swepston, 'Economic, Social and Cultural Rights', p. 42.
143. Individual Direct Request concerning Convention No. 169, Indigenous and Tribal Peoples, Costa Rica, submitted 2004, para. 8.
144. Tomei and Swepston, *Guide*, p. 14.
145. 'Note by the International Labour Office, Indigenous and Tribal Peoples and Land Rights', submitted to the United Nations Working Group on Indigenous Populations, 3rd Session, 1986, p. 62.
146. Lerner, 'The 1989 ILO Convention on Indigenous Populations: New Standards?', p. 237.
147. Swepston, 'Economic, Social and Cultural Rights', p. 43.
148. With the exception of Article 17(2) dealing with transmission of land. See Provisional Record No. 25 of 1989, 25/16–18.
149. See *Kitok* v. *Sweden* (197/1985), *Ominayak* v. *Canada* (167/1984), *I. Länsman et al.* v. *Finland* (511/1992), *J. Länsman et al.* v. *Finland* (671/1995), as well as General Comment No. 23 [50], para. 7.
150. Thornberry, *Indigenous Peoples and Human Rights* (Manchester: Manchester University Press, 2002), p. 351.
151. Report of the Committee set up to examine the representation alleging non-observance by Peru of the Indigenous and Tribal People's Convention, 1989 (No. 169), made under Article 24 of the ILO Constitution by the General Confederation of Workers of Peru (CGTP), submitted 1997, Doc. No. (ilolex) 161997PER169.
152. 76th Session, Report IV (2A), p. 30.
153. 76th Session, Report IV (1), p. 4.
154. ILO Guide on the Convention, p. 18
155. Thornberry, *Indigenous Peoples*, p. 353.

156. International Labour Organisation, Report VI(1), p. 69.
157. Knop, *Diversity and Self-Determination*, p. 246.
158. L. Hannikainen, 'The Status of Minorities, Indigenous Peoples and Immigrant and Refugee Groups in Four Nordic States' 65 (1996) *Nordic Journal of International Law* 1–71 at 53.
159. Thornberry, *Indigenous Peoples*, p. 354.
160. ILO Guide on the Convention, p. 19.
161. 75th Session, Report VI(1), 110–11.
162. Swepston, 'Economic, Social and Cultural Rights', p. 43.
163. Provisional Record No. 25 of 1989, 25/23, para. 163.
164. International Labour Office, *Handbook of Procedures relating to International Labour Conventions and Recommendations*, International Labour Standards Department, Geneva: 1995, section I, para. 8.
165. CEACR, Individual Observation concerning Convention No. 169, Indigenous and Tribal Peoples, Colombia, published 1996.
166. Report of the Committee set up to examine the representation alleging non-observance by Denmark of the Indigenous and Tribal Peoples Convention, 1989 (No. 169), made under Article 24 of the ILO Constitution by the National Confederation of Trade Unions of Greenland (Sulinermik Inuussutissarsiuteqartut Kattuffiat–SIK) (SIK), submitted 2000, Document No (ILO): 162000DNK169, para. 36.
167. *Ibid.*
168. ILO Guide on the Convention, p. vi.
169. *Ibid.*, p. 20.
170. See CEACR, Individual Observation concerning Convention No. 169, Indigenous and Tribal Peoples, Mexico, published 1997, para. 7; CEACR, Individual Observation concerning Convention No. 169, Indigenous and Tribal Peoples, Colombia, published 1999, para. 2; also, CEACR, Individual Observation concerning Convention No. 169, Indigenous and Tribal Peoples, Mexico, published 1999, para. 11; also, CEACR: Individual Observation concerning Convention No. 169, Indigenous and Tribal Peoples, Peru, published 1999, para. 7; also, CEACR, Individual Observation concerning Convention No. 169, Indigenous and Tribal Peoples, Mexico, published 2000, para. 4.
171. Report of the Committee set up to examine the representation alleging non-observance by Bolivia of the Indigenous and Tribal Peoples Convention, 1989 (No. 169), made under Article 24 of the ILO Constitution by the Bolivian Central of Workers (COB), submitted 1998, Doc. No. (ilolex) 161998BOL169.
172. *Ibid.*, para. 38.
173. *Ibid.*, paras. 39 and 44.
174. Report of the Committee set up to examine the representation alleging non-observance by Mexico of the Indigenous and Tribal Peoples Convention, 1989 (No. 169), made under Article 24 of the ILO Constitution by the Radical Trade Union of Metal and Associated Workers, submitted 1998, Doc. No. (ilolex) 161998MEX169.

175. *Ibid.*, para. 40.
176. Report of the Committee set up to examine the representation alleging non-observance by Peru of the Indigenous and Tribal People's Convention, 1989 (No. 169), made under Article 24 of the ILO Constitution by the General Confederation of Workers of Peru (CGTP), submitted 1997, Doc. No. (ilolex) 161997PER169.
177. For example, CEACR, Individual Direct Request concerning Convention No. 169, Indigenous and Tribal Peoples, Honduras, submitted 2003, para. 17; *ibid.*, Ecuador, para. 22.
178. Report of the Committee set up to examine the representation alleging non-observance by Mexico of the Indigenous and Tribal Peoples Convention, 1989 (No. 169), made under Article 24 of the ILO Constitution by the Trade Union Delegation, D-III-57, section XI of the National Trade Union of Education Workers (SNTE), Radio Education, Doc. No. (ilolex) 161998MEX169, para. 32.
179. *Ibid.*, para. 45.
180. CEACR: Individual Observation concerning Convention No. 169, Indigenous and Tribal Peoples, Mexico, published 1999, paras. 8–9.
181. Swepston, 'Economic, Social and Cultural Rights', p. 45.
182. *Ibid.*, p. 45–6.
183. Article 22.1 of Convention No. 107.
184. Article 22.2 of Convention No. 107.
185. 'Application of the Indigenous and Tribal Peoples Convention 1989 (No. 169)' in International Labour Conference, Report of the Committee of Experts on the Application of Conventions and Recommendations, 87th Session (1999), Report III (Part 1A), Geneva, paras. 98–107.
186. *Ibid.*, paras. 100–1.
187. Tomei and Swepston, *Guide*, p. viii. This example was also referred to in the ILO, General Report of the Conference Committee on the Application of Conventions and Recommendations, 1999, para. 103.
188. *Ibid.*
189. D. V. Baluarte, 'Balancing Indigenous Rights and a State's Right to Develop in Latin America: The Inter-American Rights Regime and ILO Convention 169' (2004) 4 *Sustainable Development Law and Policy* 9–15.
190. This has been one of the main utilities of the ILO Convention No. 169 in Norway. See J. A. Velin, 'Making the ILO Convention on Indigenous People Work, Sami People Seek their Due' (1997) 21 *The World of Work, The Magazine of the ILO* 11–13.
191. For example, the Regional Fund for the Development of Indigenous Peoples of Latin America and the Caribbean, a multi-agency mechanism for the distribution of funds received by donors to indigenous peoples: ILO Guide on the Convention, p. xi.
192. Report of the Committee of Experts on the Application of Conventions and Recommendations, p. 102.

3 Emerging law: The United Nations draft Declaration on indigenous peoples

The formation of the United Nations draft Declaration on the rights of indigenous peoples[1] started in 1985 with the United Nations Working Group on Indigenous Populations (WGIP), a working group of the then Sub-Commission on Prevention of Discrimination and Protection of Minorities.[2] With relaxed rules of participation and real enthusiasm among participants, the WGIP attracted up to 700 individuals; it grew to 'one of the largest regular human rights meetings organised by the United Nations' and 'made indigenous peoples a permanent presence within that world-wide governmental organisation'.[3] With the help of very supportive chairpersons, indigenous representatives had from the beginning almost equal rights to the states in expressing their views on the text. Initially comprising seven principles,[4] the text gradually expanded into a Preamble with eighteen paragraphs and nine parts with forty-five operative clauses. After several changes the draft Declaration is an ambitious text that challenges state sovereignty at a deep level. It recognises a wide range of collective indigenous rights including: the right of self-determination; prohibition of genocide and ethnocide; a wide range of collective land rights including rights to natural resources; intellectual property rights; and the recognition of distinct indigenous political and judicial systems and self-government arrangements. Essentially it is the outcome of a 'partnership between experts and indigenous peoples'.[5] States gradually withdrew from the drafting process, attending in small numbers and often reluctant to engage in a dialogue on the provisions. In 1993 the WGIP members agreed on the final text of the draft Declaration.[6] After a technical review by the Secretariat,[7] the draft was adopted by the Sub-Commission at its 46th session in 1994;[8] after that it went to the then Commission on Human Rights. Regrouped at the Commission level member states pushed for the establishment of yet another working group to further elaborate the Declaration.[9] All sessions of the Commission Drafting Group proved hard.[10] Finally, ten years after its establishment and under pressure from the United Nations, the Commission Drafting Group adopted the draft Declaration at the beginning of 2006 and passed it to the newly created Human Rights Council. The Declaration was one of the first instruments the Human Rights Council adopted in its first meeting in June 2006. Later in 2006 the Third Committee of the UN General Assembly voted to defer action concerning the Declaration in order to allow time for further considerations thereon.

Process and status of the draft Declaration

Due to the stricter rules of participation in the Commission, it was initially feared that indigenous representatives would not be able to participate in the Commission Drafting Group as actively as in the WGIP and that the draft would become substantially weakened. Working groups of the Commission on Human Rights did not customarily admit non-governmental organisations, unless they had consultative status with the ECOSOC. Even properly accredited NGOs could not ordinarily submit formal proposals at drafting sessions, where decisions were taken by a consensus of the participating governments. Yet, General Assembly Resolution 49/214[11] encouraged the participation of indigenous representatives in the Commission Drafting Group, irrespective of the consultative status of their organisations[12] and on the basis of procedures established by the Commission. Still, problems on occasions arose with the participation of specific groups. Although the relevant state had to be consulted before the coordinator approved the participation of any indigenous group,[13] Resolution 1995/32 did not require state consent for the accreditation of NGO delegations. Over 100 indigenous organisations were able to participate in the Drafting Working Group.[14]

Indigenous representatives pushed for equal rights with the states in the Drafting Working Group. The modalities of participation and organisation of work in the group was a matter of importance for them and often caused confrontations with states and the chairperson.[15] Largely because of their perseverance and often after laborious negotiations, indigenous representatives were eventually given the floor as much as states, were given access to informal consultations with governments and had their proposals included in the annual reports to the Commission. Their participation in the elaboration of the draft

Declaration has always been seen as essential, not least because it legitimised the process and the final outcome. Discussions were characterised by considerable disagreement and struggle, which resulted in the very slow adoption of the Declaration.

Several states were eager to push for changes, highlighting the inconsistencies of language and repetitions in the text and of course their own objections. Indigenous representatives were resisting any changes insisting that the text represented their minimum aspirations, as acknowledged in article 43 which states that 'the rights recognised herein constitute the minimum standards for survival, dignity and well-being of the indigenous peoples of the world'. Gradually some indigenous representatives were persuaded to accept changes in the text, provided that the integrity of the text was maintained and that the proposals were:

> reasonable, necessary and improve or strengthen the text, and that they should be consistent with the fundamental principles of equality, non-discrimination and the prohibition of racial discrimination.[16]

The reforms in the UN human rights structure and the end of the original timeframe for the Drafting Working Group created a lot of pressure for the adoption of the draft Declaration. At the end of 2004, seven states, New Zealand, Denmark, Finland, Iceland, Norway, Sweden and Switzerland, put forward an amended text of the draft under consideration that represented a compromise between the ambitious text and the restrictive proposals put forward by France, Australia, USA and UK. Although some indigenous peoples and some states disagreed with the proposals, a middle ground started emerging. The following year, the Chairperson took the initiative and sent to the Human Rights Council his proposed text without reaching consensus about its language.[17] In its first session in June 2006, the Human Rights Council adopted the proposed text of the Chairperson[18] by a roll-call vote of 30 states in favour to two against with 12 abstentions. Surprisingly, of the 47 states members of the Human Rights Council, the United Kingdom, France and Japan voted in favour of its adoption, while Canada and the Russian Federation voted against it. The Canadian delegate justified Canada's vote on the grounds of alleged lack of widespread support for the draft.[19] Certainly the lack of consensus became apparent in the discussion on the possible adoption of the Declaration by the Third Committee of the UN General Assembly in November 2006. An initiative led by Namibia and co-sponsored by a number of African countries resulted in a draft resolution to defer consideration and action on the Declaration 'in order to allow time for further consultaions'. This was a disappointing development for all supporters of the already diluted text of the draft Declaration. The end of 2006 found the Declaration on uncertain ground.

The contents of the draft Declaration

From its first article, the draft Declaration makes clear that its provisions are based on established international law norms. Article 1 proclaims that 'indigenous peoples have the right to the full enjoyment, as a collective and as individuals, of all human rights and fundamental freedoms recognised in the Charter of the United Nations, the Universal Declaration of Human Rights and international human rights law'. Although the text refers to general human rights instruments, it makes no reference to ILO Convention No. 169: indigenous peoples have not forgotten their lack of substantial participation during the formulation of the Convention, neither do they agree with some provisions of ILO Convention No. 169, especially the 'statement of coverage' in article 1.[20]

Peoples, membership, self-identification, nomadic peoples

Unlike the ILO Conventions, the draft Declaration does not include a definition or a 'statement of coverage' of indigenous peoples, even though several characteristics of indigenousness are scattered in the text. Also, cultural diversity rather than evolutionary stage is the key concept of the text.[21] Similarly to the UNESCO *Declaration on Race and Racial Prejudice* the Preamble stresses that 'indigenous peoples are equal to all other peoples' and that doctrines, policies or practices of racial superiority are 'false, legally invalid, morally condemnable and socially unjust'. As in ILO Convention No. 169, the criterion that defines indigenous peoples is that of self-identification; the draft Declaration adds a collective element: Article 8 entitles indigenous peoples 'not to be subjected to forced assimilation or destruction of their cultures'. Article 33 goes further: it gives the right to indigenous peoples 'to determine their own identity or citizenship in accordance with their customs or traditions'. Article 8 is closely linked to Article 9, which asserts that the right to belong to an indigenous community or nation is recognised to peoples and individuals 'in accordance with the traditions and customs of the community or nation concerned'. Several states found it difficult to accept that the community would have the right to accept and decline membership to an individual, as traditionally this has been seen as the individual's choice.[22] States have put forward arguments of individual choice versus group pressure for inclusion. It is doubtful whether the provision 'implicitly safeguards the option not to identify as indigenous', as Prichard suggests.[23] Nevertheless, the individual can protect herself from the group through Article 1 of the draft Declaration which protects rights and freedoms gained 'under international human rights law'.

Just as ILO Convention No. 169, the draft Declaration also provides protection to nomadic peoples and includes several articles that are relevant to them. The right of indigenous peoples to maintain and develop 'contacts, relations and cooperation, including activities for spiritual, cultural, political, economic and social purposes with their own members as well as with other peoples across borders'[24] – an article of particular importance for nomadic peoples – goes further than Article 32 of the ILO Convention No. 169. Article 32 has 'governments' as its focus, whereas Article 36 of the draft Declaration explicitly recognises the right to indigenous peoples; more importantly, Article 36 includes the right to develop cooperation for political purposes. Although there is some practice of indigenous political institutions across borders,[25] states have traditionally been reluctant to accept political contacts of minorities across borders. However, this reluctance does not seem to have been carried to the draft Declaration: for example, the USA stated that they accept this principle 'subject to non-discriminatory enforcement of custom and immigration laws'.[26]

More uncertain is the protection the Declaration offers to individuals whose ancestors were tribal but who have undergone – voluntarily or not – a process of cultural adaptation and now live in the mainstream. Thornberry notes that, on the one hand, the Declaration repeatedly refers to the right to development of indigenous peoples according to their needs and interests and in accordance with their aspirations and needs.[27] Moreover, the text refers to 'future' as well as past and present manifestations of culture;[28] and human rights instruments do not attempt to freeze processes of cultural development.[29] On the other hand, the text of the Declaration is heavily structured around the idea of a traditional community, with its claims to territory and natural resources, its juridical customs, community institutions etc. Still, there is some protection for the individual who does not necessarily live in an indigenous environment, including language education, labour rights and economic rights. Thornberry concludes:

> While the draft Declaration focuses largely on the traditional and the territorial, there is enough to make their prescriptions relevant also for those who have

been marginalized from their communities and the dominant society by social processes.[30]

Individual and collective rights

Certainly, the whole essence of the draft Declaration is the recognition of indigenous collective rights. The collective essence of the text is established in the very first articles by recognising rights to indigenous *peoples*. Recognised collective rights include among others, the right to self-determination, wide land rights, the right of indigenous peoples to belong to indigenous communities or nations,[31] to live in freedom, peace and security as distinct peoples,[32] to determine their own citizenship and the protection of membership of their institutions,[33] to maintain and develop their cultural knowledge and expressions,[34] and to be consulted when legislative and administrative measures affecting them are devised and implemented.[35]

As expected, the Commission Drafting Group's discussions on collective rights have been difficult and controversial. Several governments supported the collective approach to indigenous rights, but many still objected to the inclusion of collective rights in the draft Declaration. A few states, including France and Japan, argued that international law does not recognise collective rights.[36] As seen in the previous chapter, this argument does not fully agree with current standards of international law. Collective rights exist in various international instruments, notably the International Covenants and the African Charter on Human and Peoples' Rights. Rights solidly recognized as collective include the right to self-determination, the right to development, rights to peace and security, the environment and the culture of humankind. Also, in addition to purely collective rights, instruments such as the UN Charter and the Genocide Convention protect groups, rather than merely individuals.

Other states recognised the existence of collective rights, but feared that their inclusion would lead to the weakening of the respective individual rights.[37] A solution repeatedly suggested by the USA was the adoption of a language similar to that in the UN Declaration on the Rights of Persons belonging to National or Ethnic, Religious and Linguistic Minorities that recognises individual rights exercised individually or in community with others.[38] Such language would lower the standards of international law on indigenous rights, as both ILO Conventions No. 107 and No. 169 have already recognised a wide range of indigenous collective rights. Also, adoption of a language that emphasises individual rights would nullify the *raison d'être* of the Declaration. The Declaration has been created in order to cover gaps in existing international law on indigenous rights, to translate opinions of well-respected international bodies into law and to crystallise any additional protection indigenous peoples need for their survival and development. Mere repetition of the rights indigenous peoples already enjoy through the human rights instruments and even the minority rights instruments would compromise its value. The text adopted by the Human Rights Council has watered down the collective element, including references both to collective and individual rights of indigenous peoples.

Still, the Declaration contains certain provisions that place vast power in the communities. For instance, Article 35 entitles indigenous peoples to collectively 'determine the responsibilities of individuals to their communities'. States have expressed caution and have stressed that indigenous peoples cannot use this provision for action inconsistent with recognised human rights and fundamental freedoms.[39] It is interesting that although Article 35 does not include the limitation of international human rights, Article 34 does:

> Indigenous peoples have the right to promote, develop and maintain their institutional structures and their distinctive customs, spirituality, procedures, practices and, in cases where they exist, juridical systems or customs, in accordance with internationally recognised human rights standards.

This article goes further than the corresponding Article 8 of ILO *Convention No. 169*: apart from being more detailed about the rights of indigenous peoples, it does not require compatibility with the national legal system, but only compatibility with international human rights standards. Still, some indigenous representatives have even expressed their reluctance with this requirement, on the ground that it limits their exercise of self-determination and perpetuates existing stereotypes of indigenous peoples, since other peoples are not explicitly subjected to such a requirement.[40]

An explicit reference to the limitations of international human rights is not necessary. The Declaration does not stand on its own, but forms part of the wider human rights system and is therefore susceptible to the checks, guarantees and limits this system sets. This is clear in preambular paragraph 19 that encourages states 'to comply with and effectively implement all their obligations as they apply to indigenous peoples under international instruments, in particular those related to human rights, in consultation and cooperation with the peoples concerned'. This is a provision of wide scope; since indigenous communities form part of the state, they also have the duty to comply with international human rights norms. Also, Article 1 includes a guarantee for individual rights. The article can be interpreted as implying that nothing in the draft Declaration can lower existing standards on the rights of peoples *as well as individuals*. Several states have expressed support for the principle of article 1.[41]

A question posed by Anaya concerns the process of deciding whether the indigenous structure, custom and right is in conflict with international human rights. Who will decide whether this is the case – and how will it be done?[42] This issue has been addressed in the previous chapter. Suffice to say that firstly, I believe, the individual whose rights are in question must be the first point of reference; secondly, the group must be allowed to exercise its own interpretive and decision-making processes in the application of universal human rights norms;[43] and thirdly, conflicts between international human rights and indigenous rights would put in motion the Lovelace test[44] of proportionality, necessity, equity and balance of rights.

Self-determination

Central to the draft Declaration is the right of self-determination. Indigenous peoples have repeatedly stressed that they cannot accept the draft Declaration without recognising this right; for many of them, the success of the draft Declaration depends on such recognition.

As with collective rights, self-determination presupposes recognition of indigenous as peoples.[45] Contrary to the report of indigenous representatives,[46] the report of the 2000 session of the Drafting Working Group included an explanatory statement clarifying that no consensus has been reached on the use of the term 'indigenous peoples' and therefore the term was used in brackets.[47] This echoed the evasion of ILO Convention No. 169 to take a position on the matter. The ILO always claimed that it was not the appropriate body to clarify the situation, but the same cannot be said for the United Nations. The term 'indigenous peoples' was finally included in the text adopted by the Human Rights Council but still caused problems in the discussions of the Third Committee of the General Assembly.

The draft Declaration does not restrict the recognition of indigenous self-determination to one implicit reference, far from it. Contrary to Convention No. 169, the Declaration includes both clear statements and indirect references to the right. Preambular paragraph 13 recognises 'that indigenous peoples have the right freely to determine their relationship with States in a spirit of coexistence, mutual benefit and full respect'. More explicitly, preambular paragraph 16 acknowledges that the UN Charter and the International Covenants 'affirm the fundamental importance of the right of self-determination of all peoples, by virtue of which they freely determine their political status and freely pursue their economic, social and cultural development', whereas the next paragraph affirms that 'nothing in this Declaration can be used to deny any peoples their right of self-determination exercised in conformity with international law'. Still, the main binding provision establishing the right to self-determination is included in Article 3 of the draft Declaration. During the initial draft, the language of this right was not as strong, but it gradually evolved to be a replication of Common Article 1 of both International Covenants:

> Indigenous peoples have the right of self-determination. By virtue of this right they freely determine their political status and freely pursue their economic, social and cultural development.

Article 3 was the subject of extensive polemics at many discussions during sessions of the working groups. Later working groups evidenced some narrowing of the various views[48] and several states including Colombia,[49] Bolivia,[50] Fiji,[51] Switzerland,[52] Pakistan,[53] Finland,[54] Norway,[55] Cuba,[56] Guatemala[57] and Mexico,[58] all agreed with the inclusion of the right to self-determination in the draft Declaration. Certainly, in the time since the working groups began their work some major changes in state positions were seen. Canada stated in 2001 that they 'accepted a right of self-determination for indigenous peoples which respected the political, constitutional and territorial integrity of democratic States',[59] while the Russian Federation encountered 'no difficulties in accepting the right of self-determination, although exercise of that right must be subject to the territorial integrity of States'.[60] Because of these statements their later objections to the adoption of the Declaration surprised many. Many states set the limitation of the right as a prerequisite for their support.[61] Such possibilities were discussed extensively in the 2004 session of the Commission Drafting Group, where Denmark, Finland, Iceland, New Zealand, Norway, Sweden and Switzerland suggested the addition of two paragraphs in Article 3. Similar to Article 2 of the (1993) Vienna Declaration and Programme of Action, the first paragraph would refer to the historical circumstances of colonisation, whereas the second paragraph would follow the language of the (1970) Declaration on Friendly Relations among States and would link self-determination with the 'political unity' and 'territorial integrity' of states conducting themselves in a democratic manner.[62] Although several indigenous representatives insisted that there should be no changes to the current language, the seven states' proposal fuelled discussions and counter-suggestions,[63] especially about the position of any limitation and the language to be used.[64] A few indigenous representatives discussed the explicit reference in the Preamble to territorial integrity as included in the 1970 Declaration on Friendly Relations, provided Article 3 of the Declaration also followed paragraphs 2 and 3 of Common Article 1 of the International Covenants, which refer to the right to natural wealth and resources and non-self-governing territories.[65] However, Australia and the USA insisted on the explicit references to self-government and autonomy in Article 3 of the draft Declaration,[66] although the USA also accepted indigenous self-determination as a 'special' right,[67] a concept that could work to indigenous benefit.[68] The text that was finally put forward to the Human Rights Council includes three provisions on self-determination. The first, Article 3, follows the language of Article 1 of the International Covenants. Article 4 proclaims that indigenous peoples 'in exercising the right to self-determination, have the right to autonomy or self-government'. The provision includes the first reference in an international instrument of 'a right to' autonomy, since the latter is regarded as an application of self-determination. The provision envisages autonomy in matters relating to indigenous 'internal and local affairs as well as ways and means for financing their autonomous functions'. The difference between 'effective participation' found in the UN Declaration on Minorities[69] and the right to autonomy in Article 4 is justified by the difference in the concepts and needs of minorities and indigenous peoples. Article 34 provided indigenous peoples with the right to their 'institutional structures', their customs, spirituality, traditions, procedures, practices, juridical systems or customs. Although autonomy is not mentioned, the Article goes much further than ILO Convention No. 169, which merely urges the governments to 'establish means for the full development of these peoples' own institutions and initiatives'.[70] Originally the text elaborated on the various areas where autonomy could be granted, but after persistent objections by the USA, Canada, Brazil and Japan, such references have been deleted.[71]

Even in provisions on participation, emphasis has been shifted from the principles of participation and consultation of ILO Convention

No. 169 to indigenous institutions and autonomy. Article 5 recognises the right of indigenous peoples to participate fully in the political, economic, social and cultural life of the state and to maintain and strengthen their institutions. Article 18 specifies that participation will take place through representatives chosen by indigenous peoples in accordance with indigenous procedures and their decision-making institutions. The original text gave indigenous peoples the collective right to determine their citizenship 'in accordance with their customs and traditions' but this was not included in the text adopted by the Human Rights Council.

Indigenous consent is required in Article 19 when 'devising legislative or administrative measures that may affect' their communities; 'free and informed consent' is required 'before adopting and implementing such measures'. Indigenous consent is also required: when taking measures that concern the development or utilisation of their lands and resources;[72] when displacing them;[73] for states' measures to preserve their sacred places;[74] and when hazardous materials are stored or disposed of in indigenous areas.[75] Brölmann and Zieck agree that the draft Declaration is geared more towards autonomy than participation. They note:

> although these measures can be interpreted as a means to ensure the national government is a 'representative' one, the participation envisaged seems predominantly geared to preserving indigenous autonomy. Indicative in this respect is that the gist of the participation of indigenous peoples in national affairs is confined to those instances where, without such participation, interference by the state in the 'internal affairs' of the indigenous community would be possible.[76]

Protection of indigenous peoples

Following the debate on the draft Declaration, one would be forgiven to believe that its content focuses solely on ambitious rights, such as collective rights and self-determination. However, of particular relevance to indigenous communities are the provisions protecting basic rights such as the right to life and security. Keeping in mind indigenous experiences, the drafters of the Declaration went deeper into some issues than other human rights and minority instruments have done.[77] Aspects of the right to life are still very important to indigenous peoples, as many states provide them with cultural rights, but continue to discriminate and persecute them, as recent concluding observations of the Human Rights Committee for, among others, Congo[78] and Thailand[79] have demonstrated. Articles 7 and 8 establish a collective right to freedom, peace and security and prohibition of genocide or any other form of violence towards indigenous peoples. Reports of killings and even genocide of indigenous peoples, including the case of the Chittagong Hill Tribes in Bangladesh and the Yanomami Indians in Brazil, demonstrate the need for such provision. The provision might not be of great use to claims for political and legal redress from governments and corporations involved in genocide against indigenous peoples in the past,[80] but it explicitly condemns such practices and will hopefully contribute to their elimination in the future. Article 7 also includes the prohibition of 'forcibly removing indigenous children from the group to another group'. This reflects well-documented experiences of many indigenous children who were taken away from their families forcibly and without the consent of their parents and were adopted by non-indigenous families. The Report on the Stolen Generation in Australia[81] has exposed the forcible removal of indigenous children from their families, and the legislation that justified such practices. After their removal, indigenous children were forced to adopt a non-indigenous way of life, were not told they were indigenous or were told their parents had died or did not care about them. Every attempt was made to denigrate their aboriginality and they were not even allowed to use their language. Harsh living conditions, strict institutional rules and exploitation often added to the torments of indigenous children, ironically all occurring in the name of civilisation.[82]

Also of special importance are the rights of indigenous women. Articles 21 and 22 make references to children as well as women. Article 44 confirms that all the rights in the Declaration are guaranteed both to men and women equally. Unfortunately, indigenous women often suffer serious violations of their rights. The 2006 Concluding Observations of the Human Rights Committee confirmed that Aboriginal women in Canada are far more likely to experience a violent death than other Canadian women. No precise and updated statistical data on violence against Aboriginal women was confirmed, while the police had reportedly failed to recognise and respond adequately to the specific threats faced by women.[83] The Committee on Discrimination against Women has also noted the disproportionate incidents of violence against indigenous women and the disproportionately large number of indigenous women in prisons.[84]

Unfortunately, the original reference to ethnocide has not been maintained.[85] The drafters of the (1948) Convention on the Prevention and Punishment of the Crime of Genocide did not include cultural genocide in the final text, even though the issue was discussed.[86] The Declaration of San José equated ethnocide with cultural genocide and defined it as the denial to an ethnic group of its right to enjoy, develop and transmit its own culture and language.[87] Most commentators have long used the two terms interchangeably, but a few see cultural genocide as linked to mass ethnic murder on a grand scale and ethnocide to be linked to 'milder' forms of destruction of the group's identity.[88] States have been reluctant to accept such an explicit prohibition of ethnocide on the basis that it is not part of current standards.[89] Indeed, the prohibition of cultural genocide and ethnocide is not explicitly recognised in any human rights instruments, but derives easily from Article 27 of the International Covenant on Civil and Political Rights (ICCPR): members of minorities can only enjoy their culture if their characteristics are not forcibly erased. Such prohibition is also implied in the UN Declaration on Minorities in its protection of the existence and identity of minorities.[90] Other human rights instruments also protect against aspects of cultural genocide.[91] In this respect, the explicit prohibition of cultural genocide seems a logical evolution, in view of the prohibition of many aspects of it, including assimilationist policies, and given that the prohibition of genocide is already well-established. Indeed, UN monitoring bodies have recently highlighted cases of forced sterilisations of indigenous women.[92] Even though Article 8 does not mention ethnocide, its content points in this direction. The article prohibits 'forced assimilation and destruction of cultures' and the list in paragraph 2 is quite broad: both aims and effects are part of the crime and even forms of propaganda and integration by other cultures are prohibited. The provision provides indigenous peoples with the right to prevention and redress; the notion of 'redress' is quite vague and a potentially controversial area, especially for past acts of ethnocide.[93] Finally, states have noted that the article would be better placed among other provisions protecting cultural rights, but indigenous representatives insisted that the importance of the right and the past experiences of indigenous peoples made the prominent position of the article appropriate.[94]

The original text included a provision protecting indigenous children and peoples in periods of armed conflict. Indigenous communities often live at the borders of a state and are often the victims of ethnic conflict; on some occasions they are used as a human shield. The provision would complement recent renewed interest on children used as soldiers[95] and prohibit the recruitment of children below the age of eighteen; several States have expressed their objections to the specific age limitation on the grounds that current standards prohibit recruitment until a younger age. Several states have opposed any additional protection on the grounds that indigenous children should be treated as all other citizens during armed conflicts.[96]

Article 30 prohibits any military activity taking place in indigenous lands without the free consent of their peoples. The United Nations Environment Programme has expressed its support for this article and has suggested that it 'would be an important factor to consider in developing and promoting national environmental policy for the military sector'.[97] Showing the extent of the problem, the Commission on Human Rights asked in 2005 for more focus on the dire consequences of indigenous peoples in situations of armed conflicts.[98]

Cultural and linguistic identity

The idea of cultural diversity is paramount in the Declaration: paragraph 2 of the Preamble stresses the contribution of all peoples to the diversity and richness of civilisations and cultures, which constitutes the common heritage of humankind. Indigenous identities are not simply to be tolerated, but celebrated. Article 15 entitles indigenous peoples 'to the dignity and diversity of their cultures, traditions, histories and aspirations reflected in education and public information' and urges states to take effective measures to promote tolerance, understanding and good relations with all segments of society. At the same time, however, the draft Declaration is also cautious not to present indigenous peoples as objects of the past. It recognises that cultures evolve and does not attempt to freeze cultural development; rather to give indigenous peoples the control to determine their own cultural evolution.[99] The draft Declaration seems to endorse the idea of concentric circles analysed in the previous chapter; although the text of the Declaration gives recognition to indigenous communities and their claims to separate territory and resources, judicial customs and community institutions, there is the implicit recognition that such communities are not totally independent from the rest of the society. Thus, the Declaration also gives rights of full participation to indigenous peoples in all aspects of the life of the state[100] even though, contrary to the earlier draft, it does not recognise dual (state and indigenous) citizenship. Several states expressed hesitations about accepting the concept of dual citizenship,[101] as they believe it to be incompatible with state sovereignty. Finland, on the other hand, had accepted that 'it could be possible to have separate indigenous citizenship, in addition to the citizenship of the home country'.[102] The Finnish delegate had used the example of a Sami individual living in Finland to highlight the possibility of dual citizenships.

The paramount concept of indigenous control and autonomy is also reflected in cultural rights.[103] The focus on control and indigenous institutions has driven some indigenous peoples to see their cultural claims under their right to self-determination. During the working group sessions indigenous representatives have used the language of Article 1 of the International Covenants to suggest that the right of self-determination also includes 'economic, social and cultural development'. This tactic will be analysed in detail in the specific chapter on self-determination. Suffice to note that using the right of self-determination as the legal ground for cultural rights can prove dangerous, especially in view of the many objections to the recognition of indigenous self-determination in the Declaration.

The provisions on education, language and media are prime examples of the understanding of indigenous identities as concentric circles, analysed in chapter 1. According to Article 14, indigenous children have the right to all levels and forms of education of the state; at the same time, indigenous peoples have the right to establish their own educational systems and institutions, providing education in their own languages, following their own cultural methods of teaching and learning. The aim is that indigenous children will get the general knowledge that all other children of the state receive as well as the knowledge deriving from their indigenous cultures; so indigenous children will develop knowledge concerning both their indigenous culture and their national culture. This reflects Article 13 of the *International Covenant on Economic, Social and Cultural Rights*.[104] The draft Declaration also includes a general provision that entitles indigenous peoples to use, develop and transmit to future generations their languages and writing systems[105] and to use their languages in their media.[106] These provisions reflect Article 27 of the ICCPR as well as the extensive work of the Human Rights Committee on language rights.[107] As with education and language, indigenous peoples also have the right to establish their own media and have the right to equal access to all forms of non-indigenous media.[108]

Contrary to well-accepted rights, the Declaration also includes provisions that go beyond existing international law norms. The recognition of the collective right of restitution in Article 11 and the repatriation of human remains in Article 12 form parts of the wider debate on historical claims and the return of cultural objects to their original owners.[109] In their proposals in the 2004 session of the Commission Drafting Group, states suggested the substitution of the phrase 'the right to restitution' with 'the right to effective redress', but the original language largely remained. By contrast, the final draft adopted by the Human Rights Council does not include the strong language on full intellectual property rights.[110] The initial provision entitled indigenous peoples to 'full ownership, control and protection of their cultural and intellectual property'. Currently, Article 31 provides indigenous peoples with the right to 'maintain, control, protect and develop their intellectual property', but does not recognise indigenous ownership. Similarly, Article 24 recognises indigenous rights to their traditional medicines and the conservation of their medical plants, animals and minerals, but fails to recognises indigenous ownership on these issues. Still, even in its diluted form, the draft Declaration goes beyond ILO Convention No. 169, which does not include any such provisions.[111]

Land and resources

References to land rights are scattered throughout the draft Declaration.[112] The abundance of references to land rights reflects on the comments made by United Nations treaty bodies on prevailing discrimination on indigenous land rights.[113] It also highlights the importance of these rights for indigenous peoples and the interdependency of land rights and the enjoyment of other indigenous rights. This is also reflected in the Preamble of the draft Declaration: paragraph 5 refers to the dispossession of indigenous lands, territories and resources and links them with the deterioration of indigenous rights; there are also references to the need for indigenous control over their lands (paragraph 9), including demilitarisation (paragraph 11). The Preamble also urges the protection of indigenous 'inherent' land rights because they are linked to indigenous political, economic and social structures as well as indigenous cultures, spiritual traditions, histories and philosophies (paragraph 6). Land rights are mentioned in provisions on cultural genocide (Article 8), on the prohibition of forcible removal (Article 10), on the prohibition of military activities (Article 30) and on access to religious sites and burial sites (Article 12).

Important rights to land ownership and possession are recognised in the draft Declaration. The text uses the rights already recognised in ILO Convention No. 169 but takes them further. For example, both instruments recognise the special bond between indigenous and their lands, but the draft Declaration elaborates and expands on 'the special importance of [indigenous peoples'] relationship with their lands' of ILO No. 169. Article 25 recognises the 'distinctive spiritual and material relationship [of indigenous peoples] with their traditionally owned or otherwise occupied and used lands, territories, waters, coastal areas and other resources. The provision expands the concept of lands to include mineral and other resources that indigenous peoples have owned, occupied or even merely used in the past. Originally the Declaration went beyond the right of indigenous peoples to be consulted in matters of mineral resources, as recognised in Article 15 of ILO Convention No. 169: it recognised the right to free and informed *consent* of indigenous peoples in all matters related to mineral resources and indigenous rights of ownership, management and control over mineral resources of lands that they have traditionally owned or occupied or used (Article 26). However, after continuous strong opposition by states, the right to sub-surface resources has been removed from the text.[114] Article 26.2 nevertheless recognises the right of indigenous peoples to own, use, develop and control the resources that they possess, while Article 32 asks states to obtain free, prior and informed consent from indigenous peoples on projects relevant to 'the development, utilisation or exploitation of their mineral, water or other resources'.

However, other rights have been recognised for the first time in the draft Declaration: for example, Article 28 recognises the right to redress, and possible restitution, for the lands, territories and resources which have been traditionally owned, occupied, used or damaged without their peoples' free, prior and informed consent. The redress will usually be 'just and fair compensation'. Other controversial provisions include recognition of collective ownership and broad control on matters related to lands that indigenous peoples have occupied. The text also recognises the indigenous right to environmental management. According to some commentators, the draft Declaration successfully demonstrates 'the merging of human rights and environmental law in an integrated and holistic way'.[115]

More flexible are states when it comes to the recognition of past treaties between indigenous peoples and states, an issue not included in ILO Convention No. 169. Article 37 of the draft Declaration recognises the right of indigenous peoples to the recognition, observance and enforcement of treaties, agreements and other constructive arrangements concluded with states or their successors and to have states respecting and honouring such documents. Even though states have expressed their willingness to recognise treaties, they have sidetracked the main issue, which is whether the treaties will be recognised as domestic or international instruments. Contrary to the previous draft the final draft does not suggest the submission of relevant disputes to international bodies.[116] Originally, the text also referred to interpretation of the treaties according to 'the initial spirit and consent' which it elevated to the sole criteria for interpreting treaties between indigenous peoples and states, even though Canada, for example, only included them as two of the criteria for the interpretation of the treaties.[117] This phrase was not included in the final text adopted by the Human Rights Council.

Concluding comments

Kymlicka has suggested that 'indigenous peoples may get moral victories from international law, but the real power remains vested in the hands of sovereign States, who can and do ignore international norms'.[118] This has so far been evident in the elaboration and the delay in adopting the draft Declaration. The draft constitutes the outcome of lengthy deliberations between experts and leaders on indigenous rights. Its provisions are based on the experiences of indigenous peoples and lay out rights that would improve the lives of indigenous communities considerably. Compared to the original text which had formed the basis for discussion in the Commission Drafting Group for eleven years and which Thornberry argued 'in the spectrum from reform to revolution ... reaches towards the upper revolutionary end, among the passionate colours',[119] the text finally put forward for adoption is more modest. Nevertheless, it includes ground-breaking provisions on self-determination, land rights, redress for past injustices and intellectual property rights. The eleven years of deliberations within the Commission Drafting Group managed to reduce some important fears of states, even though many states still voiced their concerns during discussions on the draft Declaration in the General Assembly. States also raised their concerns about the way in which the text was sent to the Human Rights Council, as the Chairperson submitted his proposed text without waiting for consensus. Notwithstanding their enthusiasm with the prospect of the declaration being adopted, indigenous representatives have also been rather disappointed by the process. For them, the process was synonymous with control, voice and empowerment,[120] goals that they are hoping to achieve with the Declaration.

Indeed the lengthy process of adoption of the text by the Commission Drafting Group raised a dilemma for the transnational indigenous movement, a dilemma that confirms the multiple, different and sometimes opposing forces that exist within the movement: indigenous leaders had to decide whether a compromised text was a more realistic option or whether they would still delay the adoption of the Declaration in order to fight for a stronger text. Indeed after ten years of deliberations in the Commission Drafting Group, some indigenous representatives believed that there should be a pause in the deliberations of the Commission Drafting Group so that all parties could consider the current text. At the 2005 session of the then Human Rights Commission, states had to decide on the renewal of the mandate of the Commission Drafting Group. Even though, as expected, a few states unsuccessfully tried to stop the process, 127 indigenous groups had, surprisingly, also signed a petition asking for a pause in the work of the Drafting Group. Finally, the Commission decided that the Commission Drafting Group should have another year of deliberations and after such pressure to conclude its work, the Chairperson took the initiative to submit his proposed text. If the General Assembly does not adopt the Declaration, the tactic used will have proved disastrous for the protection of indigenous rights.

All parties, including states, indigenous representatives and the international community, realise the importance of the Declaration, even as a draft. Anaya views the draft as 'an authoritative statement of norms concerning indigenous peoples on the basis of generally applicable human rights principles';[121] indigenous representatives consider its contents 'comprehensive' and 'reflecting the legitimate aspirations of indigenous peoples as a whole'.[122] This is how the provisions of the Declaration are used in the following chapters of this book, as a manifestation of indigenous claims. The draft also constitutes the basis of the debate on indigenous rights and is widely referred to in the literature. For this reason, Thornberry rightly observes that the draft has more authority than that of a mere draft instrument.[123]

The Declaration is also important as the outcome of a partnership among indigenous peoples, states and academics. Indeed, Turpel stresses the 'power-sharing between the human rights experts who comprised the Working Group and the indigenous peoples and State representatives who took part in its work'.[124] Knop also comments on the remarkable achievement of indigenous peoples to put their rights high into the United Nations agenda.[125] The drafting process of the Declaration has had important consequences beyond indigenous communities. It has substantially changed the representation of indigenous peoples in the international arena and has gradually expanded their international legal personality. Through their participation in the drafting process, indigenous peoples have strengthened their autonomy and their will to operate as an entity separate from the state in which they live and have demonstrated that they have the necessary organisation to establish relations with other entities.[126] The fact that a group of individuals has managed to become a true collective participant in the evolution of international law cannot be underestimated; it carries major consequences for the participation of other actors in the creation, development and enforcement of international law.[127] Such consequences are also evident in the evolution of general human rights standards through, among other ways, continuous debate on concepts such as self-determination, culture and development. The thematic analysis that follows engages in this debate and elaborates on the advancement of human rights standards.

Notes

1. Within the regional context, another similar attempt represents the Inter-American Declaration on the Rights of Indigenous Peoples. However, this instrument is not as important as the draft Declaration, mainly because it is restricted to the regional level, but also because it is not based on indigenous participation. It will be important for indigenous peoples, if both Declarations complement each other in the years to come.
2. UN Doc. E/CN.4/Sub.2/1985/22, Annex II.
3. S. Wiessner, 'Rights and Status of Indigenous Peoples: A Global Comparative and International Legal Analysis' (1999) 12 *Harvard Human Rights Journal* 57–128 at 103.
4. The right to full and effective enjoyment of universally recognised human rights; the right to equality and freedom from discrimination; the collective right to exist and be protected against genocide as well as the individual right to life; rights related to religious ceremonies and access to sacred sites; the right to all forms of education; the right to preserve cultural identity and traditions and to pursue education; and the recognition of the dignity and diversity of indigenous cultures. See UN Doc. E/CN.4/Sub.2/1985/22, Annex II.
5. J. Burger, 'The United Nations Draft *Declaration* on the Rights of Indigenous Peoples' (1996) 6 *St. Thomas Law Review* 209–29 at 210.
6. UN Doc. E/CN.4/1993/29, Annex I.
7. See the technical review at UN Doc. E/CN.4/Sub.2/1994/2.
8. Resolution 1994/45, 26 August 1994.
9. 'Establishing a Working Group to Elaborate a Draft United Nations Declaration on the Rights of Indigenous Peoples', March 1995, Commission on Human

Rights, Report on the 51st Session, UN Doc. E/1995/23 and also UN Doc. E/CN.4/1995/L.11/Add.2 para.1 (1995). As quoted in R. L. Barsh, 'Indigenous Peoples and the UN Commission on Human Rights: A Case of Immovable Object and the Irresistible Force' (1996) 18 *Human Rights Quarterly* 782–813.

10. These two articles are Article 5, recognising that 'every indigenous individual has the right to a nationality', and Article 9.
11. Adopted in 23 December 1994, the Resolution was entitled 'International Decade of the World's Indigenous Peoples'. See UN Doc. A/RES/49/214, 17 February 1995.
12. Para. 3 of the Annex of the Resolution.
13. Para. 5.
14. For more on participation in the Working Group of the Commission, see Barsh, 'Indigenous Peoples and the UN Commission on Human Rights' at 783–6.
15. Problems have arisen concerning the organisation of work, especially with respect to informal private governmental meetings without indigenous participation during the hours of the meetings, see the Provisional Report of the 2000 session in Draft Report of the working group established in accordance with Commission on Human Rights Resolution 1995/32, E/CN.4/2000/WG.15/CPR.1, paras. 22–5; see also Report of the 1999 session in Report of the Working Group established in accordance with Commission on Human Rights Resolution 1995/32, E/CN.4/2000/84, paras. 18–24. For governmental drafts being used as the basis of the discussion rather than the draft Declaration as adopted by the Sub-Commission, see Report of the 1997 session in Report of the Working Group established in accordance with Commission on Human Rights Resolution 1995/32, E/CN.4/1998/106 as well as Report of the 1998 session in Report of the Working Group established in accordance with Commission on Human Rights Resolution 1995/32, E/CN.4/1999/82, paras. 80–3. For requests for the equal and full participation of indigenous representatives in the meetings, see Report of the 1996 session in Report of the Working Group established in accordance with Commission on Human Rights Resolution 1995/32, E/CN.4/1997/102, paras. 20–41.
16. See Report of the 1999 session, E/CN.4/2000/84, para. 124; also repeated in the 2000 Session, see Draft Report of the 2000 Session, E/CN.4/2000/WG.15/CPR.1, para. 34.
17. Report of the working group established in accordance with Commission on Human Rights Resolution 1995/32 of 3 March 1995 at its 11th session, UN Doc. E/CN.4/2006/79.
18. Report to the General Assembly on the First Session of the Human Rights Council, UN Doc. A/HRC/1/L/10, pp. 52–6.
19. L. Schlein, 'Canada says draft UN Declaration on indigenous rights needs more work', www.canada.com, 19 June 2006. The Declaration is now being considered by the General Assembly.
20. See 1995 session of the Commission Drafting Group, UN Doc. E/CN.4/1996/84, para. 40.

21. Thornberry, *Indigenous Peoples and Human Rights* (Manchester: Manchester University Press, 2002).
22. *Lovelace* v. *Canada*, Communication No. 24/1977; views adopted on 30 July 1981, UN Doc. A/36/40; for an analysis see Thornberry, *Indigenous Peoples*, p. 156.
23. Pritchard, *The Draft Declaration*, p. 54.
24. Article 36 of the draft Declaration.
25. For example, the Sámi Council.
26. Report of the 1996 session, UN Doc. E/CN.4/1997/102, para. 304.
27. Preamble and Articles 3, 20, 21, 23, 26, 29, 30, 32, 34 and 38.
28. Article 12.
29. Human Rights Committee General Comment 23: Länsman case.
30. Thornberry, *Indigenous Peoples*, p. 378.
31. Article 9.
32. Article 7.
33. Article 33.
34. Article 31.
35. Article 19.
36. See France, Japan and Sweden in UN Doc. E/CN.4/1997/102, paras. 108–13.
37. See Report of the 1996 session, UN Doc. E/CN.4/1997/102, paras. 108–13.
38. *Ibid.*, paras. 103–29; also see E/CN.4/1999/82, para. 49.
39. *Ibid.*, paras. 332, 334, 338, 340.
40. *Ibid.*, para. 224.
41. *Ibid.*, paras. 104, 107, 109.
42. Anaya, *Indigenous Peoples*, p. 133.
43. J. Anaya, 'International Human Rights and Indigenous Peoples: The Move towards the Multicultural State' (2004) 21 *Arizona Journal of International and Comparative Law* 13–61 at 26.
44. *Lovelace* v. *Canada*, UN Doc. CCPR/C/OP/1 (1988).
45. For a discussion on the 'battle of the -s' in another forum, the Vienna World Conference, see R. Barsh, 'Indigenous Peoples in Vienna: What's Next after the Battle of the "s"?' in J. Patel (ed.), *Addressing Discrimination in the Vienna Declaration* (Tokyo: IMADR, 1995), pp. 23–30.
46. *Ibid.*
47. Report of the Working Group established in accordance with Commission on Human Rights Resolution 1995/32, UN Doc. E/CN.4/2001/85, p. 29.
48. In 1999, the chairperson concluded that the positions of participants in the working group had moved closer. Although differences still existed, he commented that they had become more clearly defined. See Report of the 1999 session of the Commission Working Group, UN Doc. E/CN.4/2000/84, paras. 82–4.
49. Report of the Commission Working Group, UN Doc. E/CN.4/1997/102 (1996) para. 332.
50. *Ibid.*, para. 317.
51. *Ibid.*, para. 330.

52. Report of the Commission Working Group, UN Doc. E/CN.4/2000/84 (1999) para. 64.
53. *Ibid.*, para. 67.
54. *Ibid.*, para. 70.
55. Report of the Commission Working Group, UN Doc. E/CN.4/2001/85 (2001) para. 82.
56. *Ibid.*, para. 70.
57. Report of the Commission Working Group, UN Doc. E/CN.4/2004/85 (2004) para. 16.
58. *Ibid.*, para. 17.
59. Report of the Commission Working Group, UN Doc. E/CN.4/2000/84 (1999) para. 50.
60. *Ibid.*, para. 61.
61. Report of the Commission Working Group, UN Doc. E/CN.4/2003/92 (2003) paras. 19–20.
62. Information provided by States' Working Group established in accordance with Commission on Human Rights Resolution 1995/32 of 3 March 1995, UN Doc. E/CN.4/2004/WG.15/CRP.1 of 6 September 2004.
63. For example, Chairperson's Summary of Proposals, Commission Working Group, UN Doc. E/CN.4/2004/WG.15/CRP.4 (2004); also see in the same meeting information provided by the Sámi Council and Tebtebba Foundation, endorsed by the Sámi Parliament, UN Doc. E/CN.4/2004/WG.15/CRP.5 (2004).
64. Indigenous Peoples' Proposed Amendments relating to the Right of Self-Determination, (preambular para. 15, new preambular para. and Art. 3), September 20, 2004, Proposal submitted to the 2005 session of the Drafting Working Group by the African, Arctic, Asian, Latin American and Pacific Indigenous Caucuses and other indigenous Organisations (on file with author).
65. Dalee Sambo and Millani Trask proposals combined, written statement distributed during the 2005 session of the Drafting Working Group (on file with author).
66. Statement of Australia and the USA.
67. 2nd Intervention of the USA on self-determination, statement made in the 2005 session of the Drafting Working Group (on file with author).
68. See the discussion in chapter 4 of this book.
69. Articles 2.2 and 2.3.
70. Article 6 of the ILO Convention No. 169.
71. See Report on the 1996 session of the Commission Drafting Group, UN Doc. E/CN.4/1997/102, paras. 325, 332, 334 and 338.
72. Article 32.
73. Article 10.
74. Article 11.
75. Article 29.2.
76. C. M. Brölmann and M. Y. A. Zieck, 'Some Remarks on the Draft Declaration on the Rights of Indigenous Peoples' (1995) 8 *Leiden Journal of International Law* 103–13 at 106.

77. For example, Finland has stated that Articles 10 and 11 providing special protection for indigenous peoples during periods of armed conflict reflected on the realities of the Sámi. Unfortunately, these Articles did not survive the drafting process. See 'Standard Setting Activities: Evolution of Standards concerning the Rights of Indigenous Populations: Information received by Governments', UN Doc. E/CN.4/Sub.2/AC.4/1993/1, paras. 4–5.
78. 'Concluding Observations of the Human Rights Committee, Democratic Republic of Congo', UN Doc. CCPR/C/COD/CO/3 of 27 March 2006, para. 26.
79. 'Concluding Observations of the Human Rights Committee', UN Doc. CCPR/CO/84/THA of 8 July 2005, para. 24.
80. For example, after receiving an apology in 2004, the Hereros, an ethnic group from Namibia are looking for redress from the German government and corporations involved in the German colonial enterprise: see R. Anderson, 'Redressing Colonial Genocide under International Law: The Hereros' Cause of Action against Germany' (2005) 93 *California Law Review* 1155–89.
81. Australian Human Rights and Equal Opportunities Commission, *Bringing Them Home, Report of the National Enquiry into the Separation of Aboriginal and Torres Strait Islander Children from their Families*, (AGPS: Canberra, 1997).
82. *Ibid.*
83. 'Concluding Observations by the Human Rights Committee', UN Doc. CCPR/C/CAN/CO/5 of 20 April 2006, paras. 23–4.
84. 'Concluding Comments of the Committee on the Elimination of Discrimination against Women, Australia', UN Doc. CEDAW/C/AUL/CO/5 of 3 February 2006, para. 18.
85. For more, see C. C. Tennant and M. E. Turpel, 'A Case Study of Indigenous Peoples: Genocide, Ethnocide and Self-determination' (1990) 59 *Nordic Journal of International Law* 287–319.
86. Thornberry, *The Rights of Minorities*, pp. 71–3.
87. See 'Technical Review of the draft Declaration', UN Doc. E/CN.4/Sub.2/1994/2, para. 36.
88. B. Sautman, ' "Cultural Genocide" and Tibet' (2003) 38 *Texas International Law Journal* 173–95 at 189.
89. See UN Doc. E/CN.4/1996/84, para. 84; also see UN Doc. E/CN.4/1997/102, paras. 188, 176, 184.
90. The Secretariat of the Working Group on Indigenous Populations affirmed this in the 1994 Technical Review of the draft Declaration. See UN Doc. E/CN.4/Sub.2/1994/2, para. 36.
91. Prohibition of illicit transfer of children is included in Article 2(e) of the Genocide Convention and Article 9.1 of the Convention on the Rights of the Child; the use of indigenous languages is protected in several instruments; and so is the history, traditions, language and culture of minorities.
92. 'Concluding Observations of the Committee on Economic, Social and Cultural Rights, People's Repubic of China (including Hong Kong and Macao)', UN Doc. E/C.12/1/Add. 107 of 13 May 2005, para. 36. Also,

'Concluding Observations of the Human Rights Committee, Peru', CCPR/CO/70/PER of 15 November 2000, para. 21.

93. See Report of the Expert Seminar on Remedies available to the Victims of Racial Discrimination, A/CONF.189/PC.1/8, especially paras. 51–9.
94. Statement of Inuit Circumpolar Conference (ICC) during the 8th Session of the Drafting Working Group, Geneva 2–13 December 2002: see http://www.inuit.org/index.asp?lang=eng&num=229, accessed November 2005.
95. See Optional Protocol to the Convention on the Rights of the Child on the involvement of children in armed conflicts, adopted by the General Assembly Resolution 54/263 (2000), Annex I. Also see General Recommendation of the Committee against the Rights of the Child on 'Children and Armed Conflict', adopted in September 1998.
96. See Report of the 1995 session of the Commission Drafting Group, UN Doc. E/CN.4/1996/84, para. 69; also Report on the 1996 session, UN Doc. E/CN.4/1997/102, paras. 173–94.
97. Consideration of a draft United Nations Declaration on the Rights of Indigenous Peoples: information received by inter-governmental organizations, UN Doc. E/CN.4/1995/WG.15/3, 3–4.
98. Commission on Human Rights Resolution 2005/52 adopted on 20 April 2005.
99. As evidenced by recognising the 'future' as well as present and past manifestation of their cultures in Article 11, the right of indigenous peoples to 'develop their own indigenous decision-making institutions' in Article 18 and the references to the non-economic development in Articles 20, 23, 29, 31, 32, 34 and 36.
100. Article 5 of the draft Declaration.
101. See the 1996 session of the Commission Drafting Working Group, E/CN.4/1997/102, paras. 130–44.
102. See the 1995 session of the Commission Drafting Working Group, E/CN.4/1996/84, para. 91.
103. See more extensive discussion in chapter 5 of this book.
104. See 'Children and Families of Ethnic Minorities, Immigrants and Indigenous Peoples', Summary Report of the Seventh Innocenti Global Conference, 6–15 October 1996 (Florence, Geneva: UNESCO, 1997); also R. B. Douglas and E. T. K. Douglas, 'The Rights of the Indigenous Child: Reconciling the United Nations Convention on the Rights of the Child and the (Draft) Declaration on the Rights of Indigenous People with Early Education Policies for Indigenous Children' (1995) 3 *International Journal of Children's Rights* 197–211.
105. Article 13 of the draft Declaration.
106. Article 16 of the draft Declaration.
107. Questions that have been put forward by the Human Rights Committee include: the status of minority languages; the use of language in non-official matters; use of language in communication media; use of language in the school system. See A. Spiliopoulou Åkermark, *Justifications of Minority Protection in International Law* (The Hague: Kluwer International, 1996), p. 143.

108. Article 16 of the draft Declaration.
109. These issues are analysed in detail in chapter 5.
110. Also to be considered in detail in chapter 5. See J. Burger and P. Hunt, 'Towards the International Protection of Indigenous Peoples' Rights' (1994) 12 *Netherlands Quarterly of Human Rights* 405–23 at 417–19.
111. For more detailed analysis, see chapter 5.
112. Some of the issues raised in these provisions will be analysed in detail in chapter 6.
113. For example, 'Concluding Observations of the Human Rights Committee, Colombia', UN Doc. CCPR/CO/80/COL of 26 May 2004, para. 20.
114. *Ibid.*, para. 33.
115. J. Sutherland, D. Craig and D. Posey, 'Emerging New Legal Standards for Comprehensive Rights' (1997) 27 *Environmental Policy and Law* 13–30 at 24.
116. 'Study on Treaties, Agreements and other Constructive Arrangements between States and Indigenous Populations', Final Report by Miguel Alfonso Martinez, Special Rapporteur, UN Doc. E/CN.4/Sub.2/1999/20.
117. See the 1996 session of the Drafting Working Group, UN Doc. E/CN.4/107/102, para.285.
118. W. Kymlicka, 'Theorizing Indigenous Rights' (1999) 49 *University of Toronto Law Journal* 281–93 at 293.
119. Thornberry, *Indigenous Peoples*, p. 375.
120. J. Debeljak, 'Barriers to the Recognition of Indigenous Peoples' Human Rights at the United Nations' (2000) 26 *Monash University Law Review* 159–94 at 184.
121. Anaya, *Indigenous Peoples*, p. 65.
122. UN Doc. E/CN.4/Sub.2/1994/30, para. 133.
123. Thornberry, *Indigenous Peoples*.
124. M.E. Turpel, 'Draft Declaration on the Rights of Indigenous Peoples – Commentary' [1994] 1 *Canadian Native Law Reporter* 50–2 at 50.
125. Knop, *Diversity and Self-Determination*, p. 254 n. 212.
126. A. Meijknecht, *Towards International Personality: The Position of Minorities and Indigenous Peoples in International Law* (Oxford: Intersentia, 2001).
127. R. McCorquodale, 'An Inclusive International System' (2004) 17 *Leiden Journal of International Law* 477–504 at 493.

PART II

Thematic analysis

4 Do indigenous peoples have the right to self-determination?

Introduction

Indigenous representatives have repeatedly stressed that they view the recognition of their right to self-determination as essential for their survival and development[1] and 'the key to the implementation of solutions for their problems'.[2] Article 3 of the draft Declaration which currently recognises a right of self-determination has been referred to as 'the heart of the Declaration',[3] its 'cornerstone',[4] the pillar upon which all other provisions of the draft Declaration rest[5] and the 'pre-requisite for the full enjoyment of all human rights' of indigenous peoples.[6] It is unfortunate that such a central claim to the indigenous movement is such a contested right in international law.

Self-determination is a thorny topic in international law with remarkable contradictions. While it has been liberally used as a slogan of universal application, its application always seems to be set with difficulties of considerable complexity. Falk notes that the successful creation of new states as a result of struggles for self-determination has 'both strained conceptual boundaries and created an increasingly awkward gap between doctrinal and experiential accounts of self-determination, resulting, as might be expected, in controversy and confusion'.[7] Indeed, currently there are no standard answers as to the modalities of the right. Although this creates confusion, it also encapsulates the richness and diversity of the ways self-determination can operate.[8] It is this fluidity of the right that has allowed the development of some 'dialogic spaces'[9] in which a discourse on indigenous claims can take place. The present chapter attempts to examine whether these spaces allow for indigenous self-determination. By reviewing the legal instruments on self-determination, I argue that although current international law does not give a positive answer to indigenous claims for self-determination, it does leave the door open for a positive next step.

Are indigenous peoples beneficiaries of the right?

The issue

One of the most powerful arguments for the recognition of indigenous self-determination is the 'historical and rectificatory justice' argument which puts the state's authority over indigenous groups in doubt.[10] Indigenous peoples perceive the recognition of their right to self-determination as a formal proclamation of denouncing the policies of destruction and assimilation that they have experienced in the past and an acknowledgment that they can determine their life without interference by states. As an indigenous representative stated in the 1995 Commission Working Group:

> The fourth principle is self-determination: it could be said that at the heart of all violations of human rights has been the failure to respect our integrity, defining our needs and controlling our lives.[11]

Another set of arguments focus more on the respect of indigenous identity.[12] Indigenous identity, it is argued, can only be protected by indigenous control over the matters that affect them. Indigenous peoples have been excluded from participating in the formation and evolution of international law. Since the early 1980s, they have been pushing for their own interpretation of international law concepts. Notions of respect, freedom and autonomy are paramount in their understanding of self-determination; the inherent and inalienable nature of the right is also important: rather than providing self-determination, states can only recognise it.[13] Related to this is the argument that all cultures are incommensurable; therefore, it is not appropriate for one culture, i.e. the dominant one, to evaluate the rules and norms of another culture, i.e. the indigenous culture.[14]

Legally, indigenous claims for self-determination are based on Article 1 of both International Covenants, a binding provision for most states. Paragraph 1 proclaims:

> All peoples have the right to self-determination. By virtue of that right, they can freely determine their political status and freely pursue their economic, social and cultural development.

Paragraph 2 establishes the free disposal by peoples of natural wealth and resources and states that 'in no case may a people be deprived of its own means of substance'; paragraph 3 mandates states to promote and respect the right to self-determination in conformity with the UN Charter. The inclusion of the right in the first Article of the Covenants indicates its importance. It is noteworthy that the provision does not contain any reference to territorial integrity, although the principle is included in Article 5.1 of the Covenant.[15]

During the drafting process of the International Covenants it was made clear that minorities are not included in the 'peoples' of Article 1;[16] minority rights are dealt with in Article 27 of the ICCPR, whereas peoples' rights are dealt with in Article 1 of both International Covenants.[17] It is widely accepted in the legal literature that indigenous peoples are not mere minorities.[18] Notwithstanding this, there is still an attempt to equate indigenous rights with minority rights by a few states, such as the USA, whose delegates have repeatedly asked for a minority language to be used in indigenous documents.[19] Admittedly, 'the relationship between minorities and the indigenous is one of fuzzy edges rather than bright lines'[20] and indigenous peoples have repeatedly used instruments for the protection of minorities; yet, it is beyond doubt that the indigenous need additional protection in international law to address their particular characteristics that distinguish them from other groups.[21]

No clear recognition of indigenous as 'peoples' in international law

Although the treatment of the indigenous as more than mere minorities is more or less settled, the question whether indigenous rights extend to those of 'peoples', including self-determination, is still very much open, as it involves substantial transfer of political and economic power from the centralised state to the indigenous communities. Several states argue that indigenous peoples cannot be perceived as 'peoples' for the purposes of Article 1 of the International Covenants, because there is no international instrument that explicitly recognises them as beneficiaries of Article 1.[22] Recognition of indigenous self-determination, they claim, would be contrary to UN General Assembly Resolution 41/120, which prescribes that new standards should be compatible with existing international law and should attract broad international support.[23] Argentina's statement in the early meetings of the Commission Drafting Group is indicative:

> [Argentina] believes that recognition of this right in favour of indigenous peoples simply because they are indigenous peoples is nowhere supported by the practice of the states or by current international law.[24]

Early attempts to include indigenous peoples among the beneficiaries of self-determination were not successful. In the 1960s, the Belgian thesis saw self-determination beyond colonialism[25] and was supportive of indigenous claims for self-determination on the basis that their treatment was comparable to that of colonised territories.[26] However, the Blue thesis prevailed: its supporters perceived self-determination strictly within the parameters of overseas colonies,[27] argued that indigenous peoples were fully integrated politically, noted that their problems were economic rather than political and stressed the principles of territorial integrity and state sovereignty. Since then, the question of whether indigenous peoples are 'peoples' for the purposes of Article 1 has been raised before the Human Rights Committee twice, but both communications were declared inadmissible on other grounds.[28] McGoldrick has criticised the failure of the Committee to provide guidance, especially due to its 'unique position'.[29] In 2000 when the issue was raised again in the *Apirana Mahuika* case, the Committee repeated that the examination of the right to self-determination is not within its mandate, but noted that 'the provisions of Article 1 may be relevant in the interpretation of other rights protected by the Covenant, in particular Article 27'.[30] In this manner, the Committee recognised the link between the right of self-determination with the scope of Article 27 of the ICCPR. A stretched interpretation of the Committee's comment could suggest an implicit recognition of the link between self-determination to *some beneficiaries* of Article 27, arguably indigenous peoples.

Another element that also advances the view that indigenous are beneficiaries of the right to self-determination is the growing trend of international documents to refer to indigenous as 'peoples'. The 1991 World Bank Operational Directive 4.20[31] and the new draft Operational Policy 4.10 on 'Indigenous Peoples';[32] the final documents of the World Conference against Racism, Racial Discrimination, Xenophobia and Related Intolerance;[33] the UNDP Indigenous Peoples Programme and its Draft Guidelines for Support to Indigenous Peoples;[34] the IFAD Regional Programme in Support of Indigenous Peoples in the Amazon Basin;[35] the 2003 UNESCO Public Meeting on Education Rights of Indigenous Peoples;[36] all these refer to indigenous peoples. Unfortunately, these documents are not binding. The only binding document that includes the term 'indigenous peoples' is ILO Convention No. 169, which is, however, followed by the qualification that the use of the term 'peoples' should have no implication as regards the right of self-determination.[37] The ILO has stated that their intention was to be neutral on the future development of a right to self-determination for indigenous peoples in international law, as this does not fall within their mandate. The recognition of indigenous as 'peoples' in the international documents – even with the qualification – is an affirmation of their group identity and characteristics[38] and an indication that the bodies which adopt these documents support indigenous claims. However, it is doubtful whether these documents can be perceived as evidence that international law has recognised indigenous as beneficiaries of the right to self-determination.

Employment of the definition of 'peoples' in international law

A second way of evaluating whether indigenous are 'peoples' for the purpose of self-determination is to assess whether they fall within the definition of 'peoples' given by international law. Unfortunately, no international instrument explicitly defines who is 'a people' for the purpose of self-determination. In 1956, Jennings expressed his frustration:

> Nearly forty years ago a Professor of Political Science who was also President of the United States, President Wilson, enunciated a doctrine which was ridiculous, but which was widely accepted as a sensible proposition, the doctrine of self-determination. On the surface it seemed reasonable: let the people decide. It was in fact ridiculous because the people cannot decide until someone decides who are the people.[39]

Notwithstanding the confusion created by the lack of definition, such an exercise would be neither possible, nor necessarily desirable. Kamenca has rightly noted that 'nations and peoples, like genetic populations, are recent, contingent and have also been formed and reformed constantly throughout history'.[40] Definitions in international human rights law are restrictive and cannot include all relevant cases; rigid definitions result in excluding certain groups from the protection they should enjoy.

Stavenhagen advocates the establishment of specific criteria that would draw the balance between the 'maximalist approach' (allowing the right to all claimants) and the 'minimalist approach' (of a strict definition).[41] Well-accepted descriptions provide such criteria. In his UN study,[42] Espiel described a 'people' as 'a specific type of human community sharing a common desire to establish an entity capable of functioning to ensure a common future'.[43] Similar is the description of 'a people' in a subsequent UN study by Cristescu[44] as a 'social entity possessing a clear identity with its own characteristics including some relationship with the territory, even if the peoples in question have been wrongfully expelled from it and artificially replaced by another population'.[45] According to Cristescu, 'a people' satisfies two of the classic elements of state character, an identifiable and distinct population and territory, but may lack political organisation and recognised capacity to engage in foreign relations.[46] The descriptions reveal two sets of requirements for the notion of 'a people': objective ones which encompass factors such as common language, culture, religion, race or ethnicity, territory and history; and subjective requirements, which include consciousness as a distinct people and a collective will to exist as a distinct people.[47] Taking Scheinin's warning into account that being indigenous does not automatically qualify the group as 'a people',[48] indigenous communities in general do satisfy the above criteria: all of them constitute groups distinct from the rest of the populations of the state in which they live; most, if not all, are aware of their distinctiveness and want to maintain it; and they share a common vision. In addition, most of them live in well-defined areas, often apart from the rest of the population and have a special bond with the lands they live in or the lands they have been expelled from.[49]

However, there is a tendency to overlook the intellectual criteria and focus on the guidance international documents have given on the matter.[50] States' insistence that 'indigenous are not peoples for the purposes of Article 1 of the International Covenants' implies a distinction between 'peoples' in general and 'peoples' for the purpose of the right to self-determination. Who are 'peoples' in the latter category will depend on positive law.

Employment of international documents

Unfortunately, positive law does not help either: international law documents have been really vague about the modalities of the right to self-determination, including who its beneficiaries are. Despite two references to self-determination in the UN Charter and its implementation through a system established for non-self-governing territories,[51] no clarifications were given either about its beneficiaries, or its content. In the 1960s, several Declarations tried to advance decolonisation.[52] Among them, the 1960 Declaration on the Granting of Independence to Colonial Countries and Peoples (Declaration against Colonialism)[53] attempted to clarify the content and the beneficiaries of self-determination. The Declaration recognised for the first time that 'all peoples have the right to self-determination; by virtue of that right they freely determine their political status and freely pursue their economic, social and cultural development' and identified the beneficiaries of the right as peoples under 'alien subjugation, domination and exploitation'. Although the Declaration is a soft law instrument, it is of particular importance as a 'form of an authoritative interpretation of the Charter, rather than a recommendation'.[54] The strong language of the Declaration reflects its importance as well as the immediacy of the states' obligation towards self-determination.[55]

Indigenous peoples arguably satisfy the beneficiaries of self-determination given by the Declaration, as they have been victims of subjugation, domination and exploitation from the dominant populations that live in the state.[56] Rather unclear is whether they are victims of 'alien' domination. If 'alien' is interpreted in cultural, rather than purely territorial terms, then they satisfy this criterion, as they have been oppressed by nations of a different culture. Recognising indigenous peoples as beneficiaries of the Declaration is also consistent with its preamble which prescribes that the impetus for self-determination is the denial of freedom and independence of the beneficiaries, their exploitation, the abuse of their human rights and the impeding of their social, economic and cultural development.[57]

However, the basic hurdle for indigenous self-determination is considered to be the reference to territorial integrity. Article 6 provides that any attempt 'aimed at the partial or total disruption of the national unity and the territorial integrity of a country is incompatible with the purposes and principles of the Charter'; Article 7 reaffirms the principle of territorial integrity. Therefore, the exercise of the right of self-determination cannot be a threat to territorial integrity. At the time when the Declaration was adopted, self-determination was equated to decolonisation; therefore, this provision was interpreted as allowing only nations that constitute the whole population of the state to be considered as 'peoples'. This so far has been a major obstacle to indigenous claims for self-determination, as they seldom constitute the whole population of the territory in which they live.

Resolution 1541 (XV),[58] adopted the very next day after the Declaration against Colonialism also provided some guidance as to the beneficiaries of self-determination. The resolution recognised the right of self-determination to non-self-governing territories, i.e. 'a territory which is geographically separate and is distinct ethnically and/or culturally from the country administering it' and placed arbitrarily 'in a position or status of subordination' to the administering state. There are a few indigenous territories officially recognised by the United Nations as non-self-governing territories;[59] they would avoid the problems of Article 1.1 as they fall within Articles 1.3 and 73. Besides these though, most indigenous groups also satisfy the criteria set in Resolution 1541(XV): they suffer from arbitrary discrimination in their everyday life and are ethnically distinct from the rest of the population living within the state. In addition, as mentioned above, usually they are geographically separate from the administering state, living in a national federation or in partitioned – officially or de facto – lands;[60] so, if 'geographically separate' is not interpreted to involve international borders, they satisfy this criterion too. Brownlie finds this interpretation consistent with the practice of the United Nations: he has noted that the argument of colonial powers that a colonised territory was part of France, Portugal or Spain did not stop the process of decolonisation: 'The status of Algeria as part of France made no difference to the general assessment of Algeria as a unit of self-determination.'[61] Likewise, the states' argument that indigenous territories are part of the states' territories should arguably make no difference to the recognition of indigenous self-determination.

In 1970, the Declaration on Principles of International Law concerning Friendly Relations and Cooperation among States in accordance with the Charter of the United Nations[62] (Declaration on Friendly Relations) expanded the beneficiaries of the right to 'peoples under colonial or *racist regimes* or other forms of alien domination' (emphasis added).[63] Even though the drafters of the Declaration had in mind specific exclusionary regimes,[64] the provision again can be interpreted in favour of indigenous claims for self-determination: indigenous peoples have been living in states the structures and policies of which consistently discriminate against them on the basis of their race. Once again though, if self-determination is understood as independence, indigenous claims are hampered by the principle of territorial integrity, included in paragraph 7:

> Nothing in the foregoing paragraphs shall be construed as authorising or encouraging any action which would dismember or impair, totally or in part, the territorial integrity or political unity of sovereign and independent states, conducting themselves in compliance with the principle of equal rights and self-determination of peoples as described above and thus, possessed by a government representing the whole people belonging to the territory without distinction as to race, creed or colour.

This provision has been at the centre of the debate on secession, which will be analysed later. Suffice to say here that, on the one hand, secession is prohibited since it would affect territorial integrity; on the other hand, the provision seems to leave the door open for secession, if the government of the state in which the people live does not represent them and continually discriminates against them.

In 1975, the Final Act of the Conference on Security and Cooperation in Europe[65] (Helsinki Declaration) confirmed the expansion of the beneficiaries of self-determination beyond colonised peoples: the agreement of 35 independent states that they recognised the right of self-determination to their peoples implies that 'peoples' living in independent states are also entitled to the right; thus, the right is not only perceived within the colonial context. Yet, in the Declaration the right of self-determination remains overshadowed by the concepts of inviolability of frontiers, territorial integrity and non-interference: according to Principles III, IV and VI, self-determination is to be enjoyed by all the peoples of the existing state and not by particular groups within the state; these groups will enjoy the protection of human rights and protection given to minorities, affirmed in the Declaration in Principle VII.

Among the other regional instruments, only the African Charter on Human and Peoples' Rights recognised self-determination for '*all* peoples' (emphasis added).[66] Thornberry and Hannum both agree that the Charter referred to 'whole peoples' of the states, rather than ethnic or other groups.[67] The prevalence of territorial integrity over self-determination within the context of Africa was reaffirmed by the International Court of Justice in the *Frontier Dispute* case between Burkina Faso and Mali, where the Court affirmed that 'the maintenance of the territorial status quo in Africa is often seen as the wisest course'.[68] Nevertheless, recent commentators provide African examples with a looser interpretation of territorial integrity in favour of self-determination.[69]

Another international judicial body, the Inter-American Commission on Human Rights specifically addressed indigenous self-determination. In the *Miskito Indians* case,[70] the Commission held that present international law does not recognise the right of self-determination to any ethnic group:

> The present status of international law does not recognise observance of the principle of self-determination of peoples, which it considers to be the right of a people to independently chose their form of political organisation and to freely establish the means it deems appropriate to bring about their economic, social, cultural development. This does not mean however, that it recognises the right of self-determination of any ethnic group as such.[71]

The (1993) Vienna Declaration and Program of Action,[72] emanating from the 1993 United Nations World Conference on Human Rights, referred to self-determination in Article 2. After a verbatim restatement of Article 1 of the International Covenants, the Declaration affirmed the right of peoples to take legitimate action, in accordance with the UN Charter, to realise their right of self-determination,[73] but also included the usual restrictions of territorial integrity and political unity. Although its language echoes the 1970 Declaration on Principles of International Law concerning Friendly Relations, there is one significant change: the 1970 Declaration referred to a government representing the whole people without distinction as to race, creed or colour, whereas the Vienna Declaration expanded the disclaimer to a government representing the whole people without distinction of *any kind*.[74]

More recently, the 1996 General Recommendation XXI (48)[75] adopted by the Committee against Racial Discrimination in 1996 concluded that:

> ... international law has not recognised a general right to peoples unilaterally to declare secession from a State. In this respect, the Committee follows the views expressed in An Agenda for Peace (paras. 17 and following), namely that a fragmentation of States may be detrimental to the protection of human rights, as well as the preservation of peace and security. This does not however, exclude the possibility of arrangements reached by free agreements of all parties concerned.[76]

The Declaration does not discuss whether secession could be possible in specific cases.

The hurdle of territorial integrity

The above analysis demonstrates that the recognition of the right of a people to self-determination does not per se lead to the disintegration of the state. However, it is due to the fear that it could do so that most states have difficulties in giving it recognition, since indigenous communities constitute part of the state. Many states have stressed the incompatibility of indigenous self-determination with the principle of territorial integrity.[77] As proof of their fears, they refer to the statement made by the Crees of Quebec:

> We do not want to secede from Canada; but if Quebec becomes a separate state, we will insist on our right of self-determination, our right to choose which, if any, state we determine to associate ourselves with.[78]

Academic opinion seems to agree that current international law does not explicitly recognise a right of sub-national groups to self-determination through secession. In 1992, Franck, Higgins, Pellet, Shaw and Tomuschat all reached the conclusion that self-determination allows for independence only to colonial peoples or to those whose territory is the subject of *foreign* occupation; outside this context the achievement of sovereignty in law is a matter of fact.[79] Five years later, Abi-Saab, Franck, Pellet and Shaw noted though that neither does international law explicitly prohibit secession and stressed that the international community often recognises states formed by secession.[80] Crawford agreed with the 1992 opinion: international practice has no example of a unilateral right to secede;[81] thus, he concluded that the focus of the right to self-determination must be on the participation of peoples in the political system of the state.[82] Hannum also supports this view: cases where a new state has been recognised are either cases of independence after agreement of the parties concerned (USSR, Ethiopia, Czechoslovakia) or cases where the state has stopped to exist (Yugoslavia). 'State practice and the weight of authority', he has concluded, 'require that there is no right to secession'.[83] Higgins has also used state practice and territorial integrity to reject the claim that minorities can be peoples with the right to secede,[84] but not without criticism. In particular, Knop criticises Higgins' approach as rigid and inconsistent with her understanding of international law as a process.[85] Contrary to Higgins, Hannum and Crawford, Dinstein has used the same means to reach the opposite conclusion: to him, the Soviet, Yugoslav and Czechoslovak experiences show that 'there is no reason to disallow *in limine* the exercise of the right of self-determination when the desire to dismantle a multinational state is shared by a number of peoples living within its boundaries'.[86] So it seems that indigenous communities would have great difficulties in gathering support for secessionist claims. Indigenous communities only form part of the state they live in, usually not even the majority of the population.

Yet, one can see a more positive reaction when it comes to secession as a final resort for remedial reasons.[87] Even back in 1920, the Åland Islands judgment acknowledged such the possibility of remedial secession by stating that 'the separation of a minority from the State of which it forms part and its incorporation in another State can only be considered as an altogether exceptional solution, a last resort when the State lacks either the will or the power to enact and apply just and effective guarantees'.[88] United Nations instruments, including the 1970 Declaration on Friendly Relations and the Vienna Declaration, have left room for remedial secession. One could argue that these instruments are not legally binding and recall the lack of state practice to support remedial secession. Yet, de Kirgis has argued that the United Nations Declarations purport to and probably reflect an *opinio juris*, strong evidence of which may overcome differences in state practice in human rights.[89] According to him, there is a striking contrast between earlier and later (after 1970) formulations of the principles of territorial integrity that suggests that:

> from about 1970 on, there could be a right of 'peoples' – still not well defined – to secede from an established State that does not have a fully representative government, or at least to secede from a State whose government excludes people of any race, creed or colour from political representation, when those people are the ones asserting the right and they have a claim to a defined territory.[90]

Several authors accept the possibility of remedial secession under certain circumstances. Musgrave accepts it in cases of oppression and non-representation in government,[91] whereas Shaw accepts it in 'extremely exceptional circumstances'.[92] After rejecting the right to secession for sub-national groups, Franck conditionally recognises the possibility of remedial secession, if 'the people' occupies a distinct territory and is persistently and egregiously denied political and social equality as well as the opportunity to retain its cultural identity.[93] Schachter also stresses the territorial element: the community must inhabit a region that largely supports separation in the given circumstances.[94] Espiel accepts it if 'beneath the guise of ostensible national unity, colonial and alien domination does in fact exist, whatever legal formula may be used in an attempt to conceal it, the right of the subject people concerned cannot be disregarded'.[95] Heraclides has gathered the specific conditions under which a remedial right to secession can be recognised: there must be systematic exploitation of or discrimination against a sizeable, well-defined minority; the minority must be a distinct self-defined community or society, compactly inhabiting a region which overwhelmingly supports separatism; secession must present a realistic prospect of conflict resolution and of peace within and between the new and the old state; and the central government must have rejected all compromise solutions.[96]

Recent judgments have also acknowledged the growing consensus amongst international lawyers that even beyond colonialism, traditionally perceived alien domination and occupation, there is a possibility of a right to secession for remedial reasons. In the *Crime of Genocide* case,[97] self-determination was raised in a non-colonial situation without meeting the objection of the Court.[98] More explicitly, in *Loizidou* v. *Turkey*, Judge Wildhaber commented:

> Until recently in international practice the right of self-determination was in practical terms identical to and indeed restricted to, a right to decolonisation. In recent years a consensus has seemed to emerge that peoples may also exercise a right to self-determination if their human rights are consistently and flagrantly violated or if they are without representation at all or are massively under-represented in an undemocratic and discriminatory way.[99]

The African Commission on Human and Peoples' Rights has also indirectly recognised the idea of remedial secession. In *Katangese Peoples Congress* v. *Zaire*, the Commission held that:

> in the absence of concrete evidence of violations of human rights to the point that the territorial integrity of Zaire should be called into question and in the absence of evidence that the people of Katanga are denied the right to participate in government . . ., the Commission holds the view that Katanga is obliged to exercise a variant of self-determination that is compatible with the sovereignty and territorial integrity of Zaire.[100]

In the national level, the Supreme Court of Canada ruled in 1998 that:

> A right to secession only arises under the principle of self-determination of people at international law where 'a people' is governed as part of a colonial empire; where 'a people' is subject to alien subjugation, domination or exploitation; and possibly where 'a people' is denied any meaningful exercise of its right to self-determination within the state of which it forms a part.[101]

Crawford, a strong advocate of the right to self-determination within the context of colonialism, has also discussed the possibility of secession in cases of *carence de souveraineté*. Although he insists that there is an exhaustive definition of the beneficiaries of the *right* to self-determination in the trust and mandated territories and territories treated as non-self-governing under chapter XI of the UN Charter, the beneficiaries of the *principle* of self-determination are subject to the discretion of the interpreter. Obviously Crawford perceives the principle of self-determination as 'a reservoir from which apparent gaps in the corpus of international law may be filled'.[102] The interpreter, Crawford maintains, may choose to accept as beneficiaries victims of *carence de souveraineté*, namely 'territories forming distinct political–geographical areas, whose inhabitants do not share in the government either of the region or of the State to which the region belongs, with the result that the territory becomes in effect, with respect to the remainder of the State, non-self-governing'.[103] Crawford names Bangladesh as the sole example for remedial secession.[104] Bangladesh is also used by Kingsbury who concludes that:

> ... practice [suggests] that self-determination in the strong form as a right to establish a separate State may be an extraordinary remedy in distinct territories suffering massive human rights violations orchestrated by governing authorities based elsewhere in the state.[105]

Could indigenous peoples be perceived as victims of *carence de souveraineté*? Anaya believes so, even though he notes that remedial secession can operate in various ways.[106] I would adopt a different approach: I believe that the answer can only be given on an ad hoc basis.[107] However, even for a group that fulfils the criteria one must keep in mind Crawford's opinion that the interpreter *may* recognise the group's right to self-determination including secession. Therefore, it is up to the interpreter to decide whether a right of indigenous peoples to self-determination as independence should be recognised.

Who would be the interpreter of the law of self-determination in this instance? Who will determine whether indigenous peoples are a case of *carence de souveraineté*, so they have a right of secession? In the first instance it will be the state in which they live. Thornberry highlights the problems: the right of secession could be granted, if the government is not representative. If the assessment whether this test has been met lies with the government, not many governments will accept that they have failed. Moreover, any reform of the state to make it more representative takes away the possibility of secession; thus, the test of representation is far too easy a test for governments to satisfy.[108]

A more reliable interpreter of the law of self-determination is the international community, as represented by the United Nations General Assembly. Following the refusal of Portugal and Spain to voluntarily identify their non-self-governing territories, the General Assembly has become the body responsible for deciding which entities fall within non-self-governing territories by applying the criteria in Resolution 1541 (XV). In accordance with these criteria, the General Assembly has made several decisions that particular territories fall within Chapter XI. These concerned certain overseas territories of Spain and Portugal and subsequently certain French territories, of which the most recent is Caledonia.[109] Unfortunately, so far, the General Assembly has not made a ruling in any case outside the colonial context.

In essence, recognising indigenous peoples as victims of *carence de souveraineté* involves a subjective judgment about the level of lack of representation of the indigenous community in the state. Even more challenging are the judgments involved in: the Heraclides test of secession as a means of conflict resolution; the Musgrave test of indigenous oppression; the Espiel test of colonial domination; the Shaw test of extremely exceptional circumstances; and the Wildhaber test of consistent and flagrant violation of human rights. All these tests involve subjective judgments to be made by the General Assembly, a highly political body comprised of states; obviously, they would be very reluctant to encourage the expansion of the right to secession to include sub-national groups, as it could prove suicidal for them.[110] The recent example of Kosovo confirms this: even though it concerned a well-defined territory that overwhelmingly supported secession after years of well-reported oppression and gross violations of human rights and after a series of negotiations that were not successful,[111] the international community did not recognise the right to remedial secession.[112] If the right to secession was not recognised for the people of Kosovo, is it not improbable that it would be recognised in cases of indigenous communities? As Thornberry pragmatically notes, 'even this cautious and careful account of criteria appears as a possibility rather than a probability in terms of a normative development of general international law'.[113]

In short, international law seems to reluctantly allow a theoretical possibility for remedial secession to beneficiaries of self-determination. Even if this right exists – and state practice has not yet confirmed it does – claimants would have to fulfil a series of tests, before their case is even seriously considered. The principle of territorial integrity is a serious obstacle to the possibility of secession for any sub-national group, including indigenous communities.

Does this conclusion refute the claim for indigenous self-determination? Does 'secession' cover the scope of the right to self-determination? One should think so by reading selected United Nations documents, statements of state delegations and opinions of international lawyers, as 'secession' is often used interchangeably with 'self-determination'. If this is the case, then indigenous communities will have to satisfy the different tests put forward for remedial secession in order to be recognised as beneficiaries of the right to self-determination; even then recognition of their right will be difficult in practice. If, however, the scope of self-determination is not wholly covered by secession, then the tests for secession need not be satisfied, as indigenous peoples can be the beneficiaries of the right to self-determination, irrespective of whether this right reaches secession or stops short of it. Clearly, the question of who can be the beneficiaries of the right is very much dependent on the meaning of self-determination. Gilbert agrees, he has warned that 'the error in the self-determination debate has been to focus on the beneficiaries ... rather than the conditions justifying whatever form of self-determination is appropriate to the group'.[114] Therefore, the discussion has to turn to the meaning of self-determination and the different forms it can take.

The scope of the right to self-determination

The minimalist approach: self-determination as independence

There are numerous understandings of the meaning of self-determination that cannot be easily grouped. Admittedly, for a long period the prevailing understanding of self-determination equated it with independence. States have repeatedly argued that the right has a fixed meaning in international law, namely independence, which does not allow for expansion.[115] A few states,[116] including Japan, have specifically placed this meaning within the context of decolonisation:

> The concept of self-determination was set forth in the context of decolonisation, mainly for colonised people who requested independence from states.[117]

The historical account of the international instruments on self-determination confirms that this understanding is too restrictive. Crawford clarifies that 'as a matter of ordinary treaty interpretation, one cannot interpret Article 1 of the International Covenants as limited to the colonial case'.[118] Article 1 paragraph 1 refers to 'all peoples', rather than some (colonised) peoples, since paragraph 3 specifies that the phrase 'all peoples' includes colonial peoples. Further, if paragraph 1 refers only to colonised peoples, so would paragraph 2, in which case we would be led to the illogical conclusion that only colonised peoples have the right of permanent sovereignty over natural resources.

Contrary to Article 1 of both International Covenants, it seems that the Declaration against Colonialism[119] openly equated self-determination with decolonisation. Even though it defined self-determination in a broad manner as the *right* of peoples to 'freely determine their political status and freely pursue their economic, social and political development',[120] the title of the Declaration, its recommendation in paragraph 5 for immediate steps for 'independence', the inclusion of the principle of territorial integrity and the description of the beneficiaries, limited to peoples under 'alien subjugation, domination and exploitation',[121] point in this direction. Resolution 1541,[122] adopted the very next day, was also in line with the major need of the time, decolonisation, as evident from a similar description of the beneficiaries and the explicit reference to territorial integrity. The 1965 Declaration on the Inadmissibility of Intervention in the Domestic Affairs of States and the Protection of Their Independence and Sovereignty increased the ambiguity.[123] The language of the Declaration was somewhat unfortunate: although it added peoples in racist regimes to the list of beneficiaries of self-determination, it confused human rights with states' rights. The Declaration proclaimed that 'every *State* has the inalienable right to self-determination' (emphasis added)[124] ignoring that self-determination is a *people's* right, rather than a *government's* right.[125] The 1970 Declaration on Principles of International Law concerning Friendly Relations and Cooperation among States[126] also focused on liberation extending the right to peoples whose government does not represent 'the whole people without distinction as to race, creed or colour'.[127] The apartheid system of South Africa had become the focus of the international community at that time and again the meaning of self-determination accommodated this preoccupation. The Declaration obviously perceived self-determination in its external aspect as it listed the ways in which the right could be implemented, as: a) establishment of a sovereign and independent state; b) free association; c) integration with an independent state; or d) emergence into any other political status freely determined by a people.[128] Thus, independence was the prevailing understanding of the right of self-determination in 1976, when the International Covenants[129] were finally adopted, even though again its description of the right allowed space for a wider scope.

In the following years there was a gradual shift in international documents and legal literature towards an alternative meaning of the right to self-determination. One of the first instruments that recorded this shift was the 1975 Final Act of the Conference on Security and Cooperation in Europe (Helsinki Declaration).[130] Principle VII reads:

> By virtue of the principle of equal rights and self-determination of peoples, all peoples always have the right, in full freedom to determine, when and as they wish, their internal and external status, without external interference, and to pursue as they wish their political, economic, social and cultural development.[131]

The Declaration projected self-determination as an ongoing process that urges peoples to adapt to new structures, demands and needs; as the right of peoples to decide on a certain form of governance or an international status and/or re-evaluate their decisions. Moreover, the Declaration drew a clear connection between the exercise of self-determination and the existence of other human rights in a more forceful way than previous documents. Not only should peoples be free of any external interference, they should also be free of any internal interference. This new meaning corresponded to the international realities of the Cold War and Western states' interest in emphasising the principles of democracy, free elections and participation.

In 1984, the Human Rights Committee reaffirmed the special relationship of the right to self-determination with all other human rights. In General Comment 12/27 the Committee noted that the right is placed 'apart and before all of the other rights' in the Covenant, is inalienable of all peoples and poses corresponding obligations. The Comment also highlighted the link between self-determination and economic development. In this manner, the Committee implied that self-determination is a much wider right than simple independence. The General Comment also refers to the 1970 Declaration on Principles of International Law concerning Friendly Relations and Cooperation among States. Does the reference to the 1970 Declaration imply a restrictive understanding of self-determination? McGoldrick refutes such a possibility. He notes:

> The mere reference by the HRC in its General Comment to the 1970 Declaration could not sensibly be taken to suggest either that the two instruments are of the same scope or that the scope of the ICCPR has been narrowed by the 1970 Declaration.[132]

In the early 1990s, with the collapse of the former Soviet Union and Yugoslavia and the emergence of new states in Eastern Europe claims for independence resurfaced. However, this time it was different from the 1960s: it was clearly understood that self-determination was not only about independence. Several documents focused on participatory structures within the state,[133] encouraged democracy by monitoring elections,[134] referred to the possibility of autonomous regimes[135] and stressed the link between the ongoing process of self-determination and human rights guarantees.[136] And even though the (1993) Vienna Declaration and Program of Action[137] and (CERD) General Recommendation XXI (48)[138] issued the same year, both focused on secession, the latter clearly recognised that minorities have the right to internal self-determination.

Nevertheless, some indigenous representatives, together with some commentators,[139] insist on viewing self-determination within the context of colonialism. I appreciate Anghie's position that the structures of colonialism continue to exist, although in other, more informal, but still persistent ways.[140] However, colonialism as a political process that is formally recognised in international law (as opposed to its economic, cultural or other form) has more or less been completed. Therefore, as a strategy, I believe that insisting on the concept of colonisation for the purposes of indigenous self-determination is counter-productive. The process of decolonisation was about (re)-establishing an independent state; indigenous peoples ask for their right to determine their political status, which is a much broader concept than mere independence. Indigenous self-determination is about a process with various applications. Also, decolonisation has more or less been completed: in contrast, indigenous self-determination is a new concept that is dynamic and involves new ideas and nuances.[141] On the practical level, the argument of decolonisation can easily be distorted and can lead to the denial of indigenous protection: in the Commission Drafting Group, the representative of Bangladesh has used the idea that 'indigenous peoples have suffered under decolonisation' to actually deny recognition of indigenous peoples living within Bangladesh. He argued that since colonialism is restricted to European colonies, Bangladesh does not have any indigenous peoples.[142]

Knop makes the distinction between the right to self-determination as part of corrective justice and as a new right: colonial peoples ask for the restitution of their earlier right, whereas non-colonial peoples ask for a new right.[143] Although this favours indigenous claims for restitution of their earlier sovereignty, it fails to recognise the need to accommodate the claims they have which derive from a new understanding of the right (for example, autonomy claims). Kingsbury calls this understanding of self-determination 'a reductionist approach';[144] self-determination should not be understood in terms of the end result but also in terms of process and political legitimisation.

Indeed, a focus on independence gives the state the central role on the international stage and ignores the dramatic changes that have occurred in the last few decades and their consequent challenges to territorial integrity and state sovereignty as principles that secure the existing status quo.[145] The decline of the state is reflected in many aspects of international law: two obvious examples are the widespread recognition that the international community can intervene in a state's so called 'internal affairs' for human rights purposes and the gradual expansion of the bodies with international legal personality.[146] Accordingly, the meaning of self-determination cannot continue to be centred on the state and the creation of a state. Rather, Kingsbury advocates a 'relational approach' to self-determination, an approach focusing on the constructive relationship between the state and the indigenous group.[147] Using this approach, he gives another dimension to the position of the Crees that they would claim secession if Quebec seceded from Canada: since the Crees have an evolving relationship with the state of Canada, if Quebec seceded, the nature of this relationship would change; they could have the right to exercise their right of self-determination to determine their future, which might well entail a future within the State of Canada. Thus, the claim to self-determination is considered in practice as relational and remedial, triggered by the disruption in the relationship between them and the State in which they live.[148] Young has also advocated understanding self-determination as 'relational autonomy in the context of non-domination'.[149] This approach is also very similar to the Daes explanation of indigenous self-determination. She defines it as:

> . . . the right to negotiate freely [indigenous] peoples' political status and representation in the states in which they live. This might be best described as a kind of 'belated state-building', through which indigenous peoples are able to join with all the other peoples that make up the state on mutually agreed and just terms, after many years of isolation and exclusion.[150]

A UN seminar on Racism against Indigenous also recognised that 'self-determination includes, inter alia, the right and the power of indigenous to negotiate with states on an equal basis the standards and mechanisms that will govern relationships between them.'[151]

Apart from its state-centred nature, the restrictive understanding of self-determination has another drawback: equating self-determination with independence, an option recognised only with regard to populations of whole states, completely ignores the *raison d'être* of human rights; human rights are established to protect human beings, rather than states. As Falk suggests, 'it is the underlying legitimacy of peoples, not the transient legitimacy of governments that constitutes the purpose and rationale for the instruments protecting human rights.'[152] Self-determination cannot be recognised – directly or indirectly – as belonging to states; otherwise, as Crawford notes, the right could become a pretence for governments to abuse their populations in the name of self-determination.[153]

Several states have voiced their agreement with the broader understanding of the right. The delegate of Liechtenstein stated in 2001 that 'the right to self-determination was exercised in many different ways, and it needed to be understood that self-determination was not synonymous with independent statehood'.[154] Other states have stated that perceiving self-determination only within the colonial context:

> . . . would lead to freezing international law in time and inhibit progress. It was argued by some governments and most indigenous organisations that the right to self-determination was also applicable to internal non-colonial situations.[155]

At the same time though, several states perceive this evolution in a negative light. For example, in 2002, Australia, Canada, New Zealand, the Russian Federation and the United Kingdom maintained that the meaning of the right is still unclear.[156] The representative of the United States has also stated:

> Under contemporary international law, the term self-determination is open to varying interpretations depending on the specific context . . . while current views among scholars and governments may be changing on the meaning of self-determination, there is not yet international consensus.[157]

Consequently, some states argue that they cannot grant the right of self-determination to indigenous peoples, as they cannot undertake obligations that are not predetermined and clear.[158]

It is my firm belief that the evolution of the right to self-determination must not only be recognised, but also welcomed. Clarity in international law cannot be used as a cover to what Bedjaoui calls 'legal paganism'.[159] If totally cut off from international life, international law would be a selective set of rules serving only to perpetuate one kind of reality. Higgins stresses the importance of law as a process where policy considerations are taken into account, rather than as a set of strict and clear-cut rules.[160] Through this prism, international law is 'the entire decision-making process and not just a reference to the trend of past decisions which are termed "rules"'.[161] This flexibility should not of course be interpreted as allowing political concerns to determine the scope of every human right. Allowing the international community – rather than states unilaterally – to interpret each right in accordance with the current realities, albeit always within the contours set by the standards of international law, is consistent with the dynamic character of international law.[162] Especially the international law of human rights is 'an open discourse, incorporating moral, theoretical and hortatory elements, rarely capable of precisely resolving disagreements, unlike idealised domestic, court-centred processes'.[163] International human rights instruments set basic, general rules that are interpreted and applied ad hoc in any case. Notions like sovereignty, freedom, participation, and the right to expression all have a certain degree of generality which to the eyes of the sceptical can appear as vagueness. This generality allows them to evolve according to international realities and needs. For these reasons, understanding the right to self-determination to mean purely independence, either in the context of colonialism or beyond, is too limited.

The maximalist approach: self-determination as an umbrella right

At the other end of the spectrum lie maximalist perceptions of the right to self-determination. Among the many different understandings and nuances that are given to self-determination, one identifiable trend is a very broad understanding of the right that usually includes an economic[164] and/or a cultural aspect.[165] This maximalist understanding is entrenched in claims made on the basis of self-determination: for democracy and political rights; distinct political and judicial systems; territorial integrity; political independence and non-intervention; or concerning the name of a country and border adjustments; religious freedom; and educational provisions. In its distorted form, nationalism, fundamentalism, racism and even ethnic cleansing have all been justified in the name of self-determination.[166]

Many indigenous statements follow the maximalist approach. Although self-determination has rightly been understood by indigenous peoples as 'the right to be in control of their lives and their own destiny',[167] this has been used by some as the basis of all indigenous claims. A 1987 Declaration of indigenous peoples stated:

> The right of self-determination is fundamental to the enjoyment of all human rights. From the right of self-determination flow the right to permanent sovereignty over land – including aboriginal, ancestral and historic lands – and other natural resources, the right to develop and maintain governing institutions, the right to life and physical integrity, way of life and religion.[168]

The preamble of the (1992) Indigenous Peoples Earth Charter proclaims:

> We indigenous peoples maintain our inherent right to self-determination. We have always had the right to decide our own forms of government, to use

our own ways to raise and educate our children, to our own identity without interference.[169]

Similar is the spirit of the (1993) Mataatua Declaration on Cultural and Intellectual Property Rights of Indigenous Peoples:

We declare that indigenous peoples of the world have the right to self-determination, and in exercising that right must be recognised as the exclusive owners of their cultural and intellectual property.[170]

Commentators such as Spiry have confirmed the wide use of the right:

... self-determination is used today to refer to a people's control of its own destiny. As such it is used to refer to a wide range of rights, including: the right to use the native language; to develop the native culture; to use and own lands and resources; and to achieve political autonomy, self-government and ultimate independence, even where that may entail secession from an existing state.[171]

The maximalist approach appears to be supported by the language of Common Article 1 of the International Covenants, which defines self-determination as the right of peoples 'to pursue their economic, cultural and social development'. It is also in line with many instruments that call for attention to the connection between self-determination and human rights. Undoubtedly, this approach has important qualities: it views self-determination as an evolving concept and attempts to adjust its meaning according to current international needs; and it aims to restore global justice, the ultimate goal of human rights, by accommodating the claims of vulnerable groups.

However, it also has serious downsides. First, using self-determination as an umbrella right[172] is a poor legislative method that runs the danger of distorting its meaning and scope. Higgins finds this ever-expanding method irresponsible:[173] although she agrees with the flexibility of the approach, she believes that concepts should be used with care and rejects the idea that self-determination can be all things to all men. Stavenhagen takes a similar approach and warns that using self-determination as an umbrella right 'will end up demeaning and devaluing the idea of self-determination itself, and will thereby only harm those collectivities who require it the most'.[174] Peru's statement on indigenous self-determination demonstrates the validity of this argument:

... self-determination would not be national in character, rather it would have a cultural and social identity within a national formation. Government delegations would find this approach much more fruitful.[175]

By seemingly accepting the right, Peru clearly avoided any recognition of the politically sensitive scope of self-determination. Peru thereby disregarded the real meaning of the right and contrary to how it appears, this statement works to the detriment of indigenous self-determination.

Linking the right to self-determination with a wide range of claims is also a poor tactic. Claims that are justified by loose links with established rights, and even more so with a right as controversial as self-determination, are not convincing. Very often, other human rights can serve as a legitimate basis for these claims, but the use of self-determination obscures this.

This is the case, for example, with the 'cultural aspect' of the right to self-determination: the right to language, education, religion and the generic right to a culture are usually more appropriate to use for claims related to cultural freedom and its various expressions, educational issues and religious practices. Other separate issues, for example cultural cooperation and assistance through international and bilateral channels, are also established firmly in UNESCO instruments. Adding a cultural aspect to the right of self-determination fails to provide a solid basis for culture-related claims and adds nothing to the human rights canon; on the contrary, it practically disempowers a series of cultural rights by drawing attention away from them and hinders their further interpretation and evolution.[176]

To summarise, there is currently a wide range of understandings of the right to self-determination, which leads to substantially different outcomes as to the use and beneficiaries of the right. These understandings vary from the minimalist one, which limits the scope and the beneficiaries of the right, to the maximalist one, which ferociously advocates a broad understanding of the right to self-determination. Both these extremes offer important advantages: the minimalist approach offers certainty and clarity to the right of self-determination, whereas the maximalist approach offers space for evolution and adjustment of the right to meet contemporary and future international realities. However, both approaches also have important limitations. The analysis so far has demonstrated that the right to self-determination cannot be seen as merely independence; neither can it be seen as an umbrella-right that accommodates all claims. A balance needs to be found that will use the advantages of both approaches and deal with their weaknesses.

Re-evaluating the meaning of the right

In finding such a balance it is necessary to re-evaluate the meaning of the right of self-determination. In what follows I aim to set out the main characteristics that constitute such a re-evaluated meaning.

Self-determination is a right and a principle

Positive law leaves little doubt that self-determination is a legal right, as confirmed by its inclusion as such in the International Covenants, its recognition as such in several United Nations resolutions, judgments of the International Court of Justice,[177] statements by governments and other evidence of practice. Its vague meaning and inconsistent application cannot take away its legal status: legal rules are made to be general to allow for a wide spectrum of application.[178] However, self-determination is also a principle of international law, a notion often neglected in the myriads of related statements.

The discussion between principles and rights or rather rules has mainly dominated the area of jurisprudence.[179] Dworkin defines a principle as 'a standard that is to be observed, not because it will advance or secure an economic, political, or social situation deemed desirable, but because it is a requirement of justice or fairness or some other dimension of morality'.[180] This is to be distinguished from a policy that is 'that kind of standard that sets out a goal to be reached, generally an improvement in some economic, political, or social feature of the community'.[181] Self-determination is a standard to be observed in the name of justice and fairness. This makes it a principle. It is interesting that according to the UN Charter, self-determination is also a means to ensure friendly relations among nations. Therefore, it is also a policy. The question here is what is the function of a legal principle as opposed to a legal rule; in other words, what is the difference between self-determination as a principle and self-determination as a right.

According to Dworkin, the difference between legal principles and rules concerns a logical distinction. Both principles and rules point to particular decisions about legal obligations in particular circumstances, but they differ in the *character* of the direction they give. Dworkin believes that rules are applicable in an all-or-nothing fashion, whereas principles do not set out legal consequences that follow automatically when the conditions provided are met.[182] Indeed, a right when applied would point towards the right decision concerning a claim, whereas a principle would be one important factor to take into account when reaching a decision. Raz offers a similar understanding: rules prescribe relatively specific acts whereas principles relatively unspecific acts;[183] an act 'is highly unspecific if it can be performed on different occasions by the performance of a great many heterogeneous generic acts on each occasion'. Therefore, Raz takes out the restrictive definitiveness of Dworkin's rules: he notes that principles and rules can conflict with one another.[184] The logical distinction also leads to a further difference: principles have a dimension of weight or importance that rules do not have.[185] Dworkin warns though that sometimes a rule and a principle can play much the same role and the difference between them is almost a matter of form alone.[186]

In international law, Schachter follows a similar line of thought: he distinguishes between three types of legally relevant norms, namely rules, principles and ends.[187] Rules are 'norms that dictate a specific result', even though the terms of the rules are open to different interpretations.[188] Principles 'lack this element of definiteness, because of their generality and their abstract nature'.[189] Their terms have a wide range of applications and they leave room for varying interpretation in many situations. Schachter notes that particular situations can be covered by more than one principle, each pointing towards a different conclusion. In short, the difference between the principles and rules concerns, according to Schachter, their level of generality: principles are much more general than rules, are usually in a higher hierarchical order than rules, and are one of the criteria for deciding on a matter rather than the main reason. Crawford relates this to self-determination: he accepts that the concept is multifaceted: a political principle, a legal principle and a legal right.[190] Further, he seems to recognise that the level of generality will determine in which categories the concept will fall on every occasion. Alston also recognises the dual application of self-determination as a right and as a principle.[191] The multi-faceted nature of the concept is also supported by positive law: for example, the United Nations Charter refers to the principle; the International Covenants focus on the right; whereas the Helsinki Declaration recognizes both principle and right.[192]

The validity of self-determination as a *human right* does not abolish its validity as a *principle* of international law. Notions such as the respect for human life and dignity or equality have been treated as both general principles and human rights. The same applies to self-determination. Stavenhagen maintains:

Self-determination is an idée force of powerful magnitude, a philosophical stance, a moral value, a social movement, a potent ideology, that also may be expressed, in one of its many guises, as a legal right in international law.[193]

Cassese believes that a legal principle, such as self-determination, contributes to the interpretation of human rights and also 'fills the gaps' when there is no other right (rule) applicable.[194] Hall also notes that the principles of law are 'a reservoir from which apparent gaps in the corpus of international law may be filled'. In this manner, principles confirm the completeness and distinctiveness of international law as a system where 'every international situation is capable of being determined as a matter of law'.[195]

Indeed, as a principle, self-determination does not set out specific legal consequences for non-compliance, being more abstract and general. It is related to the freedom that peoples should have to determine their lives and destinies and as such, it incorporates political, economic, cultural and social claims of all kinds. It does not give a specific result, but is yet another factor that must be seriously considered, when reaching a decision, possibly together with other principles of international law including territorial integrity, national sovereignty and respect for the rights of others. In contrast, as a human right, self-determination is much more definite and clear, provides its beneficiaries with a specific claim and dictates a specific result.[196] The principle of self-determination is related to a wide range of claims, which can be based on a range of other rights, such as the right to a culture, the right to education, the right to language; in contrast, claims based on the right to self-determination must be directly related to that concept and cannot be better accommodated by recourse to such other rights.

The political core of the right to self-determination

After reaffirming the inclusiveness of the principle and the constraints of the right, sorting out the meaning of the right to self-determination becomes easier. If one looks carefully at the usage of self-determination, it will be noted that the right has essentially been linked to political power. Indeed, most authors divide the meaning of the right in its external and its internal aspect, both relating to the political status of a 'people'.[197] Dinstein maintains:

Whereas it is explicitly enunciated in [Article 1 of the International Covenants] that the right of self-determination has certain economic, social and cultural ramifications, it is uncontrovertible that the core of the right is political in nature. The gist of self-determination is political control of the people's destiny (accompanied by other forms of control).[198]

Brownlie also gives a similar definition to the right as 'the right of a community which has a distinct character to have this character reflected in the institutions of the government under which it lives'.[199] The political substance of the right is also reflected in most writings on indigenous self-determination. Harhoff transposes this meaning to the indigenous context; he maintains that indigenous self-determination refers 'to collective rights of indigenous peoples to political control of their future, and there is no reason to replace this by other labels.'[200] Kingsbury focuses on the constructive relationship between the state and the indigenous group,[201] whereas Daes views self-determination as the right to negotiate indigenous peoples' political status and representation in the states where they live.[202] Anaya, a prominent advocate of a wide interpretation of self-determination, also accepts that self-determination must be seen 'in relation to the institutions of government under which they live'.[203] The common thread in all these definitions is the political element.

An objection to the political focus of the right could derive from the description of the right in Article 1 of the International Covenants, as it refers to the right to pursue political but also economic, social and cultural development. Although this is a valid argument, a closer look at the language of the provisions reveals a focus on the process of *pursuing* development, rather than the *type* of development pursued, whether political, economic and cultural. Pursuing development essentially involves establishing policy priorities and trade-offs in policy allocations and benefits; this is political in nature. Political, but also economic and social policies can only be decided and implemented through a political process, where the state and its institutions are involved. As Held notes, 'State institutions must be viewed as necessary devices for enacting legislation, promulgating new policies, containing inevitable conflicts between particular interests, and preventing civil society from falling victim to new forms of inequality and tyranny'.[204] Of course, Held recognises that 'a multiplicity of social spheres' play a role in these decisions.[205] Further, Held relates politics to the decision-making process and 'those who press their claims upon it'.[206] He maintains:

Politics is a phenomenon found in and between all groups, institutions and societies, involving all spheres of human endeavour, public and private. It is manifested in the activities of cooperation, negotiation and struggle over the use, production and distribution of resources ... Politics is about power; about the forces which influence and reflect its distribution and use; and about the effect of this on resource use and distribution ... Where politics is regarded more narrowly as a sphere apart from economy or culture, that is, as governmental activity and institutions, a vast domain of what we would consider politics is excluded from view.[207]

This understanding of politics makes clear that pursuing development is essentially a political process; accordingly, the right to take part in this process is also political.

The political core of the right to self-determination has been reflected in some, though by no means all, indigenous statements in the United Nations. The caucus of Australian indigenous peoples stated in 1997:

At the micro level, self-determination has to do with renewed legal and political relationships. These are already being negotiated in many of the countries represented in this working group. At a micro level, self-determination concerns decision-making structures and processes in relation to a range of rather non-exceptional matters.[208]

It is commonly accepted that under this meaning, the right to self-determination incorporates two aspects, an external and an internal one. It is also commonly perceived that the forms of the external aspect are covered by the 1970 Declaration, namely establishment of a sovereign and independent state; free association; integration with an independent state; or emergence into any other political status freely determined by a people.[209] On the other hand, the internal aspect is believed to refer to the right to democratic governance and the right to participation in the public affairs of the state. Anaya cautions that this distinction implies a restrictive and exclusive universe of 'peoples' and communities that are mutually exclusive spheres.[210] Organising self-determination into compact internal versus external spheres is distorting in today's world of multiple human associational patterns. Instead, he distinguishes between constitutive self-determination, which is relevant to the occasional procedures leading to the creation of or change in the institutions of government, and ongoing self-determination, relevant to the form and functioning of the governing constitutional order.[211] This distinction by Anaya is helpful and takes the focus away from independence. Addressing Anaya's criticisms, the following section addresses accepted applications of the right to self-determination, but also goes beyond the traditional boundaries of the right and explores additional applications of the right.

Internal aspect of indigenous self-determination

Although democracy has been reflected in several human rights provisions, it was not until the end of the Cold War that the right to democratic governance was elaborated. From a rather vague concept democracy was rapidly transformed to a system of rules, articulated in a series of documents and recognised in state practice[212] and the practice of international organisations.[213] In 1988, the UN General Assembly adopted for the first time a resolution on 'Enhancing the effectiveness of the principle of periodic and genuine elections'; since then the General Assembly has adopted at least one resolution annually dealing with some aspect of democracy and the Commission on Human Rights and now the Human Rights Council have examined democracy increasingly from a human rights perspective. The importance of the concept has since been validated by its explicit proclamation in the OAS Inter-American Democratic Charter of the right to democracy;[214] the inclusion in the Treaty of the European Union that the Union is founded on the principles of, inter alia, democracy;[215] the CSCE Charter of Paris;[216] and the 1991 Harare Declaration of the Commonwealth.[217]

Democracy entails fair and periodic elections; the right to vote and be elected is included in Article 25 of the ICCPR and Article 3 of the ECHR. Even when they satisfy the multiple standards set by the international community,[218] mere elections cannot fulfil the democratic element. The concept of electoral majority is inherently disadvantageous for minorities' participation and their involvement in the political structures of the nation state.[219] Being the non-dominant groups, indigenous groups would seldom 'win' in competitive elections; if elections are the only way of ensuring democracy, then minorities and indigenous peoples are left impotent.[220] A formal model of democracy based on the idea that the state's decisions are taken to please the majority of its population has been proven totally ineffective in Eastern Europe.[221] Elections, referenda and other ways of reaching decisions are not always conducive, even within the context of deliberative[222] or consensus models.[223] The quest for consensus that these models advocate have been criticised as ineffective in conflicts based on race, as consensus is not always possible.[224] International law has subscribed to an inclusive model, which requires that the government of a state be representative of all people rather than some people.[225] Both the UN Declaration on Minorities,[226] the UN Commission on Human Rights[227] and the OSCE[228] have concluded that the issue of minorities can be resolved only within a democratic framework. This entails that democracy is relevant not only to majorities, but also to minorities. This also applies to indigenous groups. The European Court on Human Rights has also pointed out that in a democracy the views of the majority will not always prevail: 'a balance must be achieved which ensures the fair and proper treatment of minorities and avoids any abuse of a dominant position'.[229]

In their efforts to achieve such a balance, several states, including Norway, Fiji, the United States and New Zealand have taken measures to include indigenous voices in parliaments.[230] Different arrangements suit different circumstances: designated parliamentary seats whose number is proportionate to the Maori electorate together with a system of mixed member proportional representation has been considered the best option in New Zealand. In contrast, designated seats would not work in the US state of Maine as indigenous would be elected to a parliament of what is considered a separate nation; there, a 'tribal delegate' of each of the two largest Indian First Nations in the state joins the state parliament; the delegates there are not elected and are not members of the parliament.[231]

Unfortunately the majority of states do not have special arrangements; some do not even include indigenous individuals on their electoral roll. In some cases, indigenous individuals cannot vote as they do not enjoy citizenship rights;[232] even more often, the policies of extinction, exclusion and forced assimilation have led to anger and rejection of the state by indigenous peoples who do not want to take part in the process. In other cases, indigenous peoples do not have adequate knowledge of the electoral process, as it is alien to their political systems. In such cases, simple measures to improve the numbers of indigenous individuals in the electoral rolls and to enhance the indigenous understanding of the national democratic processes could go a long way. Other measures to improve indigenous participation in the democratic process were recently discussed by the Legislative Assembly of Queensland, Australia.[233] They include: periodical reviews of the electoral system; the promotion of a more active indigenous role in political parties; more employment and training opportunities for indigenous peoples in political bodies; veto powers for indigenous communities; indigenous direct input in legislative and policy processes; the enhancement of indigenous participation in local government; and youth participation in political processes. The nature of the measures confirm that democracy and participation cannot be separated. This is also reflected in the structure of Article 25 of ICCPR: its first paragraph establishes the right to participation, whereas the next paragraph focuses on elections.

It is interesting to note that although on the national level such measures are often not linked to the right to self-determination for fear of additional controversy,[234] at the international level many states are really eager to 'fill' the meaning of the right to self-determination with democracy and participation, as an attempt to set the external aspect of the right – and secession – aside. In 1999, Canada defined self-determination as 'the right which can continue to be enjoyed in a functioning democracy in which citizens participate in the political system and have the opportunity to have input in the political processes that affect them'.[235] The same year Norway favoured a similar understanding of the right as 'the right of peoples to participate at all levels of decision-making in legislative and administrative matters and the maintenance and development of their political and economic systems'.[236] Politics aside, the connection between the right of self-determination and the right of political participation has also been recorded by the Human Rights Committee.[237] The draft Declaration on indigenous rights includes several provisions on political participation including: Article 5, which follows the provision on self-determination, and Articles 18 and 19. The distance between these provisions in the text derives from the different clusters to which provisions belong – the right to self-determination to the general and fundamental principles, the participation articles to the more detailed parts of the Declaration.[238]

Even though minorities do not have the right to unconditionally choose the modalities of their participation in the public life of the state,[239] mere participation is not adequate: indigenous peoples have the expectation that their participation will be *effective* as specified in the UN Declaration on Minorities; the Declaration also highlights that minorities should be given a significant role in the formulation, passage and implementation of public policies.[240] Effective participation is also required by the CSCE. The Flensburg Proposals also emphasise that decision makers must proactively consult members of minorities that are affected by their decisions and must also create opportunities for them to effectively participate in the decision-making process.[241] Human rights bodies pay special attention to whether minorities have been included in decision making in matters that affect them and to whether any decisions have been taken after real public debate. Measures to ensure their effective participation are wide-ranging, as the 'conduct of public affairs' is 'a broad concept which relates to the exercise of legislative, executive and administrative powers ... [covering] all aspects of public administration, and the formulation and implementation of policy at international, national, regional and local level'.[242] Some of these measures are mentioned in the (1999) Geneva Declaration of Experts on Minorities and include: advisory and decision-making bodies in which minorities are represented; elected bodies and assemblies of national minority affairs; local and autonomous administration; autonomy on a territorial basis, including the existence of consultative, legislative and executive bodies chosen through free and periodical elections; self-administration by a national minority in relation to aspects concerning its identity in situations where autonomy on a territorial basis does not apply; and decentralised or local forms of government.[243] Unfortunately, the draft Declaration on indigenous rights does not include a reference to 'effective', but to 'full' participation (Article 5).

In all the documents on minority rights, the right to participation is recognised as an individual right. The Human Rights Committee has actually juxtaposed the individual nature of the right to participation and the collective nature of the right to self-determination. However, ILO Convention No. 169 recognizes participatory rights to indigenous as a group. Being one of the mean thrusts of the Convention, participation underlies many provisions, the most important of which is Article 6. Article 6 establishes the duty of states to create measures for the free participation of indigenous peoples to 'at least the same extent as other sectors of the population, at all levels of decision-making in elective institutions and administrative and other bodies responsible for policies and programs which concern them'. It also requires the establishment of indigenous representative institutions and their consultation whenever legislative measures are considered which may affect the people directly.[244] Consultations must be in good faith and in a form appropriate to the circumstances, with the objective of achieving agreement or consent to the proposed measures. The Convention also gives the right to indigenous peoples to decide their own priorities for and to exercise control of the process of development.[245] The draft Declaration on the rights of indigenous peoples also recognises the collective element of participation; according to it, indigenous peoples should 'have the right to participate in decision-making in matters which affect their rights through representatives chosen by themselves' (Article 18) and the right to 'autonomy or self-government in matters relating to their internal or local affairs' (Article 4). Scheinin applauds the inclusion of a collective element in the right of participation. In his individual opinion in *Diergaardt et al.* v. *Namibia*,[246] he notes that:

> there are situations where Article 25 calls for special arrangements for rights of participation to be enjoyed by members of minorities and in particular indigenous peoples. When such a situation arises it is not sufficient under Article 25 to afford individual members of such communities the individual right to vote in general elections. Some forms of local, regional or cultural autonomy may be called for in order to comply with the requirement of effective rights of participation.[247]

A particular form of participation that 'allows minorities claiming a distinct identity to exercise direct control over affairs of special concern to them, while allowing the larger entity to exercise those powers which cover common interests' is autonomy.[248] It is the addition of 'rules of self-rule or self-government, with own institutions and a vaguely defined independence of action'.[249] States are reluctant to accept any obligation to provide autonomy, as evident in Chile's statement in 1994 about the inclusion of the term in the draft Declaration:

> in place of the phrase 'right of self-determination' and 'autonomy' of indigenous peoples, the most appropriate wording might be 'the right to special political participation with regard to the specific affairs of those peoples or matters which may affect their development[250]

There is no recognised 'right to autonomy' in international law. Autonomy has so far been viewed as an application of the right to self-determination open to minorities, either through customary, statutory or constitutional law.[251] In most instances, the state's formal legal systems define the powers and scope of the autonomous regime. Indeed, neither the 1992 United Nations Declaration on Minorities nor the 1995 Framework Convention on National Minorities explicitly refer to autonomy; the need for autonomy can still be argued on the basis of the condition of 'effective participation'. The (1990) Geneva Meeting of Experts on Minorities and the (1990) Copenhagen Document refer to autonomy as 'one of the possible means' to protect minority identity;[252] whereas the (1993) Recommendation 1201 of the Parliamentary Assembly of the Council of Europe reluctantly suggests autonomy or special status 'matching the specific historical and territorial situation and in accordance with the domestic legislation of the State'.[253] Only the Lund Recommendations on Effective Participation by National Minorities in Political Life are somewhat more forthcoming on 'self-government' and discuss territorial and non-territorial arrangements.

Autonomy can take various forms.[254] It ranges from group-based autonomy, when the members of a group are bound by different rules on certain matters, such as cultural or family issues, to territorial autonomy, where all inhabitants of the autonomous region are subject to a particular status, irrespective of their ethnic or linguistic identity; and can reach a 'fully' autonomous regime, when there is a locally elected legislative assembly, local administrative authorities and local independent courts.[255]

Autonomy has several advantages. Experience has shown that it can be a means to respond successfully and in a flexible way to concerns about minority rights while maintaining the territorial integrity of existing states.[256] It can also be a means to protect the group's distinct identity. For some, it is the optimum solution for indigenous groups. The Human Rights Committee has positively commented on examples of devolution concerning indigenous communities.[257] Alfredsson goes as far as saying that 'the degree of autonomy of indigenous peoples within states becomes an indicator of the probability of their survival'.[258] This view appears to be shared by the drafters of the Declaration on the rights of indigenous peoples. Article 31 provides indigenous peoples with a wide 'right to autonomy or self-government' in matters relating to their internal and local affairs.

Indeed, there are several indigenous autonomous regimes that work very well. The home rule of Greenland has long been viewed as a successful regime that has improved the situation of the Greenlanders. Under the Home Rule Act, Greenland decides on all areas of policy, including its vast raw material and its environment, apart from nationality, justice, monetary affairs, defence and foreign policy. The 1999 establishment of Nunavut in Canada,[259] where the indigenous Inuit have won self-government as a territory within the federal system, has also been welcomed. The Sámi Parliament in Norway is a positive example of personal autonomy. Established in 1989, the Parliament has 39 indigenous representatives elected from 13 constituencies covering the whole of Norway. The Parliament deals with any matter that in its view particularly affects the Sámi, whereas the Sámediggi administration deals with issues such as Sámi education, culture, language, environment and cultural preservation, economic development and international cooperation. The Parliament and its administration is an effective political institution and an important advisory body to the Norwegian central authorities.[260]

However, autonomy is not a panacea for indigenous problems around the world. It also has disadvantages, not least that it promotes segregation and separation and fails to encourage dialogue.[261] As autonomous regimes protect historical differences, they can lead to a stagnated image of the group and can discourage the evolution of the group's culture. Steiner notes that 'a state composed of segregated autonomy regimes would resemble more a museum of social and cultural antiquities than any human rights ideal'.[262] In such situations, autonomy can 'dramatize grotesquely' the particular characteristics of groups, foment inter-group dissent and can be used to promote a narrow view of 'stability'.[263]

Moreover, autonomy can be a way for the State to dispose of its obligations – financial and other – towards the group. The reference to autonomy in matters relating to 'ways and means for financing their autonomous function' in Article 4 of the draft Declaration can be used as an excuse by states to refuse any financial help to indigenous groups, even though Article 39 ensures that indigenous peoples have financial and technical support from states. The 1999 Federal Law on the Guarantees of the Rights of Indigenous Numerically Small Peoples of the Russian Federation allows indigenous peoples to establish 'the territorial bodies of public self-government' and enjoy the right 'on a voluntary basis to organise [their] communities'. Although this could be an opportunity for greater control, unfortunately it has acted as a boomerang for indigenous communities in the Russian Federation. The autonomies that have been created are mostly self-supporting; as they do not have the means to operate,[264] no significant progress has been noted; only this time the state cannot be blamed for not recognizing indigenous rights.[265]

An interesting issue concerns cases when indigenous autonomous regimes violate standards of democratic governance. What happens, for example, when indigenous groups do not wish to select their leaders according to democratic principles, but their own principles? As discussed in the first chapter, these questions can only be solved on an ad hoc basis using the *Lovelace* criteria for guidance.

External aspect of indigenous self-determination

The external aspect of self-determination has so far focused on independence. The shortcomings of focusing on independence have been elaborated in depth in previous sections of this chapter. It has also been established that the right to secede is currently very limited in international law. Only remedial secession can potentially be recognised for indigenous groups, provided they have exhausted all other political and diplomatic avenues.

If the external aspect of self-determination is covered by independence and since independence is only a theoretical possibility, would it not be more realistic to accept that indigenous peoples have a qualified right to self-determination, especially as the recognition of an unqualified right to self-determination seems at the moment unlikely? Several states have suggested such a compromise. During the sessions of the Commission Drafting Group the USA accepted the recognition of internal self-determination,[266] whereas Australia proposed self-management instead of self-determination.[267] Other states also accepted the internal aspects of self-determination.[268] Norway, Cuba and Spain[269] supported the inclusion of the right of self-determination in the draft Declaration followed by a reference to the 1970 Declaration on Friendly Relations or to the principle of territorial integrity. Authors have also supported a qualified right to self-determination, either because they see claims for indigenous self-determination essentially as claims for autonomy (Eide)[270] or because of the pandemonium secession would bring (Spiry,[271] Nettheim[272]); or as a better strategy for the improvement of the indigenous situation (Hannum).[273]

Any advantages in excluding the external aspect or secession would also have had significant negative consequences: first, such an exclusion would be discriminatory; second, it would be unnecessary; and third, it would set aside innovative and important ways of exercising self-determination.

Indeed, it has been repeatedly stressed that the recognition of a qualified right to self-determination would deny to indigenous peoples the rights that all other 'peoples' have and would thus maintain patterns of discrimination and injustice against them. Indigenous representatives have repeatedly noted:

> The right of indigenous peoples to self-determination is equal to the right of non-indigenous peoples to self-determination. We should resist efforts to re-define or to dilute for indigenous peoples a right that has already been recognised for all others. The Declaration must carefully avoid establishing a category of second class rights for indigenous peoples.[274]

A similar statement was made in 1992 by the representative of the Four Directions Council:

> When speaking of the right to self-determination of indigenous peoples, we are not creating new law, but merely clarifying the applications of principles which are as old as the United Nations itself. Our purpose ... is simply to ensure that indigenous peoples are not deprived of a fundamental right which is secured to all other peoples.[275]

In 1996, Ted Moses on behalf of the Grand Council of the Crees warned:

> There cannot be a double standard on the right of self-determination in international law. In particular, there cannot be a double standard based on race or our present status as dispossessed peoples residing in nation-states founded upon principles such as *terra nullius*, conquest and extinguishment.[276]

Several authors support this argument. Daes and Spiry have referred to the UN treatment of peoples' self-determination within the context of Eastern Europe and have concluded that a rejection of indigenous self-determination would be a strange and arguably racist UN policy.[277] Scott also maintains that refusing the term 'peoples' to indigenous peoples 'has at least the effect of creating discriminatory access to the special kind of freedom that other peoples enjoy, namely that of the human right to self-determination.'[278]

Apart from discriminatory, the rejection of external self-determination is also unnecessary. Most indigenous representatives have emphasised that independence is neither a desirable nor a possible option:

> Indigenous peoples are not geographically or economically situated in a way that makes independence particularly attractive. Most, if not all indigenous peoples are consequently seeking democratic reforms and power sharing within existing states.[279]

In her explanatory report of the draft Declaration on indigenous rights, Daes has clarified the position of most indigenous groups:

> Most indigenous peoples also acknowledge the benefits of a partnership with existing states, in view of their small size, limited resources and vulnerability. It is not realistic to fear indigenous peoples' exercise of the right to self-determination. It is far more realistic to fear that the denial of indigenous' rights to self-determination will leave the most marginalised and excluded of all the world's peoples without a legal, peaceful weapon to press for genuine democracy in the states in which they live.[280]

Authors that support the unqualified recognition of indigenous self-determination also agree that independence is not the solution. Kingsbury does not see separate statehood as the optimal outcome, but he views indigenous self-determination as an ongoing process whose arrangements need re-evaluation at frequent intervals.[281] Anaya also notes the wide range of possibilities and emphasises that secession will rarely be a cure better than the disease.[282]

Even for the small minority of indigenous communities striving for independence, secession can only possibly be contemplated when the state grossly, continuously and irrevocably fails to fulfil the minimum of its obligations towards the group. Therefore, international law and practice already protect the states from secession, so that yet another reference to territorial integrity would be unnecessary, save for calming states' fears. The draft Declaration has tried to find a compromise; in its current form, the text mentions autonomy, establishment of distinct institutions and participation (Articles 4 and 5), but without confining the right only to these applications.

Emerging applications of the right to self-determination

The recognition of a qualified right to self-determination would leave out legitimate and innovative ways of exercising the right to self-determination in its external aspect. Indigenous peoples have reminded the international community that the list is not exhaustive. Away from the focus on a state-centred meaning and within the context of the evolution of the right to self-determination, new applications of the right are being added to already accepted ones. As Alfredsson has noted: 'The tentative listing of suggested forms and expressions of self-determination is undoubtedly not exhaustive and definitely not final.'[283]

The meaning of self-determination must remain open to new aspects. A reductionist approach where the right is only perceived as the addition of the prescribed applications is not uncommon among states. In its report to the Committee on Economic, Social and Cultural Rights, Greece divided self-determination into three aspects, an external, an internal and an economic one, and proposed an analysis whereby the external aspect contained only rights appropriate to peoples under a colonial or racist regime or under occupation or peoples who have been integrated by force. Similarly, the internal aspect involved the free choosing of the social system, the form of government and free elections.[284] This, it is suggested, is a poor understanding of the right. The scope of the right is not exhausted by its already experienced applications. Accordingly, any claim must be considered in relation to the meaning of the right itself, namely the right to determine a people's political status, rather than in relation to specific applications.

Anaya has rightly noted that self-determination is 'capable of embracing much more nuanced interpretations and applications'.[285] Other commentators including Daes, Falk and Thornberry, have talked about the need for flexibility in understanding indigenous self-determination. Harhoff has noted that indigenous self-determination 'reflects new dimensions in international society and requires new thinking in international law',[286] whereas Kingsbury has urged the reformulation of the right so that it opens the way to a 'wider range of relations between an indigenous peoples and an existing state'.[287]

States have not stayed indifferent to these arguments. Canada stated in 1996:

> We must take into account the variety of circumstances in which both states and indigenous peoples find themselves world-wide. We must avoid any prescriptive solutions, as desirable as these may seem, but allow the right of self-determination to be implemented flexibly through negotiations between governments and indigenous groups.[288]

In this context, the external aspect of the right of self-determination cannot be wholly covered by the applications set out in the Declaration against Colonialism. For example, indigenous representatives have repeatedly raised claims for their autonomous representation in the international arena. Indeed, the representative of the Grand Council of Crees attends United Nations fora as 'ambassador',[289] whereas the delegations of some Nordic states in relevant United Nations fora always include indigenous representatives. More importantly, the indigenous movement has managed to be on an almost equal standing with the states in the three United Nations fora relevant to indigenous matters. Indigenous representatives attend official and unofficial meetings and have managed to limit the closed meetings solely for states.[290] They take the floor on an equal basis with the states and have the right to reply. When indigenous peoples threatened to leave the Commission Drafting Group, because their participation was hindered by the chairperson, several governments took the floor to emphasise the importance of the indigenous participation in the process.[291] Also, the Permanent Forum on Indigenous Issues is comprised of eight indigenous representatives chosen by indigenous peoples and eight experts chosen by states.[292] This ensures that indigenous peoples have an input in decisions of the United Nations relevant to their future. Falk goes further and advocates the establishment of a special international tribunal or special procedures to determine conflicts between states and indigenous peoples outside the national system.[293] These new procedures must recognise indigenous peoples as equals, rather than maintain the existing statist character of international arenas.

Similarly, the draft Declaration raises rights that expand the content of self-determination, such as developing transnational contacts, relations and cooperation across borders for political reasons (Article 36).

Over the last 25 years, cross-border activities between sub-national territorial entities have increased enormously, especially under the legal and political umbrella of the Council of Europe. In 1980, the member states of the Council of Europe decided on an Outline Convention on Cross-border Co-operation between Territorial Communities or Authorities, which aims 'to facilitate and foster cross-border cooperation between territorial communities or authorities'.[294] Cooperation between states and the subsequent creation of cross-country political institutions fall within the right of peoples to decide on the relations they wish to have as a collectivity with other groups and states, in other words, their right to self-determination.

The internal aspect of the right of self-determination also incorporates applications that have not yet been explored in depth. Such applications have been envisaged by Harhoff; he has supported a right of self-determination that would allow for the establishment of: a local legislative body with powers to regulate specific matters in its own name and immune from state interference; a local executive body with powers to administer and carry out the local acts; and a judiciary with executive authority to decide legal questions on the validity and interpretation of local acts and orders.[295] The draft Declaration does not go that far, but it does establish the right of indigenous peoples to distinct political, legal, economic, social and cultural institutions (Article 5); indigenous political, economic and social systems or institutions (Article 20); indigenous educational systems and institutions (Article 14) and their representative institutions (Article 19).

In recognising the benefits of indigenous systems and institutions more states are gradually allowing for indigenous judicial institutions to coexist with the national judicial systems. In Australia, the Community Justice Group project allows Aboriginal mechanisms of justice and social control to coexist with the Anglo-Australian legal system. The indigenous Community Justice Group applies indigenous law and customary practices in family-related dispute settlement, crime prevention and community development projects in coordination with state agencies and bodies and offers information and advice to the judiciary, Community Corrections Boards and other state decision-making bodies. Together with other such projects in Australia, it has contributed to the decline in crime rate and level of violence, especially in juvenile crime and to the change in social patterns and indigenous perceptions about the justice system. In Greenland, the judicial system differs significantly from the Danish system. Citizens are called on to act as judges and counsel in disputes, including family and criminal cases, and local police handle the prosecuting function.[296] In South Africa, the (2003) Traditional Courts Act authorised and established a hierarchy of customary courts whose jurisdiction extends to criminal and civil cases; the courts will be operated by members of the community and decisions will be based on the customary laws of the community in line with the constitutional values of democracy and equality. Other states that recognise the distinct legal systems of indigenous peoples include Guatemala and Ecuador.[297]

An argument could be put forward that the recognition of indigenous judicial institutions forms part of 'cultural self-determination', an aspect rejected earlier in this chapter.[298] Judicial systems are indeed part of the culture of indigenous peoples, but the formation of such institutions falls within the political sphere of self-determination. Therefore, such claims are based on the right to self-determination in conjunction with the right to a culture, rather than on a right to cultural self-determination. Claims based on two rights are not uncommon in international human rights. Similar would be the answer of international law to claims for cultural autonomy and the establishment of other indigenous cultural institutions.

Self-determination is often used interchangeably with secession. If the right to self-determination is covered by secession, then subnational groups, including indigenous peoples, cannot have this right, as it conflicts with the principle of territorial integrity. This section has shown that this is not the case. Reading self-determination as secession echoes an earlier period of international history, where state sovereignty reigned and decolonisation was an urgent need. Since then, self-determination has evolved considerably. The scope of the right is in the political realm, but the right of peoples to decide on their political status includes a wide range of possibilities. International law has already acknowledged some of them in international instruments: at the early stage, independence, integration or association with another state were identified; later, democratic governance and political participation, which sometimes takes the form of autonomy, were elevated to be the main applications of the right. There are other normative formulations of the right, which have not yet been explored.[299] The indigenous debate has revealed some new possibilities, including gathering of autonomous international personality, the creation of distinct legal and political systems, and the possibility of indigenous citizenship. This understanding of the right to self-determination is consistent with its past, but is also able to address important issues of the present and is open to future possibilities.

Concluding comments

As secession occupies a small part of the scope of the right to self-determination and since territorial integrity does not conflict with any other exercise of the right, sub-national groups can be recognised as beneficiaries of the right to self-determination as included in Article 1 of both *International Covenants*, albeit prima facie not secession. Therefore, if indigenous peoples are recognised as beneficiaries of the right to self-determination, they will not automatically have the right to secede. Just as 'all peoples' of Article 1 of the International Covenants, they would have to satisfy a number of difficult tests before their claim for secession gained any international support. After the obstacle of territorial integrity is removed, the road to indigenous recognition seems open: indigenous peoples in general satisfy the logical and intellectual criteria of 'peoples'. Also, difficulties posed by international instruments can be overcome by innovative interpretations that would be consistent with the spirit of international law and correspond to current international realities.

Indeed, there is a move towards recognising indigenous self-determination, evident in the international literature as much as the political scene. As the experts consulted by Canada noted, current international law increasingly guarantees indigenous peoples greater territorial rights, the exact substance and extent of which are at present difficult to ascertain.[300] Gradually, more states recognise at the national level that justice requires some form of territorial autonomy for sub-national groups.[301] In its concluding observations, the Human Rights Committee has repeatedly linked indigenous peoples to the right to self-determination;[302] and states have gradually started analysing indigenous issues within Article 1 of the *International Covenants*: for example, Finland discussed in its report to the Human Rights Committee in 2004 Sámi issues within the realm of Article 1,[303] while Denmark stated in 2002 that the right of peoples to self-determination is applicable to indigenous peoples.[304] During the informal debates of the working group on the draft Declaration a number of states from various parts of the world, including Colombia,[305] Bolivia,[306] Fiji,[307] Switzerland,[308] Pakistan,[309] Finland,[310] Norway,[311] Cuba,[312] Guatemala[313] and Mexico,[314] all agreed with the inclusion of the right to self-determination in the draft

Declaration on the rights of indigenous peoples. More importantly, 30 out of the 47 states members of the Human Rights Council, including the United Kingdom, France and Japan, voted in favour of the adoption of a draft Declaration that includes an indigenous right to self-determination.

These developments cannot conceal how difficult the road ahead is, as is evident from the recent delay to take action at General Assembly level. A partly tactical argument that attempts to sideline all political considerations views indigenous peoples as a special case, a suggestion that has recently been gathering momentum. Falk explains why indigenous should be perceived as a special case:

> [Indigenous peoples] have overwhelmingly been marginalised as outside the framework of normal political behaviour. The promises associated with the mainstream right of self-determination have almost no relevance to them: this creates a high degree of normative confusion as a fundamental aspiration of these peoples is inevitably some form of self-determination, but not the prevailing one. In other words, the semantic confusion that is implicit in statist views of self-determination has been used to avoid confronting the actual situations of either captive nations and even more insistently, the various lamentable situations of indigenous peoples.[315]

Kingsbury also asserts the special status of indigenous peoples.[316] According to this approach, the way forward would be the recognition of 'a special' right to self-determination, related, but different to the traditional understanding of the right. This seems to be in accordance with Anaya's argument: he explains the need for indigenous self-determination on the basis of injustice and oppression that indigenous peoples have suffered; these can only be erased by recognising their right to determine their future, namely their right to self-determination.[317] He adds:

> . . . once diverse cultural groupings are acknowledged and valued, their associational patterns and community aspirations become factors that must be reflected in the governing institutional order if self-determination notions are to prevail.[318]

Pentassuglia also agrees that the question of indigenous self-determination is a *sui generis* one. He maintains that although the ramifications of ILO Convention No. 169 on self-determination and the draft Declaration are still being debated in the United Nations and even though important states appear united in rejecting full independence, overall the term 'peoples' associated with indigenous serves the general purpose of conceptualising a demand for protection through guarantees appropriate to the specific characteristics of indigenous peoples.[319]

Two decades ago suggesting that indigenous peoples can be perceived as a special case for the purposes of international law would be unrealistic. However, the international community has shown evidence of endorsing this view; the most notable example being the establishment of the Permanent Forum, a body largely comprised of indigenous representatives. Such a body in such a high position in the hierarchy of the United Nations can only be explained in terms of indigenous 'special circumstances'. No other vulnerable group has received such treatment from the United Nations or any other international organisation; this can be taken as proof that the international community is willing to accept the special status of indigenous peoples, which could possibly expand into a 'special' right of self-determination.

Recognition of indigenous self-determination based on their distinct past may attract more positive responses from the states, mainly because recognising the right on such basis avoids opening the floodgates for other groups' claims to self-determination. However, another element of this approach – also attractive to some states – is the vague nature of what is offered. It is not clear what this 'special' right would entail. Would it add to the existing status of indigenous peoples or would it be just a gesture of goodwill with no real substance? Would this right allow for more participation and indigenous control over matters that affect them? When indigenous peoples invoke such a general right as self-determination, 'they inevitably take on board its non-indigenous dimensions'.[320] The concept cannot have one meaning for all peoples and another for indigenous peoples. Also, this tactic would again isolate indigenous peoples from the 'peoples' of Article 1 of the International Covenants. However, indigenous peoples partly ask for indigenous self-determination as a recognition that they are 'peoples' like all other beneficiaries of Article 1 of the International Covenants, as a matter of equality. Recognising them as 'a special case' goes against this. Brownlie on the other hand makes the opposite argument: he maintains that this approach 'smacks of nominalism and a sort of snobbery'.[321]

If the current provisions on self-determination do not get eventual support in the General Assembly, the only other realistic option would be the inclusion in the text of guarantees that indigenous self-determination will not lead to secession. Canada stated in 2001 that they 'accepted a right of self-determination for indigenous peoples which respected the political, constitutional and territorial integrity of democratic states'[322] and the Russian Federation noted that 'his delegation had no difficulties in accepting the right of self-determination, although exercise of that right must be subject to the territorial integrity of states'.[323] In 2003, several states also indicated that they would agree with the inclusion of the right to self-determination in the draft Declaration provided there was an explicit reference to territorial integrity.[324] Such an inclusion might speed the adoption of the Declaration by the General Assembly. Even though international standards can be interpreted as allowing indigenous self-determination, there is no doubt that the adoption of the draft Declaration with the inclusion of a provision on indigenous self-determination will be a major step towards the realisation of indigenous self-determination both at the domestic and the international level.

Notes

1. Report of the Working Group on Indigenous Populations on its First Session, UN Doc. E/CN.4/Sub.2/1982/33 (1983), para. 70.
2. *Ibid.*, para. 72.
3. Statement of the Representative of the Chittagong Hill Tracts Peace Campaign in Report of the Working Group established in accordance with Commission on Human Rights Resolution 1995/32, UN Doc. E/CN.4/1997/102 (1996), para. 339.
4. Statement of the Representative of the Indigenous World Association, *ibid.* para. 319.
5. Representative of the Aboriginal and Torres Strait Islander Commission in Report of 1997 Commission Working Group, E/CN.4/1997/102 (1996), para. 62.
6. Report of 1995 Commission Working Group, E/CN.4/1996/84 (1996), para. 51.
7. R. Falk, *Human Rights Horizons, The Pursuit of Justice in a Globalising World* (New York: Routledge, 2000), p. 98.
8. K. Knop, *Diversity and Self-determination in International Law* (Cambridge: Cambridge University Press, 2002), p. 2.
9. Quoting S. Spiliopoulou Åkermark, 'The World Bank and Indigenous Peoples' in N. Ghanea and A. Xanthaki (eds.), *Minorities, Peoples and Self-Determination* (Dordrecht: Martinus Nijhoff, 2005), pp. 15–33.
10. M. Moore, 'Internal Minorities and Indigenous Self-Determination' in A. Eisenberg and J. Spinner-Halev (eds.), *Minorities within Minorities: Equality, Rights and Diversity*, (Cambridge: Cambridge University Press, 2005), pp. 271–93.
11. Statement made on behalf of the Office of the Aboriginal and Torres Strait Islander Social Justice Commissioner, Geneva, 24 November 1995 (1995 Commission Working Group), on file with author.
12. Moore, 'Internal Minorities'.
13. See Statement by the International Indian Treaty Council in Consideration of the Draft United Nations Declaration on the Rights of Indigenous Peoples:

Information Received by Non-Governmental Organisations, UN Doc. E/CN.4/1995/WG 15/4 (1995), para. 24.

14. Moore, 'Internal Minorities'.
15. Article 5.1 of the ICCPR reads:

    Nothing in the present Covenant may be interpreted as implying for any State, group or person any right to engage in any activity or perform any act aimed at the destruction of any of the rights or freedoms recognised herein or at their limitation to a greater extent than is provided for in the present Covenant.

16. P. Thornberry, *Indigenous Peoples and Human Rights* (Manchester: Manchester University Press, 2002), p. 126.
17. Brownlie argues that the concepts of 'nationalities', 'minorities', 'peoples' and 'indigenous populations' all involve essentially the same idea. I. Brownlie, 'The Rights of Peoples in Modern International Law' in J. Crawford (ed.), *The Rights of Peoples* (Oxford: Clarendon Press, 1988), pp. 1–16 at p. 5.
18. Thornberry, *Indigenous Peoples*, pp. 52–5; Brownlie, 'Rights of Peoples'; T. Makkonen, *Identity, Difference and Otherness: The Concepts of 'People', 'Indigenous People' and 'Minority' in International Law* (Helsinki: Helsinki University Press, 2000); G. Alfredsson, 'Minorities, Indigenous and Tribal Peoples, and Peoples: Definitions of Terms as a Matter of International Law' in Ghanea and Xanthaki (eds.), *Minorities, Peoples*, pp. 163–72.
19. In 1998, the US representative stated that 'her government urged the working group to follow the approach taken by the Declaration on the Rights of Persons belonging to National or Ethnic, Religious and Linguistic Minorities, and refer to "persons belonging to indigenous groups" rather than "peoples".' See Report of Commission Working Group, E/CN.4/1999/82 (1999), para. 40.
20. Thornberry, *Indigenous Peoples*, p. 54.
21. For an analysis of these characteristics see Thornberry, *Indigenous Peoples*, pp. 33–60.
22. For example, see statements of: the USA in the Report of Commission Working Group, UN Doc. E/CN.4/2000/84 (1999), para. 49; Argentina in Consideration of a Draft United Nations Declaration on the Rights of Indigenous peoples, Information received by the Governments, UN Doc. E/CN.4/1995/WG.15/2 (1995), para. 6; France in Report of Commission Working Group UN Doc. E/CN.4/1997/102 (1996), para. 329; Morocco in Consideration of a Draft United Nations Declaration on the Rights of Indigenous peoples, Information received by the Governments, UN Doc. E/CN.4/1995/WG.15/2/Add.1, para. 3; Japan in Report of the Commission Working Group UN Doc. E/CN.4/1997/102 (1996), para. 340.
23. Setting International Standards in the Field of Human Rights, GA Res. 41/ 121 (1986), UN Doc. A/41/120 (1986).
24. See Information Received by Governments, Argentina, UN Doc. E/CN.4/1995/WG.15/2, para. 6.
25. The Belgian delegate stated in the Fourth Committee that 'similar problems' to the overseas colonies '[e]xisted wherever there are under-developed ethnic groups ... in America as well as in Asia or Africa.' He observed that

'more than half the sixty members of the United Nations had backward indigenous peoples in their territories', although only eight had admitted to be administering states under chapter eleven. See 7 UNGAO C.4 (253rd meeting), UN Doc. A/2361 (1952), 22–3.

26. The Belgian view could be interpreted as a means to protect Belgium's interests in the Belgian Congo. It was a response to the criticisms by the developing states about the exploitation of the natural resources of the colonies. Belgium at the time was exploiting Congo's natural resources, mainly the copper of Katanga. If Belgium enabled Katanga to secede from a possibly independent Congo, then, they could still exploit the copper of Katanga. See P. Thornberry, 'Self-Determination, Minorities, Human Rights: A Review of International Instruments' (1989) 38 *International and Comparative Law Quarterly* 867–89 at 874.
27. See UN GAOR, Official Record of the General Assembly, 7th session, 4th Committee, 55.
28. *AD* v. *Canada* (1989) 79 *International Law Review*, 261 and *Kitok* v. *Sweden*, CCPR/C/33/D/197/1985. For an analysis of the first case, see M. E. Turpel, 'Indigenous Peoples' Rights to Political Participation and Self-Determination' (1992) 25 *Cornell International Law Journal* 579–602.
29. D. McGoldrick, *The Human Rights Committee, its Role in the Development of the ICCPR* (Oxford: Clarendon Press, 1991), p. 250.
30. Communication No. 547/1993: New Zealand. 15/11/2000. CCPR/C/70/D/547/1993 (Jurisprudence) UN Doc CCPR/C/70/D/541/1993 Human Rights Committee, para. 9.2.
31. Operational Directive 4.20 (1991) is available at www.worldbank.org. Also see I. Shihata, *The World Bank Inspection Panel* (Oxford: Oxford University Press, 1994). For the World Bank and indigenous peoples, see Spiliopoulou Åkermark, 'World Bank and Indigenous Peoples'.
32. World Bank, draft Operational Policy 4.10 and draft Bank Procedures 4.10 on Indigenous Peoples (2001), available at www.worldbank.org.
33. Durban Declaration of the World Conference against Racism, Racial Discrimination, Xenophobia and Related Intolerance, paras. 22, 23, 39 and 43 and Program of Action, paras. 15–23, although the Declaration includes a qualification in paragraph 24 which notes that the use of the term in the final document 'cannot be construed as having any implications as to rights under international law'. See http://www.unhchr.ch/html/racism/02-documents-cnt.html (accessed on 10/09/2004).
34. See http://www.undp.org/csopp/CSO/NewFiles/ipundppol.html (accessed on 10/09/2004).
35. (PRIA) TAG-234 (Bolivia, Brazil, Colombia, Venezuela), see http://www.ifad.org/evaluation/public_html/eksyst/doc/tag/tag234be.htm (accessed on 15/09/2004).
36. The meeting took place on 17 November 2003 in the Headquarters of UNESCO in Geneva. See http://portal.unesco.org/culture/en/ev.php-URL_ID=2946&URL_DO=DO_TOPIC&URL_SECTION=201.html, (accessed on the 15/12/2004).

37. International Labour Conference, Provisional Record No. 25, 76th Session (1989), p. 7
38. S.J. Anaya, 'Canada's Fiduciary Obligations Toward Indigenous Peoples in Quebec under International Law in General' in S.J. Anaya, R. Falk and D. Pharand (eds.), *Canada's Fiduciary Obligation to Aboriginal Peoples in the Comment of Accession to Sovereignty to Quebec, Papers prepared as part of the Research Program of the Royal Commission on Aboriginal Peoples*, (Canada: Minister of Supply and Services Canada, 1995), p. 22.
39. I. Jennings, *The Approach to Self-Government* (Cambridge: Cambridge University Press, 1956), pp. 55–6.
40. E. Kamenca, 'Human Rights, Peoples Rights' in Crawford (ed.), *The Rights of Peoples*, p. 133; see also P. Allott, 'The Nation as Mind Politic' (1992) 24 *New York University Journal of International Law and Politics* 1361–98.
41. R. Stavenhagen, 'Self-determination: Right or Demon?' in D. Clark and R. Williamson, *Self-determination: International Perspectives* (London: Macmillan Press, 1996), pp. 1–11 at p. 7.
42. G.H. Espiel, 'Study on the Implementation of United Nations Resolutions Relating to the Right of Peoples under Colonial or Alien Domination to Self-determination', UN Doc. E/CN.4/Sub.2/ 405/Rev.1 (1980).
43. Para 56.
44. UN ESCOR, 137 UN Doc E/CN.4/Sub.2/ 404, (vol. 1).
45. *Ibid.*, para. 279.
46. See L. R. Barsh, 'Indigenous North America and Contemporary International Law' (1983) 63 *Oregon Law Review* 73–125 at 94.
47. C. Iorns, 'Indigenous Peoples and Self-Determination: Challenging State Sovereignty' (1992) 24 *Case Western Reserve Journal of International Law* 199–348 at 288–9; also see H-J. Heintze, 'International Law and Indigenous Peoples' (1995) 45 *Law and the State* 37–67 at 41.
48. M. Scheinin, 'What are Indigenous Peoples?' in Ghanea and Xanthaki (eds.), *Minorities, Peoples*, pp. 1–15.
49. Hannum and Daes agree that indigenous are peoples: H. Hannum, 'Self-Determination in the Post-Colonial Era' in Clark and Williamson (eds.), *Self-Determination, International Perspectives*, pp. 12–44, p. 28, and E-I. Daes, 'The Right of Indigenous peoples to "Self-Determination" in the Contemporary World Order' in Clark and Williamson (eds.), *Self-Determination*, pp. 47–57, at p. 51; also Scheinin, 'What are Indigenous Peoples?'.
50. Draft Report of the 1995 Commission Working Group, E/CN.4/1995/WG.15/ CRP.4 (1995), para. 13.
51. For a discussion on non-self-governing territories, see 'Report by J. Crawford: "State Practice and International Law in Relation to Unilateral Secession"' in A. Bayevsky, *Self-Determination in International Law: Quebec and Lessons Learned* (Dordrecht: Kluwer Law International, 2000), pp. 31–61, at pp. 37–8.
52. Such as UNGA Resolutions 421 (V) of 4 December 1950, Res. 545 (VI) of 5 February 1952, Res. 637 (VII) of 16 December 1952, Res. 567 (VI) of 18

January 1952, Res. 648 (VII) of 10 December 1952, Res. 742 (VIII) of 27 November 1953 and Res. 1188 (XII) of 11 December 1957.

53. GA Res. 1514, UN GAOR, 15th Session, Supp. no. 16, at 66, 67, UN Doc. A/L.323 and Add.1–6 (1960).
54. I. Brownlie and G. S. Goodwill-Gill (eds.), *Basic Documents on Human Rights* (Oxford: Oxford University Press) p. 24.
55. R. Higgins, *The Development of International Law through the Political Organs of the United Nations* (Oxford: Oxford University Press, 1963), p. 100.
56. E. Spiry, 'From "Self-Determination" to a Right to "Self-Development" for Indigenous Groups' (1995) 38 *German Yearbook of International Law* 129–52 at 136; also G. T. Morris, 'In Support of the Right of Self-Determination for Indigenous Peoples under International Law' (1986) 29 *German Yearbook of International Law* 277–316 at 309. On the other hand, if 'alien' is interpreted in terms of territory, then indigenous communities do not satisfy this criterion.
57. Iorns, 'Challenging State Sovereignty', 296.
58. Resolution 1541 (XV) on Principles Which Should Guide Members in Determining whether or not an Obligation Exists to Transmit the Information Called for under Article 73e of the Charter of 15 December 1960, UN GAOR, 15th Session, Supplement No. 16 (A/4684), p. 29.
59. Tokelau and New Caledonia are two examples. See Tokelau, Working Paper prepared by the Secretariat, Special Committee on the Situation with Regard to the Implementation of the Declaration on the Granting of Independence to Colonial Countries and Peoples, UN Doc. A/AC.109/2003/10 (2003); New Caledonia, Working Paper prepared by the Secretariat, Special Committee on the Situation with Regard to the Implementation of the Declaration on the Granting of Independence to Colonial Countries and Peoples, UN Doc. A/AC.109/2003/7 (2003). Also see N. Maclellan, 'Indigenous Peoples in the Pacific and the World Conference on Racism' in http://www.tebtebba.org and *Indigenous Affairs* 41/85.
60. Iorns, 'Challenging State Sovereignty', 255.
61. Unpublished opinion by I. Brownlie quoted in Iorns, 'Challenging State Sovereignty', 294.
62. GA Res. 2625, UN GAOR, 25th Sess., Supp. 28 (1971), 9 ILM 1292.
63. Paragraph 7 of the chapter on 'The Principle of Equal Rights and Self-Determination of Peoples'. Other similar Declarations followed, such as UNGA resolution 3103 (XXVIII), adopted on 12 December 1973, entitled 'Basic Principles of the Legal Status of the Combatants struggling Against Colonial and Alien Domination and Racist Regimes'.
64. Spiry, 'From Self-Determination', 135.
65. Conference on Security and Cooperation, Final Act, 1 August 1975, 14 ILM 1292.
66. Neither the European Convention for Protection of Human Rights and Fundamental Freedoms (1950), nor the American Convention on Human Rights (1969) refer to the right of self-determination.

67. Thornberry reaches this conclusion from the Charter, the comments of African leaders and the Constitutions of many African states. See Thornberry, 'Self-Determination, Minorities', 887. Hannum believes that territorial integrity and national unity have been proclaimed as more fundamental than self-determination because of the extreme heterogeneity of most African states and the resulting difficulties in developing a sense of statehood in the post-independence period. H. Hannum, *Autonomy, Sovereignty and Self-Determination: The Accommodation of Conflicting Rights* (Philadelphia: University of Pennsylvania Press, 1990), pp. 46–7. Also see G. Shivji, *The Concept of Human Rights in Africa* (London: Codesria, 1989), p. 77.
68. *Frontier Dispute* case (*Burkina Faso* v. *Mali*), Judgment, ICJ Reports (1986) at 567. For an analysis of the judgments of the International Court of Justice on self-determination see A. Cassese, 'The International Court of Justice and the Right of Peoples to Self-Determination' in V. Lowe and M. Fitzmaurice (eds.), *Fifty Years of the International Court of Justice, Essays in Honour of Sir Robert Jennings* (Cambridge: Grotius Publications, 1996), pp. 351–63 and J. Crawford, 'The General Assembly, the International Court and Self-determination' in Lowe, Fitzmaurice, *International Court of Justice*, pp. 585–605.
69. But *contra* J. Klabbers and R. Lefeber, 'Africa: Lost between Self-Determination and *Uti Possedetis*' in C. Brolmann, R. Lefeber and M. Zieck (eds.), *Peoples and Minorities in International Law* (Dordrecht: Martinus Nijhoff Publishers, 1993), pp. 37–76; also see A. G. Kouevi, 'The Right of Self-determination of Indigenous Peoples: Natural or Granted? An African perspective' in P. Aikio and M. Scheinin (eds.), *Operationalizing the Right of Indigenous Peoples to Self-Determination* (Turku/ Åbo: Åbo Akademi University, 2000), pp. 143–53.
70. Inter-American Commission on Human Rights, Report on the Situation of Human Rights of a Segment of the Nicaraguan Population of Miskito Origin, OAS Docs. OEA/Ser.L/V/II.62, doc. 10 and rev. 3 (1983) and OEA/Ser.L/V/II.62, doc. 26 (1984). See H. Hannum, 'The Protection of Indigenous Rights in the Inter-American System' in D. J. Harris and S. Livingstone (eds.), *The Inter-American System of Human Rights* (Oxford: Clarendon Press, 1998), pp. 323–43 at pp. 328–31.
71. *Ibid.*, pp. 78–9.
72. The *Vienna Declaration and Program of Action* was the outcome of the (1993) Second World Conference on Human Rights, where 180 States participated and hundreds of non-governmental organisations attended. The Vienna Declaration and Programme of Action has been published by the United Nations Department of Public Information, Doc. DPI/1394-39399, August 1993.
73. The Declaration recognised:

> the right of peoples to take any legitimate action, in accordance with the Charter of the United Nations, to realise their inalienable right of self-determination. The World Conference on Human Rights considers the denial of self-determination as a violation of human rights and underlines the importance of the effective realisation of this right.

74. Article 1.3 reads:

    In accordance with the 1970 Declaration on principles of International Law Concerning Friendly Relations and Co-operation Among States in Accordance with the Charter of the United Nations, this [the right to self-determination] shall not be construed as authorising or encouraging any action which could dismember or impair, totally or in part, the territorial integrity or political unity of sovereign and independent states conducting themselves in compliance with the principle of equal rights and self-determination of peoples and thus, possessed of a government representing the whole peoples belonging to the territory without distinction of any kind.

75. The General Recommendation was adopted by the Committee at the 1147th meeting, on March 1996, CERD/C/49/CRP.2/Add.7 (1996).
76. *Ibid.*
77. States that have expressed such objections include: Morocco, see UN Doc. E/CN.4/1995/WG.15/2/Add.1, para. 3; Philippines, see UN Doc. E/CN.4/1997/102 (1996), 59, 312; New Zealand, see UNPO Monitor, Thursday, October 30, 1997, Morning Session, 2; France, see written statement of the French delegate, Geneva, 29 November 1995 (1995 Commission Working Group) (on file with author); Chile, see UN Doc. E/CN.4/1997/102 (1996), para. 42; Argentina, see UN Doc. E/CN.4/1997/102 (1996), para. 340. Also see E/CN.4/1996/84, para. 46.
78. Statement to the Eleventh Session of the Working Group on Indigenous Populations on Agenda Item 5 (on file with author).
79. The five experts were consulted by the Canadian Committee to examine matters relating to the accession of Quebec to sovereignty to shed light on some international aspects of the claims of Quebec for independence. See 'Expert Opinion prepared in 1992 by T. M. Franck, R. Higgins, A. Pellet, M. N. Shaw and C. Tomuschat, 'The Territorial Integrity of Quebec in the Event of the Attainment of Sovereignty' in A. Bayefsky, *Self-Determination in International Law: Quebec and Lessons Learned* (Dordrecht: Kluwer Law International, 2000), pp. 241–303 at p. 294.
80. 'Expert opinions accompanying the Amicus Curiae's Factum' in Bayevsky, *Quebec and Lessons Learned*, pp. 69–50; especially G. Abi-Saab at p. 74; T. M. Franck at p. 83; A. Pellet at pp. 91, 122; M. N. Shaw at pp. 138, 144.
81. Except Bangladesh, see below.
82. Crawford, 'State Practice and International Law'.
83. Hannum, 'Self-Determination in the Post-Colonial Era', p. 30.
84. R. Higgins, *Problems and Processes: International Law and How We Use It* (Oxford: Clarendon Press, 1994), pp. 124–7.
85. Knop, *Diversity and Self-Determination*, pp. 95–105.
86. Y. Dinstein, 'Self-determination revisited' in *International Law in an Evolving World* (Montevideo: Fondacion de Cultura Universitaria, 1994), pp. 241–52.
87. Rather than based on a majority vote of the population of a given subdivision or territory.
88. Report of the Committee of Rapporteurs, LN Council Doc. B7/21/68/106[VII] (16 April 1921) at 28. Also see J. Crawford, 'The Right of Self-determination

in International Law: Its Development and Future' in P. Alston (ed.), *Peoples' Rights* (Oxford: Oxford University Press, 2001) pp. 7–67 at p. 17.

89. Frederic Kirgis, 'The Degrees of Self-Determination in the United Nations Era' (1994) 88 *American Journal of International Law* 304–10 at 306.
90. *Ibid.*
91. T. D. Musgrave, *Self-Determination and National Minorities* (Oxford: Clarendon Press, 1997), pp. 188–92.
92. 'Report by Malcolm N. Shaw: "Re: Order in Council P. C. 1996–1997 of 30 September 1996"' in Bayevsky, *Quebec and Lessons Learned*, pp. 125–50 at p. 138.
93. T. M. Franck, 'Postmodern Tribalism and the Right to Secede' in Brölmann, Lefeber, Zieck, *Peoples and Minorities*, pp. 3–27 at pp. 13–14; also, Franck Report in *Quebec and Lessons Learned*, p. 79.
94. O. Schachter, 'Sovereignty – Then and Now' in R. St. J. Macdonald (ed.), *Essays in Honour of Wane Tieya* (Dordrecht: Martinus Nijhoff, 1993), pp. 671–88 at p. 684.
95. Espiel, 'Study on Self-determination', para. 57.
96. A. Heraclides, 'Secession, Self-Determination and Non-Intervention: In Quest of a Normative Symbiosis' (1992) 45 *Journal of International Affairs* 399–420 at 400–11.
97. *Case concerning Application of the Convention on the Prevention and Punishment of the Crime of Genocide (Bosnia-Herzegovina v. Yugoslavia)* [1996] ICJ Rep., General List No. 91 (1996).
98. G. Gilbert, 'Autonomy and Minority Groups – A Legal Right in International Law?', Paper Prepared for the Seventh Session of the Working Group on Minorities of the Sub-Commission on the Promotion and Protection of Human Rights, UN Doc. E/CN.4/Sub.2/AC.5/2001/CRP.5 (2001), p. 20.
99. *Loizidou* v. *Turkey* (Merits), European Court of Human Rights, 18 December 1996 (1997) 18 *Human Rights Law Journal* 50 at 59 (concurring opinion of Judge Wildhaber, joined by Judge Ryssdal).
100. Communication 75/92, reproduced in (1996) 3 *International Human Rights Reports* at p. 136. For an analysis of the case, see O. C. Okafor, 'Entitlement, Process and Legitimacy in the Emergent Law of Secession' (2002) 9 *International Journal on Minority and Group Rights* 41–70; also see Thornberry, *Indigenous Peoples*, pp. 256–8.
101. Supreme Court of Canada, *Reference re Secession of Quebec*, Judgment of 20 August 1998, reproduced in Bayevsky, *Quebec and Lessons Learned*, pp. 455–505 at p. 504.
102. S. Hall, 'The Persistent Spectre: Natural Law, International Order and the Limits of Legal Positivism' (2001) 12 *European Journal of International Law* 269–307 at 297.
103. J. Crawford, *The Creation of States in International Law* (Oxford: Clarendon Press, 1979), p. 100–1; B. Kingsbury, 'Claims by Non-State Groups' (1992) 25 *Cornell International Law Journal* 481–513 at 487.

104. See J. Castellino, *International Law and Self-Determination* (The Hague: Martinus Nijhoff, 2000), pp. 147–72.
105. B. Kingsbury, 'Reconstructing Self-determination: A Relational Approach' in Aikio and Scheinin (eds.), *Operationalizing Self-Determination*, pp. 19–37 at p. 24.
106. J. Anaya, *Indigenous Peoples and International Law* (Oxford: OUP, 1st edn, 1996) at pp. 83–4.
107. Scheinin, 'What are Indigenous Peoples?'.
108. See P. Thornberry, 'The Democratic or Internal Aspect of Self-Determination with Some Remarks on Federalism' in C. Tomuschat (ed.), *Modern Law of Self-Determination* (London: Martinus Nijhoff, 1993) pp. 101–138 at p. 117.
109. Crawford, 'State Practice and International Law', p. 38.
110. *Ibid.*
111. Crawford, 'Self-Determination: Development and Future', pp. 38–9; P. Williams and F. Pecci, 'Earned Sovereignty: Bridging the Gap between Sovereignty and Self-Determination' (2004) 40 *Stanford Journal of International Law* 347–86 at 371; H. Quane, 'A Right to Self-Determination for the Kosovo Albanians?' (2000) 13 *Leiden Journal of International Law* 219–27. In general for Kosovo, see K. Drezov, B. Gokay and D. Kostovicova (eds.), *Kosovo: Myths, Conflict and War* (Keele: University of Keele, 1999).
112. Pentassuglia uses the example of Kosovo and the uncertainty of the use of remedial secession in the case of Bangladesh to conclude that the right of secession does not exist, even in its remedial form. However, he does refer to indigenous self-determination as a special case. G. Pentassuglia, *Minorities in International Law* (Strasbourg: Council of Europe, 2002), pp. 165–6.
113. P. Thornberry, 'The Principle of Self-Determination' in V. Lowe and C. Warbrick (eds.), *The United Nations and the Principles of International Law, Essays in Memory of Michael Akehurst*, (London: Routledge, 1995), pp. 175–203 at p. 183, n. 44.
114. Gilbert, *Autonomy and Minority Groups*, p. 28.
115. P. Thornberry, 'Self-Determination and Indigenous peoples: Objections and Responses' in Aikio and Scheinin (eds.), *Operationalizing Self-Determination*, pp. 39–64 at p. 49.
116. See Draft Report of Commission Working Group, UN Doc. E/CN.4/1995/WG.15/CRP.4 (1995), para. 13, where it is stated that 'many governments were of the view that article 3 went beyond existing international and national law and practice in that self-determination had to be placed in the historical context of decolonisation'.
117. Report of the Commission Working Group, E/CN.4/1997/102 (1996), para. 336.
118. Crawford, 'Self-Determination: Development and Future', p. 27.
119. UN Doc. A/L.323 and Add.1–6 (1960), Declaration on the Granting of Independence to Colonial Countries and Peoples, GA Res. 1514, UN GAOR, 15th Session, Supp. No. 16, p. 67.

120. *Ibid.*, para. 2.
121. *Ibid.*, para. 5.
122. Three years earlier, in 1962, the General Assembly had established a Special Committee on the Situation with regards to the Implementation of the Declaration on the Granting of Independence to Colonial Countries and Peoples, charged mainly with reporting and making recommendations but also with visiting areas of concern. GA Resolution 1541, UN GAOR, 15th Session, Supplement no 16, at 29, UN Doc. A/4651 (1960).
123. Resolution 2131 (XX) of 21 December 1965.
124. GA Resolution 1810, 17 UN GAOR Supp., no. 17 at 72, UN Doc. A/L.410 (1962); GA Res. 1654, 21 UN GAOR Supp, no. 17 at 65, UN Doc. A/L.366 and Add. 1–3 (1961).
125. Of course, as Crawford notes, to the extent that it applies, self-determination qualifies the right of governments to dispose of the 'peoples' in question in ways that conflict with their rights of self-determination. See J. Crawford, 'The Rights of Peoples: 'Peoples' or 'Governments'?' in Crawford (ed.), *The Rights of Peoples*, pp. 55–67 at p. 59.
126. GA Res. 2526, UN GAOR, 25th Sess., Supp. 28 (1971), 9 ILM 1292. Also see the 1965 Declaration on the Inadmissibility of Intervention in the Domestic Affairs of States and the Protection of their Independence and Sovereignty, which was in the same spirit.
127. *Ibid.*, para. 7.
128. *Ibid.*, para. 4.
129. UN Doc. A/6316 (1966), International Covenant on Civil and Political Rights, UNGA Res.2200 A (XX1), 16 December 1966 and International Covenant on Economic, Social and Cultural Rights, UNGA Res. 2200 A (XXI), 16 December 1966.
130. Final Act, Conference on Security and Co-operation, August 1, 1975, 14 ILM 1292.
131. Principle VIII of the Principles Guiding Relations between Participating States.
132. McGoldrick, *The Human Rights Committee*, p. 248.
133. For example, UN Doc.A/47/49 (1993), Declaration on the Rights of Persons Belonging to National or Ethnic, Religious or Linguistic Minorities, 1992, United Nations General Assembly Res. 47/135, Annex, 47 UNGAOR Supp.(No.49) p. 210; UN Doc. E/CN.4/1995/60 (1995), Resolution 1995/60 on 'ways and means of overcoming obstacles to the establishment of a democratic society and requirements for the maintenance of democracy', UN Commission on Human Rights ESCOR Supp. (No. 4) p. 183, Preamble; section VI of the (1990) Document of the Copenhagen Meeting of the Conference on the Human Dimension of the CSCE, (1990) 11 *Human Rights Law Journal* 232.
134. For example, the (1990) CSCE Document of the Copenhagen Meeting of the Conference on the Human Dimension, paras 6–1.8; the (1991) Geneva CSCE Meeting of Experts on National Minorities, http://www.osce.org/

docs/english/1973-1990/other_experts/gene91e.htm (accessed 2 August 2004), section III; CSCE Paris Summit, the Charter of Paris for a New Europe (1990), http://www.osce.org/docs/english/1990-1999/summits/paris90e.htm (accessed 2 August 2004). Also, the 1991 General Assembly OAS Resolution stated that the principles of the OAS Charter 'require the political representation of [member] States to be based on effective exercise of representative democracy'. Resolution AG/RES 1080, 21-0/91 adopted on 5 June 1991.

135. For example, Recommendation 1201 on 'an additional protocol on the rights of national minorities to the European Convention on Human Rights', Council of Europe Parliamentary Assembly Text adopted on 1 February 1993 (22nd Sitting), article 11; the (1990) CSCE Document of the Copenhagen Meeting of the Conference on the Human Dimension of the CSCE, para. 35; the (1991) Geneva CSCE Meeting of Experts on National Minorities, section 4.
136. For example, UN Doc. ICCPR/C/21/Add.3, General Comment 12(21), Human Rights Committee, GAOR, 39th Sess., Supp. 40, Annex VI; also, Doc. DPI/1394–39399, Vienna Declaration and Program of Action (1993).
137. The Vienna Declaration and Program of Action was the outcome of the (1993) Second World Conference on Human Rights, where 180 states participated and hundreds of non-governmental organisations attended.
138. CERD/C/49/CRP.2/Add.7, General Recommendation, adopted by the Committee at the 1147th meeting, on March 1996.
139. For example, M. C. Lâm, *At the Edge of the State: Indigenous Peoples and Self-Determination* (New York: Transnational Publishers, 2000). Other discussions on indigenous peoples as colonised peoples in Heintze, 'International Law and Indigenous Peoples', p. 45; C. Scott, 'Indigenous Self-Determination and Decolonisation of the International Imagination: A Plea' (1996) 18 *Human Rights Quarterly* 814–20 at 817; B. R. Howard, 'Human Rights and Indigenous People: On the Relevance of International Law for Indigenous Liberation' (1992) 35 *German Yearbook of International Law* 105 at 133; see also remarks by H. R. Berman, in 'Indigenous Peoples and the Right to Self-Determination' (1993) 87 *The American Society of International Law, Proceedings of the 87th Annual Meeting* 190–204 at 190; also Spiry, 'From Self-Determination', 137.
140. A. Anghie, *Imperialism, Sovereignty and the Making of International Law* (Cambridge: Cambridge University Press, 2004).
141. A. Xanthaki, 'The Meaning of Self-determination' in Ghanea and Xanthaki (eds.), *Minorities, Peoples*, 15–33.
142. *Ibid.*
143. *Ibid*, 69–73.
144. Kingsbury, 'Claims by Non-State Groups', 501.
145. See M. Koskenniemi, 'National Self-Determination Today: Problems of Legal Theory and Practice', (1994) 43 *International and Comparative Law Quarterly* 241–69 at 243.

146. See 'The Kurdish Issue and Beyond: Territorial Communities Rivaling the state, Remarks by S. Wiessner', (2004) 98 *American Society of International Law Proceedings* 107.
147. Kingsbury, 'Reconstructing Self-Determination', p. 24.
148. *Ibid.*
149. I. M. Young, 'Two Concepts of Self-Determination' in S. May, T. Modood and E. Squires (eds.), *Ethnicity, Nationalism and Minority Rights*, (Cambridge: Cambridge University Press, 2004), pp. 176–95.
150. See E.-I. Daes, 'Explanatory Note concerning the draft Declaration on the Rights of Indigenous Peoples', UN Doc. E/CN.4/Sub.2/1993/26/Add.1 (1993), para. 26.
151. 'The Effect of Racism and Racial Discrimination on the Social and Economic Relations between Indigenous Peoples and States', Geneva: United Nations, 1989, UN Doc. HR/PUB/89/5, 8, para (viii).
152. R. Falk, 'The Rights of Peoples (In Particular Indigenous Peoples)' in Crawford, *The Rights of Peoples*, pp. 17–37 at p. 25.
153. Crawford, 'Peoples or Governments', p. 59.
154. 'Right to Self-determination Not Synonymous with Independent Statehood, Third Committee Told as Debate Continues', Press Release GA/SHC/3651, United Nations Fifty-Sixth General Assembly, Third Committee, 27th Meeting (PM), 31/10/2001.
155. Report of Commission Working Group, UN Doc. E/CN.4/1996/84 (1996), para. 43.
156. Report of Commission Working Group, UN. Doc. E/CN.4/2003/92 (2003), para. 20, para. 22.
157. See 1995 Draft Report of Commission Working Group, UN. Doc. E/CN.4/1995/WG.15/CRP.4 (1995), para. 14.
158. Thornberry, 'Self-Determination and Indigenous Peoples', p. 49. States including Bangladesh, Japan and India have therefore asked for the definition of the right to self-determination.
159. M. Bedjaoui, *Towards an International Economic Order* (Paris: UNESCO, 1979), p. 100.
160. Higgins, *Problems and Processes*, p. 8.
161. *Ibid*, p. 2.
162. Thornberry, *Indigenous Peoples*, p. 133.
163. Thornberry, 'Self-determination and Indigenous Peoples', p. 49.
164. For example, S. Trifunovska, 'One Theme in Two Variations – Self-Determination for Minorities and Indigenous Peoples' (1997) 5 *International Journal on Minority and Group Rights* 175–97 at 182–3.
165. For example, T. Moses, 'The Right of Self-Determination and its Significance to the Survival of the Indigenous Peoples' in Aikio and Scheinin (eds.), *Operationalizing Self-Determination*, pp. 155–77.
166. G. Alfredsson, 'Different Forms of and Claims to the Right to Self-Determination' in D. Clark and R. Williamson (eds.), *Self-Determination: International Perspectives* (London: Macmillan Press, 1996), pp. 58–86 at p. 58.

167. See Report of Commission Working Group, UN Doc. E/CN.4/2000/84 (1999), para. 72. Also J. B. Henriksen, 'The Right of Self-Determination: Indigenous Peoples versus States' in Aikio and Scheinin (eds.), *Operationalizing Self-Determination*, pp. 131–141 at p. 137.
168. As quoted in J. Burger, 'Indigenous peoples: Their rights and International Action in the International Year and Beyond' in P. Morales (ed.), *Indigenous Peoples, Human Rights and Global Interdependence* (Geneva: International Centre for Human and Public Affairs, 1994), pp. 39–46 at p. 43.
169. The *Kari-oca Declaration* is the Preamble of the *Indigenous Peoples Earth Charter*, which was adopted by indigenous representatives in the World Conference of Indigenous Peoples on Territory, Environment and Development, held at Kari-Oca, Brazil on May 25–30 1992, just before the Sustainable Development at the United Nations Conference on Environment and Development (UNCED) in Rio de Janeiro. The text of the Declaration is at the http://www.dialoguebetweennations.com/IR/english/KariOcaKimberley/intro.html (accessed 2 August 2004), para. 4.
170. The Mataatua Declaration was adopted in 1993 at the end of the First International Conference on the Cultural and Intellectual Property Rights of Indigenous Peoples (12–18 June 1993, Whakatane) attended by 150 indigenous representatives from 14 states. See http://aotearoa.wellington.net.nz/imp/mata.htm (accessed 2 August 2004), Preamble, para. 5.
171. Spiry, 'From Self-Determination', 151.
172. As used by Alfredsson, 'Different Forms of Self-Determination'.
173. Higgins, *Problems and Processes*, p. 128.
174. Stavenhagen, 'Self-Determination: Right or Demon?', p. 7.
175. Statement made on 8 December 1998 by the Peruvian representative to the fourth session of the United Nations working group on the draft Declaration on the rights of indigenous peoples (on file with the author).
176. Alfredsson, 'Different Forms of Self-Determination', pp. 75–6.
177. In its 'Advisory Opinion on the Legal Consequences for States of the Continued Presence in South Africa in Namibia (South-west Africa) notwithstanding Security Council Res. 276 (1970)', Advisory Opinion of 21 June 1971; also in its 'Advisory Opinion on Western Sahara', Advisory Opinion of 16 October 1975 http://www.icj-cij.org/icjwww/idecisions.htm (accessed 2 August 2004).
178. Thornberry, 'Self-Determination and Indigenous Peoples', p. 49; however, see Crawford, 'Self-Determination: Development and Future', p. 9.
179. For example, see R. Dworkin, *Taking Rights Seriously* (Cambridge, Mass.: Harvard University Press, 1978); J. Raz, 'Legal Principles and the Limits of Law' (1972) 81 *Yale Law Journal* 823–54; H. L. A. Hart, *The Concept of Law* (Oxford: Oxford University Press, 1961), p. 119.
180. R. Dworkin, *Taking Rights Seriously* (London: Dukworth, 1977), p. 22.
181. *Ibid.*
182. *Ibid.*, p. 25.
183. Raz, 'Legal Principles', p. 838.

184. *Ibid.*, p. 829.
185. Dworkin, *Taking Rights Seriously*, p. 26.
186. *Ibid.*, p. 27.
187. O. Schachter, *International Law in Theory and Practice* (Martinus Nijhoff Publishers, 1991) p. 20.
188. *Ibid.*
189. *Ibid.*
190. J. Crawford, *The Creation of States in International Law* (Oxford: Clarendon Press, 1979), pp. 85–102 and J. Crawford, Book review of *Self-Determination of People: A Legal Reappraisal* by A. Cassese (1996) 90 *American Journal of International Law* 331.
191. P. Alston, '"Core Labour Standards" and The Transformation of the International Labour Rights Regime' (2004) 15 *European Journal of International Law* 457–522.
192. Section VIII of the Declaration.
193. See McGoldrick, *The Human Rights Committee*, p. 12.
194. A. Cassese, *Self-Determination of Peoples: A Legal Reappraisal* (Cambridge: Cambridge University Press, 1995), pp. 132–3.
195. Hall, 'The Persistent Spectre'.
196. For the consequences of non-compliance with the right of self-determination, see J. D. van der Vyer, 'The Right of Self-Determination and its Enforcement' (2004) 10 *ILSA Journal of International and Comparative Law* 421–36.
197. See, for example, Tomuschat, *Modern Law of Self-Determination.*
198. Y. Dinstein, 'Self-Determination Revisited' in *International World in an Evolving World, In Tribute to Professor Eduardo Jimenez de Arechaga* (Montevideo: Fondacion de Cultura Universitaria, 1994) p. 245.
199. I. Brownlie, 'The Rights of Peoples'.
200. F. Harhoff, 'Constitutional and International Legal Aspects of Aboriginal Rights' (1988) 57 *Nordic Journal of International Law* 289–94 at 293.
201. Kingsbury, 'Reconstructing Self-Determination', p. 24.
202. See E. -I. Daes, 'Explanatory Note Concerning the Draft Declaration on the Rights of Indigenous Peoples', UN Doc. E/CN.4/Sub.2/1993/26/Add 1 (1993), para. 26.
203. J. S. Anaya, *Indigenous Peoples in International Law* (Oxford: Oxford University Press, 2nd edn, 2004), p. 104.
204. D. Held, *Political Theory and the Modern State* (California: Stanford University Press, 1984), p. 168.
205. *Ibid.*
206. *Ibid.*, p. 243.
207. *Ibid.*, p. 247.
208. Statement of the caucus of Australian indigenous representatives, 1997 Commission Drafting Group, 7 November 1997, (on file with author).
209. *Ibid.*, para. 4.
210. Anaya, *Indigenous Peoples*, 2nd edn, p. 105.
211. *Ibid.*, pp. 106–7.

212. The trend of the 1980s and 90s moved 81 states to democratise, yet, only 47 are now considered fully democracies: Human Development Report 2002.
213. T. Franck, 'The Emerging Right to Democratic Governance' (1992) 86 *American Journal of International Law* 46–91.
214. Article 1 of OAS Inter-American Democratic Charter, adopted in Lima, 11 September 2001, 40 ILM (2001) 1289.
215. Article 6 (1). Article 7 TEU sets out a procedure for dealing with any serious and persistent breach by the member state of the principles of Article 6.
216. According to the Charter of Paris, the participating states have agreed to 'build, consolidate and strengthen democracy as the only system of government of our nations' and to 'co-operate and support each other with the aim of making democratic gains irreversible': CSCE Charter of Paris for a New Europe (1990) 30 ILM (1991) 190.
217. Among several references to democracy, paragraph 9 of the Harare Declaration pledges the states and the Commonwealth to concentrate on the protection and promotion of democracy and democratic processes.
218. See OSCE, *Existing Commitments for Democratic Elections in OSCE Participating States* (Warsaw, October 2003), http://www.osce.org/odihr/?page=elections&div=standards.
219. K. Wassendorf (ed.), *Challenging Politics: Indigenous Peoples' Experiences with Political Parties and Elections* (Copenhagen: IWGIA, 2001).
220. Commission on Human Rights Resolution 2004/38 on 'The Incompatibility Between Democracy and Racism'.
221. Continuing Dialogue on Measures to Promote and Consolidate Democracy, Report of the High Commissioner on Human Rights submitted in accordance with Commission Resolution 2001/41, Commission on Human Rights, UN Doc. E/CN.4/2003/59, para. 28.
222. Habermas understands democracy as a free association of equal citizens who engage in a rational discussion on political issues, presenting options and seeking a consensus on what is to be done: J. Habermas, *Between Facts and Norms* (Cambridge, Mass: MIT Press, 1996).
223. A. Lijphart, *Democracies: Patterns of Majoritarian and Consensus Government in 21 Countries* (New Haven: Yale University Press, 1984).
224. S. Wheatley, 'Deliberative Democracy and Minorities' (2003) 14 *European Journal of International Law* 507–27.
225. UN Declaration on Friendly Relations, GA Res. 2625 (XXV) 24 October 1970.
226. United Nations Declaration on the Rights of Persons belonging to National, Ethnic, Religious and Linguistic Minorities, GA Resolution 47/135, 18 December 1992, Preamble.
227. The UN Commission on Human Rights has concluded that the creation of the conditions for a democratic system of government are 'essential for the prevention of discrimination and the protection of minorities': 'Ways and means of overcoming obstacles to the establishment of a democratic society and requirements for the maintenance of democracy', adopted 7 March 1995, E/CN.4/RES/1995/60, Preamble.

228. See the OSCE Guidelines to assist national minority participation in the electoral process, www.osce.org/odihr/documents/guidelines/gl_nmpa_eng.pdf. See also the CSCE Copenhagen document, which provides that 'questions relating to national minorities can only be satisfactorily resolved in a democratic political framework': Copenhagen Meeting of the Human Dimension (1990) 29 ILM 1318, para. 30
229. *Chassagnou and others* v. *France*, ECHR, Reports 1999–III, para. 112.
230. Y. Ghai, *Public Participation and Minorities* (London: Minority Rights Group, 2001).
231. C. Iorns, 'Dedicated Parliamentary Seats for Indigenous Peoples: Political Representation of Indigenous Self-Determination' (2003) 10 *E Law–Murdoch University Electronic Journal of Law*, www.murdoch.edu.au/elaw/issues/v10n4/iorns104nf.html, accessed on 15 February 2005.
232. For example, until 2001 many indigenous peoples in Thailand did not have citizenship papers. C. Vaddhanuphuti, 'The Present Situation of Indigenous Peoples in Thailand' in *'Vines that won't Blind', Proceedings of a Conference held in Chiang Mai, Thailand, 1995*, IWGIA Document 80, pp. 79–88 at p. 81. The problem continues in Laos and other Asian states. For artificial barriers to the political rights of minorities, see *Ignatane* v. *Latvia*, HRC, Communication No. 884/1999, UN Doc. CCPR/C/72/D/884/1999, 31 July 2001, para. 7.4.
233. 'Hands on Parliament: A Parliamentary Committee Enquiry into Aboriginal and Torres Strait Islanders Peoples' Participation in Queensland's Democratic Processes', Legislative Assembly of Queensland, Report No. 42, September 2003.
234. Iorns, 'Parliamentary Seats', Conclusions.
235. As quoted in C. Foster, 'Articulating Self-Determination in the Draft Declaration on the Rights of Indigenous Peoples' (2001) 12 *European Journal of International Law* 141–57 at 151.
236. *Ibid.*
237. HRC General Comment on Article 25 (1999).
238. Foster, 'Articulating Self-Determination', 151.
239. *Mikmaq People* v. *Canada*, Communication No. 205/1986, Views in A/47/40 (1992). See Turpel, 'Indigenous Self-Determination'.
240. Article 2(3) of the United Nations Declaration on the Rights of Members belonging to National or Ethnic, Religious and Linguistic Minorities.
241. Proposals of the ECMI Seminar 'Towards Effective Participation of Minorities', UN Doc. E/CN.4/Sub.2/AC.5/1999/WP.4 (1999).
242. HRC General Comment on Article 25 (1999).
243. For an analysis of some of these see Y. Ghai, 'Public participation, Autonomy and Minorities' in Z. A. Skurbaty (ed.) *Beyond a One-Dimensional State: An Emerging Right to Autonomy?* (Leiden: Martinus Nijhoff, 2004), p. 3.
244. Article 6(a) states:

> In applying the provisions of the Convention, governments shall:
>
> (a) consult the peoples concerned, through appropriate procedures and in particular through their representative institutions, whenever consideration is being given to legislative measures which may affect them directly.

245. Article 7.
246. Communication No. 760/1997, UN Doc. CCPR/C/69/D/760/1996, 6 September 2000, para. 10.3.
247. *Ibid.*
248. Ghai 'Public participation, autonomy and minorities', p. 38.
249. P. Thornberry, 'Images of Autonomy and Individual and Collective Rights in International Instruments on the Rights of Minorities' in M. Suksi (ed.), *Autonomy: Applications and Implications* (The Hague: Kluwer Law International, 1998), pp. 97–124.
250. See Consideration of a Draft Contained in the Annex to Resolution 1994/45 of 26 August 1994 of the Sub-Commission on Prevention and Protection of Minorities, entitled Draft 'United Nations Declaration on the Rights of Indigenous Peoples', Information received by Governments, Chile, UN Doc. E/CN.4/1995/WG.15/2 (1995), para. 6.
251. H-J. Heintze, 'On the Legal Understanding of Autonomy' in Suksi, *Autonomy: Applications and Implications*, pp. 7–32; also Z. A. Skurbaty, 'Introduction' in Skurbaty, *One-Dimensional State*, p. xxxviii.
252. Paragraph 35.
253. Article 11 of the Recommendation. For an analysis of the references to autonomy in international minority instruments, see Thornberry, 'Images of Autonomy', pp. 97–124.
254. For the different types, see K. Myntti, 'The Right to Self-Determination and Effective Participation' in Aikio and Scheinin (eds.), *Operationalizing Self-Determination*, pp. 85–130 at p. 116; also Z. A. Skurbaty, 'Introduction', p. xlii.
255. Hannum, *Autonomy, Sovereignty*, pp. 467–8.
256. H. Hannum, 'Conceptual issues pertaining to minorities' in Skurbaty, *One-Dimensional State*, pp. 154–5.
257. Concluding Observations of the Human Rights Committee, Norway, UN Doc. CCPR/C/NOR/CO/5 (2006), para. 5; also CCPR/C/79/Add.112 (1999), para. 10.
258. As quoted in Heintze, 'International Law and Indigenous Peoples', 47.
259. For more information on Nunavut see: J. Dahl, J. Hicks and P. Jull (eds.), *Nunavut – Inuit Regain Control of their Lands and their Lives* (Copenhagen: IWGIA, 2000).
260. 'Promoting the participation of the Sámi peoples – the indigenous people of Norway – through the Sámi Parliament (the Samedigi)', Paper delivered at the Seminar on Good Governance Practices for the Promotion of Human Rights, Seoul, 15–16 September 2004.
261. Hannum, 'Conceptual Issues', p. 156.
262. H. Steiner, 'Ideals and Counter-Ideals in the Struggle over Autonomy Regimes for Minorities' (1991) 66 *Notre Dame Law Review* 1539–60 at 1547.
263. Skurbaty, 'Introduction', p. xlii.
264. ECRI (2001) 41, para. 6.
265. A. Xanthaki, 'Indigenous Rights in the Russian Federation: The Case of Numerically Small Peoples of the Russian North, Siberia and Far East' (2004) 26 *Human Rights Quarterly* 74–105.

266. The USA adopted in 2001 a position supporting the use of the term 'self-determination' both in the UN and the OAS Declarations on the rights of indigenous peoples; see Anaya, *Indigenous Peoples*, 2nd edn, pp. 111–112.
267. Written statement on Indigenous Issues submitted by International Indian Treaty Council, Commission on Human Rights, E/CN.4/2003/126 (2003); also see earlier position in Information Received by the Government of Australia, UN Doc. E/CN.4/1995/WG.15/2/ Add.2 (1995), para. 19.
268. Also see Information Received by Venezuela, UN Doc. E/CN.4/1995/WG.15/2 (1995), para. 3; and Peru, UN Doc. E/CN.4/1997/102 (1996), para. 53.
269. See Report of the Commission Working Group, UN. Doc. E/CN.4/2003/92 (2003), paras. 19–20.
270. A. Eide, 'Peaceful Group Accommodation as an Alternative to Secession in Sovereign States' in Clark and Williamson (eds.), *Self-Determination*, pp. 87–110, pp. 95–6; also A. Eide, 'The National Society, Peoples and Ethno-Nations: Semantic Confusions and Legal Consequences' (1995) 64 *Nordic Journal of International Law* 353–67 at 365.
271. Spiry, 'From Self-Determination', 151.
272. G. Nettheim, 'Peoples and Populations: Indigenous Peoples and the Rights of Peoples' in Crawford, *The Rights of Peoples*, pp. 107–26 at p. 120.
273. Hannum, *Autonomy, Sovereignty*, pp. 97–98.
274. See Recommendations concerning the August 1989 Draft Universal Declaration on the Rights of Indigenous Peoples, UN Doc. E/CN.4/Sub.2/AC.4/1990/3/Add.2 (1990).
275. Statement of the Representative of the Four Directions Council during the 10th session of the Working Group on Indigenous Populations (1992) as quoted in S. Prichard, *The United Nations Draft Declaration on the Rights of Indigenous Peoples: An Analysis* (New South Wales: Faculty of Law, University of New South Wales, 1996), p. 21.
276. Statement by T. Moses on behalf of the Grand Council of the Crees in the Commission Working Group (Geneva, 30 October 1996), on file with the author. Also see a similar statement by K. Deer, 'An Indigenous Understanding of Self-Determination' in Y. N. Kly and D. Kly (eds.), *In Pursuit of the Right to Self-Determination* (Atlanta: Clarity Press, 2000), pp. 104–6 at p. 106.
277. Spiry, 'From Self-Determination', 138; also Daes, 'The Right of Indigenous Peoples to Self-Determination', p. 51.
278. Scott, 'A Plea', 817.
279. See Statement of the Four Directions Council distributed during the 1995 Commission Working Group, on file with the author.
280. Daes in Explanatory Note concerning the draft Declaration, para. 28.
281. See B. Kingsbury, 'Self-Determination and Indigenous Peoples' (1992) 86 *American Society of International Law, Proceedings* 383–94 at 393.
282. S. J. Anaya, ' A Contemporary Definition of the International Norm of Self-Determination' (1993) 3 *Transnational Law and Contemporary Problems* 131–64 at 163.

283. Alfredsson, 'Different Forms Self-Determination', 79.
284. UN Committee on Economic, Social and Cultural Rights, Initial Reports submitted by States Parties under Articles 16 and 17 of the Covenant, Greece, UN Doc. E/1990/5/Add.56 (2002), para. 11.
285. See S. J. Anaya, 'The Capacity of International Law to Advance Ethnic or Nationality Rights Claims', 75 (1990) *Iowa Law Review* 837–44 at 842.
286. Harhoff, 'Legal Aspects of Aboriginal Rights', 294.
287. Kingsbury, 'Self-Determination and Indigenous Peoples', 393. Kingsbury has developed a flexible approach towards the general right of self-determination, see B. Kingsbury, 'Reconstructing Self-Determination', pp. 19–37.
288. Statement of Canada in the Commission Working Group (Geneva, 31 October 1996), on file with author.
289. Ambassador Ted Moses has been representing the Grand Council of the Crees, see www.gcc.ca/gcc/intrelations.php.
290. Report of the Commission Working Group, UN Doc. E/CN.4/2000/84 (1999), paras. 19–24.
291. Report of the Commission Working Group, UN Doc. E/CN.4/1997/102 (1996), paras. 20–41.
292. See http://www.un.org/esa/socdev/unpfii/aboutPFII/members.htm, accessed on 25 March 2005.
293. Falk, 'The Rights of Peoples', p. 19.
293. Crawford, 'Peoples or Governments', p. 59.
294. Article 1. In 1995, an important additional protocol was added to the Madrid Convention. For cross-border cooperation, see F. Palermo and J. Woelk, 'Cross-border Cooperation as an Indicator for Institutional Evolution of Autonomy: The case of Trentino–South Tyrol', in Skurbaty, *One-Dimensional State*, pp. 277–304.
295. F. Harhoff, 'Self-Determination, Ethics and Law' in G. Alfredsson and P. Macalister-Smith (eds.), *The Living Law of Nations* (Kehl am Rhein: N. P. Engel, 1996), pp. 169–77 at p. 176.
296. See Human Rights and Indigenous Peoples, Report of the United Nations Special Rapporteur on the situation of human rights and fundamental freedoms of indigenous people, Rodolfo Stavenhagen, submitted in accordance with Commission Resolution 2003/ 56, UN Doc. E/CN.4/2004/ 80 (2004), paras. 55–60.
297. *Ibid.*
298. J. Henriksen, 'Implementation of the Right of Self-Determination of Indigenous Peoples' (2001) 3 *Indigenous Affairs*, 6–21 at 11.
299. Kingsbury, 'Reconstructing Self-Determination', p. 21.
300. Bayefsky, *Quebec and Lessons Learned.*
301. W. Kymlicka, 'Justice and Security in the Accommodation of Minority Nationalism' in S. May, I. Modood and E. Squires (eds.), *Ethnicity, Nationalism and Minority Rights*, pp. 144–75.
302. Concluding Observations of the Human Rights Committee, Canada, UN Doc. CCPR/C/79/Add.105(1999), paras 4, 7 and 8; also Norway, UN Doc.

CCPR/C/79/Add.112 (1999), paras. 16 and 17; also Mexico, UN Doc.CCPR/C/79/Add.109, para. 19; and Australia, UN Doc. CCPR/CO/69/AUS (2000), para. 506.

303. Finland, Fifth Periodic Report, Consideration of Reports submitted by States Parties under Article 40 of the Covenant, Human Rights Committee, UN Doc. CCPR/C/FIN /2003/5 (2003), para. 93.
304. UN Committee on Economic, Social and Cultural Rights, Fourth Periodic Report submitted by States Parties under Articles 16 and 17 of the Covenant, Denmark, UN Doc. E/C.12/Add 12 (2003), para. 7.
305. Report of the Commission Working Group, UN Doc. E/CN.4/1997/102 (1996) para. 332.
306. *Ibid.*, para. 317.
307. *Ibid.*, para. 330.
308. Report of the Commission Working Group, UN Doc. E/CN.4/2000/84 (1999) para. 64.
309. *Ibid.*, para. 67.
310. *Ibid.*, para. 70.
311. Report of the Commission Working Group, UN Doc. E/CN.4/2001/85 (2001) para. 82.
312. *Ibid.*, para. 70.
313. Report of the Commission Working Group, UN Doc. E/CN.4/2004/85 (2004) para. 16.
314. *Ibid.*, UN Doc. E/CN.4/2004/85 (2004) para. 17.
315. Falk, 'The Rights of Peoples', p. 27.
316. B. Kingsbury, 'The Applicability of the International Legal Concept of "Indigenous Peoples" in Asia' in J. R. Bauer and D. Bell (eds.), *The East Asian Challenge for Human Rights* (Cambridge: Cambridge University Press, 1999), pp. 236–77.
317. *Ibid.*, 162–3.
318. Anaya, 'Contemporary Definition of Self-Determination', 155.
319. G. Pentassuglia, *Minorities in International Law* (Strasbourg: Council of Europe, 2002), pp. 168–9.
320. Thornberry, 'Self-Determination and Indigenous Peoples', p. 40.
321. I. Brownlie, *Treaties and Indigenous Peoples*, (Oxford: Clarendon Press, 1966), p. 63.
322. Report of the Commission Working Group, UN Doc. E/CN.4/2000/84 (1999) para. 50.
323. *Ibid.*, para. 61.
324. Report of the Commission Working Group, UN Doc. E/CN.4/2003/92 (2003) paras. 19–20.

5 Indigenous cultural rights

Introduction

A closer look at the United Nations monitoring bodies, the statements during the working groups relevant to indigenous peoples and the reports of the UN Special Rapporteurs reveals only the tip of the iceberg of abuses of indigenous cultural rights. Patterns of cultural violence include the seizure of traditional lands, the expropriation and the commercial use of indigenous cultural objects without permission from indigenous communities; the misinterpretation of indigenous histories, mythologies and cultures; the suppression of indigenous languages and religions; the denial of indigenous education; even the forcible removal of indigenous peoples from their families and the denial of their identity.[1]

Recent years have witnessed the further development of abusive practices. States and transnational corporations have been expanding their activities to areas previously considered remote and inaccessible, areas where indigenous peoples live. Renewed interest in indigenous cultures has also brought renewed interest in acquiring products of indigenous art and indigenous traditional science. A new wave of tourism has disrupted indigenous historical and archaeological sites and has brought about the commercialisation of indigenous cultures. Biotechnology and the demand for new medicines have also intensified the interest in traditional botanology and medicine. These factors have lead to the unregulated use of aspects of indigenous cultures by various entities, such as states, international corporations, pharmaceutical companies and individuals, for their own agendas.[2]

Indigenous peoples have repeatedly noted their struggle for maintaining their cultures. In 2005, the Indian Movement Tupac Katari stated:

After over 500 years of irrational exploitation and appropriation of traditional cultural expressions ... and traditional knowledge ... belonging to the ancestral civilizations, today, the indigenous peoples and local aboriginal communities have the moral duty to protect, develop and preserve the past, present and future manifestations of their cultural values, traditional customs, languages and expressions of folklore, which constitute an integral part of the cultural and intellectual heritage of humanity.[3]

Various United Nations bodies have expressed their support for indigenous cultural rights. Among them, the Permanent Forum re-emphasised

the importance of respect for and protection of traditional indigenous knowledge and heritage; the contribution of traditional knowledge in matters related to spirituality, the environment and the management of natural resources within ecosystems; objectively favouring the synergies between local traditional knowledge and modern science, with indigenous participation.[4]

Following the main argument of the previous chapter that cultural claims must not be constructed on the basis of the right to self-determination, but rather on the basis of cultural rights, this chapter attempts exactly this: it explores the current standards of international law concerning indigenous cultures and attempts to answer whether indigenous claims can be accommodated by current international law. After a short analysis of the various international instruments that protect indigenous rights, the chapter focuses on the intrinsic problems of international law in effectively protecting the cultures of indigenous peoples. The chapter then goes on to examine controversial claims of indigenous peoples concerning specific cultural rights, namely the prohibition of ethnocide; control over cultural matters; and restitution and repatriation of human remains.

Overview of standards relevant to indigenous peoples

General standards

Indigenous protection of their cultural rights, as with all indigenous rights, comes from three different – yet overlapping – systems of human rights protection: general human rights instruments; minority instruments; and instruments specifically for the protection of indigenous rights, i.e. the ILO Conventions. The international human rights system protects cultural rights mainly through minorities; general human rights instruments do not attempt an in-depth protection of the right to a culture.[5] The International Covenant on Economic, Social and

Cultural Rights recognises a general right to freely participate in the cultural life of the community,[6] together with the right to enjoy the benefits of scientific progress and its applications as well as the benefits of authorship of scientific, literary of artistic production. Prima facie this provision does not appear to be of great help to indigenous peoples, who strive for more than mere participation in mainstream culture. However, the Committee on Economic, Social and Cultural Rights (ESCR Committee) has covered this apparent gap by agreeing that the right to participation in cultural life also includes 'the right to benefit from cultural values created by the individual or the community'.[7] This view combined with the ESCR Committee's guidelines that states' reports should include information about the cultural heritage of indigenous peoples[8] and its frequent discussions on indigenous cultural rights increases radically the usefulness of the Covenant for indigenous peoples. Through the Committee's work, the right to participate in the cultural life 'opens possibilities of preservation and promotion of [indigenous] culture, while safeguarding access to the "outer world" in a non-discriminatory basis'.[9] The dual effect of the right is implied for example in the Concluding Observation of the Committee on the 2001 Report of Bolivia; the Committee expressed its concern about the discrimination towards indigenous peoples in education as well as its concern for the non-recognition of the cultural rights of indigenous peoples 'as a distinct group'.[10] The International Committee on the Elimination of Racial Discrimination (CERD) has also interpreted the provisions of the corresponding Convention in a way relevant to indigenous needs. The International Convention on the Elimination of All Forms of Racial Discrimination includes a rather generic prohibition of discrimination in religion, cultural rights, education and participation in cultural activities.[11] Apart from the frequent references to indigenous cultural rights in Concluding Observations,[12] the Committee has also issued General Recommendation XXIII (51) that calls for the recognition and respect of indigenous distinct cultures, histories, languages and ways of life as an enrichment of the state's cultural identity.

More explicit than the previous human rights instruments is the Convention on the Rights of the Child: the Convention refers specifically to indigenous children in three provisions: first, it recognises the right of the indigenous child to 'enjoy his/her culture' (Article 30); second, it urges for education that promotes responsible life in a free society in the spirit of understanding, peace, tolerance, equality of sexes and friendship among all peoples including persons of ethnic origin

(Article 29); and third, it urges states 'to have particular regard to the linguistic needs of the child who belongs to a minority group or who is indigenous' (Article 17). The Committee for the Rights of the Child has expanded the scope of the Convention: recently, the Committee has referred to past practices of forcibly removing indigenous children from their families;[13] has raised issues of limited access to education for indigenous children;[14] and has extensively referred to caste-based discriminatory practices against Dalit children in 'education, employment, marriage, access to public places including water sources and places of worship'.[15] Specifically, the Committee expressed serious concerns about 'the harmful effects of this prevailing form of discrimination on the physical, psychological and emotional well-being of the *Dalit* children'.[16] Also, in 2003, the Committee had a day discussion on the indigenous child, where it confirmed the need for states to take all necessary measures to protect the identity of the indigenous child and address its educational and linguistic needs.[17] Specifically on education, the Recommendations ask for the revision of school curricula to develop respect for indigenous identities, the implementation of the right of children to be taught and to read in their own language, the training of indigenous teachers and measures to address the high rate of indigenous dropping out of schools.

Notwithstanding their importance, the general human rights instruments do not address the importance of cultures for the peoples themselves as well as for the society. However, this is an important element for indigenous peoples, as violations of their cultural rights have often been based on the lack of respect towards indigenous cultures and their branding as primitive.[18] Respect for cultures has been emphasised by UNESCO documents. The (1966) UNESCO Declaration on the Principles of International Cultural Cooperation declares that 'each culture has a dignity and value which must be protected and preserved' and that 'every people has the right and duty to develop its culture'. This includes the right to define, interpret and determine the nature of future changes in the peoples' cultures. The (1978) UNESCO Declaration on Race and Racial Prejudice also emphasises the right of all individuals and *groups* (emphasis added) 'to be different' (Articles 1 and 5), whereas the UNESCO World Conference in Cultural Policies proclaimed in 1982 the 'right to cultural identity'. The (2001) UNESCO Declaration on Cultural Diversity noted that cultural diversity must be considered as a 'common heritage of humanity', and its 'defence as an ethical imperative, inseparable from respect for human dignity'. The (2005)

Convention on the Protection and Promotion of the Diversity of Cultural Expressions maintains that cultural diversity can be protected only though human rights, including the right to choose cultural expressions (Article 1). The text recommends the recognition of equal dignity and respect of all cultures, 'including the cultures of persons belonging to minorities and indigenous peoples' (Article 3) and urges states to create an environment that would encourage the protection and promotion of indigenous cultures (Articles 7 and 8). It remains to be seen whether the Convention will come into force soon.

Evidently, the general instruments give some, albeit not adequate protection to indigenous cultural rights. Although the monitoring bodies have succeeded in expanding the scope of protection included in the texts and making them more relevant to indigenous needs and despite the high value of their interpretative role, their opinions are not binding.

Minority standards

Minority instruments are more elaborate on cultural rights. Through both its Concluding Observations regarding Article 27 on minorities[19] and its semi-judicial role,[20] the Human Rights Committee has confirmed on several occasions that indigenous peoples can use the protection of minority instruments. Article 27 of the International Covenant on Civil and Political Rights (ICCPR) that recognises the right of persons belonging to minorities to enjoy their culture and practise their language has proved very useful for indigenous peoples. The UN Declaration on the Rights of Persons belonging to National or Ethnic, Religious and Linguistic Minorities (Declaration on Minorities) provides an authoritative interpretation of Article 27 of the ICCPR.[21] The Declaration underlines the importance of knowledge of the history, traditions, language and culture of the minorities existing within their territory.[22] This process of learning about the different groups within the society is mutual: minorities should learn about the wider society too. This model applies the idea of concentric circles, as analysed earlier in this book. It recognises that both the minority culture and the national culture are important to the individual; getting to know elements of both also reflects the approach of 'togetherness in difference', developed by Young.[23] Mutual knowledge brings with it respect and interconnection among different groups. In this way, 'fundamentalist' indigenous doctrines of ethnic purity and exclusiveness are discouraged.

Convention No. 169 is also quite helpful concerning indigenous cultural claims. The Convention recognises that the concept of indigenous culture is much broader than the traditional meaning of culture and allows for wider interpretations that would protect most aspects of indigenous heritage. Unfortunately, the text is not flawless: the references on cultural rights are too general; the protection is not extended to cultural objects; and intellectual and cultural property rights are omitted. Still, the Convention represents an important step for the protection of indigenous cultures.

Collective element

Article 27 of ICCPR refers to members belonging to minorities. The Human Rights Committee has emphasised the importance of the cultures of minorities and indigenous peoples. In its General Comment on Article 27, the Committee underlined the values behind the article:

> The protection of these rights is directed to ensure the survival and development of the cultural, religious and social identity of the minorities concerned, thus enriching the fabric of society as a whole. Accordingly, the Committee observes that these rights must be protected as such and should not be confused with other personal rights conferred on one and all under the Covenant.[24]

The language of the Comment affirms the collective nature of the rights conferred in Article 27 and stresses the importance of indigenous cultures for the members of the respective groups as well as the enrichment of the entire society.[25] In the *Lovelace* case, the Committee linked the loss of membership to a group with 'the loss of the cultural benefits of living in an Indian community, the emotional ties to home, family, friends and neighbours and the loss of identity'.[26] So far, indigenous cases that have appeared in front of the Human Rights Committee concerning the right to culture have focused on membership of the group[27] and land rights.[28] The latter cases will be analysed in the next chapter on indigenous land rights.

The UN Declaration on Minorities has maintained the individual character of the rights of minorities, but has emphasised further their collective element. Article 1 refers to the existence and 'the ethnic, cultural, religious and linguistic identity of minorities'. The use of the terms 'existence' and 'identity' points towards culture.[29] Although the rest of the Declaration specifically refers to 'persons belonging to minorities', the importance of the reference to 'minorities' in the first article of the Declaration should not be undermined.[30]

Positive protection

A question that is often raised is whether Article 27 creates obligations on states to take positive action to protect indigenous cultures. Spiliopoulou Åkermark discerns between two schools of thought on the matter: the minimalist or passive school represented by Nowak and Tomuschat maintains that the negative language of the provision ('should not be denied . . .') implies that states have no obligations for positive action.[31] On the other hand, the radical or active school, represented by Capotorti, Thornberry, Sohn, Ermacora and Cholewinski, argues that Article 27 implies an obligation to take positive measures. Thornberry notes that if Article 27 only established an obligation of non-interference with the cultural rights of members of minority groups, it would constitute a mere repetition of the rules prohibiting discrimination, the right to language, the right to religion and other specific rights.[32] Indeed, the effective implementation of the provision necessitates positive measures: cultural development requires considerable human and financial support and minorities and indigenous groups rarely possess them.[33] States need to take affirmative action so that the rights of Article 27 can be realised. As Bengoa argues, the state has to ensure the 'modern right to opportunity',[34] 'the just opportunity of each individual to make the best of his potential capabilities'.[35] This entails affirmative action.

This view has also been followed by the UN Special Rapporteur Capotorti[36] as well as the Human Rights Committee.[37] In its General Comment 23(50), the Committee explicitly states that states need to take positive measures to implement Article 27, not only against the acts of the state party itself, but also against acts of other persons in the state.[38] Within the scope of Article 27, the Committee often asks for information on any positive measures the states have taken concerning minorities and indigenous peoples. In 2003, the body welcomed positive measures taken by the Philippines for indigenous protection but asked for further positive protection of indigenous peoples.[39] The Committee has asked Guatemala to adopt legislation for the protection of indigenous peoples and to 'ensure that the implementation of this legislation improves the situation of members of indigenous communities in practice and not only on paper'.[40] Similar was the emphasis of the Committee on the 'practical implementation' of the constitutional protection of indigenous peoples in Venezuela 'with the view to complying with Article 27'.[41] The Committee has also asked Sri Lanka whether any 'assistance' had been given among others to Tamils to preserve their cultural identities, languages and religions[42] and Algeria to provide information 'on the measures taken to foster and preserve [the Berbers'] culture and language'.[43]

The UN Declaration on Minorities also points towards positive protection. Article 1 proclaims that states 'shall adopt appropriate and other measures to achieve' the protection of indigenous existence and identity. The language is very strong: the use of the term 'shall' indicates that the states' obligations are mandatory. It is significant that such strong language is used in the first article of the Declaration, because it sets out the spirit of the instrument. The second paragraph of the article requires that states should adapt their legislation in order to make the protection effective. Legal measures are not adequate, if not followed by implementation. The states' obligations do not stop in tolerating the existence and cultural identity of the groups; they have the obligation to encourage conditions for the promotion of the cultural identity of the group.

Article 2 of the Declaration repeats the language of Article 27 of ICCPR, yet in a more positive manner: the 'shall not be denied' of Article 27 is replaced by the positive phrase 'shall have the right to enjoy'; also, Article 2 specifies that the rights of minorities may be exercised 'in private and in public, freely and without interference or any form of discrimination'. Articles 2.2 and 2.3 establish participation rights for persons who belong to minorities, including the right to participate *effectively* in the cultural life of the minority and the right to participate effectively in matters that affect them 'in a manner not incompatible with national legislation' (emphasis added).

Regional instruments are more cautious in establishing obligations for positive action. Even though the text does not specifically refer to 'positive measures', the (1994) Council of Europe Framework Convention for the Protection of National Minorities establishes that state parties must promote the conditions necessary for members of minorities to develop their culture and preserve their identity, including their religion, language, traditions and cultural heritage' (Article 5.1). Article 12 is more forthcoming: it establishes that positive measure must be taken 'in the fields of education and research to foster knowledge of the culture, history, language and religion of their nationals'.

ILO Convention No. 169 clearly establishes state obligations for positive action. Governments have the responsibility to develop, with the participation of indigenous peoples, coordinated and systematic action to protect indigenous rights.[44] Such action includes special measures

(Article 4.1), namely measures that promote the full realisation of the cultural rights of indigenous peoples with respect to their cultural identity, their customs and traditions and their institutions (Article 2(b)). The recognition, protection and promotion of indigenous values and practices must be an important factor when applying the provisions of the Convention (Article 5). Also, with the cooperation of indigenous themselves, measures shall be adopted to mitigate the difficulties deriving from new conditions of life and work.

Obstacles to the effective protection of indigenous cultural rights by international law

Although numerous instruments offer protection to cultures and recognise cultural rights, international law is still not well-equipped to deal with cultural rights of indigenous peoples. This is largely due to three elements: first, a substantial difference between the indigenous and non-indigenous understandings of culture; second, the prevalence of the concept of cultural property inscribed in international law; and third the focus on states, rather than groups, as beneficiaries of its protection of cultural objects.

The meaning of culture

Indigenous peoples view culture as the outcome of their relationship with other human beings, plants, animals and the land. Culture is not associated with the concept of commercial exchange. All products of the human mind and heart flow from the same source – human beings, their kinship with the other beings of the world and their relationship with the land and the spiritual world. They do not represent the rulers of the world, but live in harmony and cooperation with other beings, such as the animals and the plants. The heritage of indigenous peoples is a spherical notion and not merely a collection of objects, stories and ceremonies.[45] It is 'a complete knowledge system with its own conceptions of epistemology, philosophy, and scientific and logical validity'.[46]

Culture as capital

However, the prevailing conception of culture in international law has been very different. Culture has been perceived as 'the accumulated material heritage of humankind in its entirety or of particular groups'.[47] In this perspective, culture is viewed in a single-dimensional way, as capital that creates rights either for the individual or the state or, in a rather loose way, humanity. Accordingly, the right to a culture is translated either to rights of individuals, such as the right to equal access to the accumulated cultural capital;[48] or rights of states to protect their 'national' culture; or rights of humanity to protect the culture of humankind.

Indeed, a closer look at the general human rights instruments would reveal their adherence to this understanding of culture. Some of them, including the Universal Declaration on Human Rights (Article 27.2), the International Covenant on Economic, Social and Cultural Rights (Article 15) and the International Convention on the Elimination of All Forms of Racial Discrimination (Article 5d),[49] focus on the right of the individuals to have access to culture; others, including the International Covenant on Civil and Political Rights and the International Covenant on Economic, Social and Cultural Rights (Article 1), on cultural development, are currently understood as a right of whole populations of states; and finally others, including the (1966) UNESCO Declaration of the Principles of International Cultural Co-operation (Article 1.3),[50] the (1978) Declaration on Race and Racial Prejudice (Article 5),[51] and the (1972) UNESCO Recommendation concerning the Protection at National Level of the Cultural and Natural Heritage (Article 4),[52] concentrate on the common heritage of the mankind.[53]

Conceptualising culture as accumulated property is alien to indigenous values. Therefore, the instruments that incorporate this understanding of culture cannot adequately address indigenous concerns. An exception to this represents the loosely protected right to cultural development. Unfortunately, the meaning and the beneficiaries of the right have been interpreted so far as the whole populations of states; although helpful, it cannot form a solid basis for protection of indigenous cultures.

Culture as creativity

The focus of general instruments on the individual author testifies to the understanding of culture as creativity, 'the process of artistic and scientific creation'.[54] From this perspective, the right to culture means the right of individuals to create their cultural objects without any restrictions and the right of all peoples to enjoy free access to these creations in the places where they are exhibited, including museums, galleries, libraries, theatres and concerts.

Many UNESCO instruments protect this understanding of culture; notably, the (1961) International Convention for the Protection of Performers, Producers of Phonograms and Broadcasting Organisations;

the (1971) Convention for the Protection of Producers of Phonograms against Unauthorised Duplication of their Phonograms; the (1974) Convention relating to the Distribution of Programme-carrying Signals Transmitted by Satellite; the (1976) Recommendation on the Legal Protection of Translators and Translations and the Practical Means to Improve the Status of Translators; and the (1980) Recommendation concerning the Status of the Artist. The general human rights instruments also seem to recognise this aspect of culture: Article 27.1 of the Universal Declaration establishes that everybody has the right to enjoy the arts and to share scientific advancement and Article 15 of the International Covenant on Economic, Social and Cultural Rights recognises the right of the individual to enjoy the benefits of scientific progress and its applications and the duty of states to take steps necessary 'for the conservation, the development and the diffusion of science and culture' as well as the duty to 'respect the freedom indispensable for scientific research and creative activity'. Several other international instruments define cultural objects in a manner that is compatible with the conception of culture as creativity. The most recent example is the (1995) Unidroit Convention on Stolen or Illegally Exported Cultural Objects: the Convention defines cultural objects as 'those which on religious or secular grounds, are of importance for archaeology, prehistory, history, literature, art or science'.[55]

The protection of individuals who create culture does not substantially advance the protection of indigenous cultures. Indigenous understandings of culture underline that it cannot be created by a sole individual; the community entrusts to the individual the representation of their culture. As an indigenous artist explained in the Australian courts:

> As an artist, whilst I may own copyright under western law, under Aboriginal law I must not use an image or story in such a way to undermine the rights of all the other Yalgnu [her indigenous community].[56]

Still, even though the understanding of culture as individual creativity is not shared by indigenous communities, the discourse of this idea of culture has helped the recognition of indigenous culture as popular culture. The debate on elite and popular culture has transpired in international instruments which have concluded that:

> [t]he cultural or natural heritage should be considered in its entirety as a homogeneous whole, comprising not only works of great intrinsic value, but also more modest items which have, with the passage of time, acquired cultural or natural value.[57]

This has been an important step forward for the protection of indigenous cultures, as a broader spectrum of indigenous cultural works are valued and protected as part of popular art.

Culture as way of life

The above understandings of culture have been prevalent in international standards. However, mainly through the work of UNESCO and the monitoring bodies, a third approach consistent with indigenous understandings has emerged. This views culture as:

> the sum total of the material and spiritual activities and products of a given social group which distinguishes it from other similar groups, ... a coherent self-contained system of values, and symbols as well as a set of practices that a specific cultural group reproduces over time and which provides individuals with the required signposts and meanings for behaviour and social relationships in everyday life.[58]

In this broad sense, the right to culture covers all aspects of life: it incorporates protection for knowledge, belief, art, morals, law, customs and other capacities and habits. Culture is related to language, literature, philosophy, religion, science and technology as well as 'ideological systems' (knowledge, beliefs, values, etc.).[59]

This 'holistic approach' to culture has been neglected by the majority of the instruments protecting cultural rights until the 1980s. However, gradually international law has listened more to sub-national groups and their understandings of concepts such as culture. An early example of such a trend is the (1989) UNESCO Recommendation on the Safeguarding of Traditional Culture and Folklore. The Recommendation attempts to protect traditional and popular art. It defines the term 'folklore' in Article A as:

> the totality of tradition-based creations of the cultural community, expressed by a group or individuals and recognised as reflecting the expectations of a community in so far as they reflect its cultural and social identity; its standards and values are transmitted orally, by imitation or by other means. It forms are, amongst others, language, literature, music, dance, games, mythology, rituals, customs, handicrafts, architecture and other arts.

This definition embraces the entirety that indigenous understandings of culture stand for, includes oral traditions and omits any earlier requirement of 'outstanding' value. The preamble of the recommendation recognises 'the social, economic, cultural and political importance [of folklore], its role in the history of the peoples, and its place in contemporary culture, ... the extreme fragility of the traditional forms of folklore, particularly those aspects relating to oral tradition and the risk that they might be lost' and 'the need in all countries for recognition of the role of folklore and the danger it faces from multiple factors'.

Notwithstanding its helpful elements, the use of the term 'folklore' acknowledges indigenous cultures as elements of the past that need to be protected. However, indigenous peoples have emphasised that they 'are a vital and structured whole and not the remains of traditions or customs long dead'.[60] By using the term 'folklore', we tend to 'freeze' indigenous and ignore their evolution. When indigenous peoples make claims to their own images, stories and cultural themes,

> they do not do so as Romantic authors nor as timeless homogeneous cultures insisting upon permissions and loyalties for the circulation of authorial personas in the public realm. Nor is their assertion of cultural presence made in the name of an ahistorical collective essence, but in the name of living, changing, creative peoples engaged in very concrete contemporary political struggles. The law however affords them little space to make their claims.[61]

Still, the Recommendation on the Safeguarding of Traditional Culture and Folklore was an interesting attempt to close the gap between indigenous and non-indigenous perceptions of culture. Another such attempt is the (1998) UNESCO's World Commission on Culture and Development (WCCD) Report, Our Creative Diversity. Chapter VII of the Report recognises both tangible and intangible heritage as part of indigenous culture:

> Non-physical remains such as place names or local traditions are also part of the cultural heritage. Particularly significant are the interactions between these and nature: the collective natural landscape. Only the preservation of these enables us to see indigenous cultures in a historical perspective. The cultural landscape forms a historical and cultural frame for many indigenous peoples.[62]

The greatest advocates of the third understanding of culture have been human rights monitoring bodies. The monitoring process has always pushed the boundaries. In addition, General Comment 25 (50) of the Human Rights Committee has referred to the broad nature of indigenous culture, observed that 'culture manifests itself in various forms' and mentioned indigenous traditional activities such as fishing or hunting and the right to live in reserves protected by law.[63] In the *Kitok* and *Lubicon Lake Band* cases the Committee reaffirmed this understanding of culture.[64] Likewise, General Recommendation XXIII (51) of CERD asked for the respect of 'indigenous distinct culture, history, language, and way of life as an enrichment of the state's cultural identity'.

The perception of culture as a way of life has had a great influence on the scope of cultural rights. The wide understanding of culture expands the scope of cultural rights and supports the further recognition of collective cultural rights: If culture relates to all aspects of life of a sub-national group, the collective element of the right to a culture seems generic and its recognition necessary. Consequently, any instrument that recognises collective cultural rights for minorities and indigenous peoples appears by nature to accept the wide understanding of culture. For example, Article 33 of the Document of the Copenhagen meeting of the Conference on the Human Dimension of the CSCE (1990) appears to recognise the cultural rights of *minorities* as collectivities.[65]

The concept of cultural property

Related to the understanding of culture as capital is also the liberal use of 'cultural property' in international law,[66] a term that goes against indigenous understandings of culture. As mentioned before, indigenous peoples view culture as part of the community:

> No person 'owns' or holds as 'property' living things. Our Mother Earth and our plant and animal relatives are respected sovereign living beings with rights of their own in addition to playing an essential role in our survival.[67]

For them, culture signifies the continuous relationship between human beings, animals, plants and places with which culture is connected. In this relationship, economic rights have no place:

> The European concept of the natural world, knowledge and culture as 'property' (therefore commodities to be exploited freely and bought and sold at will) has resulted in disharmony between human beings and the natural world, as well as the current environmental crisis threatening all life. This concept is totally incompatible with a traditional Indigenous world view.[68]

Unfortunately several international instruments endorse the understanding of culture as capital and look on it as property. The (1954) UNESCO Convention for the Protection of Cultural Property in the Event of Armed Conflict defines cultural property as: 'irrespective of origin or ownership . . . movable or immovable property of great importance to the cultural heritage of every people'. The restrictiveness of this definition is maintained in the (1999) Second Protocol to the Convention, even though its preamble emphasises that rules in this area should reflect developments in international law.[69] The (1970) UNESCO Convention on the Means of Prohibiting and Preventing the

Illicit Import, Export, and Transfer of Ownership of Cultural Property is more detailed: cultural property is defined as 'property which, on religious or secular grounds, is specifically designated by each State as being of importance for archaeology, prehistory, history, literature, art or science'.[70] The Convention also includes a very detailed account of objects of cultural property.

The (1972) UNESCO Convention concerning the Protection of the World Cultural and Natural Heritage seems to be more 'indigenous friendly', as it uses the term cultural heritage, instead of cultural property. Its definition of cultural heritage broadens the scope of protection,[71] but still excludes some aspects of indigenous heritage. It is doubtful whether all aspects of indigenous 'individual artistic works, artefacts and handicrafts; objects of religious significance; music, folklore and design; archaeology and human remains; sacred and historical sites'[72] would be protected by the (1972) UNESCO Convention. For example, it is debatable whether human skeletons could be included in the 'products of archaeological excavations and discoveries'. Also doubtful is the inclusion of oral history in the Convention; arguably, it can be protected as part of 'sound, photographic and cinematographic archives'. More generally, both the 1970 and 1972 UNESCO Conventions make no reference to spiritual or religious criteria that might apply in identifying areas of cultural heritage, although these are the main criteria for indigenous heritage.[73] Also, the 1972 Convention specifically protects objects of outstanding or monumental value, whereas indigenous peoples view all cultural objects as worthy of protection. These omissions by the Convention leave many cultural objects open to the possibility of uncontrollable use and abuse.[74] An illustrative example is unauthorised filmings of indigenous religious ceremonies and secret recordings of songs and rituals: the Convention protects photographs, films and sound recordings that have a historical value (hence the use of the term 'archive'), but it is arguable whether indigenous have any protection against unauthorised filmings and recordings.

The United Nations Special Rapporteur on Indigenous Cultural and Intellectual Property has urged the use of the term 'indigenous cultural heritage', rather than 'cultural property'. She has defined 'cultural heritage' as:

> everything that belongs to the distinct identity of a people and is therefore theirs to share, if they wish, with other peoples. It includes all of those things which international law regards as the creative production of human thought

and craftsmanship, such as songs, stories, scientific knowledge and artworks. It also includes inheritances from the past and from nature, such as human remains, the natural features of the landscape, and naturally-occurring species of plants and animals with which a people has long been connected.[75]

In an elaboration of the draft Declaration on the rights of indigenous peoples, a similar change of terminology was initiated by the secretariat: it was suggested that the term cultural, intellectual, religious and spiritual 'property' be replaced by the term 'heritage'.[76] However, this suggestion was not followed through.

Even though the gradual shift from cultural 'property' to cultural 'heritage' is welcomed, this change in terminology indicates the drafters giving a focus to each specific instrument, rather than their concern with the development of a coherent system in international law for protecting cultural rights.[77] The instruments demonstrate 'narrow-targeted responses to specific problems which do not provide a single, generally agreed definition of cultural heritage and fail to recognise the deeper implications of the concepts applied'.[78] This uncertainty is not evident in other parts of the relevant law. The consistent use of 'cultural heritage' and the elaboration of its scope will further clarify the rights that indigenous peoples have under current law and will contribute to their further development.

Ownership of culture

International instruments on the protection of culture are also quite vague about who can benefit from their provisions. In their overwhelming majority, they seem to recognise only two owners of culture: the individual and the state. Although this dichotomy has been consistent with international realities in the past, the last two decades have opened the way for the recognition of sub-national groups in international law. This, however, has not been reflected in all international instruments relevant to the protection of culture.

The (1954) UNESCO Convention for the Protection of Cultural Property in the Event of Armed Conflict refers to the cultural property 'of every people'; however, the discussions on the drafting of the Convention indicate that the conferees used the terms 'peoples' and 'state' interchangeably.[79] The (1966) UNESCO Declaration on the Principles of International Cultural Cooperation also refers to nations and peoples,[80] but it is rather doubtful that its protection includes subnational groups, rather than whole population of the states.

The (1970) UNESCO Convention on the Means of Prohibiting and Preventing Illicit Import, Export and Transfer of Ownership and Cultural Property[81] is not much clearer. Paragraph 2 of its preamble notes that 'it is essential for every state to become increasingly aware of the moral obligations to respect its own cultural heritage and *that of all nations*' (emphasis added). If the term 'nations' refers to sub-national groups, paragraph 2 implies a state obligation towards among others indigenous cultures. Article 4 defines as part of the 'cultural heritage of each State' property that belongs to the following categories:

a. cultural property created by the individual or collective genius of nations of the State concerned, and cultural property of importance to the State concerned created within the territory of that State by foreign nationals or stateless persons resident within such territory;
b. cultural property found within the national territory;
c. cultural property acquired by archaeological, ethnological and natural science missions, with the consent of the competent authorities of the country of origin of such property;
d. cultural property which has been the subject of a freely agreed exchange;
e. cultural property received as a gift or purchased legally with the consent of the competent authorities of the country of origin of such property.

Even though paragraph (a) refers to *nations* within the state, which implies the recognition of sub-national cultural property, the existence of such cultural property creates international rights for the state, rather than for the sub-national groups. If state authorities decide so, indigenous heritage can be removed from the territory of the state, exchanged or given as a gift to other states without even asking for the consent of indigenous communities. Also, requests for the repatriation of cultural objects can only be made by states. Further, even if a state decides to raise such an issue, there are many hurdles to overcome until a successful accomodation is reached. The Convention prescribes that both states involved in a dispute must be parties to the Convention and the removal of the object must have occurred after the Convention came into force in both states, certainly after 1972. However, most of the largest art-importing states, such as France, Germany, Japan and the United Kingdom, are not parties; even more, most of the violations on indigenous art occurred before 1972. The (1972) UNESCO Convention concerning the Protection of the World Cultural and Natural Heritage is equally state centred and most articles create rights to states parties.[82]

However, not all relevant instruments are restrictive for indigenous claims; non-legally binding instruments are more open to indigenous cultures. The (1974) UNESCO Recommendation concerning Education for International Understanding, Cooperation and Peace and Education relating to Human Rights and Fundamental Freedoms clearly links culture with nations rather than states. Article 17 urges member states to 'promote, at various stages and in various types of education, study of different cultures, their reciprocal influences, their perspectives and ways of life, in order to encourage mutual appreciation of the differences between them'. Still, the article does not create a specific state obligation to promote the study of all cultures within the state. For example, the state could include in its educational system the study of many cultures around the world, but ignore indigenous cultures at home.

Also, the (1989) UNESCO Recommendation on the Safeguarding of Traditional Culture and Folklore appears to successfully reflect the notion of multiculturalism: the link between culture and the state is not predominant in the document. The recommendation proclaims that 'folklore, as a form of cultural expression, must be safeguarded by and for the group (familial, occupational, national, regional, religious, ethnic etc.) whose identity it expresses' (Article B). Thus, the provision indirectly recognises that cultures can belong to sub-groups. On preservation of culture Article D notes:

> preservation is concerned with protection of folk traditions and *those who are the transmitters*, having regard to the fact that each people has the right to each own culture and that its adherence to that culture is often eroded by the impact of the industrialised culture purveyed by the mass media. Measures must be taken to guarantee the status of and economic support for folk traditions both in the communities, which produce them, and beyond [emphasis added].

To this end, states are encouraged to proceed to specific activities that would ensure the preservation of folklore.

It becomes obvious that apart from human rights instruments, most other international binding instruments do not seem to positively acknowledge and protect indigenous cultures. On the contrary, they seem to neglect sub-national cultures and to perceive every cultural object existing in the state as part of the state. In this respect, not only do they fail to help indigenous claims, they also support states' control over indigenous cultural objects. Arguably, this approach constitutes another form of cultural appropriation of indigenous cultural objects by states, a matter that the international community has accepted so far with relative indifference. Recently though, international law and scholarship have accepted the need to re-evaluate the understandings of culture in international law. The Recommendation on Folklore, the report on Our Creative Diversity, the study of the Special Rapporteur and the work of the human rights monitoring bodies point in this direction. Indeed, human rights instruments protect a 'right to a culture' and their monitoring bodies have expanded their scope and translated the rather generic protection into ways that accommodate indigenous claims. Although these are helpful, they are of a non-binding nature. Convention No. 169 does address important indigenous questions and is of a binding nature; but this instrument has only been ratified by seventeen states, limiting its scope considerably.

It is important to note that the three understandings of culture are not mutually exclusive and that this section does not argue for the elimination of any of the above meanings from international instruments. My argument is that all understandings must be included in international instruments, so that all understandings are protected. Neither has this section argued for the elimination or the undermining of the individual right to culture; it has argued for the better recognition of collective cultural rights of indigenous groups. All notions of culture and aspects of cultural rights complement one another and ensure the comprehensive protection of all aspects and actors of culture. Unfortunately, many international instruments still neglect that culture can also be seen as a way of life. This makes the protection of indigenous cultural interests a very difficult task. It seems to me that the lacuna in the existing law could be rectified in two ways: firstly, by new and binding, or overwhelmingly accepted, interpretations of the existing instruments and, secondly, by the establishment of new standards that would address indigenous concerns.[83] This approach can also be supported by a closer look at specific indigenous cultural claims that have proved very controversial.

Specific issues concerning cultural rights

Although some issues related to culture are very important, such as rights related to education, religion, language and media, minority instruments have addressed these issues to a large degree and are quite helpful in accommodating indigenous claims. In contrast, the right of indigenous peoples to cultural autonomy, the misappropriation and misuse of cultural heritage, the right to repatriation of cultural objects, including human remains, and traditional medicine rights have been overlooked, partly because they stretch the contours of current international standards.

Indigenous cultural autonomy

Indigenous peoples ask for the establishment and development of their own separate cultural institutions and systems. The danger of claiming cultural rights on the basis of self-determination has been analysed earlier. Nevertheless, cultural autonomy is based on rights of control, participation and consultation in conjunction with cultural rights. Within the scope of Article 27 of the ICCPR, the Human Rights Committee has repeatedly asked for indigenous control over matters that concern them[84] and has praised the devolution of responsibility on such matters to indigenous institutions.[85] Even though the UN Declaration on Minorities does not clearly recognise cultural autonomy, Article 2.3 recognises the right of minorities to participate effectively in decisions that affect them at the national and the regional level, whereas Article 2 opens the way towards indigenous cultural self-government appropriate to ensure 'effective' participation.[86] The condition of 'effective participation' through local and national organisations seems to include the possibility of the creation of autonomy. Further, Article 5 recognises that national policies, national programmes and programmes of cooperation and assistance amongst states should be planned and implemented with due regard for the legitimate interests of minorities. This article can be read as establishing the obligation of states, which take part in development assistance plans, to examine the possible consequences and effects on minorities and their culture.[87] In this respect, the establishment of community-based institutions for supervising research, promoting education and training and conserving collections of important objects and documents seems within the boundaries of international law. In some states, such as the United States and Panama, a number of indigenous communities have enacted laws for regulating archaeological and cultural research.[88]

European political instruments are also important as they demonstrate the accepted trends on cultural autonomy. The CSCE Copenhagen Concluding Document explicitly mentions the possibility of establishing appropriate local or autonomous administrations for minority issues, including for cultural issues. Self-administration and the establishment of advisory or decision-making bodies in which minorities are represented, particularly with respect to cultural issues, were also included in the recommendations of the Geneva Experts Meeting on National Minorities. The possibility of autonomy was reaffirmed in the (1992) Helsinki Follow-up, again with specific references to full participation in cultural, social and economic life.

The possibility of indigenous cultural autonomy also derives from ILO Convention No. 169. Myntti disagrees; he argues that the omission of the term 'cultural autonomy' from the text rules out the possibility.[89] Article 6 establishes that indigenous communities must be consulted on matters that affect them directly, through their representatives and following the appropriate procedures. The consultations must be undertaken in good faith; in a form appropriate to the circumstances; and be directed towards reaching an agreement. The Convention also recognises that indigenous peoples 'should enjoy as much control as possible over their own economic, social and cultural development'. The degree of control will vary according to the circumstances; yet, it must be the highest degree possible under the specific circumstances. The Committee of Experts has interpreted the provision in such a way that it creates an obligation for effective participation backed up with appropriate mechanisms and implementation procedures,[90] including cultural autonomy.

Even when indigenous do not have their separate cultural systems recognised, they should give their informed consent for matters that affect them. According to the draft Declaration, indigenous peoples must give their consent for matters that affect them. Article 19 requires that they give their free and informed consent before the adoption and implementation of any legislative and administrative measures;[91] so too with the right to autonomy (Article 4); and the right to distinct cultural institutions (Article 5). Finally, membership of an indigenous group will be determined by the traditions and cultures of the group (Article 9). Several recent efforts have been made at the United Nations to elaborate further the need for indigenous control over their cultures. Chairperson Daes of the working group on indigenous populations (WGIP) has elaborated 'Principles and Guidelines for the Protection of the Heritage of Indigenous Peoples'.[92] These principles, which take into account indigenous peoples' articulated demands,[93] urge states to recognise indigenous peoples as the primary guardians and interpreters of their cultures and the true collective owners of their works, arts and ideas.

However, on occasions, indigenous cultural rights clash with other rights as well as established legal principles. The issue of compatibility of indigenous customs with other human rights has already been raised earlier in this book. Suffice to say that this limitation is included in current standards of international law,[94] as several states, including the USA,[95] France,[96] Switzerland,[97] Sweden[98] and the Netherlands,[99] Canada[100] and Russia,[101] have repeatedly stressed.

Misappropriation and misuse of indigenous cultural heritage

Indigenous practices, representations, expressions, knowledge and skills as well as traditional craftsmanship fall within the protection of intangible cultural property.[102] Article 11 of the draft Declaration provides indigenous peoples with the right to practice and revitalise their traditions and customs and to protect and develop the past, present and future manifestations of their cultures, such as archaeological and historical sites, artifacts, designs, ceremonies, technologies and visual and performing arts and literature. Also, Article 12 recognises the indigenous right to protect their religions and cultural sites and to control their ceremonial objects.'

It has been argued that because indigenous songs, ceremonies, cultural practices and objects have not been created for the marketplace and are within the public domain, they cannot have the protection of intellectual property systems. However, as these cultural practices have been captured by anthropologists in field notes or on tape and are used in publications, they find a place in the body of scholarship for the benefit of mankind. Therefore, scientists should be able to copyright this specific material.[103]

The ongoing and escalating exploitation of intangible heritage has led to claims by developing states, for whom such heritage has been important for their economies, to lobby for changes in the existing intellectual property regimes. However, developed states have resisted the giving of protection to intangible cultural heritage by intellectual property rights systems, on the basis that such heritage is in the public domain. Article 1 of the 1952 Universal Copyright Convention provided some indirect protection via national legislation. Such legislation has been enacted in some countries.[104]

The (1989) UNESCO Recommendation on the Safeguarding of Traditional Culture and Folklore was the first multilateral instrument to cover exclusively intangible cultural heritage. The Recommendation refers to the importance of intangible heritage to the cultural identity of groups, acknowledges 'traditional' societies as creators and emphasises the need to protect the cultural community from which folklore originates. However, it gives an outdated, static definition of folklore and places too much emphasis on safeguarding the interests of third parties like scientific researchers and governmental officials at the expense of persons who actually produce the folklore. It fails to require prior and informed consent from the traditional owners for use or exploitation; on the contrary, the underlying principle of the Recommendation is the wide circulation of folklore to foster awareness.[105]

For some time, the WIPO and UNESCO have been trying to convince states that a sui generis system of international intellectual property regime is needed for the protection of intangible cultural heritage; the new system would cover expressions and productions, rather than merely works and would allow communities to find appropriate responses for accessing and protecting indigenous heritage. Gibson elaborates on the main problems concerning the existing system:

> Efforts at protecting traditional knowledge within intellectual property frameworks largely presume the objective to be the defence of that knowledge against misappropriation, through safeguarding that knowledge and its origin within an ethic of sharing it as a global resource, rather than realising positive rights in traditional knowledge development and management according to the customary law of the community. However, the subject matter of protection for indigenous groups is not necessarily captured within this conceptualisation of the problem. Furthermore, even within the framework of intellectual property protection, construction of traditional knowledge as 'information' for the purposes of the trade-related system of intellectual property largely neglects the legitimate interests of communities, concerning customary management, cultural integrity, and traditional knowledge development.[106]

The (2003) UNESCO Convention for the Safeguarding of the Intangible Cultural Heritage was a positive step to address the problems of the international intellectual property system. The Convention builds on the 1972 World Heritage Convention, but moves further towards an alternative system for the protection of cultural heritage in international law. It attempts to sidestep the existing system and place cultural heritage within the rubric of human rights. Contrary to the 1972 Convention, the 2003 Convention does not limit its protection to cultural heritage of 'outstanding universal value'. The 2003 text also acknowledges the link between groups and cultural heritage and even though states are still the focus, they are also asked to seek the participation of communities and groups. Unfortunately so far the Convention has not been signed by states where issues of indigenous cultural objects often arise.

Western preoccupations with individual expression are critical to the intellectual property rights system, but at odds with indigenous collective experiences of cultural expression. National copyright law systems usually require individual authorship and original forms of expression, which do not sit well with indigenous cultural forms. So, copyright protection may not apply to traditional knowledge, where the material is deemed unoriginal and in the public domain, or where the misappropriation is a legitimate adaptation under copyright law. Also, current rules defy duration, as after a certain period of time the object becomes part of the public domain. They also require a fixed object, rather than oral and expressive forms of culture.[107] Therefore, by applying intellectual property rights laws, we are led to unfair results.

The focus on individual expression is also evident in international human rights. The use and dissemination of art, cultural exchange and cultural interaction are seen as important principles of human rights and have been enshrined in provisions on freedom of culture and free access to the benefits of artistic and scientific work.[108] To the indigenous complaints of false representation of their cultural manifestations, many critics emphasise the need for the artist's imagination to be free of all constraints. Every expression in the world must be accessible for her to digest and transform it into her own work. As long as the artist does not copy somebody else's work, she is free to use any themes, plots, ideas and characters she chooses. Any attempts to restrict the sources of inspiration would be a violation of personal autonomy.[109]

The use of indigenous materials for academic reasons can also be justified on grounds of academic freedom. Cultural objects, practices and even the genetic information of indigenous peoples are of special interest for researchers in academic institutions and universities. To indigenous protest, researchers pronounce their right to academic freedom. The (1997) UNESCO Recommendation concerning the Status of Higher-Education Teaching Personnel proclaims that 'institutions of higher education and more particularly universities, are communities of scholars preserving, disseminating and expressing freely their opinions on traditional knowledge and culture . . .'.[110] Restrictions on academic freedom would also be contrary to the right to education as protected by Article 26 of the Universal Declaration and Article 13 of the International Covenant on Economic, Social and Cultural Rights.

Still, all the above rights are subject to limitations. According to Article 29(2) and (3) of the Universal Declaration, the right of expression can be limited by reason of the rights and freedoms of the others, morality, public order, and general welfare in a democratic society. The International Covenant on Civil and Political Rights also includes restrictions to rights because of the rights and reputations of others, national security, public order, public health or morals. The Convention also contains an additional restriction of the right to expression: it prohibits war propaganda and the advocacy of racial, national, and religious hatred. Likewise, the Racial Discrimination Convention restricts the right of expression in the case of group defamation or language that incites racial hatred, and outlaws organisations that disseminate literature espousing ideas based on theories of racial superiority. Similar restrictions are also included in all regional human rights instruments. Of special interest are the restrictions included in the (1997) UNESCO Recommendation concerning the Status of Higher-Education Teaching Personnel; the text asserts that higher education personnel must exercise their rights 'in accordance with their professional responsibility and subject to nationally and internationally recognised professional principles of intellectual rigour, scientific inquiry and research ethics'.[111]

It seems, therefore, that the use and appropriation of indigenous cultural heritage can be justified on the basis of certain human rights; thus, there is a conflict of the rights of indigenous communities and the rights of others, including the right of artistic, academic and scientific expression and freedom. Conflicts of rights or between rights and principles are not uncommon in international law. Although predetermined formulas are not useful, some criteria have been developed to deal with such situations. Daes has recognised the need to educate the public and the scientific and academic associations to respect the cultural heritage of indigenous peoples. Indigenous cultural objects should only be retained by universities, museums, private institutions and individuals provided there has been a recorded agreement with the indigenous community about the sharing and the interpretation of the object. The objects should always be displayed in a manner deemed appropriate by the indigenous peoples concerned. Where objects have been removed or recorded in the past and their traditional owners cannot be identified anymore, the traditional owners are presumed to be the entire people associated with the territory from which the objects were removed or made.[112] Applying the principle of proportionality in such a way that the core of both rights is maintained is important. Through consultation and negotiation the following should be further explored: ways to ensure that indigenous cultural objects are not used without the informed consent of their owners; an insistence on respect for ethical and professional standards of research and artistic expression; the establishment of national and international sui generis systems to protect indigenous communities and their intellectual property rights; continuous efforts to find new ways to make indigenous cultural objects accessible to the general public while maintaining their links with the community. To this end, the principles of non-discrimination, of recognition of the original indigenous owner and of respect towards the cultural object and the community are paramount.

Repatriation of indigenous cultural objects

Many cultural objects belonging to indigenous heritage are currently in the hands of state or private collections. Many indigenous cultural objects are stored in museums and cultural or scientific institutions; on many occasions, their interpretation falls outside the beliefs and struggles of indigenous peoples. This is particularly important in view of the educational role museums have in developing public perceptions of indigenous cultures.[113] According to Daes,[114] museum collections should be used to strengthen respect for indigenous identity, rather than perpetuate colonial stereotypes and dispossession. Moreover, in contrast to the state, indigenous seldom benefit from the exhibition of their cultural objects. Of particular importance for indigenous peoples are human remains and other objects found in graves. It is estimated that 200,000 Native American human remains are held in federal agency and museum collections.[115]

In addition to state cultural and scientific bodies, private entities, including art dealers, tourists and scholars, also try to acquire culturally important objects, without the consent of their traditional owners. On occasions, indigenous individuals have agreed to sell their cultural heritage, contrary to their customs and tribal wishes. In addition, indigenous artefacts are copied and reproduced in large numbers by non-indigenous persons for commercial reasons without respect for their symbols and meanings, while indigenous images and themes are appropriated without consent or compensation.[116] Some states have enacted laws prohibiting exportation of indigenous heritage, but unfortunately they have not always proved effective.

Faced with this reality, indigenous peoples are asking for the repatriation of indigenous cultural objects to their traditional owners.[117] As one indigenous organisation has stated:

> The topic of repatriation is important as it is difficult to teach our children to be proud of who they are as native people if museums continue to believe that they can 'own' the remains of our ancestors and our sacred objects.[118]

Fulfilling indigenous aspirations, the draft Declaration addresses, albeit cautiously, the issue of restitution. Article 11 suggests that 'States shall provide redress though effective measures, which may include restitution' with respect to indigenous cultural, intellectual, religious and spiritual property. A similar language is used with respect to indigenous cultural objects. According to Article 12, states shall seek to enable the repatriation of indigenous cultural objects. However, on issues of human remains, the language is much stronger. Article 12.2 provides indigenous peoples with 'the right to the repatriation of their human remains', even though several governments have expressed their reluctance to accept such a right.[119] During the elaboration of the draft Declaration Canada had stated:

> ... we believe that states should make best efforts, in accordance with applicable international and domestic law, to facilitate the return to indigenous people of their cultural property.[120]

The representative of the United States has stated that an open-ended obligation for restitution of cultural and similar property is not a present rule of international law.[121]

If these provisions are adopted, they will represent an important evolution in international law. No instrument has included any reference to the repatriation of human remains, while, as seen earlier, only states have had a recognised right to restitution. The (1954) Convention for the Protection of Cultural Property in the Event of Armed Conflict only applies to states; as does the (1970) Convention on the Means of Prohibiting and Preventing the Illicit Import, Export and Transfer of Cultural Property. The text provides that state parties must 'take appropriate steps to recover and return any cultural property that has been illegally acquired'.[122] Although the (1995) Unidroit Convention on Stolen and Illegally Exported Cultural Objects explicitly asks for the return of any 'sacred or communally important cultural object belonging to and used by a tribal or indigenous community in a Contracting State as part of that community's traditional or ritual use', such objects will be returned to the state, rather than the indigenous community. The Convention recognises the right of the state to request the restitution of the cultural object and to decide on the practicalities of the restitution. This can lead to a situation where the indigenous object is returned to the state, but not to the indigenous group who are the traditional owners. The (1972) UNESCO Convention Concerning the Protection of the World Cultural and Natural Heritage also establishes an inventory of property forming part of the cultural and natural heritage of each state.[123] In its resolution 46/10 of 22 October 1991, the United Nations General Assembly reaffirmed the importance of inventories as an essential tool in the identification and recovery of cultural property. However, such inventories can have the opposite result for indigenous communities: as the state declares its ownership of such objects, the violation of indigenous cultural rights is perpetuated.

The concept of common heritage has often been used as an important argument against intellectual property claims of indigenous peoples in general, and in specific claims for repatriation of cultural objects. The (1999) Castellón Declaration on New Prospects for the Common Heritage of Humanity[124] argued that the common heritage

> belongs to humanity as a whole and cannot be appropriated ... [it] must be safeguarded and its exploitation monitored by humanity, in its name, for itself, in its exclusive interest, that is in the interest of every human being, every people and every nation, without discrimination.[125]

This statement raises the main objection of indigenous peoples – and of some states –[126] against the concept of common heritage: if the sole criterion for determining the future of a cultural object is the interest of humanity, any state can argue that humanity will benefit more from the exhibiting of indigenous cultural objects in a state museum – an argument used particularly by rich states, whose museums surpass indigenous exhibition centres in terms of access and technology. A decision based solely on such considerations completely neglects the importance and deep meaning of these cultural objects to their communities. The Castellón Declaration weakens the 'common interest' criterion by adding the principle of equity:[127] the decision on the cultural object should take into account the benefits to every state, every individual and every people. Although the reference to the 'benefit of every people' is important for indigenous claims, the addition of the benefit of every state in the same article allows for a restrictive interpretation. It implies that the wishes of any indigenous community which has been the creator of a cultural object should be on an equal footing with the interests of the state and ultimately the interests of humanity, even though they have had no special bearing on the creation of the object. In addition, the interests of humanity cannot be easily assessed and can easily be manipulated to serve the interests of states.

The Daes Principles and Guidelines supported the return of indigenous cultural property to their traditional owners and urged states to assist indigenous communities to this end. Daes suggested a UNESCO programme to mediate the recovery of moveable cultural heritage from across international borders at the request of the traditional owners of the property concerned. According to Daes, human remains and associated funeral objects must also be returned to their descendants and territories in a culturally appropriate manner. Also, documentation must be retained and displayed in a manner appropriate to indigenous traditions.[128]

The recognition of rights to restitution and repatriation is of great importance to indigenous communities, as they contribute to the end of abuse and the return of respect and appropriate use of cultural heritage. International law does not currently provide sub-national groups with the right to restitution of their cultural objects. However, several international instruments prescribe the return of cultural objects to the states from which they originate. It seems that the recognition of restitution rights for indigenous cultural objects to their traditional owners would constitute a drastic evolution of international law. It is doubtful whether states would commit themselves to such a principle, particularly states that are involved in such issues. In contrast, compensation and access to benefits would be a more viable solution. Redress for victims of acts of discrimination has been widely discussed recently and has been one of the main themes of the 2001 World Conference on Racism.[129] Further elaboration of the concepts and norms in the matter will clarify international standards and could pave the way for repatriation of cultural objects in the future.

Indigenous biodiversity rights

The Declaration of Principles adopted by the Indigenous Peoples Preparatory Meeting in 1987 urged indigenous control of their biodiversity and sharing of the benefits of biodiversity. Such rights were also mentioned in the Mataatua Declaration on the Cultural and Intellectual Property Rights of Indigenous Peoples which elaborates on indigenous intellectual property claims. These rights are transcribed in Articles 24 and 31 of the draft Declaration.[130] Apart from its proclamation of the prohibition of discrimination in medical health, Article 24 recognises rights of control of indigenous medicines and health practices, including plants, animals and minerals, while Article 31 protects indigenous sciences, technologies, genetic seeds, medicines, flora and fauna. States have expressly noted their disagreement with these provisions. The USA had stated that such claims, 'would appear to extend [indigenous] rights beyond those normally accorded to other members of the state'[131] Canada has explained its position in a more elaborate manner:

There is in place today a complex multilateral system for the protection of intellectual property rights. Consideration will need to be given by States party to existing international agreements relating to intellectual property regimes before changes could be made. Rights of third parties, already recognised under such regimes, must also be acknowledged and addressed in any discussion which proposes to amend them . . . At present only a broad statement of principle should be included in the draft Declaration. Such a principle might be to the effect that indigenous people have the right to a fair and equitable sharing of the benefits arising from the utilization, including commercial utilization, of their traditional knowledge.[132]

Specialists have also defended the current system;[133] arguments on the need for worldwide access to products that enhance physical well-being are also relevant.[134] Indigenous peoples are under no illusions; recognition of their biodiversity rights is an upwards struggle:

The intellectual property rights system totally ignores the close inter-relationship between indigenous peoples, their knowledge, genetic resources and the environment. The proponents of intellectual property rights are only concerned with the benefits they will gain from the commercial exploitation of these resources.[135]

Over the past decade, traditional knowledge has won a growing interest from the international community. Currently more than eleven UN agencies do work on these issues[136] and several recent Declarations urge the recognition of indigenous intellectual property rights.[137] The framework of intellectual property rights analysed in earlier sections is inadequate to protect adequately indigenous biodiversity rights. Partly because of its Eurocentric nature, its individualistic approach to intellectual property rights, and its rather sectional perception of those rights, it only provides limited protection for indigenous biodiversity rights. For example, the protection of confidential information has been used to give indigenous communities the right to prevent unauthorised use of traditional knowledge.[138] Also, a community that has adequate proprietary control over its indigenous knowledge and genetic resources can legitimately assert ownership and demand compensation for the exploitation of its resources; it can also enter into contracts with pharmaceutical and biotechnological companies and government agencies.[139] However, such control is usually not given to indigenous communities, but is limited to states.

The (1992) Convention on Biological Diversity attempts to address the issue of control. The Convention is the primary international instrument whose mandate includes addressing issues regarding respect for and preservation and maintenance of knowledge, innovations and practices of indigenous communities relevant to biological diversity.[140] The Preamble of the Convention acknowledges the close and traditional dependence of many indigenous communities on biological resources, the vital role that such resources play in their lives and livelihoods and the important contribution that traditional knowledge can make to the conservation and sustainable use of biological diversity. Article 8 (j) of the Convention on Biological Diversity establishes that any contracting party shall:

> subject to its national legislation, respect, preserve and maintain knowledge, innovations and practices of indigenous and local communities embodying traditional lifestyles relevant for the conservation and sustainable use of biological diversity and promote their wider application with the approval and involvement of the holders of such knowledge, innovations and practices and encourage the equitable sharing of the benefits arising from the utilisation of such knowledge, innovations and practices.

The provision has been of prime importance, as it has legitimised indigenous bio-diversity rights. However, the text is vague and does not give any normative protection beyond declaring the rights. Although it purports to create a different system, for some even contradictory to the existing intellectual property rights system, it has been argued that the Convention perpetuates the 'steady, unhindered and available supply of the South's biological resources' by acknowledging developing countries' and to a lesser degree indigenous communities' sovereignty over their natural resources and obliging them to conserve such resources for the needs of developed countries.[141] Irrespective of the validity of such criticism, Article 8(j) does not go as far as Articles 24 and 31 of the draft Declaration.

It seems that even though indigenous biodiversity rights are still in an embryonic state, steps have already been taken for the establishment of a sui generis intellectual property rights system for indigenous peoples that would coexist with the existing intellectual property system.[142] Such a system will allow some control to indigenous peoples over the use of their knowledge without overly shaking the intellectual property system.

Concluding comments

Indigenous cultural claims are not fully accommodated by current international law. Although the overwhelming majority are either consistent with existing instruments or represent a logical evolution of those instruments' standards, several claims seem quite radical. A great obstacle to indigenous claims lies in the different understanding of culture contained in many general international instruments, which treat culture as property owned by the state or by the individual. Thus, they ignore to a large degree indigenous control and ownership of their cultures. Although several minority instruments protect the right of indigenous peoples to a culture, they do not address specific indigenous concerns. The ILO Convention No. 169 represents a positive step forward, but its limited application restricts the effectiveness of the instrument. Fortunately, current trends in international law indicate a shift in the way culture is perceived: cultural pluralism within the state is recognised and respected and cultural rights are gradually being defined in a broader way. The indigenous movement has brought specific indigenous concerns to the agendas of international bodies who are currently trying to interpret their existing systems in a manner that accommodates such concerns or to devise new systems and instruments that would address such issues. Several international actors perceive indigenous claims as legitimate and are currently eager to accommodate them. Development of existing law would contribute to the future enjoyment of indigenous cultural rights in full.

Notes

1. R. J. Coombe, 'The Properties of Culture and the Politics of Possessing Identity: Native Claims in the Cultural Appropriation Controversy' (1993) 6 *Canadian Journal of Law and Jurisprudence* 249–85 at 272.
2. Study on the protection of the cultural and intellectual property of indigenous peoples by Erica-Irene Daes, Special Rapporteur of the Sub-Commission on Prevention of Discrimination and Protection of Minorities and Chairperson of the Working Group on Indigenous Populations, UN Doc. E/CN.4/Sub.2/1993/28, paras. 18–20.
3. Review of developments pertaining to the promotion and protection of the rights of indigenous peoples, including their human rights and fundamental freedoms: Principal Theme: 'Indigenous Peoples and the International and Domestic Protection of Traditional Knowledge', UN Doc. E/CN.4/Sub.2/AC.4/2005/CRP.5 of 18 July 2005, p. 2.

4. Report of the First Session of the Permanent Forum, UN Doc. E/2002/43/Rev.1, para. 26.
5. R. Coomaraswamy, 'Identity Within: Cultural Relativism, Minority Rights and the Empowerment of Women' (2002–2003) 34 *George Washington International Law Review* 483–513 at 488.
6. Also Article 27.2 of the Universal Declaration on Human Rights.
7. Report of the International Committee on the Seventh Session, UN Doc. E/1993/22, paras. 202 and 223.
8. Revised Guidelines regarding the Form and Contents of Reports to be submitted by State Parties under Articles 16 and 17 of the International Covenant on Economic, Social and Cultural Rights, UN Doc. E/C.12/1991/1.
9. P. Thornberry, *Indigenous Peoples and Human Rights* (Manchester: Manchester University Press, 2002), p. 197.
10. Concluding observations of the Committee on Economic, Social and Cultural Rights, Bolivia, UN Doc. E/C.12/1/Add.60 of 21 May 2001, para. 14.
11. Article 5.
12. For example see recent questions on inter-cultural indigenous education in Argentina, UN Doc. CERD/C/65/CO/1 of 10 December 2004; about the effect of relocation on indigenous cultural rights, UN Doc. CERD/C/LAO/CO/15, para.18; indigenous peoples' right to use their languages, UN Doc. CERD/C/VEN/CO/18 of 1 November 2005.
13. Concluding Observations of the Committee on the Rights of the Child, Australia, CRC/C/15/Add. 268 of 13 September 2005, paras. 31 and 32.
14. Concluding Observations of the Committee on the Rights of the Child, Ecuador, CRC/C/15/Add. 262 of 13 September 2005, paras. 73 and 74.
15. Concluding Observations of the Committee on the Rights of the Child, Nepal, CRC/C/15/Add. 261 of 3 June 2005, para. 36.
16. *Ibid.*
17. Recommendations, Day of General Discussion on the Rights of Indigenous Children, 3 October 2003.
18. For example, F. Shyllon, 'The Right to a Cultural Past: African Viewpoints' in H. Niec (ed.), *Cultural Rights and Wrongs* (Paris: UNESCO, 1998), pp. 103–19 at p. 103.
19. Recent examples where the Committee talked about indigenous rights within the scope of Article 27 include: Concluding Observations of the Human Rights Committee, Thailand, UN Doc. CCPR/CO/84/THA of 8 July 2005, para. 24; Concluding Observations of the Human Rights Committee, Finland, UN Doc. CCPR/CO/82/FIN of 2 December 2004, para. 17; Concluding Observations of the Human Rights Committee, Suriname, UN Doc. CCPR/CO/80/SURI of 4 May 2004, para. 21.
20. See Human Rights Committee, *Lovelace* v. *Canada*, Communication No. 24/1977, Views in A/36/40 (1981); *Bernard Ominayak, Chief of the Lubicon Lake Band v. Canada*, Communication No. 167/1984, views in A/45/40 (1990); *Kitok v. Sweden*, Communication No. 197/1985, views in A/43/40 (1988); also *Ilmari*

Länsman et al. v. *Finland*, Communication No. 511/1992, views in A/50/40 (1995); *Hopu* v. *France*, Communication No. 549/1993, UN Doc CCPR/C.60/D/549/1993/Rev.1 (1997).

21. I. Brownlie, *Principles of Public International Law* (Oxford: Oxford University Press, 4th edn 1990), p. 699.
22. P. Thornberry, 'The UN Declaration on the Rights of Persons belonging to National or Ethnic, Religious and Linguistic Minorities: Background, Analysis, Observations and an Update' in A. Phillips and A. Rosas (eds.), *Universal Minority Rights* (London and Abo: Minority Rights Group and Abo Akademi University, 1995), pp. 26–7.
23. See chapter 2.
24. Paragraph 9.
25. See above, chapter 1.
26. *Lovelace* v. *Canada.*
27. *Lovelace* case and *Kitok* case.
28. *Kitok* case, *Lubicon Lake Band* case, *Länsman* case, and *Hopu* case.
29. W. Mannens, 'A Structure called Culture' in Y. Donders, K. Henrard, A. Meijknecht and S. Tempelman (eds.), *Law and Cultural Diversity*, SIM Special No. 25 (Utrecht: SIM, 1999).
30. Thornberry, 'The UN Declaration on Minorities', pp. 13–76.
31. See A. Spiliopoulou Åkermark, *Justifications of Minority Protection in International Law* (The Hague: Kluwer International, 1996), p. 128. Also see R. Cholewinski, 'State Duty towards Ethnic Minorities: Positive or Negative?' (1988) 10 *Human Rights Quarterly* 344–71; also, P. Thornberry, *International Law and the Rights of Minorities* (Oxford: Clarendon Press, 1991), pp. 185–6.
32. Thornberry, *International Law and Minorities*, p. 181.
33. See Study by the Special Rapporteur A. Capotorti on the Rights of Persons Belonging to Ethnic, Religious and Linguistic Minorities for the UN Sub-Commission on Prevention of Discrimination and Protection of Minorities, UN Doc. E/CN4/Sub2/384/Add.1-7, Add. 2, para. 132.
34. Preliminary report on the relationship between the enjoyment of human rights, in particular economic, social and cultural rights, and income distribution, prepared by Mr J. José Bengoa, in conformity with Resolution 1994/40 of the Sub-commission and Decision 1995/105 of the Commission on Human Rights, UN Doc. E/CN.4/Sub.2/1995/14, para. 9.
35. UN Doc. E/CN.4/Sub.2/1994/21, para. 63.
36. Capotorti Study, para. 136.
37. Y.M. Donders, *Towards a Right to Cultural Identity?* (Antwerp: Intersentia, 2002), p. 169.
38. Human Rights Committee, *General Comment 23(50)*, UN Doc. CCPR/C/21/Rev.1/Add.5, para. 6.2.
39. Concluding Observations of the Human Rights Committee, Philippines, UN Doc. CCPR/CO/79/PHIL of 1 December 2003, para. 16.
40. Concluding Observations of the Human Rights Committee, Guatemala, UN Doc. CCPR/CO/72/GTM of 27 August 2001, para. 29.

41. Concluding Observations of the Human Rights Committee, Venezuela, UN Doc. CCPR/CO/71/VEN of 26 April 2001, para. 28.
42. See 1991 Report of the Human Rights Committee, A/46/40 (1991), para. 488–9.
43. See 1992 Report of the Human Rights Committee, A/47/40 (1992), para. 64. Also see Reports of the Human Rights Committee, A/33/40 (1978), para. 538; A/35/40 (1980), para. 186; A/38/40 (1983), paras. 200 and 218; A/48/40 (1993), para. 509; A/40/40 (1985), paras. 514–15; and A/50/40 (1995), para. 303.
44. Article 2 of the Convention.
45. Daes 1993 study, para. 21.
46. Preliminary Report of the Special Rapporteur, Mrs E.-I. Daes, submitted in conformity with Sub-Commission Resolution 1993/44 and Decision 1994/105 of the Commission on Human Rights, UN Doc. E/CN.4/Sub.2/1994/31, para. 8.
47. R. Stavenhagen, 'Cultural Rights: A Social Science Perspective' in H. Niec, *Cultural Rights and Wrongs* (Leicester: Institute of Art and Law and UNESCO, 1998), pp. 1–20 at p. 3.
48. Cultural development is linked to economic growth and social conditions.
49. This article prohibits discrimination with respect to the ownership of property, individually or collectively and promotes non-discrimination towards the 'right to equal participation in cultural activities' (Article 5, e, vi).
50. Article 1.3 asserts that 'In their rich variety and diversity, and their reciprocal influences they exert on each other, all cultures form part of the common heritage belonging to all mankind'.
51. Article 5 defines 'culture, as a product of all human beings and a common heritage of mankind'.
52. Paragraph 6 of the preamble of the Convention states that 'every country in whose territory there are components of the cultural and natural heritage has an obligation to safeguard this part of mankind's heritage and to ensure that it is handed down to future generations'.
53. The (1952) UNESCO Convention for the Protection of Cultural Property in the event of Armed Conflict, the (1972) UNESCO Convention concerning the Protection of the World Cultural and Natural Heritage, the (1968) UNESCO Recommendation Concerning the Preservation of Cultural Property Endangered by Public or Private Works, the (1972) UNESCO Recommendation concerning the Protection at National Level of the Cultural and Natural Heritage, the (1975) Recommendation on Participation by the People at Large in Cultural Life and their Contribution to it and the (1989) UNESCO Recommendation on the Safeguarding of Traditional Culture and Folklore which also includes references to the universal heritage of humanity.
54. Stavenhagen, 'Cultural Rights', p. 4.
55. Article 2 of the Convention.
56. *Milpurrurru* v. *Indofurn Pty Ltd and Others*. See M. Blakeney, 'Protecting Expressions of Australian Aboriginal Folklore under Copyright Law' (1995) 17 *European Intellectual Property Review* 442–5 at 443.
57. Article 5 of the Recommendation.
58. Stavenhagen, 'Cultural Rights', p. 5.

59. Thornberry, *International Law and Minorities*, p. 188.
60. Report of the Working Group on Indigenous Peoples to the World Conference on Human Rights, Vienna 18 June 1993, Preambular para. 4.
61. Coombe, 'Properties of Culture', 268–9.
62. *Ibid.*, 176.
63. Human Rights Committee, General Comment 23 (50th Session, 1994), Report of Human Rights Committee, Vol. 1, GAOR, 49th Session, Supplement no. 40, (A/49/40), 107–10.
64. See *Kitok* case; also, Human Rights Committee, *Bernard Ominayak, Chief of the Lubicon Lake Band v. Canada*, Communication No. 167/1984, adopted on 26 March 1984.
65. Article 33 of the Copenhagen Document proclaims that 'the participating States will protect the ethnic, cultural, linguistic and religious identity of national minorities on their territory and create conditions for the promotion of that identity'.
66. The (1954) UNESCO Convention for the Protection of Cultural Property in the event of Armed Conflict and its 1999 Second Protocol; the (1970) UNESCO Convention on the Means of Prohibiting and Preventing the Illicit Import, Export, and Transfer of Ownership of Cultural Property.
67. See International Indian Treaty Council (IITC), IITC Discussion Paper on Biological Diversity and Biological Ethics, 30 August 1996, p. 5 (on file with author).
68. *Ibid.*
69. See paragraph 4 of the Preamble and Article 1.b. of the (1999) Second Protocol to the Hague Convention of the 1954 for the Protection of Cultural Property in the Event of Armed Conflict (1999) 38 *International Legal Materials* 769–82 at 769.
70. Article 1 of the Convention lists the following categories:

> rare collections and specimens of fauna, flora, minerals and anatomy, and objects of palaeontological interest;
> property relating to history, including the history of science and technology and military and social history, to the life of national leaders, thinkers, scientists and artists and to events of national importance;
> products of archaeological excavations (including regular and clandestine) or of archaeological discoveries;
> elements of artistic or historical monuments or archaeological sites which have been dismembered;
> antiquities more than one hundred years old, such as inscriptions, coins and engraved seals;
> objects of ethnological interest;
> property of artistic interest, such as:
>
> (i) pictures, paintings and drawings produced entirely by hand on any support and in any material (excluding industrial designs and manufactured articles donated by hand);
> (ii) original works of statuary art and sculpture in any material;
> (iii) original engravings, prints and lithographs;
> (iv) original artistic assemblages and montages in any material;

rare manuscripts and incunabula, old books, documents and publications of special interest (historical, artistic, scientific, literary, etc.) singly or in collections;
postage, revenue and similar stamps, singly or in collections;
archives, including sound, photographic and cinematographic archives;
articles of furniture more than one hundred years old and old musical instruments.

71. Cultural heritage is defined as:

Monuments: architectural works, works of monumental sculpture and painting, elements or structures of an archaeological nature, inscriptions, cave dwellings and combinations of features, which are of outstanding universal value from the point of view of history, art or science;

Groups of buildings: groups of separate or connected buildings which, because of their architecture, their homogeneity or their place in the landscape, are of outstanding universal value from the point of view of history, art or science;

Sites: works of man or the combined works of nature and man including archaeological sites which are of outstanding universal value from the historical, aesthetic, ethnological or anthropological point of view.

72. Working paper on the question of the ownership and control of the cultural property of indigenous peoples prepared by Ms. E.-I. Daes, UN Doc. E/CN.4/Sub.2/1991/34, para. 6.
73. *Ibid.*, para. 5.
74. *Ibid.*, paras. 7–8.
75. Daes 1993 study, para. 24.
76. See Technical Review of the United Nations draft Declaration on the rights of indigenous peoples, E/CN.4/Sub.2/1994/2, para. 16.
77. L. V. Prott and P. J. O'Keefe, *Law and the Cultural Heritage*, Vol. I (Professional Books, 1984) p. 8.
78. J. Blake, 'On Defining the Cultural Heritage' (2000) 49 *International and Comparative Law Quarterly* 61–85 at 85.
79. R. Clements, 'Misconceptions of Culture: Native Peoples and Cultural Property under Canadian Law' (1991) 49 *University of Toronto Faculty of Law Review* 1–26 at 12.
80. The Declaration states that 'every *people* has the right and duty to protect its culture' (emphasis added). Although it links cultures with nations and establishes a more detailed right to a culture than the International Covenant on Economic, Social and Cultural Rights, it does not specify the obligations of the 'governments, authorities, organisations, associations and institutions responsible for cultural activities' (para. 9). Moreover, the instrument emphasises both at its beginning and end the principle of non-intervention in the domestic affairs of states, independence and sovereignty.
81. The Convention notes at the very beginning (paragraph 2 of the Preamble) that 'the interchange of cultural property among *nations* ... enriches the cultural life of *all peoples* and inspires mutual respect and appreciation among *nations*' (emphasis added).

82. Most Articles of the Convention are addressed to the states parties.
83. See Report of the Technical Meeting on the Protection of the Heritage of Indigenous People, (Geneva, 6–7 March 1997), UN Doc. E/CN.4/Sub.2/1997/15, para. 5.
84. A/49/40 (1994), para. 182.
85. *Ibid.*, para. 89.
86. Thornberry, 'The UN Declaration', p. 22.
87. Spiliopoulou Åkermark, *Justifications of Minority Protection*, p. 184.
88. See Daes 1993 study, paras. 107–8.
89. See K. Myntti. 'National Minorities, Indigenous Peoples and Various Modes of Political Participation' in F. Horn (ed.), *Minorities and the Right to Political Participation* (Rovaniemi, Northern Institute for Environmental and Minority Law, 1996), pp. 1–26 at p. 21.
90. International Labour Conference, 75th Session (1988), *Partial Revision of the Indigenous and Tribal Populations Convention 1957 (no. 107), Report* VI(1), 29–30.
91. Article 20 para. (b) of the draft.
92. See 'Principles and Guidelines for the protection of the Heritage of Indigenous Peoples', Report of the Technical Meeting on the Protection of the Heritage of Indigenous people, (Geneva, 6–7 March 1997), UN Doc. E/CN.4/Sub.2/1997/15, Annex.
93. The Mataatua Declaration on Cultural and Intellectual Property Rights of Indigenous Peoples, First International Conference on the Cultural and Intellectual Property Rights of Indigenous Peoples, UN Doc. E/CN.4/Sub.2/AC.4/1993/CRP.5 (1993).
94. Article 4 of the Declaration on Minorities, and Articles 8.2 and 9.1 of ILO Convention No. 169.
95. Such statements have been issued by the US delegates in every session of the working group on the draft Declaration of indigenous peoples.
96. See 1995 Commission Drafting Group, Report of the working group established in accordance with Commission on Human Rights Resolution 1995/32, UN Doc. E/CN.4/1997/102, para. 67.
97. *Ibid.*, para. 69.
98. *Ibid.*, para 76.
99. *Ibid.*, para 78.
100. *Ibid.*, para 80.
101. *Ibid.*, para 91.
102. According to the definition of the 2003 UNESCO Convention for the Safeguarding of the Intangible Cultural Heritage.
103. S. Hutt, 'If Geronimo was Jewish: Equal Protection and the Cultural Property Rights of Native Americans' (2004) 24 *Northern Illinois University Law Review* 527–62 at 554.
104. For example, the (1990) Native American Graves Protection and Repatriation Act, the National Historic Preservation Act and the Indian Arts and Craft Art in the USA; see R. Grad, 'Indigenous Rights and Intellectual Property Law: A Comparison of the United States and Australia' (2003) 13 *Duke*

Journal of Comparative and International Law 203–31. Also, the (2000) Law 20 in Panama on 'Special Intellectual Property Regime Governing the Collective Rights of Indigenous Peoples for the Protection and Defense of their Cultural Identity and their Traditional Knowledge and Other Provisions', see A. Lopez, 'For the Recovery and Protection of Traditional Indigenous Knowledge', Paper delivered at the International Workshop on Traditional Knowledge, Panama City, 21–23 September 2005, UN Doc. PFII/2005/WS.TK/6.

105. A. F. Vrdoljak, 'Minorities, Cultural Rights and the Protection of Intangible Cultural Heritage', Paper presented at the ESIL Research Forum on International Law, Conference on Contemporary Issues, Graduate Institute of International Studies, Geneva, 26–28 May 2005.
106. J. Gibson, 'Community and the Exhaustion of Culture, Creative Territories in Traditional Cultural Expressions', Paper delivered at the AHRB Copyright Research Network 2005 Workshop on Protection of Traditional Culture and Knowledge at Birkbeck University. See http://www.copyright.bbk.ac.uk/contents/publications/workingpapers.shtml (accessed on 30 November 2005), p. 4.
107. For an elaboration of these principles, see Grad, 'Indigenous Rights and Intellectual Property Law'.
108. Article 27 of the Universal Declaration; Articles 15 and 19.2 of the International Covenant on Economic, Social and Cultural Rights; the 1950 Agreement on the Importance of Educational, Scientific and Cultural Materials (the Florence Agreement); the 1974 UNESCO Recommendation on the Status of Scientific Researchers; the 1980 UNESCO Recommendation on the Status of the Artist; the (1997) UNESCO Recommendation concerning the Status of Higher-Education Teaching Personnel.
109. Coombe, 'Properties of Culture', pp. 251–5.
110. (1997) UNESCO Recommendation concerning the Status of Higher-Education Teaching Personnel, Article 4.
111. *Ibid.*, Article 29.
112. Daes Preliminary Report (n. 46 above), paras. 19–24.
113. Hutt, 'If Geronimo was Jewish'.
114. Daes 1993 study, pp. 6–8.
115. Hutt, 'If Geronimo was Jewish', p. 555.
116. Blakeney, 'Protecting Expressions of Aboriginal Australian Folklore'.
117. Daes 1993 study.
118. Statement of the Cultural Council of Marican Indians, Alaska Natives and Native Hawaiians, Working Group on Indigenous Populations, 12th Session, 25–29 July 1994.
119. See Japan, Sweden, Australia, Brazil, France, the USA, UN Doc. E/CN.4/1997/102, paras. 68, 76, 83, 66, 90 respectively. Also, the UK and New Zealand, see (1999) 28 *doCip Update* 3.
120. See 'Canada Comments' distributed in the Commission Drafting Group on October 24, 1996, on file with the author.

121. See 'US Comments on Articles 1, 2, 12–14, 24, 29 and 42–44' distributed in the Commission Drafting Group on 24 October 1996, on file with the author.
122. Article 7(b)(ii) of the Convention.
123. Article 11.1. of the Convention.
124. The Castellón International Colloquium on New Prospects for the Common Heritage of Humanity, held from 12 to 14 June 1999, was organised by UNESCO and the International Bancaja Centre for Peace and Development. The Castellón Declaration was the outcome of this conference.
125. Paragraph 6 (i) and (iii) of the Declaration.
126. For example, Greece would agree with indigenous claims for the repatriation of cultural objects and has been struggling for some time for the repatriation of the Parthenon marbles. See T. E. George, 'Using Customary International Law to Identify "Fetishistic" Claims to Cultural Property' (2005) 80 *New York University Law Review* 1207–36.
127. Paragraph 6 (v) of the Declaration reads: 'Advantages derived from the use of the common heritage of humanity must be of equitable benefit to every State, every individual and every people'.
128. See Daes Principles and Guidelines (n. 92 above), paras. 19–24.
129. See 'Draft Declaration and Programme of Action of the World Conference, Elements for a draft Declaration and Programme of Action for the World Conference', Note by the Secretary-General, UN Doc. A/CONF.189/WG.1/3, 22 February 2001, section XVI; also see 'United Nations Strategies to Combat Racism and Racial Discrimination: Past Experiences and Present Perspectives', Background paper prepared by Mr Theodor van Boven, UN Doc.E/CN.4/1999/WG.1/BP.7, para. 6(vi); also, 'The Causes of, and Remedies for, Racial Discrimination', Background paper prepared by Mr Michael Banton, UN Doc. E/CN.4/1999/WG.1/BP.7.
130. Paragraph 21 of the Declaration of Principles states: 'All indigenous nations and peoples have the right to their own traditional medicine, including the right to the protection of vital medicinal plants, animals and minerals . . .'.
131. 1996 Drafting Working Group, US Comments.
132. 1996 Drafting Working Group, Canada Comments.
133. For example, see J. Frow, 'Public Domain and Collective Rights in Culture' (1998) 13 *Intellectual Property Journal* 39–52.
134. R. J. Ostergard, 'Intellectual Property: A Universal Human Right?' (1999) 21 *Human Rights Quarterly* 156–78.
135. Quoted in S. Prichard, *The United Nations Draft Declaration on the Rights of Indigenous Peoples: An Analysis* (New South Wales: ATSIC, University of New South Wales, 1996), p. 153.
136. Paper on 'The Convention on Biological Diversity and Traditional Knowledge' by the Secretariat of the Convention on Biological Diversity, delivered at the International Workshop on Traditional Knowledge,

Panama City, 21–23 September 2005, UN Doc. PFII/2005/WS.TK/1. Also, see paper on 'Local and Indigenous Knowledge of the Natural World, An Overview of Programmes and Projects', Paper delivered by the Secretariat of UNESCO, *ibid.*; also 'Information Note' by the Secretariat of the WIPO, *ibid.*

137. For example, chapter 26 of the Report of the United Nations Conference on Environment and Development (Rio de Janeiro, 3–14 June 1992); and United Nations Technical Conference on Practical Experience in the Realisation of Sustainable and Environmentally Sound Self-Development of Indigenous Peoples, Santiago, Chile, 18–22 May 1992, E/CN.4/Sub.2/1992/31, Section V, Recommendation 10. For the work of the WIPO in this field, see 'Protection of Traditional Knowledge: A Global Intellectual Property Issue', Document prepared by the International Bureau of the WIPO in the Roundtable on Intellectual Property and Traditional Knowledge, organised by the World Intellectual Property Organisation, Geneva, November 1–2 1999, WIPO Doc. WIPO/IPTK/RT/99/2.
138. WIPO Information Note in the 2005 Workshop on Traditional Knowledge.
139. R. N. Nwabueze, 'Ethnopharmacology, Patents and the Politics of Plants' Genetic Resources' (2003–4) 11 *Cardozo Journal of International and Comparative Law* 585–632 at 606.
140. Convention on Biological Diversity, Conference of the Parties Decision VI/10 on 'Article 8(j) and Related Provisions', preambular paragraph 8.
141. Nwabueze, 'Ethnopharmacology, Patents and the Politics of Plants', 603.
142. P. Drahos, 'Indigenous Knowledge, Intellectual Property and Biopiracy: Is a Global Bio-Collecting Society an Answer?' (2000) 22 *European Intellectual Property Rights* 245–50.

6 Indigenous land rights

Introduction

It was not until the latter part of the twentieth century that efforts were made to seriously consider land claims of indigenous peoples and to work towards their resolution. During the 1996 Commission Drafting Group, a representative of the indigenous communities of the Pacific expressed the general position of indigenous peoples:

> First of all, it must be legally accepted that we are the first settlers, first dwellers or proprietors of our land. Second, we are a collective group who were imposed upon by uninvited external forces who disrupted the normal march of our history.[1]

For some indigenous communities, land rights are the central claim in their struggle for more protection. Largely, this is because of their special relationship with the land on which they live, a relationship confirmed by the UN Human Rights Committee,[2] the UN Special Rapporteur on Indigenous Issues[3] and ILO Convention No. 169.[4] As indigenous peoples have explained:

> The land is the basis for the creation stories, for religion, spirituality, art and culture. It is also the basis for relationships between people and with earlier and future generations. The loss of land, or damage to land, can cause immense hardship to indigenous people.[5]

> Land was indigenous peoples' sacred mother, life giver and the source of their survival, and therefore [land rights] were the heart and soul of the draft.[6]

Land rights often have ramifications for the physical survival of the group. These communities are amongst the poorest in the world and control over their lands alleviates many of the financial problems they face and, consequently, contributes to the elimination of social problems. Burger believes that 'unless indigenous peoples can reassert their right to control their own development and future and win back sufficient lands and resources, there can be no real progress in their standards of living'.[7] The importance of recognising indigenous land rights also underlies claims for equality and non-discrimination. Many states have taken measures that provide lesser protection to indigenous land rights than to the rest of the population. The UN Committee on the Elimination of All Forms of Racial Discrimination has repeatedly highlighted such cases.

Unfortunately, the differences between indigenous and national land systems and the negative financial consequences indigenous land rights can have for states and transnational corporations have resulted in their strong opposition to such recognition. This chapter explores the main issues relevant to indigenous land claims and identifies the existing contours of international law on the matter. International bodies have been very reluctant to establish clear standards on property rights, therefore such rights enjoy rather vague and general protection. Both ILO Conventions include specific and strong protection for indigenous land rights, as demonstrated in the analysis earlier in this book. The ILO monitoring bodies have confirmed and even broadened such protection, also seen earlier. In order to complete the picture this chapter looks at the position of the other United Nations bodies and states' domestic practice. It attempts to highlight trends concerning indigenous land rights. Domestic practice contributes to the interpretation of international law norms. An analysis of that practice is therefore helpful.

Legal basis for indigenous land claims

It is widely argued that land rights form part of indigenous peoples' right to self-determination.[8] Certainly, they themselves pursue their land rights on the basis of their right to self-determination. Although there is no consensus, of all the various aspects maximalists integrate into the right of self-determination in addition to the internal and external ones, the economic aspect is the most accepted. Whether it is attached to the right of self-determination per se[9] or is perceived as part of internal self-determination,[10] economic self-determination appears essential to indigenous peoples as the main legal basis for: permanent sovereignty over their lands; the exercise of their traditional activities and indigenous practices for sustainable development; the enjoyment of the natural resources of the lands they live in; and the sharing of the benefits of such resources.[11]

There is quite a solid legal basis for accepting an economic side to the right of self-determination. The main justification is offered in Article 1 of the International Covenants. Paragraph 1 establishes the right of peoples to develop their own economic status, while paragraph 2 reads:

> All peoples may, for their own ends, freely dispose of their natural wealth and resources without prejudice to any obligations arising out of international economic co-operation, based upon the principle of mutual benefit, and international law. In no case may a people be deprived of its own means of subsistence.

Also, Article 47 of the International Covenant on Civil and Political Rights (ICCPR) and Article 25 of the International Covenant on Economic, Social and Cultural Rights (ICESCR) include a common statement which reads:

> Nothing in the present Covenant shall be interpreted as impairing the inherent right of all peoples to enjoy and utilise freely their natural wealth and resources.

However, even though important economic rights are proclaimed in the above articles, no explicit link is established in the text between these economic aspects and the right to self-determination. Neither does General Assembly Resolution 1803 (XVII) of 14 December 1962 on Permanent Sovereignty over Natural Resources, that refers to 'the right of peoples and nations to permanent sovereignty over their natural resources',[12] make such a link. Moreover, in *Nauru* v. *Australia*,[13] Nauru argued that the exploitation of certain phosphate lands in Nauru constituted a violation, among others, of the international standards generally recognised as applicable to the implementation of the *principle* of self-determination' and of the obligation 'to respect the right of the Nauruan people to permanent sovereignty over their natural wealth and resources'. In other words, the Human Rights Committee linked the issues in question with the *principle* of self-determination rather than the *right* to self-determination. Consequently, it can be argued that claims related to natural wealth resources and in general to economic development do not fall within the right to self-determination, but within the right to development. It can be further argued that Common Article 1.2 of the International Covenants does not refer to an economic aspect of the right to self-determination, but simply to the right of development; so do Articles 47 of ICCPR and Article 25 of ICESCR.

The right of development was first proclaimed in the (1986) Declaration on the Right to Development[14] as 'an alienable human right by virtue of which every human person and all peoples are entitled to participate in, contribute to, and enjoy economic, social, cultural and political development, in which all human rights and fundamental freedoms can be fully realised'. Its establishment as a human right faced strong opposition by some states; it took seven years until a consensus on the right of development as a human right was reached in 1993 at the UN World Conference on Human Rights. The Vienna Declaration and Programme of Action reaffirmed the right as a 'universal and inalienable right and an integral part of fundamental human rights'.[15]

Unfortunately, the text of the Declaration on the Right to Development is quite blurred about the contours of the right to self-determination and those of the right to development. In the Preamble, development is defined as:

> a comprehensive economic, social, cultural and political process, which aims at the constant improvement of the well-being of the entire population and of all individuals on the basis of their active, free and meaningful participation in development and in the fair distribution of benefits resulting therefrom.[16]

Following this definition, any claims on control, benefits and participation to natural wealth and resources, such as land, would fall within the right to development. However, Article 1.2. reads:

> The human right to development also implies the full realisation of the right of peoples to self-determination, which includes, subject to the relevant provisions of both International Covenants, the exercise of their inalienable right to full sovereignty over all their natural wealth and resources.

Thus, Article 1.2 suggests that claims relating to natural wealth and resources fall within the scope of the right to self-determination. The confusion about the scope of the right to development and the right to self-determination does not stop here. Although several states rightly link Article 1 of both International Covenants with economic development and natural resources,[17] they are not unanimous as to whether this is part of the right to self-determination or the right to development. For example, in its report to the Human Rights Committee, Peru stated on Article 1 that self-determination gives the state the right to decide on its political and *economic* regime;[18] but the Philippines pronounced Article 1 of both International Covenants as 'the right to self-determination *and free disposal of natural wealth and resources*', implying the existence of two separate rights.[19] Indigenous representatives have also used the right to self-determination and the right to development interchangeably as a basis for claims concerning ownership of their lands or resources.[20] Following from the analysis earlier on the meaning of the right of self-determination, a clear distinction between the right to self-determination, restricted to political power, and the right to development, encompassing economic claims, could prove helpful.

Admittedly, there are valid objections to the position described above; the first one relates to the language of the texts. Article 1.1 of the International Covenants proclaims that self-determination is the right of peoples 'to pursue their political, *economic*, social and cultural development' (emphasis added). Yet, as argued earlier, the emphasis of the text must be on the *pursuance* rather than the actual *development*. The pursuance takes place through political means (right to self-determination), whereas the development per se belongs to the economic, social etc. spheres (right to development). Otherwise, if the language of Article 1 is taken literally, then the right to self-determination covers all aspects of development, in which case the right of peoples to development becomes completely void. Still, a sceptic would insist that the position of paragraph 1.2 in the middle of an article on self-determination is another reminder that this paragraph refers to an aspect of the right to self-determination. However, it has not been denied that the right to self-determination and the right to development are very closely related, even though, following my position, they do have distinct scopes. The sceptic would also put forward the endorsement of the economic aspect to the right of self-determination by UN bodies. For example, in its General Comment 12, the Human Rights Committee maintained that paragraph 2 of Article 1 'affirms a particular aspect of the economic content of the right to self-determination'.[21] Again, it can be argued that the opinions of the Human Rights Committee are not binding; nevertheless, they do have weight as interpretations by the authorised monitoring bodies of particular treaties.

Even if problems with the existing instruments are resolved, a more fundamental objection has been raised. Knopp warns that a rejection of economic self-determination disregards important feminist and Third World critiques on the interdependence of political and economic self-determination.[22] The 'liberal' revolutions in Eastern Europe, and their focus on internal political self-determination, and the parallel disappearance of the communist bloc removed from the international agenda the idea of economic independence of populations of states, an essential element for real democracy. Chinkin and Wright have criticised the focus on political self-determination arguing that 'food, shelter, clean water, a healthy environment, and a stable existence must be the first priorities in how we define or "determine" the self in both individuals and groups'.[23] Does the rejection of economic self-determination take away the legal basis of such claims? I think not. Just as with cultural claims, claims for food, shelter, clean water, a stable environment, economic independence and control are not diminished by my position; on the contrary, they are strengthened because they find a more appropriate direct basis. The right to development, the right to a clean environment and the right to food are all third generation rights that are linked to the principle of self-determination, as all rights are, but have still been recognised for their own value in the international human rights system. These rights better accommodate such claims.

Still, one can counter-argue that all the above-mentioned human rights present important weaknesses and therefore cannot be used as fruitful bases for claims. Their meaning is still contested; their beneficiaries are vague; and so are their duty bearers.[24] In particular, the right to development has very similar weaknesses to the right to self-determination.[25] Minimalists view the right to development as an economic right, whereas maximalists give it an economic, social, political and cultural dimension. Its beneficiaries are also not clear, especially those aspects related to natural resources and even more so to sub-surface resources; and its duty bearers are very elusive, especially since states are eager to focus on 'international assistance and co-operation', rather than on their individual responsibilities.[26] Consequently, by transferring economic claims from the scope of self-determination to the scope of the right to development are we just transferring the problem instead of solving it? I think not. Contrary to self-determination, claims for economic development and benefit sharing are at the heart of the right to development. Essentially, the validity of the claims is strengthened; it is their basis that changes. In other words, the right to development provides a solid basis for such claims, and such claims present the perfect opportunity for the advancement of the right to development.

In any case, indigenous peoples have not yet been recognised as beneficiaries, neither of the right to self-determination, nor the right to development in international law. In addition, land rights per se have not been the focus of international human rights. For indigenous peoples, most helpful are undoubtedly ILO Conventions No. 107 and

No. 169. Unfortunately, few states are parties to these two instruments. Nevertheless, the Conventions have acted as an important political tool for the development of indigenous rights. Property rights are notably absent from both the International Covenants. Other universal instruments only protect the individual right to property; consequently, they are not helpful to indigenous claims.

The United Nations bodies have sidestepped the difficulties that self-determination and development pose and have covered the legal gap in the protection of land rights by applying general human rights, especially provisions on the prohibition of discrimination, minorities' right to their culture and the right to property. Indeed, although not addressing directly collective land rights, the UN's ICCPR and ICESCR and the UN International Convention for the Elimination of All Forms of Racial Discrimination contain important provisions relevant to indigenous land rights. For example, the Human Rights Committee has repeatedly been using Article 27 of the ICCPR to deal with violations of indigenous land rights.[27] The Committee on the Elimination of All Forms of Racial Discrimination (CERD) has also encouraged states to 'recognise and protect the right of indigenous peoples to own, develop, control and use their communal lands, territories and resources; the Committee has urged states where indigenous have been deprived of their lands and territories without their free and informed consent, to take steps to return these lands and territories.[28] States are also bound by the standards set in the UN Declaration on Minorities. Apart from human rights instruments, protection to indigenous land rights is also provided by instruments on environment and development, especially the Convention on Biological Diversity, the Rio Declaration and Agenda 21.

Important issues related to indigenous land claims

Collective ownership

Doctrine of *terra nullius*

The doctrine of *terra nullius*, a legal construction used by states in the past to legitimize colonisation and dispossess indigenous peoples from their lands has now been rejected both at the national and the international level. *Terra nullius* was allowed by international law, as affirmed by the decision of the Permanent Court of Justice in the (1933) *Eastern Greenland* case.[29] In 1975, the International Court of Justice ruled in the *Western Sahara* case[30] that the doctrine of *terra nullius* had been erroneously and invalidly applied, because indigenous tribes inhabited the territory at the time of arrival of new settlers. More recently, in *Mabo* v. *Queensland (No. 2)*[31] the Australian High Court discussed the legal and other effects of the doctrine of *terra nullius*. The case concerned a claim by members of the Meriam people to rights in land in the Murray islands in the Torres Strait, off the Queensland coast. The Australian High Court held by a majority that when the Imperial Crown acquired sovereignty in 1879 over the islands, the land rights of indigenous peoples survived the change of sovereignty and were not extinguished. The Court also rejected the view that the Aboriginal peoples were so low in the scale of social organisation that they did not possess rights and interests in land. The *Mabo* decision has had a tremendous impact on the Australian society[32] and has been a landmark case for the recognition of indigenous rights all over the world.[33]

Non-recognition of ownership

Currently, some states do not recognise ownership to any individual or group within the state. In Vietnam, for example, the 1988 Land Law established that land is the property of the entire people and is subject to exclusive administration by the state. A leasehold system has been in operation since 1986 and indigenous individuals, as all other citizens, can inherit, transfer, sell, rent or sublet lands.[34] In such cases, where indigenous peoples are not discriminated against by other sections of the populations, although their rights are restricted, international law is of limited help. An instrument that could be of particular use is the Universal Declaration on Human Rights, which establishes the right of everyone 'to own property alone as well as in association with others' and the right not to be arbitrarily deprived of one's property.[35] The provision recognises the right to property in both its individual and its collective form. Unfortunately, the protection of Article 17 is qualified, as it protects only from *arbitrary* deprivation of property. This is, according to Lucas, deprivation without any reasonable cause or justification imposed by the mere exercise of power, without giving those affected the right to be heard and to have their interests considered.[36] Most deprivations of indigenous lands, including non-respect of past treaties between indigenous nations and settlers and the application of *terra nullius*, fall within this category. However, the term 'arbitrarily' does not include a guarantee against taxation, naturalisation or the seizure of land.[37] This is a weakness of the Declaration, however more serious is its lack of any of route redress.

Indigenous peoples could also use the (1948) Convention on the Prevention and Punishment of the Crime of Genocide (Genocide Convention). The Convention includes in the definition of genocide the deliberate infliction on a group of 'conditions of life calculated to bring about its physical destruction in whole or in part'. Prohibition of indigenous land ownership severely harms the demographic and social situation of these communities and raises fears for their survival. Yet, the Convention sets as an intrinsic element of genocide the 'intent to destroy'; it would be very difficult to prove that restrictions of indigenous land rights actually aim at the destruction of indigenous groups. As mentioned earlier, the draft Declaration establishes the 'aim or effect' rather than the intent to destroy indigenous communities as the main criterion in defining genocide.[38]

Strong legal ammunition for indigenous peoples is provided by ILO Convention No. 107. Article 11 recognises the right to ownership, 'collective or individual, of the members of the populations concerned over the lands which these populations traditionally occupy'. Even stronger is ILO Convention No. 169. Article 14 recognizes 'the rights of ownership and possession of the peoples concerned over the lands which they traditionally occupy.'[39] Article 13 of the Convention provides for respect for the 'special importance . . . of [indigenous peoples'] relationship with the lands and territories . . . and in particular the collective aspects of this relationship'. The article encapsulates a powerful argument on indigenous land ownership: ownership of their lands must be established irrespective of the land rights of other persons in the state, because of this special bond between indigenous peoples and their lands. Non-establishment of land ownership would violate indigenous cultural rights.

Recognition of individual ownership

Article 13 of ILO Convention No. 169 does not just require ownership, but *collective* ownership. This could prove very useful for indigenous peoples in states where only individual ownership is allowed. In Thailand, for example, individual ownership is protected and indigenous peoples cannot always acquire even this title because of legal restrictions and lack of citizenship. Population increase, expansion of commercial farming, plantations and migration of lowland Thais into the northern provinces have made problems related to indigenous land acute.[40] Lack of collective ownership dilutes the control indigenous communities have over their lands. As the ILO noted in a 1998 representation,[41] when lands held collectively by indigenous and tribal peoples are divided and assigned to individuals, the exercise of indigenous rights tends to be weakened and, in general, they ultimately lose all or most of their lands.[42]

Non-establishment of collective indigenous ownership also contravenes Article 27 of the ICCPR and the right of minorities to exercise their cultures. On numerous occasions, the Human Rights Committee has included indigenous land rights in the right to a culture.[44] Its jurisprudence provides important support for indigenous land rights. However, in 2000, the Committee qualified its protection of indigenous land rights: in *Diergaardt et al.* v. *Namibia* the Committee suggested that a long link between the land and indigenous peoples is not adequate; the special link has to be 'the result of a relationship that would have given rise to a distinctive culture'.[44] The Inter-American Court on Human Rights has recently joined the United Nations in supporting collective indigenous rights. In *Awas Tingni*,[45] the Court ruled in favour of collective indigenous rights. In its judgment, the Court found that the right of property includes the collective property of indigenous peoples, even if this property has not been formally recognised by domestic law.[46]

Native title

In common law countries, recognition of collective land rights often takes place through the legal construction of native title. Native (or aboriginal) title is essentially 'the right to exclusive use and occupation of the land held pursuant to that title for a variety of purposes'.[47] Exclusive use and occupancy of land from time immemorial gives rise to native title, a title that is good against all but the Sovereign. In Australia, the *Mabo (No. 2)* case ruled that Aboriginal peoples and Torres Strait islanders who live in a traditional society may possess native title to land that has not been alienated or appropriated by the Crown for its own use.[48] The Canadian Supreme Court also affirmed in *Delgamuukw* v. *The Queen* (1997)[49] that native title is a legal interest in the land itself and can compete with other types of proprietary interest.[50] The form of the title depends on the type of traditional conduct of the Aboriginal group claiming it: an indigenous group that has been living on a certain territory ever since that group first occupied it has the right to continue to live on it. An indigenous group that has been using an area to hunt has the right to continue to do so, but cannot claim full ownership of this specific area. Native title can exist in specific lands, where it has not been extinguished by an act of government, in vacant or unallocated

Crown land, in forests, beaches, national parks, public reserves, in some types of pastoral leases, in land held by government agencies and land held in trust for Aboriginal communities and any other public or Crown lands. Native title may also exist in inland or offshore waters, such as oceans, seas, lakes, rivers and other waters that are not privately owned.[51] Lokan highlights the positive aspects of the native title:

> By defining native title rights primarily at the level of the community, native title doctrine reinforces the community's identity. At a practical level, it further provides an incentive for the community to remain cohesive, since members who leave the community may lose their ability to enjoy the rights and benefits that are associated with membership. This is a marked departure from the individual basis of common law property rights in most other contexts.[52]

Still, there are some important limitations to the right: native title cannot prevail over other individuals' valid rights, including ownership of a property in the land, a pastoral lease or a mining license; neither does it prevail in areas where individuals enjoy exclusive possession of the land, freehold ownership - essentially, most houses in cities and towns and most farms - and residential, commercial and certain other types of leases. Also native title does not prevail over legislation and does not prevail in cases where the public has the right to access places such as parks, recreation reserves and beaches; it is not recognised where there are schools, hospitals and roads.[53]

Moreover, states have the power to 'extinguish' land rights and titles of indigenous peoples without their consent.[54] National legal systems have developed a set of guidelines about when and under which circumstances extinguishment can occur. In *Sparrow*,[55] the Court held that legislation that restricts native rights is allowed, so long as the restriction is justified and pursues an objective which is 'compelling and substantial',[56] constitutional and 'absolutely necessary to accomplish the required limitation'.[57] According to the Court, while the conservation and management of fisheries constitutes a valid objective, 'public interest' is so vague that it does not provide meaningful guidance and so broad that it is unattainable as a test for justifying limitations on constitutional rights.[58] However, *Delgamuukw* expanded the legislative objectives that allow indigenous title to be infringed; according to the Court they included:

> ...the development of agriculture, forestry, mining and hydro-electric power, the general economic development of the interior of British Columbia, protection of the environment or endangered species, the building of infrastructure and the settlement of foreign populations to support these aims.[59]

Such a long list of grounds for restriction of indigenous land rights falls below the international standards, which insist that limitations on human rights must be interpreted and applied restrictively. The United Nations Committee on Human Rights has identified the extinguishment of indigenous land rights as a violation of indigenous rights. In its 1999 report, the Committee recommended to Canada that 'the practice of extinguishing inherent aboriginal rights be abandoned, as it is incompatible with Article 1 of the Covenant'.[60] In 2006, the same Committee noted that alternative policies to extinguishment of indigenous rights also amount to violation of indigenous rights.[61] Another way that certain states use to limit indigenous land rights is the doctrine of plenary power, namely the unlimited power of states to control or regulate the use of indigenous lands, without regard to constitutional limits on governmental power, which would otherwise be applicable.[62] In 2006, the Human Rights Committee asked the United States whether such a principle set forth in US practice complies with Articles 1 and 27 of the ICCPR.[63] In this manner, the Committee clearly indicated its dissatisfaction with the application of such doctrine.

Indeed, the whole concept of native title raises issues of discrimination against indigenous peoples. If the title is inferior to other land rights recognised for the rest of the population, the state has to justify the difference of treatment on the basis of necessity and for legitimate purposes. Article 5 of the International Convention for the Elimination of All Forms of Racial Discrimination clearly establishes non-discrimination concerning 'the right to own property alone as well as in association with others';[64] the Convention prohibits discrimination both in law and in fact.[65] In its Advisory Opinion on Minority Schools in Albania, the International Court of Justice noted that 'equality in law precludes discrimination of any kind; whereas equality in fact may involve the necessity of different treatment in order to attain a result which establishes an equilibrium between different situations'.[66] UN Special Rapporteur Daes has also stressed that the concept of native title 'is itself discriminatory in that it provides only defective, vulnerable and inferior legal status for indigenous land and resource ownership'.[67]

CERD has repeatedly raised issues of discrimination in the relevant Australian legislation. After the *Mabo* decision, the (1993) Native Title Act[68] attempted to find the balance between indigenous land rights and third party interests. After consultations with indigenous leaders, the act allowed validation of prior land dealings, a discriminatory measure for indigenous peoples, but provided two measures for indigenous recovery of their land rights: the freehold standard, which required native title to be treated in the same way as freehold title; and the right to negotiate about certain land use in the future. Unfortunately, both the freehold standard and the right to negotiate were restricted in the (1998) Native Title Amendment Act. Also, the 1998 Act expanded the extinguishment of native title to privately owned land (including family homes or freehold farms), residential, commercial and certain other leases and in areas where the government has built roads or other public works.[69] CERD has been highly critical of the 1998 Act and has issued no less than three decisions condemning it.[70] According to the committee, the Australian native title is a discriminatory legal arrangement, since other land rights are better protected against interference and forced alienation.[71] All is not bleak though: other states have recently expanded their protection of native title; for example, recent Malaysian case law has confirmed that native title prevails over other interests.[72]

Problems of proof

Problems of proof of indigenous ownership often occur in disputes over indigenous land rights. The passage of time can also increase the differences of view between indigenous peoples and states. The problem of the Sámi land rights in Finland has been ongoing for a while. After initiating several studies, the state insists that lands claimed by Saami are public lands belonging to the state. Finland has recently stated:

> From a legal perspective, it would be inappropriate to have the question of the titles of the Sámi to the land resolved by means of instituting court proceedings. The outcome of the proceedings could involve uncertainties relating e.g. to questions of evidence. Instead, adequate historical research based on archives could provide a sound basis for political decision-making.[73]

Indeed, courts often face problems in judging on the existence of a legal title. Differences in values between indigenous and non-indigenous peoples lead to a chasm between indigenous land systems and current national policies. Problems arise in transforming the link between the people and the land into a legal right. Most legal systems require a registered title to prove ownership of land. It is often assumed that land not formally registered belongs to the state; such assumptions have widely affected indigenous land rights in Latin America.[74] Indigenous have to demonstrate possession and intent, usually established by acts showing a sufficient assertion of physical dominion over the land, ranging from construction of fences, cultivation of crops or grazing of animals, in general acts that demonstrate substantial maintenance or connection between them and the land. However, indigenous communities do not generally use their lands for such activities. Thus, the existing standards presuppose value-based judgments about the 'efficient use' of the land and other conditions to which indigenous peoples can prove vulnerable: the legal title can be refused to indigenous communities on the ground that they have not invested sufficient labour or derived sufficient production to show assertion of physical dominion.[75]

Fortunately, the Court noted in *Mabo (No. 2)* that the nature and incidents of native title must be ascertained as a matter of fact by reference to the laws and customs of the indigenous inhabitants who possess that title.[76] This means that possession must be considered according to indigenous interpretations. National courts in other parts of the world have also reached similar conclusions. In the United States, it was held that the legal question concerning occupancy of the land would be solved 'in accordance with the way of life, customs and usages of [the indigenous people] who are its users and occupiers'.[77] In Canada, the majority found in *Delgamuukw* that occupancy sufficient to support aboriginal title should be based on both 'the physical occupation of the land in question' and 'the pattern of land holdings in Aboriginal law'.[78] In establishing occupation, the court will take into consideration the group size, manner of life, the material resources that are utilised by technology and the character of the land claimed.[79] Many Latin American states have designed measures that take into account indigenous customary norms in administrative and legal proceedings dealing with land rights.[80]

Moreover, in *Delgamuukw* the Court asked for exclusive occupancy. Proof of exclusion of others from the land would be useful, including through war, own laws (such as trespass laws), and recognition of the boundaries of indigenous land by neighboring groups. A joint title between two nations has also been confirmed as possible.[81] In *Delgamuukw*, the Court further accepted the use of indigenous oral histories as proof of historical facts and ruled that 'this kind of evidence can be accommodated and placed on an equal footing with the types of historical evidence that courts are familiar with, which largely consists of historical documents'. This constitutes an important victory for indigenous peoples.[82]

National courts have also asked for continued occupation of the land prior to the assertion of the occupants. *Delgamuukw* ruled that occupation includes physical presence on the land and must be proved to the confines of the territories. This ruling fails to address the problem of indigenous peoples that have been removed from their traditional areas. If the *Dulgamuukw* ruling prevails and physical occupation is necessary to prove native title, groups that have been removed would lose their claims even for compensation. This would be quite unfair, especially since they may still be very close to the territory that was taken away from them. The situation in Australia is similar. Although Toohey J questioned the criterion of current physical presence in *Mabo (No. 2)*,[83] Australian courts have been demanding high levels of proof of continuous occupation, to the extent that many Australian aborigines cannot obtain legal title.

All these conditions in national laws and courts should always be in accordance with standards of international law. For example, Article 13 of ILO Convention No. 169 does not require continuous actual presence in the territory in question. CERD has highlighted the situation and asked Australia to acknowledge the customs and traditions of indigenous peoples in this respect.[84] More generally, conditions of exclusivity and continuity must not discriminate against indigenous peoples, either directly or indirectly either in law or in practice; such are the requirements of the Convention against Racial Discrimination.

Indeed, there is a growing trend to adapt the rules of evidence and requirements of proof to indigenous perceptions. This suggests that the courts are attempting to take into account the cultural identity of indigenous communities and beginning to show some willingness to consider indigenous perceptions of land ownership and occupation.

Demarcation, a formal process to formally identify locations and boundaries of indigenous lands and to physically mark such boundaries on the ground, can be very helpful in issues of proof. In 1988, the Preparatory Meeting of Indigenous Organisations noted the importance of demarcation:

> In most instances, the territories of indigenous peoples are not clearly identified or demarcated within the national legal system of States. This situation perpetuates uncertainty and facilitates States governments and other third parties to infringe upon the territorial rights of indigenous peoples.[85]

Demarcation is encouraged by international law. Article 14 (2) of ILO Convention No. 169 urges governments to 'take steps as necessary to identify the lands which the peoples concerned traditionally occupy'. The importance of demarcation has been noted repeatedly by the Inter-American Commission on Human Rights in its 1997 Report on Brazil[86] and the Inter-American Court of Human Rights in the *Awas Tingni* v. *Nicaragua*[87] and most recently, the *Moiwana Village* case, where the Court ordered Suriname to delimitate and demarcate the traditional territories of an indigenous group.[88] Recently, CERD has also commented on Venezuela's efforts to demarcate indigenous lands, as in the promulgation of the Indigenous Peoples Habitat and Lands, Demarcation and Protection Act.[89] The Human Rights Committee has recently commented on the slow pace of demarcation of indigenous lands in Brazil as well as the forced evictions of indigenous populations from their land and the lack of legal remedies to reverse these evictions and compensate the victimised populations for the loss of their residence and subsistence.[90] Also, the draft Declaration urges states to take measures to identify indigenous lands (Article 27).

Non-implementation of strong legislation

Finally, some States recognise collective ownership, through native title or otherwise, but do not follow up these proclamations with a strong system of implementation. In 1997, the Philippines introduced the Indigenous Peoples Rights Act drafted on the basis of ILO Convention No. 169. The Act provides indigenous peoples with a wide range of rights over ancestral domains and ancestral rights, including ownership over their lands and resources. The Act has been a major breakthrough for the protection of indigenous peoples, but the government has not allocated funds for its implementation and has even adopted subsequent policies that have contradicted it.[91] A similar fate has met the 2001 Cambodian Land Law; in the spirit of ILO Convention No. 169, Article 26 of the law proclaims that ownership of indigenous lands is recognised by the state as collective ownership; this right includes all components of individual ownership. Although the law is very important, it has not been implemented yet. Similar weaknesses in the implementation of the relevant legislation exist in the Russian Federation.[92] In 2004, the Committee on Economic, Social and Cultural Rights blamed the lack of implementation of strong communal indigenous land rights in Ecuador for its negative effects on indigenous health and the equilibrium of the ecosystem.[93]

Rights of consultation and participation

The right of indigenous peoples to negotiate and participate in decision making is of paramount importance, as it is linked to fundamental principles of law, such as democracy, constitutionalism and the rule of law, and the protection of sub-national groups.[94] Rights of consultation and participation touch upon the internal aspect of the right to self-determination and go beyond mere voting, as the right of every citizen to take part in the conduct of public affairs must be realised on a basis of equality and in circumstances in which persons 'are able to develop and express their identities as members of different communities within larger societies'.[95] Although groups do not have an unconditional right to choose the modalities of their participation in the conduct of the public affairs,[96] the Human Rights Committee has emphasized in its General Comment 23(50) the importance of *effective* participation of members of minorities in decisions that affect them,[97] as has the UN Minority Declaration.[98] The Human Rights Committee has noted that 'indigenous populations should have the opportunity to participate in decision-making in matters that concern them'[99] and has positively commented on examples of devolution concerning indigenous communities.[100] Lack of participation is a violation of Article 5(c) of the International Convention against All Forms of Racial Discrimination. In its General Recommendation XXIII (1997), CERD stressed the importance of ensuring that 'members of indigenous peoples have equal rights in respect of effective participation in public life, and that no decisions directly relating to their rights and interests are taken without their informed consent'.[101] The Committee called on states to 'recognise and protect the rights of indigenous peoples to own, develop, control and use their common lands, territories and resources'. Standards of participation and consultation and comments by international bodies on this matter are also applicable to decisions related to land rights.

Earlier, we saw how the CEACR of the ILO has focused on issues of indigenous participation and consultation related to land rights. The United Nations bodies have also repeatedly highlighted such issues.[102] Recently, CERD indicated that mere participation of indigenous peoples is not adequate. In the Concluding Observations on the 2005 Nigeria Report, CERD criticised states for lack of *meaningful* consultation with indigenous peoples about the effects of oil production activities in their areas.[103] This was the essence of the CERD concerns about the Australian Native Title Amendment Act 1998.[104] The Committee had warned against the restriction of the right of indigenous title holders to negotiate non-indigenous land uses and in particular the *level* of negotiations between the government and indigenous communities before the adoption of the Act. The Australian government replied that further negotiations with indigenous peoples were not deemed appropriate for reasons of parity in the treatment of indigenous and pastoralists.[105] The government also noted that indigenous peoples have the same participatory rights as the rest of the population.[106] The reply of the government ignores the obligation of the state to take positive measures to ensure that discrimination against racial groups does not occur in law and in practice. CERD issued a further decision, Decision 2 (55),[107] reaffirming its earlier decision. In its Concluding Observations on Australia's report, the Committee reiterated in 2000:

> its recommendation that the States party ensure effective participation by indigenous communities in decisions affecting their land rights, as required under article 5(c) of the Convention and General Recommendation XXIII of the Committee, which stresses the importance of ensuring the 'informed consent' of indigenous peoples.[108]

The view of CERD is in agreement with ILO Convention No. 169 and its requirement that governments consult indigenous populations 'through appropriate procedures and in particular through their representative institutions' for matters that affect them;[109] Convention No. 169 also recognises the right of indigenous peoples to decide their own priorities and to exercise control over their development 'as far as possible'.[110] The draft Declaration also includes indigenous rights of participation and consultation with particular reference to land rights.[111] The Inter-American system has also stressed the importance of consultation with and participation of indigenous people in land issues that affect them in the *Awas Tingni* case.[112] In 1998, the Inter-American Commission of Human Rights found that Nicaragua had violated Awas Tingni rights to property by granting a concession to a company to carry out road construction work and logging exploitation without the consent of the Awas Tingni community.[113] Subsequent failure by the government to resolve the situation led to a 2001 decision of the Inter-American Court of Human Rights that confirmed the violation of land rights, including the right of the Awas Tingni indigenous peoples to participation and consultation. Other international bodies that have spoken in favour of indigenous participation in land rights include the 1992 United Nations Conference on Environment and Development (UNCED); the European Community;[114] and several international agencies working in sectors such as hydropower, forestry and conservation.[115]

Do international standards go so far as to require that indigenous peoples *consent* in matters related to the lands they live in? A 2005 legal commentary notes that 'the principle of free, prior informed consent is acknowledged in several international human rights law instruments'[116] and argues that such a right 'is grounded in and is a function of indigenous peoples' inherent and prior rights to freely determine their political status, freely pursue their economic, social and cultural development and freely dispose of their natural wealth and resources – a complex of inextricably related and interdependent rights encapsulated in the right to self-determination, to their lands, territories and resources'.[117] Indeed, Article 7 of the ILO Convention No. 169 recognises indigenous peoples' right 'to decide their own priorities for the process of development' and 'to exercise control, to the extent possible, over their own economic, social and cultural development'. The 'to the extent possible' weakens the provision. The Convention clearly requires consent of indigenous peoples for relocation (Article 16). Both the United Nations draft Declaration on the rights of indigenous peoples and the Inter-American Declaration on Indigenous Rights go further and ask for prior and informed consent before relocation and development projects. United Nations bodies have also gradually started referring to the requirement of consent, rather than consultation. In its General Recommendation CERD called upon states to ensure that 'no decisions directly relating to their rights and interests are taken without their informed consent'. The Committee on Economic, Social and Cultural Rights has also recently asked for the consent of indigenous peoples in matters of resource exploitation.[118] In 2005, the Inter-American Court on Human Rights also asked for the consent of indigenous peoples in demarcating their territories.[119] Although other international bodies have acknowledged the need for prior informed consent by indigenous peoples and several such national laws have been adopted in the Philippines, New Zealand and Colombia,[120] it may be too far-reaching to suggest that prior and informed consent is required in all matters affecting indigenous land rights. Such consent, however, gradually seems to emerge in relation to development projects directly affecting indigenous peoples and is already a standard – albeit with exceptions – concerning the relocation of indigenous peoples.

Even if current standards fall short of requiring indigenous consent in all matters that relate to their land rights, mere consultation is not adequate. Consultation not in good faith or without intending to address the concerns of the indigenous community falls below the existing standards. The duty to consult entails more than mere information sharing, but can take several forms, including discussions or meetings with local leaders and individuals or with local organisations or communities, establishment of local advisory boards, indigenous membership on protected area management boards, informed involvement in development of management plans, active participation in development of management plans or local authorisation of protected area establishment, management plans, policies, and regulations.[121] It may also include: exchanges of information and opinions related to specific proposals; development and negotiation of consultation protocols; site visits to explain the nature of the proposals; and the undertaking of traditional use studies. Effective consultations will involve entire communities rather than special groups within the indigenous group. National policies concerning formal consultation institutions and procedures for indigenous participation have to show flexibility and willingness to adjust to local cultural and political conditions.[122]

Rights of use, management and resources

Claims of indigenous peoples for the use and management of the lands they live in have a similar legal basis to indigenous land ownership. The Human Rights Committee has proclaimed that violation of the indigenous right to engage in traditional economic activities amounts to a violation of their right to enjoy their culture.[123] While the regulation of economic activity is normally a matter for state, the Committee has repeated that if the activity in question is 'an essential element in the culture of an ethnic community',[124] there is a violation of Article 27 of the ICCPR. The Committee has also suggested that when it comes to traditional activities, equal rights to indigenous and non-indigenous persons may have adverse consequences for the traditional activities of the former; the traditional rights of indigenous peoples must have priority.[125] This was affirmed in the Committee's criticism in their 2005 comments on Thailand's (1992) Master Plan on Community Development, Environment and Narcotic Crop Control in Highland Areas and its negative impact on indigenous peoples' livelihood and way of life.[126] This demonstrates how reluctant the Committee is to accept restrictions on indigenous traditional activities, even for a legitimate reason. In 2000, the Committee had noted that:

> in many areas native title rights and interests remain unresolved [and] in order to secure the rights of its indigenous population under article 27 ... the

necessary steps should be taken to restore and protect the titles and interests of indigenous persons in their native lands . . . [S]ecuring continuation and sustainability of traditional forms of economy of indigenous minorities (hunting, fishing and gathering), and protection of sites of religious or cultural significance for such minorities, [are rights] that must be protected under article 27 . . .[127]

The Committee has also demonstrated interest in the Sámi traditional means of subsistence in Finland – in particular reindeer breeding – and has asked whether the divisions of lands in private and public endanger their traditional culture, way of life, and hence their identity.[128] The UN Committee on Economic, Social and Cultural Rights has also urged Norway to ensure that the Finnmark Act gives due regard to the rights of the Sámi people to participate in the management and control of natural resources in the county of Finnmark.[129]

Article 14(1) of ILO Convention No. 169 follows the same line as the Human Rights Committee. It urges states to take measures to safeguard indigenous rights to use lands not exclusively occupied by them, but to which they have traditionally had access for their subsistence and traditional activities. Particular reference is made to the situation of nomadic peoples and shifting cultivators. The draft Declaration includes even wider protection of indigenous rights to pursue traditional activities.[130]

The ways in which traditional economic activities are exercised do not have to remain old-fashioned; the Human Rights Committee has clarified that within the scope of Article 27, traditional economic developments can be adapted to modern developments. McGoldrick has reflected on the omission of the Committee to refer to the margin of appreciation of the states concerning Article 27; he has noted that 'any reference to the doctrine of 'margin of appreciation' in the Committee's jurisprudence remains conspicuous by its absence'.[131] In the *Selbu* case,[132] the Norwegian Supreme Court held that when considering whether the conditions for establishing a right to reindeer herding in a particular area based on immemorial usage are met, one has to take into account the special conditions for Sámi reindeer herding, including the nomadic lifestyle and the lack of visible signs of activity due to their traditional way of life. Prior to this judgment it had been difficult for people engaged in reindeer herding to obtain rights in cases where there was competing use of the land in question. The *Selbu* case is considered to be a milestone and will be an important source of law in similar cases.[133]

Contrary to Norwegian jurisprudence, Canadian jurisprudence is more cautious. Although Canadian courts have recognised the indigenous right to use land for traditional activities,[134] *Van der Peet* established that the activity in question must satisfy the 'distinctive culture test', i.e. be integral to the pre-contact indigenous culture of the indigenous community.[135] Lokan maintains that the test

> attempts to find the dividing line between matters of such significance to indigenous peoples that they should be within the zone of privilege where laws of general application do not intrude, and those matters where the normal sovereignty of the States is undiluted.[136]

Eisenberg has rightly criticised the test.[137] Apart from its ethnocentric focus,[138] the distinctive culture test sets the pole higher than international law standards: no international body requires such a strong link between the indigenous culture during the time before the settlers arrived and today, and no instrument has established the time of contact with the newcomers as a landmark for indigenous rights. In *Diergaardt*, the Human Rights Committee asked for proof that the link between indigenous and their land was 'the result of a relationship that would have given rise to a distinctive culture';[139] this test does not go as far as the 'distinctive culture test'.

Unfortunately, neglect of international standards on the protection of indigenous traditional activities is not uncommon. Indigenous peoples often face severe restrictions in exercising their traditional activities, especially if the lands they live in have rich natural resources.[140] States repeatedly use the argument of economic development and alleged necessity to restrict indigenous rights. For example, in 2002, in his reply to human rights concerns of the Human Rights Committee the representative of Vietnam said that:

> The human rights obligations under the Covenant were universal, but they existed alongside the collective right to self-determination and the right to determine a country's process of development.[141]

The question whether indigenous peoples can claim rights over the natural resources of the lands they live in is not a resolved issue in international law. The draft Declaration on Indigenous Rights recognises the right of indigenous peoples to their lands, territories and resources (Article 26.1) and their right to 'own, use, develop, and control the resources that they possess' (Article 26.2). It also expects indigenous consent for the 'development, utilisation or exploitation of their resources' (Article 32). The use of natural resources continues to be one of the most controversial issues in international law, mainly because of the pivotal economic repercussions.[142] Common Article 1(2) of both the International Covenants recognises the right of *peoples* to freely dispose of their natural wealth and resources' and not to 'be deprived of [their] own means of subsistence', while Article 47 of the ICCPR gives *peoples* the right 'to enjoy and utilise fully and freely their natural wealth and resources'. As international law does not clarify who 'a people' is, there is disagreement between indigenous peoples and states on whether indigenous are the beneficiaries of these articles. The Human Rights Committee has indicated that indigenous peoples fall within the scope of Articles 1(2) and 47: in its comments on reports on Canada, Mexico and Australia, the Committee has dealt with the right to natural resources of indigenous peoples calling upon their right to self-determination, as enshrined in Article 1 of the International Covenants.[143] Traditionally though, in cases concerning the negative effects of multinational companies on indigenous rights, the Committee has sidestepped the controversial issue of indigenous rights to natural resources and has used the 'safer' right to traditional activities and the right of minorities to a culture. In *Ominayak* v. *Canada*,[144] the Committee found that a Canadian Government lease over Indian land that was to be used for commercial timber activities would violate Article 27 because it would destroy the traditional life of the Lubicon Lake Band. Although no violation was found in *Länsman* v. *Finland*,[145] the Committee warned that any future mining activities on a large scale 'may constitute a violation of the authors' right under Article 27, in particular of their right to enjoy their culture'. Making a shift, in *Hopu* v. *France*[146] the Committee used the right to family and privacy, as they could not use Article 27 of the ICCPR;[147] the Committee held that a construction of a hotel located on indigenous ancestral grounds would violate the right to family and privacy, because it would destroy the owners' traditional burial grounds, which can play an important role in a person's identity.[148]

ILO Convention No. 107 is not very clear on the matter of natural resources; however, ILO Convention No. 169 is as helpful as it is realistic on the matter. Article 15 of ILO Convention No. 169 recognises that governments often retain some of the natural resources for their own exclusive ownership, but provides indigenous peoples with rights 'to the natural resources pertaining to their lands. These rights include the right of these peoples to participate in the use, management and conservation of these resources'. Paragraph 2 notes that even when states own mineral resources, consultations before permitting exploitation or even exploration must take place. Thus, whilst recognising the principle of state sovereignty over resources, the provision also notes the need for prior consultation with indigenous peoples. In a 1999 case against Bolivia, the ILO Governing Body held that states must

> undertake to ensure that the indigenous communities concerned are consulted promptly and adequately on the extent and implications of exploration and exploitation activities, whether these are mining, petroleum or forestry activities.[149]

The ILO Governing Body has suggested that environmental, cultural, social and spiritual impact studies, conducted jointly with indigenous peoples,[150] and appropriate consultations with indigenous peoples should take place before any exploration and exploitation of natural resources in areas traditionally occupied by them.[151] The Committee of Experts of the ILO has also commented in several of its observations on projects that had negative impacts on indigenous peoples.[152] The approach of the ILO Convention is in line with the United Nations Declaration on Development. Article 2 (3) of the Declaration establishes states' right and duty to formulate development policies aiming at the development of the whole population and all individuals 'on the basis of their active, free and meaningful participation in development and in the fair distribution of the benefits resulting therefrom'. The Commission on Human Rights has in its Resolution 2000/5 reaffirmed the importance of the right to development for individuals and peoples alike. A number of international monetary organisations have recently been paying attention to the effects of their policies on indigenous rights. After years of criticism, the World Bank adopted Operational Directive 4.20, designed to condition Bank projects to ensure borrower government adherence to indigenous standards.[153] In 1998, the Asian Development Bank also adopted a similar policy on indigenous peoples.[154]

Even though indigenous rights currently form part of the debate on development projects, such projects continue to take place without consideration of their effect on indigenous peoples. Contrary to pronouncements by states, such projects also often have catastrophic effects on the whole population of states, putting in question the 'wider good' on which they are justified. Colchester et al. note:

> contrary to the expectations of those who have favoured land markets as an engine for 'development', there is widespread evidence that land and resource mobilisation has actually increased poverty, landlessness and environmental damage in indigenous areas.[155]

Nevertheless, environmental degradation is still used by states to curtail indigenous rights, rather than development projects. For example, the practice of indigenous shifting cultivation is seen as unacceptable as being environmentally destructive; therefore, indigenous peoples are pushed to engage in fixed cultivation.[156] The representatives of Vietnam stated in CERD Committee in August 2001:

> Unfortunately the mountain peoples employed traditional cultivation methods and burned the forests, thereby causing major environmental disasters in the form of floods affecting millions of people living downstream along the Mekong river. The Government was therefore endeavouring to persuade ethnic groups to adopt a settled method of cultivation, even though the latter would require large-scale investment from the Government so as to ensure adequate water supplies for rice-growing.[157]

Such forms of 'persuasion' go against the protection of 'customary use of biological resources in accordance with traditional cultural practices' in the Convention on Biological Diversity (Article 10(c)). The provision requires recognition of indigenous control over and use of natural resources within the context of respect for indigenous self-determination and self-government.[158] Also, paragraph 22 of the 1992 Declaration on Environment and Development (Rio Declaration) maintains:

> Indigenous peoples and their communities and other local communities have a vital role in environmental management and development because of their knowledge and traditional practices. States should recognise and duly support their identity, culture and interests and enable their effective participation in the achievement of sustainable development.

Human Rights bodies have specifically addressed the issue of environmental degradation in relation to indigenous peoples. In *Lubicon Lake Band* and in *Länsman*, the Human Rights Committee affirmed that the environment forms part of the traditional way of life and culture of indigenous peoples and must be protected as such. Spiliopoulou has concluded that even though the protection of the environment is not part of Article 27 of the ICCPR, 'the application of Article 27 is highly relevant for the environmental protection of considerable areas in many countries'. Other bodies have also commented on the issue. The Committee on Social, Economic and Cultural Rights has noted that 'the traditional lands of indigenous peoples have been reduced or occupied, without their consent, by timber, mining and oil companies, at the expense of the exercise of their culture and the equilibrium of the ecosystem'.[159] CERD has also expressed its deep concern 'about the adverse effects on the environment of ethnic communities through large-scale exploitation of natural resources in the Delta Region and other River States, in particular, the Ogoni areas'.[160]

Removal and relocation

In several states, indigenous peoples are removed from their territories.[161] States' justifications for forced relocations vary from economic reasons to environmental reasons, natural disasters or internal strife. In some cases, indigenous peoples are the victims of the interests of multinational corporations; they are often the ones that pay the price of economic progress made without their consent or even consultation with them.

Forced removals have tremendous consequences for the physical and cultural survival of indigenous groups and make them 'internally displaced persons'. Internally displaced persons have been defined as:

> Persons that have been forced to flee their homes suddenly or unexpectedly in large numbers, as a result of armed conflict, internal strife, systematic violations of human rights or natural or man-made disasters; and who are within the territory of their own country.[162]

There is no international instrument that explicitly protects against relocation.[163] The right not to be internally displaced falls within the freedom of movement and the right to choose one's residence, as guaranteed in Article 13 (1) of the Universal Declaration, Article 12 (1) of the ICCPR,[164] Article VIII of the American Declaration, Article 22 (1) of the American Convention, Article 2 (1) of the Fourth Protocol to the European Convention and Article 12 (1) of the African Charter. Although movement and residence are subject to restrictions 'which are provided by law, are necessary to protect national security, public order (*ordre public*), public health or morals or the rights and freedoms of others, and are consistent with the other rights recognized . . .',[165] such limitation clauses must be interpreted restrictively. It is doubtful whether the development of the economic life of states constitutes an adequate reason to cause such negative changes to a group's life.

In the last decade, United Nations bodies have renewed their efforts to address internal displacement. The UN Security Council has 'affirmed the right of refugees and displaced persons to return to their homes'.[166] The Vienna Declaration and Programme of Action of the World Conference on Human Rights[167] called upon States to give special attention and find lasting solutions to the problems of internally displaced persons. In 1994, the Sub-Commission on Prevention of Discrimination and Protection of Minorities expressed its concern over the growing number of internally displaced persons and affirmed 'the right of persons to remain in peace in their own homes, on their own lands and in their own countries'.[168] Several regional initiatives in Latin America, Europe and Africa have also expressed similar concerns.[169] In 1998, the UN Guiding Principles on Internal Displacement affirmed that every person has the right to be protected against arbitrary displacement from his place of habitual residence and referred to states' obligations for the realisation of this human rights.[170] Currently, United Nations monitoring bodies often refer to relocations of indigenous peoples. The Human Rights Committee has raised issues of compensation for the displacement of the Thule community in Greenland.[171] Human Rights monitoring bodies have recently highlighted relocations of indigenous peoples in Colombia,[172] Brazil[173] and Venezuela.[174] In the concluding observation on Laos, CERD elaborated on the obligations of states concerning relocations:

> The Committee recommends that the State party ... study all possible alternatives with a view to avoiding displacement; that it ensure that the persons concerned are made fully aware of the reasons for and modalities of their displacement and of the measures taken for compensation and resettlement; that it endeavour to obtain the free and informed consent of the persons and groups concerned; and that it make remedies available to them ... The preparation of a legislative framework setting out the rights of the persons and groups concerned, together with information and consultation procedures, would be particularly useful.[175]

In this respect, the Committee followed the standards set by ILO Convention No. 169. Article 12 of ILO Convention No. 107 prohibits 'removal', 'except in accordance with national laws and regulations for reasons relating to national security or in the interest of national economic development or of the health of the said populations'. The variety and vagueness of exceptions and the lack of consultation requirement weakens the prohibition considerably; however, as seen earlier, the Committee of Experts has interpreted the provision in a way that corresponds more to corresponding Article 16 of ILO Convention No. 169. Article 16 allows relocation of indigenous peoples, but only as an exceptional measure. The decision whether the measure is necessary will probably be made by the state, however with the free and informed consent of the group in question. When the consent of indigenous peoples cannot be obtained, 'such relocation shall take place only following appropriate procedures established by national laws and regulations, including public inquiries where appropriate, which provide for the effective representation of the people concerned'. The Article prescribes that indigenous peoples should 'where possible' have the option of return, 'as soon as the conditions for relocation have ceased to exist' and, where return is not possible, a right to lands of 'at least' equal quality and legal status to the former lands, or to compensation in kind or in money.

Contrary to ILO Convention No. 169, the draft Declaration does not set any conditions for forced relocation of indigenous groups. This omission has been the subject of criticism. It has been suggested that the requirement of a public hearing with effective participation contained in Article 16(2) of ILO Convention No. 169 may be the best safeguard for the protection of indigenous land rights, because it ensures that removals will be subjected to a judicial process rather than executive decree. In this respect, the protection of Article 10 of the draft Declaration is viewed as weaker than that of Article 16 of Convention No. 169. However, it appears that Article 10 excludes any possible relocation without the consent of indigenous groups, whereas Convention No. 169 allows states to go ahead with it, even without indigenous consent. The importance of indigenous consent on the matter is also stressed by the repetition of the condition in Article 30 of the draft Declaration. A reference to an independent arbitration for issues of relocation has been suggested,[176] yet this suggestion again allows the possibility of relocations, especially since the independence of any national tribunal can be questionable. Thus, the current language of the draft Declaration protects indigenous groups more than ILO Convention No. 169.

Restitution and compensation

Article 10 of the draft Declaration on the rights of indigenous peoples also refers to no relocation without compensation and, where possible, the option of the return of indigenous peoples to their original lands. The right to restitution is not well established in international law, even though compensation is.[177] Several international bodies have focused generally on reparations for human rights violations. A United Nations study on reparations by Theo van Boven noted that 'restitution shall be provided to violations of human rights. Restitution requires, inter alia, restoration of liberty, citizenship or residence, employment or property'.[178] In the landmark *Velasquez* case, the Inter-American Court on

Human Rights held that 'reparation of harm brought about by the violation of an international obligation consists in full restitution which includes the restoration of the prior situation'.[179] Among other bodies, the Human Rights Committee has also repeatedly called for reparation for violations of human rights recognised in the Covenant.[180]

ILO Convention No. 169 is quite cautious on the issue of restitution. Article 16(3) prescribes that 'whenever possible', indigenous peoples 'shall have the right to return to their traditional lands, as soon as the grounds for relocation cease to exist'. Although this is a positive step, the Convention avoids referring to the restitution of indigenous lands that have been taken away from them in the past. There is a view that this can be deduced from Article 16 in conjunction with Article 14(3) that requires 'adequate procedures ... within the national system to resolve land claims' by indigenous peoples. This provision does not establish any temporal restriction, thus it can be argued that it even refers to claims originating well in the past. Anaya suggests:

> Article 14(3) is the response to the historical processes that have afflicted indigenous peoples, processes that have trampled on their cultural attachment to ancestral lands, disregarded or minimised their legitimate property interests, and left them without adequate means of subsistence. In the light of the acknowledged centrality of lands and resources to indigenous cultures and economies, the requirement to provide meaningful redress for indigenous land claims implies an obligation on the part of states to provide remedies that include for indigenous peoples the option of regaining lands and access to natural resources.[181]

Yet, Article 14 does not fully support Anaya's position. Restitution is considered with respect to relocation only, rather than dispossession. In other words, the Convention does not go so far as giving indigenous peoples who have lost their lands the right to restitution.

Can the general principle of restitution also apply to violations of indigenous land rights? Waldron questions indigenous justifications for restitution.[182] He argues that the First Occupancy claim that justifies restitution on the basis of indigenous historical priority is 'inherently objectionable', as it incites chauvinistic feelings and is 'historically precarious', since it is not possible to prove which group was first on the land. The second basis for indigenous restitution, the Established Order Claim, justifies restitution claims on the basis of prior occupancy. However, Waldron argues, 'while this principle condemns injustice at one particular point in time, it can equally work to vindicate established patterns of settlement that are founded upon that injustice'.[183] In contrast, Falk is supportive of such indigenous claims. He has noted that claims for restitution of past injustices represent 'a search for intergenerational equity' and give rise to 'a greater sense of time consciousness with respect to past and future, making such intergenerational concerns part of the subject matter of justice and hence of humane governance'.[184] Ted Moses of the Grand Council of the Crees explains the indigenous position:

> The function of article 27 is to reverse the process of dispossession. It does not send the non-indigenous occupiers back to their homelands, rather it establishes a process of restitution that leads to the removal of the taint upon the sovereignty of the States, and seeks to return wherever possible, ownership to the original owners. Where this is not possible, compensation with the consent of indigenous peoples is a defined resolution.
>
> What is so controversial and unreasonable about that?[185]

Restitution in indigenous cases gives rise to conflicts with interests of third parties. The balancing between indigenous need to restitution and non-indigenous rights and recent history in these same lands drives states to close their ears to voices for restitution.[186] The statement by the United States highlights the point:

> We doubt... whether restitution is a viable means for resolving such issues in most States. For this reason, we believe that the Declaration should call on States to consider the possibility of negotiated settlements, including restitution, as appropriate.[187]

Canada also has pushed for the alternative of compensation:

> While the article mentions the right of restitution or compensation in the form of lands and resources of equal quality, size and legal status, consideration might also be given to allowing for alternatives which provide for fair and just compensation.[188]

Indeed, compensation is considered a less complicated option. Theo van Boven has explicitly referred to the entitlement of indigenous peoples to compensation in cases of damage resulting from exploration and exploitation programmes pertaining to their lands, and in cases of their relocation.[189] He has also noted the interaction of individual and collective aspects in indigenous rights and, consequently, a necessity for provisions 'to entitle groups of victims or victimized communities to present collective claims for damages and to receive collective reparation accordingly'.[190]

Compensation is often examined by international and national judicial bodies when assessing the legitimacy of an interference with property.[191] Pursuant to the non-discriminatory principle, indigenous peoples should have at least the same right to compensation as the rest of the population when they lose their land rights. In General Recommendation XXIII (51), CERD recognised the right to just, fair and prompt compensation for violations of indigenous land rights.[192] Leading cases in several states, including Australia,[193] Canada[194] and the USA,[195] have affirmed the right of indigenous peoples to compensation when their land rights have been legally restricted. It must be noted that states' arguments that shift the obligation for compensation to transnational organisations violating indigenous rights are not valid. Although the Transnational Corporations' Code of Conduct urges corporations to respect social and cultural objectives, values and traditions of the countries in which they operate and to respect the human rights and fundamental freedoms in the countries in which they operate,[196] the prime responsibility for protection of human rights lies with states.

Concluding comments

The above analysis has demonstrated that although international human rights instruments do not include strong protection of indigenous land rights, interpretation of these instruments by their monitoring bodies has expanded their scope and has to a degree accommodated indigenous claims. Unfortunately, their role is restricted to interpretation rather than law-creation. Still, the contribution of such documents cannot be underestimated. Through the elaboration of existing routes, new avenues for the protection of indigenous lands are explored. Apart from international norms, national case law has also been helpful, even though at times falling short of international standards. National courts are still in the process of coming to terms in dealing with indigenous land rights; although on a few occasions they fall below international standards, they are usually useful in interpreting and elaborating international standards. The ILO Conventions are certainly helpful; Convention No. 169 in particular goes quite far in its protection of indigenous rights and sets out specific rules on important aspects of land rights, including ownership, use and management of indigenous lands. Although the draft Declaration offers a very extensive range of rights, it still does not cover all indigenous concerns related to land rights: it includes no provision for shared use of land or pastoral peoples similar to Article 14(1) of ILO Convention No. 169; no provision encouraging additional land to allow for future growth and development, similar to Article 19 of the Convention No. 169; and no obligation on states to assist indigenous peoples in developing their lands, similar to Article 19.[197] Yet, the limited application of Convention No. 169 seriously restricts its possible impact on indigenous land rights. Thus, even though most indigenous claims seems to be in broad agreement with current international law standards, new instruments would help clarify and consolidate these standards.

Notes

1. Statement of Kekula P. Bray-Crawford of Hawaii, representing the indigenous peoples of the Pacific, Commission Drafting Group, 21 October–1 November 1996 (on file with author).
2. Human Rights Committee, General Comment No. 23(50), UN Doc. CPR/C/21/Rev.1/Add.5, para. 7.
3. M. Cobo, *Study of the Problem of Discrimination Against Indigenous Populations*, Volume V (Geneva: United Nations, 1981), paras. 196–7.
4. Article 15.
5. ATSIC, *Native Title Amendment Bill 1997, Issues for Indigenous Peoples* (Australia: ATSIC, 1997), p. 5.
6. Statement made by the International Indian Treaty Council, Report of the Commission Drafting Group, UN Doc. E/CN.4/1997/102, para. 248.
7. J. Burger, 'The Economic Rights of Indigenous Peoples' in L. van der Vlist (ed.), *Voices of the Earth, Indigenous Peoples, New Partners and the Right to Self-Determination in Practice* (Utrecht: The Netherlands Centre for Indigenous Peoples, 1994), p. 195.
8. For example, see J. Castellino, 'Conceptual Difficulties and the Right to Indigenous Self-Determination' in N. Ghanea and A. Xanthaki (eds.), *Minorities, Peoples and Self-Determination* (Dordrecht: Martinus Nijhoff, 2005), pp. 55–74.
9. A. Rosas, 'The Right to Self-Determination' in A. Eide, C. Krause and A. Rosas (eds.), *Economic, Social and Cultural Rights, A Textbook* (Dordrecht: Martinus Nijhoff, 1995), pp. 79–86 at p. 83.
10. E. Spiry, 'From "Self-Determination" to a Right to "Self-Development" for Indigenous Groups' (1995) 38 *German Yearbook of International Law* 129–52 at 136; Spiry notes that 'the label "internal self-determination" is biased, and should be abandoned in favour of more "neutral" and objective expressions, such as "self-government" or, if we include economic rights, . . . "self-development" or "self-preservation" '.
11. Report of the Working Group on Indigenous Populations, UN Doc. E/CN.4/Sub.2/2001/17 para. 38; also see J. Henriksen, 'Implementation of the Right of Self-Determination of Indigenous Peoples' (2001) 3 *Indigenous Affairs* 6–21 at 10.

12. G. Alfredsson, 'Different Forms of and Claims to the Right to Self-Determination' in D. Clark and R. Williamson (eds.), *Self-Determination: International Perspectives* (London: Macmillan Press, 1996), pp. 58–86 at p. 74.
13. *Certain Phosphate Lands in Nauru (Nauru* v. *Australia)*, Preliminary Objections, Judgment, *ICJ Reports* (1993), 243. The parties reached settlement and the proceedings before the Court were discontinued.
14. The Declaration on the Right to Development was adopted by the General Assembly in its Resolution 41/128 of 4 December 1986.
15. Vienna Declaration and Programme of Action, World Conference on Human Rights, Vienna, 14–25 June 1993, UN Doc. A/CONF.157/23 (1993), para. 10.
16. Paragraph 2 of the Preamble.
17. Human Rights Committee, Consideration of Reports submitted by States Parties under Article 40 of the Covenant, Venezuela, UN Doc. CCPR/C/VEN/1998/3 (1999), para. 6.
18. Human Rights Committee, Consideration of Reports submitted by States Parties under Article 40 of the Covenant, Peru, UN Doc. CCPR/C/PER/1998/4 (1999), para. 2.
19. For example, Human Rights Committee, Consideration of Reports submitted by States Parties under Article 40 of the Covenant, the Philippines, UN Doc. CCPR/C/PHIL/2002/2 (2002), p. 88; also Human Rights Committee, Consideration of Reports submitted by States Parties under Article 40 of the Covenant, Russian Federation, UN Doc. CCPR/C/RUS/2002/5 (2002), para. 6.
20. *Ibid.*
21. Compilation of General Comments and General Recommendations Adopted by Human Rights Treaty Bodies, UN Doc. HRI/GEN/1 (1992), para. 5.
22. K. Knop, *Diversity and Self-Determination in International Law* (Cambridge: Cambridge University Press, 2002), p. 19.
23. C. Chinkin and S. Wright, 'The Hunger Trap: Women, Food and Self-Determination' (1993) 14 *Michigan Journal of International Law* 262–321 at 294.
24. J. Donnelly, 'Human Rights, Democracy and Development' (1999) 21 *Human Rights Quarterly* 608–32.
25. G. Abi-Saab, 'Technological Development and the Right to Development' in L.-A. Sicilianos and M. Gavouneli (eds.), *Scientific and Technological Developments and Human Rights* (Athens: Ant. N. Sakoulas Publishers, 1996), p. 266.
26. J. Donnelly, 'In Search of a Unicorn: The Jurisprudence of the Right to Development' (1985) 12 *California International Law Review* 473–509.
27. See Human Rights Committee, *Lovelace* v. *Canada*, Communication No. 24/1977, Views in A/36/40 (1981); *Kitok* v. *Sweden*, Communication No. 197/1985, views in A/43/40 (1988); *Ominayak* v. *Canada*, Communication No. 167/1984, UN Doc. A/45/40 (1990); also *Länsman* v. *Finland*, Communication No. 511/1992, UN Doc. CCPR/C/52/0/511/1992 (1993); *Hopu* v. *France*, Communication No 549/1993, UN Doc. CCPR/C.60/D/549/1993/Rev.1 (1997).
28. Para. 5 of the General Recommendation XXIII (51) concerning Indigenous Peoples of 18 August 1997, CERD/C/51/Misc.13/Rev.4.

29. *Eastern Greenland* case (1933), *PCIJ Series* A/B, no. 53, 46. In this case, the Court held that Denmark had sovereignty over all of Greenland and dismissed the claim of Norway that part of Greenland, the Eirik Raudes Land, was *terra nullius* when Norway issued a declaration of occupation in 1931. Irrespective of the outcome, the Court accepted and discussed the idea of *terra nullius*.
30. *Western Sahara* case, *ICJ Reports* (1975), 12.
31. (1992) 107 A.L.R. 1.
32. R. P. Hill, 'Blackfellas and Whitefellas: Aboriginal Land Rights, the Mabo Decision, and the Meaning of Land' (1995) 17 *Human Rights Quarterly* 303–22.
33. Amongst the vast bibliography generally on the *Mabo No. 2* decision, see 15 (1993) 2 *Sydney Law Review*, a special issue dedicated to the *Mabo No. 2* decision; also, M. Manwaring, 'A Small Step or a Giant Leap? The Implications of Australia's First Judicial Recognition of Indigenous Land Rights: *Mabo and Others* v. *State of Queensland* (1993) 34 *Harvard International Law Journal* 177–91.
34. CERD, Summary record of the first part of the 1481st meeting: China, Viet Nam. 30/08/2001, UN Doc. CERD/C/SR.1481, para. 11.
35. Article 17.
36. E. Lucas, 'Towards an International Declaration on Land Rights' (1984) 33 *Review (International Commission of Jurists)* 61–8 at 64.
37. *Ibid.*
38. Article 8 of the draft Declaration. On the question of possible genocide concerning violations of indigenous lands, see M. A. Greer, 'Foreigners in their own Land: Cultural Land and Transnational Corporations – Emergent International Rights and Wrongs' (1998) 38 *Virginia Journal of International Law* 331–97 at 359–64.
39. Article 14 of ILO Convention No. 169.
40. M. Colchester, F. MacKay, T. Griffiths and J. Nelson, 'A Survey on Indigenous Land Tenure, A Report for the Land Tenure Service of the Food and Agricultural Organisation', December 2001, p. 63.
41. Report of the Committee set up to examine the representation alleging non-observance by Peru of the Indigenous and Tribal People's Convention, 1989 (No. 169), made under Article 24 of the ILO Constitution by the General Confederation of Workers of Peru (CGTP), Submitted 1997, Documents: GB.270/16/4 and GB.273/14/4.
42. CEACR, Individual Observation concerning Convention No. 169, Indigenous and Tribal Peoples, 1989, Peru, Published: 1999, paras. 3–6.
43. See *Kitok* v. *Sweden*, *Ominayak* v. *Canada*, *I. Länsman et al.* v. *Finland*, *J. Länsman et al.* v. *Finland* as well as General Comment No. 23 [50], para. 7.
44. In *Diergaardt et al.* v. *Namibia* (760/1997), UN Doc. Namibia 06/09/2000, CCPR/C/69/D/760/1996, para. 10.8, the Committee rejected a special link of the Rehoboth way of life to the lands covered by their claims, on the ground that although the link dated back 125 years, this link was not the result of a distinct culture.

45. Inter-American Court on Human Rights, *Mayagna (Sumo) Community of Awas Tingni* v. *Nicaragua*, Case No. 11.555P, Series C No. 79; judgment of 31 August 2001. See P. Macklem and E. Morgan, 'Indigenous Rights in the Inter-American System: The Amicus Brief of the Assembly of First Nations in Awas Tingni v. Republic of Nicaragua' (2000) 22 *Human Rights Quarterly* 569–602.
46. S. J. Anaya, *Indigenous Peoples in International Law* (Oxford: Oxford University Press. 2nd edn 2004), pp. 145–6 and 266–71.
47. *Delgamuukw* v. *British Columbia* [1997] 3 S.C.R. 1010, para. 117.
48. For Australian cases before the *Mabo* case, see R. B. Lumb, 'Aboriginal Land Rights: Judicial Approaches in Perspective' (1988) 62 *Australian Law Journal* 273–284.
49. *Delgamuukw* case [1997] 3 S.C.R. 1010, 153 D.L.R. (4th) 193, [1998] 1 C.N.L.R. 14, 37 I.L.M. 268.
50. For an overview of Canadian case law on the subject, see K. McNeil, 'Aboriginal Title and Aboriginal Rights: What's the Connection?' 36 (1997) *Alberta Law Review* 117–48.
51. See 'A Short guide to Native Title, Revised edition, March 2000', at www.nntt.govau/nntt/publictn.nsf.
52. A. Lokan, 'From Recognition to Reconciliation: The Functions of Aboriginal Rights Law' (1999) 23 *Melbourne University Law Review* 65–120 at 89.
53. Freehold estates extinguish native title rights because the rights that flow from freehold lands (including the right to exclusive possession) are inconsistent with native title based on traditions and customs. Where such inconsistency is apparent, native title rights are extinguished. See the judgment of Brennan J as well as Toohey J in *Mabo*, as explained in M. Mansell, 'Australians and Aborigines and the Mabo decision: Just who needs whom the most?' (1993) 15 *Sydney Law Review* 168–77 at 170.
54. Erica-Irene Daes, 'Indigenous Peoples and their Lands: Preliminary Working Paper', UN Doc. E/CN.4/Sub.2/1997/17, 20 June 1997 and Corr.1, p. 12.
55. *Sparrow* [1990] 1 S.C.R.
56. *Ibid.*; see L. I. Rotman, 'Defining Parameters: Aboriginal Rights, Treaty Rights, and the *Sparrow* Justificatory Test' (1997) 36 *Alberta Law Review* 149–79.
57. *Ibid.*, 417–18.
58. *Ibid.*, 412.
59. *Delgamuukw* case [1997] 3 S.C.R., 1111.
60. Concluding Observations of the Human Rights Committee: Canada. 07/04/99. UN Doc. CCPR/C/79/Add. 105, para. 8.
61. Concluding Observations of the Human Rights Committee, Canada, UN Doc. CCPR/C?CAN/CO/5 of 20 April 2006, para. 8.
62. See P. Frickey, 'The Status and Rights of Indigenous Peoples in the United States' (1999) *Zeitschrift für ausländisches öffentliches Recht und Völkerrecht (Heidelberg Journal of International Law)*, Special issue 383–404.
63. Human Rights Committee, List of issues to be taken up in connection with the consideration of the second and third periodic reports of the United

States of America, Advanced Unedited Version, CCPR/C/Q/3 of 30 March 2006.
64. Article 5(c) and (d) (v) of the Convention.
65. Articles 1.1 and 2.1(a).
66. [1935] PCIJ (series A/B), No. 64, 19. The ECJ affirmed this principle in the *South West Africa Cases (Second phase)*, 6 [1966] *ICJ Reports*, 303–4.
67. Daes, 'Indigenous Peoples and their Lands', p. 11.
68. See Report of Ms G. McDougall, Country Rapporteur to the Committee on the Elimination of All Forms of Racial Discrimination (CERD) in www.faira.org.au/cerd/racial-discrimination.html.
69. For a thorough analysis of the Native Title Amendment Act, see G. Triggs, 'Australia's Indigenous Peoples and International Law: Validity of the *Native Title Amendment Act 1998* (CTH)' 23 (1999) *Melbourne University Law Review* 372–415; for the comments of CERD concerning the Native Title Amendment Act, see http//www.faira.org.au.
70. CERD, Findings on the Native Title Amendment Act 1998, UN Doc. ERD/C/54/Misc.40/Rev.2 (28 March 1999), 6–8 and CERD 1998 Decision 1 (53) adopted on 11 August 1998, UN Doc. A/53/18; CERD Decision 2 (54) adopted on 18 March 1999, UN Doc. A/54/18; and Decision 2 (55) adopted on 16 August 1999, UN Doc. A/54/18.
71. For an elaborate analysis, see P. Thornberry, *Indigenous Peoples and Human Rights* (Manchester: Manchester University Press, 2002), pp. 218–23.
72. Colchester, MacKay, Griffiths and Nelson, *A Survey on Indigenous Land Tenure*, p. 17; A. Xanthaki, 'Land Rights of Indigenous Peoples in Southeast Asia' (2003) 2 *Melbourne Journal of International Law* 467–96.
73. Committee on Economic, Social and Cultural Rights, Implementation of the International Covenant on Economic, Social and Cultural Rights, Finland, UN Doc. E/C.12/FIN/5 of 8 February 2006, para. 69.
74. See R. Grote, 'The Status and Rights of Indigenous Peoples in Latin America', (1999) *Zeitschrift für ausländisches öffentliches Recht und Völkerrecht (Heidelberg Journal of International law)*, Special issue, 497–528 at 512.
75. Lokan, 'From Recognition to Reconciliation', pp. 74–5.
76. (1992) 107 *Australian Law Review* 1, 2 (iv).
77. *Sac and Fox Tribe of Indians of Oklahoma* v. *United States* (1967) 383 F 2d 991, at 998.
78. *Delgamuukw* case [1997] 3 S.C.R., 1099–100.
79. *Ibid.*, 1099–101.
80. See Grote, 'The Status and Rights of Indigenous Peoples in Latin America' at 511–16. For the Amazonian countries, see United Nations, Working paper prepared by Mr R. Roldan, in Report of Expert Seminar on Practical Experiences Regarding Indigenous Land Rights and Claims, held in Whitehorse, Canada in March 1996, UN Doc. E/CN.4/Sub.2/AC.4/1996/6/Add.1, 22–32.
81. *Delgamuukw* case [1997] 3 S.C.R., 1106 and 1129.
82. *Ibid.*, para. 87. For the indigenous understanding and discussion of the *Delgamuukw* case, see Assembly of First Nations, Aboriginal Title and

Comprehensive Claims, Conference Report, Winnipeg, Manitoba, 24–25 February 1998, AFN Land Rights Unit, April 1998. For analysis of the case see also M. Hehan, 'Delgamuukw v. British Columbia' (1998) 22 *Melbourne University Law Review* 763–82; also W. F. Flanagan, 'Piercing the Veil of Real Property Law: *Delgamuukw* v. *British Columbia*' (1998) 24 *Queen's Law Journal* 279–326.

83. See *Mabo No. 2* case, per Toohey J, 146–7; also see Mansell, 'Australians and Aborigines and the Mabo decision', 171.
84. Concluding Observations of the Committee on the Elimination of Racial Discrimination, Australia, UN Doc. CERD/C/AUS /CO/14 of 14 April 2005, para. 17.
85. Universal Declaration on Indigenous Rights, A Working Paper, Preparatory Meeting of Indigenous NGOs, July 25–29, 1988, Geneva, para. 19.
86. Inter-American Commission on Human Rights, *Report on the Situation of Human Rights in Brazil*, 1997, chapter VI, J.
87. Anaya, 'Indigenous Peoples in International Law', 267–71; Macklem and Morgan, 'Indigenous Rights in the Inter-American System'.
88. Inter-American Court of Human Rights, Case of *Moiwana Village* v. *Suriname*, Judgment of 15 June 2005.
89. Concluding Observations of the Committee on the Elimination of Racial Discrimination, Venezuela, UN Doc. CERD/C/VEN/CO/18 of 1 November 2005, para. 20.
90. Concluding Observations of the Human Rights Committee, Brazil, UN Doc. CCPR/C/BRA/CO/2 of 1 December 2005, para. 6.
91. D. Novellino, 'The Ominous Switch: From Indigenous Forest Management to Conservation – The case of the Batak on Palawan island, the Philippines' in M. Colchester and C. Erni (eds), *Indigenous Peoples and Protected Areas in South and Southeast Asia*, IWGIA Document No. 97, (Copenhagen: IWGIA, 1999) 250–97 at 273.
92. Concluding Observations of the Committee on Economic, Social and Cultural Rights, Russian Federation, UN Doc. E/C.12/1/Add.94 of 12 December 2003, para. 39; see also A. Xanthaki, 'Indigenous Rights in the Russian Federation: The Case of Numerically Small Peoples of the Russian North, Siberia and Far East' (2004) 26 *Human Rights Quarterly* 74–105.
93. Concluding Observations of the Committee on Economic, Social and Cultural Rights, Ecuador, UN Doc. E/C.12/1/Add.100 of 7 June 2004, para. 12.
94. See *Reference re Secession of Quebec* [1998] 2 S.C.R. 217; 161 D.L.R.(4th) 385; 37 ILM 1342, para. 90.
95. Articles 25, 26 and 27 of the *ICCPR*.
96. Human Rights Committee, *Mikmaq People* v. *Canada*, Communication No. 205/1986, Views in A/47/40 (1992).
97. Human Rights Committee, *General Comment No.23(50)*, UN Doc. CCPR/C/21/ Rev.1.Add..5, 5.
98. Article 2(3) of the *United Nations Declaration on the Rights of Members belonging to National or Ethnic, Religious and Linguistic Minorities*. At the European level, it is

included in para. 24 of the 1992 OSCE Helsinki Document and Article 15 of the Framework Convention for National Minorities.

99. Mexico, A/49/40 (1994), para. 182.
100. Norway, *ibid.*, para. 89.
101. CERD, General Recommendation XXIII Concerning Indigenous Peoples, UN Doc. CERC/C/51/Misc.13/Rev.4 (1997).
102. For example, Concluding Observations of the Human Rights Committee, Thailand, UN Doc. CCPR/CO/84/THA of 8 July 2005, para. 24 and *ibid.*, Colombia, 26/05/2004, UN Doc. CCPR/CO/80/COL of 26 May 2004, para. 20, and *ibid.*, Suriname, UN Doc. CCPR/CO/80/SURI of 4 May 2004, para. 21; also Concluding Observations of the Committee on Economic, Social and Cultural Rights, Colombia, UN Doc. E/C.12/1/Add.74 of 30 November 2001, paras. 11 and 12; Concluding Observations of the Committee on the Elimination of Racial Discrimination, Laos, UN Doc. CERD/C/LAO /CO/15 of 18 April 2005, para. 18.
103. Concluding Observations of the Committee on the Elimination of Racial Discrimination, Nigeria, UN Doc. CERD/C/NGA/CO/18 of 1 November 2005, para. 19.
104. CERD 1998 Decision 1 (53) was adopted on 11 August 1998, UN Doc. A/53/18, para. IIB1; CERD 1999 Decision 2(54) was adopted on 18 March 1999, UN Doc. A/54/18, para. 21(2), see UN Doc. CERD/C/54/Misc.40/Rev.2 (18 March 1999), 8; also CERD 1999 Decision 2 (55) was adopted on 16 August 1999, UN Doc. A/54/18, para. 23 (2).
105. See Australia's Comments on Decision 2 (54) of 18 March 1999 pursuant to Article 9 (2) of the Convention, 3–4.
106. *Ibid.*, 4.
107. CERD 1999 Decision 2 (55) was adopted on 16 August 1999, UN Doc. A/54/18, para. 23 (2).
108. Concluding Observations by the Committee on the Elimination of Racial Discrimination: Australia. 24/03/2000, CERD/C/56/Misc.42/rev.3. (Concluding Observations/Comments), para. 9; also see Concluding Observations by the Committee on the Elimination of Racial Discrimination: Botswana: 23/08/2002, UN Doc. A/57/18, paras. 304.
109. Article 6.
110. Article 7.
111. See esp. Articles 26, 27, 29 and 32.
112. Judgment of the Inter-American Court of Human Rights in the case of *The Mayagna (Sumo) Indigenous Community of Awas Tingni* v. *Republic of Nicaragua*, issued 31 August 2001.
113. Inter-American Commission of Human Rights, Report No. 27/98 (Nicaragua), quoted in *The Mayagna (Sumo) Awas Tingni Community Case, Judgment on the Preliminary Objections of February 1, 2000*, Inter-Am. Ct. H.R. Series C No. 66, para. 22.
114. The European Community adopted a Resolution on Indigenous Peoples and Development which endorses the principle that initiatives on their lands should be subject to their agreement.

115. M. Colchester, M. Sirait, B. Wijardjo et al., 'The application of FSC Principles 2 and 3 in Indonesia: Obstacles and Possibilities' (2003), Study funded by DfID and Ford Foundation, p. 151.
116. 'Legal Commentary on the Concept of Free, Prior and Informed Consent', Expanded Working Paper submitted by Mrs. Antoinella-Iulia Motoc and the Tebtebba Foundation offering guidelines to govern the practice of implementation of the principle of free, prior and informed consent of indigenous peoples in relation to development affecting their lands and natural resources, UN Doc. E/CN.4/Sub.2/AC.4/2005/WP.1 of 14 July 2005, para. 11.
117. *Ibid.*, p. 15.
118. Concluding Observations of the Committee on Economic, Social and Cultural Rights: Ecuador, UN Doc. E/C.12/1/Add.100 of 7 June 2004 para. 12; also see *Ibid.*, Colombia, UN Doc. E/EC.12/Add.74 of 30 November 2001, para. 12.
119. Inter-American Court of Human Rights, Case of *Moiwana Village* v. *Suriname*, Judgment of 15 June 2005.
120. 'Legal Commentary on the Concept of Free, Prior and Informed Consent'.
121. S. Steven (ed.), *Conservation through Cultural Survival, Indigenous Peoples and Protected areas* (Washington: Island Press, 1997), p. 274.
122. *Ibid.*, 174–5.
123. *Ominayak* v. *Canada*, Communication No. 167/1984, UN Doc. A/45/40 (1990).
124. *Ivan Kitok* v. *Sweden*, Communication No. 197/1985, UN Doc. CCPR/C/33/D/197/1985 (1988).
125. See 1995 Swedish Report to the Human Rights Committee, CCPR/C/79, paras. 18 and 26.
126. Concluding Observations of the Human Rights Committee, Thailand, UN Doc. CCPR/CO/84/THA of 8 July 2005, para. 24.
127. Concluding Observations of the Human Rights Committee, Australia, 28/07/2000, CCPR/CO/69/AUS (Concluding Observations/Comments), para. 10.
128. Concluding Observations of the Human Rights Committee, Finland. 02/12/2004, UN Doc. CCPR/CO/82/FIN of 2 December 2004, para 17.
129. Committee on Economic, Social and Cultural Rights, Norway.
130. Articles 29, 31 and 32.
131. D. McGoldrick, *The Human Rights Committee: its Role in the Development of the International Covenant on Civil and Political Rights* (Oxford: Clarendon Press, 1991), p. 1xiii.
132. *Selbu* was a plenary judgment by the Supreme Court published in *Norwegian Supreme Court Reports* (2001) p. 769. See Human Rights Committee, Fifth Periodic Report, Norway, UN Doc. CCPR/C/NOR/2004/5, 3 December 2004, para. 250.
133. *Ibid.*
134. Lokan, 'From Recognition to Reconciliation', p. 94.
135. *R.* v. *Van der Peet* [1996] 2 S.C.R. 507, para. 76.
136. Lokan, 'From Recognition to Reconciliation', p. 98.

137. A. Eisenberg, 'The Distinctive Culture Test' (2005) 12 *Human Rights Dialogue* (Special Issue on Cultural Rights), Carnegie Council on Ethics and International Affairs, 26–7.
138. *Ibid.*
139. In *Diergaardt et al.* v. *Namibia* (760/1997), UN Doc. Namibia 06/09/2000, CCPR/C/69/D/760/1996.
140. Xanthaki, 'Land Rights of South-East Asian Indigenous Peoples'.
141. Human Rights Committee, Summary record of the 2020th meeting: Viet Nam. 17/07/2002, UN Doc. CCPR/C/SR.2020 (Summary Record), para. 6.
142. E. I. Daes, 'Indigenous Peoples' Rights to Land and Natural Resources' in Ghanea and Xanthaki (eds.), *Minorities, Peoples and Self-Determination*, pp. 75–112.
143. For Canada, see UN Committee on Human Rights, Consideration of Reports submitted by States Parties under Article 40 of the Covenant, Concluding Observations of the Human Rights Committee, Canada, 07/04/99, UN Doc. CCPR/C/79/Add. 105, para. 8. For Mexico, see UN Committee on Human Rights, Consideration of Reports submitted by States Parties under Article 40 of the Covenant, Concluding Observations of the Human Rights Committee, Mexico, 27/07/99, UN Doc. CCPR/C/79/Add. 109, para. 19. For Australia, see UN Committee on Human Rights, Consideration of Reports submitted by States Parties Under Article 40 of the Covenant, Concluding Observations of the Human Rights Committee, Australia (Advanced unedited version), UN Doc. CCPR/CO/69/AUS, para. 9.
144. *Ibid.*
145. *Ibid.*
146. *Ibid.*
147. France has made a reservation to Article 27, thus no finding was possible on this ground.
148. UN Committee on Human Rights, Australia, n. 143 above, para. 11.
149. Report of the Committee set up to examine the representation alleging non-observance by Bolivia of the Indigenous and Tribal Peoples Convention, 1989 (No. 169), made under Article 24 of the ILO Constitution by the Bolivian Central of Workers (COB), Submitted 1998 (Documents: GB.272/8/1 and GB.274/16/7), para. 38.
150. *Ibid.*, paras. 39 and 44.
151. *Ibid.*
152. See CEACR, Individual Observations concerning Convention No. 169 on Indigenous and Tribal Peoples: Mexico, published 1997, para. 7; Colombia, published 1999, para. 2; Mexico, published 1999, para. 11; Peru, published 1999, para. 7; Mexico, published 2000, para. 4.
153. A. Spiliopoulou-Åkermark, 'The World Bank and Indigenous Peoples' in Ghanea and Xanthaki, *Minorities, Peoples and Self-Determination*, pp. 93–112.
154. Colchester, MacKay, Griffiths and Nelson, *A Survey on Indigenous Land Tenure*, pp. 5 and 60.
155. *Ibid.*, 60.

156. G. Clarke, 'From Ethnocide to Ethnodevelopment? Ethnic Minorities and Indigenous Peoples in Southeast Asia' (2001) 22 *Third World Quarterly* 413–36 at 424–5.
157. CERD, Summary record of the first part of the 1481st meeting: China, Viet Nam. 30/08/2001, UN Doc. CERD/C/SR.1481, para. 11.
158. Convention on Biological Diversity, *Traditional Knowledge and Biological Diversity*, UNEP/CBD/TKBD/1/2, October 1997, 18.
159. Concluding Observations of the Committee on Economic, Social and Cultural Rights, Colombia, UN Doc. E/C.12/1/Add.74 of 30 November 2001, paras. 11 and 12.
160. Concluding Observations of the Committee on the Elimination of Racial Discrimination, Nigeria, UN Doc. CERD/C/NGA/CO/18 of 1 November 2005, para. 19.
161. See 'Transnational Investments and Operations on the Lands of Indigenous Peoples', Report of the Centre on Transnational Corporation submitted pursuant to Sub-Commission Resolution 1990/26 UN Doc. E/CN.4/Sub.2/1994/40.
162. 'Internally Displaced Persons', Report of the Representative of the Secretary-General Francis M. Deng, submitted pursuant to Commission on Human Rights Resolution 1995/57, Compilation and Analysis of Legal Norms, UN Doc. E/CN.4/1996/52/Add.2, para. 8.
163. *Ibid.*, paras. 269–84. On the issue of internally displaced persons see also N. Geisler, 'The International Protection of Internally Displaced Persons' (1999) 11 *International Journal of Refugee Law* 451–78; also C. Phung, 'Internally Displaced Persons and Refugees: Conceptual Differences and Similarities' (2000) 18 *Netherlands Quarterly of Human Rights* 215–29.
164. The right to movement is also guaranteed in Article VIII of the American Declaration, Article 22 (1) of the American Convention, Article 2 (1) of the Fourth Protocol to the European Convention and Article 12 (1) of the African Charter.
165. Article 12 (3) of the ICCPR.
166. United Nations Security Council Resolution 876 (1993) passed on 19 October 1993 in relation to the situation in Abkhazia.
167. The Vienna Declaration and Programme of Action are the outcome of the World Conference on Human Rights, held in Vienna 14–25 June 1993. See UN Doc. A/CONF.157/23, Part I, para. 23.
168. Sub-Commission Resolution 1994/24, para. 1. See Report of the Sub-Commission on Prevention of Discrimination and Protection of Minorities at its Forty-Sixth Session, Geneva, 1–26 August 1994, UN. Doc. E/CN.4/Sub.2/1994/56, 67.
169. The San José Declaration, the Permanent Consultation on Internal Displacement in the Americas, the OSCE and the Organisation of African Unity have repeatedly expressed their concern about internally displaced persons.
170. See UN Doc E/CN.4/1998/53/Add.2, Principles 6–9.

171. Concluding Observations of the Human Rights Committee, Denmark, UN Doc. CCPR/CO/80/DEN of 31 October 2000, para. 10.
172. Concluding Observations of the Committee on Economic, Social and Cultural Rights, Colombia, UN Doc. E/C.12/1/Add.74 of 30 November 2001.
173. Concluding Observations of the Committee on Economic, Social and Cultural Rights, Brazil, UN Doc. E/C.12/1/Add.87 of 23 May 2003, para. 36.
174. Concluding Observations of the Committee on the Elimination of Racial Discrimination, Venezuela, UN Doc. CERD/C/VEN/CO/18 of 1 November 2005, para. 20.
175. Concluding Observations of the Committee on the Elimination of Racial Discrimination, Laos, UN Doc. CERD/C/LAO /CO/15 of 18 April 2005, para. 18.
176. *Ibid.*
177. See Article 8 of the Universal Declaration on Human Rights, Article 2(3) of the ICCPR, Article 6 of the Convention against All Forms of Racial Discrimination.
178. United Nations Study concerning the right to restitution, compensation and rehabilitation for victims of gross violations of human rights and fundamental freedoms. Final report submitted by Mr Theo van Boven, Special Rapporteur, UN Doc. E/CN.4/Sub.2/19993/8, 57.
179. Inter-American Court on Human Rights, *Velasquez Rodriguez Case, Compensatory Damages* (Art. 63(1) American Convention on Human Rights), Judgment of 21 July 1989, Inter-Am.Ct.H.R. Series C No. 7 (1990), para. 26.
180. See, for example, Human Rights Committee Communications Nos. 4/1977, 6/1977, 11/1977, 132/1982, 138/1983, 147/1983, 161/1983, 188/1984, 194/1985 as quoted by the Court in the *Velasquez* case.
181. J. S. Anaya, *Indigenous Peoples in International Law*, (Oxford University Press: Oxford, 1st edn, 1996), pp. 106–7.
182. J. Waldron, 'Indigeneity?: First Peoples and Last Occupancy', 2002 Quentin-Baxter Memorial Lecture, 5 December 2002. The lecture was published in (2003) 1 *New Zealand Journal of Public and International Law* 56–77.
183. *Ibid.*
184. R. Falk, *Predatory Globalisation, A Critique* (Cambridge: Polity Press, 1999), p. 181.
185. Statement by Ambassador Dr Ted Moses on behalf of the Grand Council of the Crees, Commission Drafting Group, 21 October–1 November 1996, (on file with the author).
186. Lokan, 'From Recognition to Reconciliation', p. 67.
187. See Delegation of the United States of America, US Comments on Articles 27, 28 and 30, Commission Drafting Group, 21 October–1 November 1996, (on file with the author).
188. See Statement of Delegation of Canada on Articles 27, 28 and 30, Commission Drafting Group, Second session, 21 October–1 November 1996, (on file with the author).
189. *Ibid.*, para. 17.

190. *Ibid.*, para. 14.
191. See D. Anderson, 'Compensation for Interference with Property' [1999] *European Human Rights Law Reports* 543–58.
192. Paragraph 5, section 2 of CERD General Recommendation XXIII (51).
193. See *Mabo* case, (1992) 107 *Australian Law Review* 85 (Deane and Gauldron JJ, concurring).
194. See *Delgamuukw* case [1997] 3 S.C.R. 1134.
195. See *Sparrow* [1990] 1 S.C.R. 1075, 1099.
196. Code of Conduct on Transnational Corporations, UN ESCOR, Organisational Session for 1988, UN Doc. E/1998/39/Add.1, paras. 13 and 14.
197. These omissions were identified by the ILO Secretariat, see Comments on the draft United Nations Declaration on the rights of indigenous peoples, Note by the International Labour Office, UN Doc. E/CN.4/1995/119, para. 26.

Conclusions

Existing norms of international law build a framework that favours the preservation of indigenous collective identity, the underlying basis of all indigenous claims. International law standards are gradually moving away from the dichotomy between the state and the individual and endorse the multiple loyalties individuals have. The variety of cultures is celebrated and sub-national groups are perceived as part of 'a heterogeneous public', rather than merely 'the other'; groups are given control and the means to contribute as equals in the evolution of the national society. Multiple loyalties act as concentric circles around the individual and allow for the re-evaluation and ultimately the evolution of cultures. In this picture, indigenous claims for collective rights and control over their affairs can be accommodated. Recognition of indigenous collective rights bestows respect for indigenous identities and allows indigenous peoples to claim back the control over matters that affect them.

The international community has recently accepted the need for specific instruments to protect indigenous rights; ILO Conventions Nos. 107 and 169 address some of the claims of these peoples. Notwithstanding its integrationist and paternalistic character, ILO Convention No. 107 recognised basic indigenous rights whose violations were pertinent at the time of its adoption and forced states parties to take systematic and coordinated action for the protection of indigenous peoples. Major contributions of ILO No. 107 were also the establishment of special measures and the inclusion of land rights. Over the years, the ILO Committee of Experts on the Application of Conventions and Recommendations has managed to push towards progressive interpretation of the provisions that reflect the current standards of international law. Nevertheless, Convention No. 107 fails to satisfy several indigenous claims, including those for self-determination, control and participation. ILO Convention No. 169 goes much further, establishes wide indigenous rights and celebrates indigenous distinctiveness. Prominent features of the Convention are the recognition of indigenous consultation and participation in matters that affect them, the recognition of indigenous institutions, special measures and wide land rights. The Convention constitutes an essential and positive step in the evolution of standards on indigenous rights. Unfortunately, the small number of states that are parties to the Convention considerably weakens its impact. The United Nations is currently trying to fill the lacuna in indigenous protection with the draft Declaration on the rights of indigenous peoples. The text has to a large degree formed the basis of the indigenous debate in the United Nations; it includes a wide range of indigenous rights and reflects to a considerable extent indigenous aspirations. Although, when adopted by the UN General Assembly, it will not be strictly binding, it may generate political pressure on states to comply with its terms.

Apart from the instruments dedicated to their protection, indigenous peoples have been successfully using general human rights instruments and minority instruments. Although both sets of rights have not been constructed with the indigenous needs in mind and do not address their specific problems, their innovative interpretation by the United Nations monitoring bodies has covered several of the gaps and has accommodated indigenous peoples. Indigenous claims appeal to the dynamic and evolving character of international law and address the need for international law to engage with new challenges in the international arena.

Overall, most indigenous claims are consistent with current international law. Where not explicitly recognised, claims tend to be compatible with the spirit of international law. Compatibility does not involve the mere repetition of rights already recognised, but reflection on and evolution of existing standards. Reflection and continuous discussions about the challenges that indigenous claims pose, about their understandings and their needs, are invaluable for indigenous rights. Indeed, this book has shown how in the last twenty years and in the course of continuing discussions with indigenous peoples in United Nations fora, states have changed their positions – in some cases drastically. The debate on indigenous rights has also had immense impact on human rights in general. Re-evaluation and revisibility should not only be expected by cultural groups, but also by the international community. The indigenous debate, as expressed in the United Nations fora and beyond, has offered such an opportunity. It has highlighted different understandings of concepts, such as self-determination, culture and land, and has lead to re-evaluation of standards concerning non-state groups. It has also contributed to wider discussions in the international arena, such as the position of non-state actors and remedies for past injustices. Standards concerning indigenous rights are still fluid; the contours of international law are constantly stretched.

The greatest challenge indigenous peoples pose for international law is undeniably their claims for self-determination. This book has adopted an alternative understanding of the right of self-determination, away from the focus on secession and the specific applications of the right. It has been argued that the right cannot be seen merely as an addition to applications that have already been experienced. Even though these are of course an indication of how self-determination can be realised, new applications are possible. The indigenous discourse has highlighted some such possibilities, for example the participation of indigenous leadership in international fora and the recognition of indigenous political institutions. Recognition of indigenous self-determination would open the way for new, dynamic applications of self-determination. On the other hand, the right cannot become the shelter of all claims. In contrast to the *principle* of self-determination, the *right* of self-determination must maintain its political focus. In this respect, the principle of subsidiarity can be relevant: some indigenous claims could benefit by being grounded on other human rights, including the right to culture and the right to development, rather than on the fickle right to self-determination.

The need for this is all the greater because currently the possibility of extending the beneficiaries of the right to include non-state groups is still doubtful. The prevailing view among states maintains that indigenous peoples do not constitute 'peoples' according to Common Article 1 of the International Covenants and thus are not entitled to an unqualified right of self-determination. A radical interpretation that would overcome the hurdle of 'whole populations' of states is possible; United Nations bodies have repeatedly linked the right of self-determination with indigenous peoples. However, at the moment such interpretations do not prevail. Recognition of indigenous self-determination nevertheless seems possible, if indigenous peoples are acknowledged as a special case on the basis of their emphasis on respect, equal partnership and redress of past injustices. Then, the right of self-determination will not extend to other non-state groups. The draft Declaration on indigenous peoples allows for such an interpretation, though it also allows states to perceive indigenous self-determination merely as autonomy and participation in the life of the state. States may be more willing to accept such an approach. Other possibilities include the recognition of a qualified right of self-determination that would exclude prima facie secession or the protection of some aspects of self-determination without actual reference to the right. The second option has been already followed by ILO Convention No. 169.

In their majority, indigenous cultural claims can be satisfied by application of existing standards. When not recognised explicitly in international law, indigenous claims seem a natural next step. For example, although indigenous protection against cultural genocide is not explicitly included in international instruments, aspects of the concept are well-established and the underlying principle of the right well-protected. Therefore, its explicit recognition would not be against international standards. However, other indigenous cultural claims challenge current international law, as the latter focuses on state or individual ownership and promotes a commercial understanding of culture. However, lately there is some evidence that United Nations bodies endorse indigenous perceptions about culture. Continuous indigenous references to minority rights have also produced a growing jurisprudence on the matter. The most difficult challenge must be claims for indigenous intellectual property rights; the solution of a sui generis system solely for indigenous intellectual property rights may again provide a realistic solution.

Indigenous land rights are also gradually being recognised in the United Nations; however, although indigenous peoples view them as part of their right to self-determination, UN monitoring bodies have mainly advanced them as part of indigenous cultural rights. In recent times, concluding observations of monitoring bodies have placed indigenous land rights in the realm of self-determination. Recognition of collective land ownership is consistent with the ILO Conventions as well as some national systems. International law agrees that legal questions concerning occupancy of lands must be solved according to indigenous customs, traditions and means of proof; international bodies have also recognised the right of indigenous peoples to their traditional activities. The explicit recognition of this right in the Declaration would strengthen this position. The issue of relocation of indigenous peoples from their lands has also been evolving gradually: exceptions to its prohibition are being limited. Another evolving issue is that of natural resources. The protection of natural resources is established in ILO Convention No. 169, albeit very tentatively. Claims for indigenous ownership of natural resources challenge national systems of state ownership. General human rights, especially the right to development, can be used as a basis for indigenous claims for sharing of benefits, if not ownership. Recognition of such right will be facilitated, especially after the explicit recognition of indigenous as 'peoples'; the Human Rights Committee and CERD have already commented on this aspect of indigenous rights and the right to benefits is gradually taking its place among the standards of international law.

Equally challenging is the issue of restitution. On the issue of restitution of cultural objects international law entrusts only states the right to ask for their return. Even this possibility is contested in states' practice and literature. Nevertheless, more than ever the international community recognises the abuse of indigenous cultural objects by commercialisation and appropriation. On land rights Convention No. 169 makes a very cautious reference to the possibility of restitution. A broad right to restitution of indigenous land rights is not currently recognised by international law and, as expected, the majority of states are very reluctant to be bound by such a rule. Nevertheless, international standards constitute only the base for indigenous protection; states can always go beyond this protection. Moreover, the debate on restitution of indigenous claims is part of a wider debate emerging in the United Nations concerning restitution and reparation for victims of past injustices; reparation has been one of the themes of the 2001 World Conference on Racism. Compensation seems currently a more viable option for indigenous peoples, although continuing discussions on the issue may lead to the emergence of a broader consensus for restitution; certainly the dynamic nature of international law allows such a prospect.

Even though not all their specific claims can be satisfied by current standards of international law, the rights of indigenous peoples to their institutions and systems, control over their affairs and input in land decisions that affect them are all based on the principles of consultation and participation. Indeed, these principles are well-founded in international law, especially in minority instruments and ILO Convention No. 169. Consultation and participation satisfy the main indigenous claim for respect and equal partnership with the states in which they live. The level of control of indigenous peoples over matters that affect them will be decided after consideration of each case and all other relevant factors, including indigenous past histories of assimilation and paternalism, rights of others and the interests of the wider society. However, these factors cannot become mere justifications for the rejection of indigenous rights. Balancing these factors must follow the test of objectiveness, reasonableness, necessity and proportionality, as developed specifically in connection with indigenous rights by the Human Rights Committee.

The indigenous rights debate has contributed to the reinstatement of the United Nations as the primary organisation protecting human rights. One of the major criticisms of the United Nations system concerns the lack of cooperation among the UN bodies;[1] the case of indigenous peoples reveals a different reality. The system has been essential in the emergence and elaboration of new standards and has modified its rules and mechanisms to accommodate indigenous peoples and their claims. At the same time, indigenous belief in the United Nations has restored some of the credibility of the organisation.[2]

The debate on indigenous rights highlights the tensions that arise in human rights and the emergence of new standards. It poses questions about controversial human rights that are not fully developed, nor framed in legal instruments. Most of all, the debate on indigenous rights asks for commitment to the common values of the international community, especially on respect and celebration of difference. This book has hopefully illustrated ways in which such commitment can be demonstrated in international law.

Notes

1. C. Chinkin, 'International Law and Human Rights' in T. Evans (ed.), *Human Rights Fifty Years on: A Reappraisal* (Manchester: Manchester University Press, 1998) pp. 105–29 at p. 116.
2. R. Falk, *On Humane Governance, Toward a New Global Politics* (Cambridge: Polity Press, 1995), p. 243.

Bibliography

Abi-Saab, G., 'Technological Development and the Right to Development' in L.-A. Sicilianos and M. Gavouneli (eds.), *Scientific and Technological Developments and Human Rights* (Athens: Ant. N. Sakoulas Publishers, 1996)

Addis, A., 'Individualism, Communitarianism, and the Rights of Ethnic Minorities' (1992) 62 *Notre Dame Law Review* 615–76

Ahmed, L., *Women and Gender in Islam: Historical Roots of a Modern Debate* (New Haven: Yale University Press, 1992)

Aikio, P. and Scheinin, M. (eds.), *Operationalizing the Right of Indigenous Peoples to Self-Determination* (Turku/ Åbo: Åbo Akademi University, 2000)

Alexy, R., 'Individual Rights and Collective Goods' in C. Nino, *The Ethics of Human Rights* (Oxford: Oxford University Press, 1991), pp. 163–81

Alfredsson, G., 'International Law, International Organisations, and Indigenous Peoples' (1982) 36 *Journal of International Affairs* 113–24

'Different Forms of and Claims to the Right to Self-Determination' in D. Clark and R. Williamson (eds.), *Self-Determination: International Perspectives* (London: Macmillan Press, 1996), pp. 58–86

'Minorities, Indigenous and Tribal Peoples, and Peoples: Definitions of Terms as a Matter of International Law' in N. Ghanea and A. Xanthaki (eds.), *Minorities, Peoples and Self-Determination* (Dordrecht: Martinus Nijhoff, 2005), pp. 163–72

Alfredsson, G. and Macalister-Smith, P. (eds.), *The Living Law of Nations* (Kehl am Rhein: N. P. Engel, 1996)

Allott, P., 'The Nation as Mind Politic' (1992) 24 *New York University Journal of International Law and Politics* 1361–98

Alston, P. (ed.), *Peoples' Rights* (Oxford: Oxford University Press, 2001)

' "Core Labour Standards" and the Transformation of the International Labour Rights Regime' (2004) 15 *European Journal of International Law* 457–522

Anaya, J. S., 'The Capacity of International Law to Advance Ethnic or Nationality Rights Claims', 75 (1990) *Iowa Law Review* 837–44

'A Contemporary Definition of the International Norm of Self-Determination' (1993) 3 *Transnational Law and Contemporary Problems* 131–64

Indigenous Peoples and International Law, (Oxford: OUP, 1st edn 1996)
'The Influence of Indigenous Peoples on the Development of International Law' in S. Garkawe, L. Kelly and W. Fisher (eds.), *Indigenous Human Rights* (Sydney Institute of Criminology, 2001), pp. 109–117
Indigenous Peoples in International Law (Oxford: Oxford University Press, 2nd edn 2004)
'International Human Rights and Indigenous Peoples: The Move towards the Multicultural State' (2004) 21 *Arizona Journal of International and Comparative Law* 13–61
Anaya, J. S., Falk R., and Pharand D. (eds.), *Canada's Fiduciary Obligation to Aboriginal Peoples in the Comment of Accession to Sovereignty to Quebec, Papers prepared as part of the Research Program of the Royal Commission on Aboriginal Peoples*, (Ottowa: Minister of Supply and Services Canada, 1995)
Anderson, D., 'Compensation for Interference with Property' [1999] *European Human Rights Law Reports* 543–58
Anderson, R., 'Redressing Colonial Genocide under International Law: The Hereros' Cause of Action against Germany' (2005) 93 *California Law Review* 1155–89
Anghie, A., *Imperialism, Sovereignty and the Making of International Law* (Cambridge: Cambridge University Press, 2004)
An-Na'im, A. (ed.), *Human Rights in Cross-Cultural Perspectives* (Philadelphia: University of Pennsylvania Press, 1992)
Australian Human Rights and Equal Opportunities Commission, *Bringing them Home: Report of the National Enquiry into the Separation of Aboriginal and Torres Strait Islander Children from their Families* (AGPS: Canberra, 1997)
Avineri, S. and de-Shalit, A. (eds.), *Communitarianism and Individualism* (Oxford: Oxford University Press, 1992)
Baluarte, D. V., 'Balancing Indigenous Rights and a State's Right to Develop in Latin America: The Inter-American Rights Regime and ILO Convention 169' (2004) 4 *Sustainable Development Law and Policy* 9–15
Barsh, L. R., 'Indigenous North America and Contemporary International Law' (1983) 63 *Oregon Law Review* 73–125
Barsh, R., 'Indigenous Peoples in Vienna: What's next after the battle of the "s"?' in J. Patel (ed.), *Addressing Discrimination in the Vienna Declaration* (Tokyo: IMADR, 1995), pp. 23–30
Barsh, R. L., 'An Advocate's Guide to the Convention on Indigenous and Tribal Peoples' (1990) 15 *Oklahoma University Law Review* 209–36
'Indigenous Peoples and the UN Commission on Human Rights: A Case of Immovable Object and Irresistible Force' (1996) 18 *Human Rights Quarterly* 782–813
Bauer, J. R. and Bell, D. (eds.), *The East Asian Challenge for Human Rights* (Cambridge University Press, 1999)
Bayefsky, A., *Self-Determination in International Law: Quebec and Lessons Learned* (Dordrecht: Kluwer Law International, 2000)

Bedjaoui, M., *Towards an International Economic Order* (Paris: UNESCO, 1979)
Bennett, G. I., 'The ILO Convention on Indigenous and Tribal Populations – The Resolution of a Problem of *Vires*' (1972–3) 46 *British Yearbook of International Law* 382–92
Berman, H. R., 'The International Labour Organization and Indigenous Peoples: Revision of ILO Convention No. 107 at the 75th Session of the International Labour Conference, 1988' (1988) 41 *The Review (International Commission of Jurists)* 48–57
Blake, J., 'On Defining the Cultural Heritage' (2000) 49 *International and Comparative Law Quarterly* 61–85
Blakeney, M., 'Protecting Expressions of Australian Aboriginal Folklore under Copyright Law' (1995) 17 *European Intellectual Property Review* 442–5
Borah, W. W., *Justice by Insurance: The General Indian Court of Colonial Mexico and the Legal Aides of the Half-Real* (Berkeley: University of California Press, 1983)
Brölmann, C., Lefeber, R. and Zieck, M. (eds.), *Peoples and Minorities in International Law* (Dordrecht: Martinus Nijhoff Publishers, 1993)
Brölmann, C. M., and Zieck, M. Y. A., 'Some Remarks on the Draft Declaration on the Rights of Indigenous Peoples' (1995) 8 *Leiden Journal of International Law* 103–13
Brownlie, I., *Treaties and Indigenous Peoples*, (Oxford: Clarendon Press, 1966)
'The Rights of Peoples in Modern International Law' in J. Crawford (ed.), *The Rights of Peoples* (Oxford: Clarendon Press, 1988), pp. 1–16
Principles of Public International Law (Oxford: Oxford University Press, 4th edn 1990)
Brownlie, I. and Goodwill-Gill, G. S. (eds.), *Basic Documents on Human Rights* (Oxford: Oxford University Press, 2002)
Brysk, A., 'Turning Weakness into Strength: The Internationalization of Indian Rights' (1996) 32 *Latin American Perspectives* 38–57
Burger, J., 'Indigenous Peoples: Their Rights and International Action in the International Year and Beyond' in P. Morales (ed.), *Indigenous Peoples, Human Rights and Global Interdependence* (Geneva: International Centre for Human and Public Affairs, 1994), pp. 39–46
'The Economic Rights of Indigenous Peoples' in L. van der Vlist (ed.), *Voices of the Earth: Indigenous Peoples, New Partners and the Right to Self-Determination in Practice* (Utrecht: The Netherlands Centre for Indigenous Peoples, 1994)
'The United Nations Draft Declaration on the Rights of Indigenous Peoples' (1996) 6 *St. Thomas Law Review* 209–29
Burger, J. and Hunt, P., 'Towards the International Protection of Indigenous Peoples' Rights' (1994) 12 *Netherlands Quarterly of Human Rights* 405–23
Cassese, A., *Self-Determination of Peoples: A Legal Reappraisal* (Cambridge: Cambridge University Press, 1995), pp. 132–3
'The International Court of Justice and the Right of Peoples to Self-Determination' in V. Lowe and M. Fitzmaurice (eds.), *Fifty Years of the International Court of Justice, Essays in Honour of Sir Robert Jennings* (Cambridge: Grotius Publications, 1996), pp. 351–63

Castellino, J., *International Law and Self-Determination* (The Hague: Martinus Nijhoff, 2000)

'Conceptual Difficulties and the Right to Indigenous Self-Determination' in N. Ghanea and A. Xanthaki (eds.), *Minorities, Peoples and Self-Determination* (Dordrecht: Martinus Nijhoff, 2005), pp. 55–74

Chakma, S., 'Permanent Forum on Indigenous Issues: Chasing the Mirage' in IWGIA, *The Indigenous World 1999–2000* (Copenhagen: IWGIA, 2000), pp. 402–419

Children and Families of Ethnic Minorities, Immigrants and Indigenous Peoples, Summary Report of the Seventh Innocenti Global Conference, 6–15 October 1996 (Florence, Geneva: UNESCO, 1997)

Chinkin, C., 'International Law and Human Rights' in T. Evans (ed.), *Human Rights Fifty Years On, A Reappraisal* (Manchester: Manchester University Press, 1998), pp. 105–129

Chinkin, C. and Wright, S., 'The Hunger Trap: Women, Food and Self-Determination' (1993) 14 *Michigan Journal of International Law* 262–321

Cholewinski, R., 'State Duty towards Ethnic Minorities: Positive or Negative?' (1988) 10 *Human Rights Quarterly* 344–71

Christodoulidis, E. (ed.), *Communitarianism and Citizenship* (Aldershot: Ashgate, 1998)

Clark D. and Williamson R. (eds.), *Self-Determination: International Perspectives* (London: Macmillan Press, 1996)

Clarke G., 'From Ethnocide to Ethnodevelopment? Ethnic minorities and Indigenous Peoples in Southeast Asia' (2001) 22 *Third World Quarterly* 413–36

Clements, R., 'Misconceptions of Culture: Native Peoples and Cultural Property under Canadian Law' (1991) 49 *University of Toronto Faculty of Law Review* 1–26

Cobo, M., *Study of the Problem of Discrimination against Indigenous Populations* (Geneva: United Nations, 1981)

Colchester, M. and Erni, C. (eds.), *Indigenous Peoples and Protected Areas in South and Southeast Asia*, IWGIA Document No. 97 (Copenhagen: IWGIA, 1999)

Colchester, M., MacKay, M., Griffiths, T. and Nelson, J., *A Survey on Indigenous Land Tenure, A Report for the Land Tenure Service of the Food and Agricultural Organisation* (December 2001)

Colchester, M., Sirait, M., Wijardjo, B. et al., *The Application of FSC Principles 2 & 3 in Indonesia: Obstacles and Possibilities*, Study funded by DfID and Ford Foundation (2003)

Coomaraswamy, R., 'Identity within: Cultural Relativism, Minority Rights and the Empowerment of Women' (2002–3) 34 *George Washington International Law Review* 483–513

Coombe, R. J., 'The Properties of Culture and the Politics of Possessing Identity: Native Claims in the Cultural Appropriation Controversy' (1993) 6 *Canadian Journal of Law and Jurisprudence* 249–85

Crawford, J., *The Creation of States in International Law* (Oxford: Clarendon Press, 1979)

'The Rights of Peoples: "Peoples" or "Governments"?' in J. Crawford (ed.), *The Rights of Peoples* (Oxford: Clarendon Press, 1988), pp. 55–67

'The General Assembly, the International Court and Self-Determination' in V. Lowe and M. Fitzmaurice (eds.), *Fifty Years of the International Court of Justice, Essays in Honour of Sir Robert Jennings* (Cambridge: Grotius Publications, 1996), pp. 585–605

Book Review of *Self-Determination of People: A Legal Reappraisal* by A. Cassese (1996) 90 *American Journal of International Law* 331–3

'State Practice and International Law in Relation to Unilateral Secession' in A. Bayevsky, *Self-Determination in International Law: Quebec and Lessons Learned* (Dordrecht: Kluwer Law International, 2000), pp. 31–61

'The Right of Self-Determination in International Law: Its Development and Future' in P. Alston (ed.), *Peoples' Rights* (Oxford: Oxford University Press, 2001), pp. 7–67

(ed.), *The Rights of Peoples* (Cambridge: Clarendon Press, 1988)

Daes, E.-I., 'The Right of Indigenous peoples to "Self-Determination" in the Contemporary World Order' in D. Clark and R. Williamson, *Self-Determination: International Perspectives* (London: Macmillan Press, 1996), pp. 47–57

'A United Nations Permanent Forum for the World's Indigenous Peoples – A Global Imperative' in G. Alfredsson, J. Grimheden, B. G. Ramcharan and A. de Zayas (eds.), *International Human Rights Monitoring Mechanisms* (Dordrecht: Martinus Nijhoff, 2002), pp. 371–9

'Indigenous Peoples' Rights to Land and Natural Resources' in N. Ghanea and A. Xanthaki (eds.), *Minorities, Peoples and Self-Determination* (Dordrecht: Martinus Nijhoff, 2005), pp. 75–112

Dahl, J., Hicks, J., and Jull, P. (eds.), *Nunavut – Inuit Regain Control of their Lands and their Lives* (Copenhagen: IWGIA, 2000)

Debeljak, J., 'Barriers to the Recognition of Indigenous Peoples' Human Rights at the United Nations' (2000) 26 *Monash University Law Review* 159–94

Deer, K., 'An Indigenous Understanding of Self-Determination' in Y. N. Kly and D. Kly (eds.), *In Pursuit of the Right to Self-Determination* (Atlanta: Clarity Press, 2000), pp. 104–6

Delanty, G., 'Re-inventing Community and Citizenship in the Global Era: A Critique of the Communitarian Concept of Community' in E. Christodoulidis (ed.), *Communitarianism and Citizenship* (Aldershot: Ashgate, 1998), pp. 33–52

Dinstein, Y., 'Self-Determination Revisited' in *International Law in an Evolving World* (Montevideo, Uruguay: Fondacion de Cultura Universitaria, 1994), pp. 241–52

Dixon, M., *Textbook on International Law* (London: Blackstone Press Ltd, 3rd edn 1996)

Donders, Y. M., *Towards a Right to Cultural Identity?* (Antwerp: Intersentia, 2002)

Donders, Y., Henrard, K., Meijknecht, A. and Tempelman, S. (eds.), *Law and Cultural Diversity*, SIM Special No. 25 (Utrecht: SIM, 1999)

Donnelly, J., 'In Search of a Unicorn: The Jurisprudence of the Right to Development' (1985) 12 *California International Law Review* 473–509

'Human Rights, Democracy and Development' (1999) 21 *Human Rights Quarterly* 608–32

'Human Rights' in J. Dryzek, B. Honig and A. Phillips (eds.), *Oxford Handbook of Political Theory* (Oxford: Oxford University Press, 2006), extracts published in http://www.du.edu/~jdonnell/papers/oxford_handbook.pdf

Douglas, R. B. and Douglas, E. T. K., 'The Rights of the Indigenous Child: Reconciling the United Nations Convention on the Rights of the Child and the (Draft) Declaration on the Rights of Indigenous People with Early Education Policies for Indigenous Children' (1995) 3 *International Journal of Children's Rights* 197–211

Drahos, P., 'Indigenous Knowledge, Intellectual Property and Biopiracy: Is a Global Bio-Collecting Society an Answer?' (2000) 22 *European Intellectual Property Rights* 245–50

Drezov, K., Gokay B. and Kostovicova D. (eds.), *Kosovo: Myths, Conflict and War* (Keele: University of Keele, 1999)

Dworkin, R., *Taking Rights Seriously* (London: Duckworth, 1977)

Taking Rights Seriously (Cambridge, Mass.: Harvard University Press, 1978)

Sovereign Virtue: The Theory and Practice of Equality (Harvard University Press, 2000)

Eide, A., 'The National Society, Peoples and Ethno-Nations: Semantic Confusions and Legal Consequences' (1995) 64 *Nordic Journal of International Law* 353–67

'Peaceful Group Accommodation as an Alternative to Secession in Sovereign States' in D. Clark and R. Williamson, *Self-Determination: International Perspectives* (London: Macmillan Press, 1996), pp. 87–110

Eide, A., Krause, C. and Rosas, A. (eds.), *Economic, Social and Cultural Rights, A Textbook* (Dordrecht: Martinus Nijhoff, 1995)

Eisenberg, A., 'Context, Cultural Difference, Sex and Social Justice' (2002) 35 *Canadian Journal of Political Science* 613–28

'The Distinctive Culture Test' (2005) 12 *Human Rights Dialogue* (Special Issue on Cultural Rights) Carnegie Council on Ethics and International Affairs 26–7

Eisenberg, A. and Spinner-Halev, J. (eds.), *Minorities Within Minorities, Equality, Rights and Diversity* (Cambridge: Cambridge University Press, 2005)

Espiel, G. H., Study on the 'Implementation of United Nations Resolutions Relating to the Right of Peoples under Colonial or Alien Domination to Self-determination', UN Doc. E/CN.4/Sub.2/ 405/Rev.1 (1980)

Estebanez, M. M. M, *International Organisations and Minority Protection in Europe* (Turku/Åbo: Åbo Akademi, 1996)

Evans, T. (ed.), *Human Rights Fifty Years on: A Reappraisal* (Manchester: Manchester University Press, 1998)

Falk, R., 'The Rights of Peoples (In particular Indigenous Peoples)' in J. Crawford (ed.), *The Rights of Peoples* (Oxford: Clarendon Press, 1988), pp. 17–37

'Cultural Foundations for the International Protection of Human Rights' in A. An-Na'im (ed.), *Human Rights in Cross-Cultural Perspectives* (Philadelphia: University of Pennsylvania Press, 1992), pp. 43–64

On Humane Governance, Toward a New Global Politics (Cambridge: Polity Press, 1995)

Predatory Globalisation, A Critique (Cambridge: Polity Press, 1999)
Human Rights Horizons, The Pursuit of Justice in a Globalising World (New York: Routledge, 2000)
Fierlbeck, K., 'The Ambivalent Potential of Cultural Identity' (1996) 29 *Canadian Journal of Political Science* 3–22
Flanagan, W. F., 'Piercing the Veil of Real Property Law: *Delgamuukw* v. *British Columbia*' (1998) 24 *Queen's Law Journal* 279–326
Foster, C., 'Articulating Self-Determination in the draft Declaration on the Rights of Indigenous Peoples' (2001) 12 *European Journal of International Law* 141–57
Franck, T. M., 'The Emerging Right to Democratic Governance' (1992) 86 *American Journal of International Law* 46–91
'Postmodern Tribalism and the Right to Secede' in C. Brolmann, R. Lefeber and M. Zieck (eds.), *Peoples and Minorities in International Law* (Dordrecht: Martinus Nijhoff Publishers, 1993), pp. 3–27
Higgins, R., Pellet, A., Shaw, M. N. and Tomuschat, C., 'The Territorial Integrity of Quebec in the Event of the Attainment of Sovereignty' in A. Bayefsky, *Self-Determination in International Law: Quebec and Lessons Learned* (Dordrecht: Kluwer Law International, 2000), pp. 241–303
Friedman, M., *Autonomy, Gender, Politics* (Oxford: Oxford University Press, 2003)
Frow, J., 'Public Domain and Collective Rights in Culture' (1998) 13 *Intellectual Property Journal* 39–52
Garet, R., 'Communality and Existence: The Rights of Groups' (1993) 56 *South California Law Review* 1001–50
Garkawe, S., Kelly, L. and Fisher, W. (eds.), *Indigenous Human Rights* (Sydney Institute of Criminology, 2001)
Gayim, E. and Myntti, K., *Indigenous and Tribal Peoples' Rights – 1993 and After* (Roveniami: Northern Institute for Environmental and Minority Law, 1993)
Geisler, N., 'The International Protection of Internally Displaced Persons' (1999) 11 *International Journal of Refugee Law* 451–78
George, T. E., 'Using Customary International Law to Identify "Fetishistic" Claims to Cultural Property' (2005) 80 *New York University Law Review* 1207–36
Ghai, Y., *Public Participation and Minorities* (London: Minority Rights Group, 2001)
'Public participation, autonomy and minorities' in Z. A. Skurbaty (ed.) *Beyond a One-Dimensional State: An Emerging Right to Autonomy?* (Leiden: Martinus Nijhoff, 2004), pp. 3–45
Ghanea, N. and Xanthaki, A. (eds.), *Minorities, Peoples and Self-Determination* (Dordrecht: Martinus Nijhoff, 2005)
Gibson, J., 'Community and the Exhaustion of Culture, Creative Territories in Traditional Cultural Expressions', Paper delivered at the AHRB Copyright Research Network 2005 Workshop on Protection of Traditional Culture and Knowledge at Birkbeck University, London, http://www.copyright.bbk.ac.uk/contents/publications/workingpapers.shtml
Gilbert, G., 'Autonomy and Minority Groups – A Legal Right in International Law?' Paper Prepared for the Seventh Session of the Working Group on

Minorities of the Sub-Commission on the Promotion and Protection of Human Rights, UN Doc. E/CN.4/Sub.2/AC.5/2001/CRP.5 (2001)
Grad, R., 'Indigenous Rights and Intellectual Property Law: A Comparison of the United States and Australia' (2003) 13 *Duke Journal of Comparative and International Law* 203–31
Green, J. A., 'The Difference Debate: Reducing Rights to Cultural Flavours' (2000) 33 *Canadian Journal of Political Science* 133–44
Greer, M. A., 'Foreigners in their own Land: Cultural Land and Transnational Corporations – Emergent International Rights and Wrongs' (1998) 38 *Virginia Journal of International Law* 359–64
Grote, A., 'The Status and Rights of Indigenous Peoples in Latin America', (1999) *Zeitschrift für ausländisches öffentliches Recht und Völkerrecht, (Heidelberg Journal of International law)*, Special issue, 497–528
Habermas, J., *Between Facts and Norms* (Cambridge, Mass.: MIT Press, 1996)
Hall, S., 'The Persistent Spectre: Natural Law, International Order and the Limits of Legal Positivism' (2001) 12 *European Journal of International Law* 269–307
Hannikainen, L., 'The Status of Minorities, Indigenous Peoples and Immigrant and Refugee Groups in four Nordic States' 65 (1996) *Nordic Journal of International Law* 1–71
Hannum, H., *Autonomy, Sovereignty and Self-Determination, The Accommodation of Conflicting Rights* (Philadelphia: University of Pennsylvania Press, 1990)
'Self-Determination in the Post-Colonial Era' in D. Clark and R. Williamson, *Self-Determination: International Perspectives* (London: Macmillan Press, 1996), pp. 12–44
'The Protection of Indigenous Rights in the Inter-American System' in D. J. Harris and S. Livingstone (eds.), *The Inter-American System of Human Rights* (Oxford: Clarendon Press, 1998), pp. 323–43
'Conceptual Issues Pertaining to Minorities' in Z. A. Skurbaty (ed.), *Beyond a One-Dimensional State: An Emerging Right to Autonomy?* (Leiden: Martinus Nijhoff, 2004), 153
Harhoff, F., ' Self-Determination, Ethics and Law' in G. Alfredsson and P. Macalister-Smith (eds.), *The Living Law of Nations* (Keln: N. P. Engel, 1996), pp. 169–77
'Constitutional and International Legal Aspects of Aboriginal Rights' (1988) 57 *Nordic Journal of International Law* 289–94
Harris, D. J. and Livingstone, S. (eds.), *The Inter-American System of Human Rights* (Oxford: Clarendon Press, 1998)
Hart, H. L. A., *The Concept of Law* (Oxford: Oxford University Press, 1961)
Hehan, M., 'Delgamuukw v. British Columbia' (1998) 22 *Melbourne University Law Review* 763–82
Heintze, H.-J., 'International Law and Indigenous Peoples' (1995) 45 *Law and the State* 37–67
'On the Legal Understanding of Autonomy' in M. Suksi (ed.), *Autonomy: Applications and Implications*, (The Hague: Kluwer Law International, 1998), pp. 7–32

Held, D., *Political Theory and the Modern State* (California: Stanford University Press, 1984)

Henriksen, J. B., 'The Right of Self-determination: Indigenous Peoples versus States' in P. Aikio and M. Scheinin (eds.), *Operationalizing the Right of Indigenous Peoples to Self-Determination* (Turku/ Åbo: Åbo Akademi University, 2000), pp. 131–41

Henriksen, J., 'Implementation of the Right of Self-Determination of Indigenous Peoples' (2001) 3 *Indigenous Affairs*, pp. 6–21

Heraclides, A., 'Secession, Self-Determination and Non-Intervention: In Quest of a Normative Symbiosis' (1992) 45 *Journal of International Affairs* 399–420

Higgins, R., *The Development of International Law through the Political Organs of the United Nations* (Oxford: Oxford University Press, 1963)

Problems and Processes: International Law and How We Use it (Oxford: Clarendon Press, 1994)

Honig, B., 'Complicating Culture' (1997) 22 *Boston Review* at http://bostonreview.net/BR22.5/honig.html

Horn, F. (ed.), *Economic, Social and Cultural Rights of the Sámi, International and National Aspects* (Rovaniemi: Northern Institute for Environmental and Minority Law, 1988)

Howard, B. R., 'Human Rights and Indigenous People: On the Relevance of International Law for Indigenous Liberation' (1992) 35 *German Yearbook of International Law* 105–6

'Indigenous Peoples and the Right to Self-Determination' (1993) 87 *The American Society of International Law, Proceedings of the 87th Annual Meeting 190–204*

Howard-Hassmann, R., 'Dignity, Community, and Human Rights' in A. An-Na'im (ed.), *Human Rights in Cross-Cultural Perspectives* (Philadelphia: University of Pennsylvania Press, 1992), pp. 81–102

Hutt, S., 'If Geronimo was Jewish: Equal Protection and the Cultural Property Rights of Native Americans' (2003) 24 *Northern Illinois University Law Review* 527–62

Idleman, S., 'Multiculturalism and the Future of Tribal Sovereignty' (2004) 35 *Columbia Human Rights Law Review* 589–660

ILO, 'The Second Session of the ILO Committee of Experts on Indigenous Labour' (1954) 70 *International Labour Review* 418–41

Iorns, C., 'Dedicated Parliamentary Seats for Indigenous Peoples: Political Representation of Indigenous Self-Determination' (2003) 10 *E Law – Murdoch University Electronic Journal of Law*, www.murdoch.edu.au/elaw/issues/v10n4/iorns104nf.html

Iorns, I. C., 'Indigenous Peoples and Self-Determination Challenging State Sovereignty' (1992) 24 *Case Western Reserve Journal of International Law* 199–348

IWGIA, *'Vines that won't Blind', Proceedings of a Conference held at Chiang Mai, Thailand, 1995*, Document 80 (Copenhagen: IWGIA, 1995)

Jennings, I., *The Approach to Self-Government* (Cambridge: Cambridge University Press, 1956)

Johnson, J., 'Why Respect Culture?' (2000) 44 *American Journal of Political Science* 405–18

Jones, P., 'Individuals, Communities and Human Rights' (2000) 26 *Review of International Studies* 199–215

Kamenca, E., 'Human Rights, Peoples' Rights' in J. Crawford (ed.), *The Rights of Peoples* (Oxford: Clarendon Press, 1988), pp. 1–16

Kargbo, F. B., 'International Peacekeeping and Child Soldiers: Problems of Security and Rebuilding' (2004) 37 *Cornell International Law Journal* 485–96

Kelly, E., 'Justice and Communitarian Identity Politics' (2001) 35 *The Journal of Value Enquiry* 71–93

Ketley, H., 'Exclusion by Definition: Access to International Tribunals for the Enforcement of the Collective Rights of Indigenous Peoples' (2001) 8 *International Journal on Minority and Group Rights* 331–68

Kingsbury, B., 'Claims by Non-State Groups' (1992) 25 *Cornell International Law Journal* 481–513

'Self-Determination and Indigenous Peoples' (1992) 86 *American Society of International Law, Proceedings* 383–94

'The Applicability of the International Legal Concept of "Indigenous Peoples" in Asia' in J. R. Bauer and D. Bell (eds.) *The East Asian Challenge for Human Rights* (Cambridge University Press, 1999), pp. 236–77

'Reconstructing Self-Determination: A Relational Approach' in P. Aikio and M. Scheinin (eds.), *Operationalizing the Right of Indigenous Peoples to Self-Determination* (Turku/ Åbo: Åbo Akademi University, 2000), pp. 19–37

Kirgis, F., 'The Degrees of Self-Determination in the United Nations Era' (1994) 88 *American Journal of International Law* 304–10

Klabbers, J. and Lefeber, R., 'Africa: Lost between Self-Determination and *Uti Possedetis*' in C. Brolmann, R. Lefeber and M. Zieck (eds.), *Peoples and Minorities in International Law* (Dordrecht: Martinus Nijhoff Publishers, 1993), pp. 37–76

Kly, Y. N. and Kly, D. (eds.), *In Pursuit of the Right to Self-Determination* (Atlanta: Clarity Press, 2000)

Knop, K., *Diversity and Self-Determination in International Law* (Cambridge: Cambridge University Press, 2002)

Koskenniemi, M., 'National Self-Determination Today: Problems of Legal Theory and Practice', (1994) 43 *International and Comparative Law Quarterly* 241–69

Kouevi, A. G., 'The Right of Self-Determination of Indigenous Peoples: Natural or Granted? An African Perspective' in P. Aikio and M. Scheinin (eds.), *Operationalizing the Right of Indigenous Peoples to Self-Determination* (Turku/ Åbo: Åbo Akademi University, 2000), pp. 143–53

Kukathas, C., 'Are there any Cultural Rights?' (1992) 20 *Political Theory* 105–39

Kymlicka, W., 'Liberal Individualism and Liberal Neutrality' (1989) 99 *Ethics* 883–905

Liberalism, Community and Culture (Oxford University Press, 1991)

'Reply to Kukathas' (1992) 20 *Political Theory* 140–6
Multicultural Citizenship: A Liberal Theory of Minority Rights (Oxford: Clarendon Press, 1995)
'Theorizing Indigenous Rights' (1999) 49 *University of Toronto Law Journal* 281–93
'Justice and Security in the Accommodation of Minority Nationalism' in S. May, T. Modood and E. Squires (eds.), *Ethnicity, Nationalism and Minority Rights*, (Cambridge: Cambridge University Press, 2004), pp. 144–75
(ed.), *The Rights of Minority Cultures* (Oxford: Oxford University Press, 1995)
Lâm, M. C., *At the Edge of the State: Indigenous Peoples and Self-Determination* (New York: Transnational Publishers, 2000)
Leary, V. A., 'Postliberal Strands in Western Human Rights Theory' in A. An-Na'im, *Human Rights in Cross-Cultural Perspectives* (Philadelphia: University of Pennsylvania Press, 1992), pp. 105–32
Legislative Assembly of Queensland, 'Hands on Parliament: A Parliamentary Committee Enquiry into Aboriginal and Torres Strait Islander Peoples' Participation in Queensland's Democratic Processes', Report No. 42, September 2003
Lerner, N., 'The 1989 ILO Convention on Indigenous Populations: New Standards?' (1991) 20 *Israel Yearbook on Human Rights* 223–41
Levy, J. T., 'Sexual Orientation, Exit and Refuge' in A. Eisenberg and J. Spinner-Halev (eds.), *Minorities Within Minorities, Equality, Rights and Diversity* (Cambridge: Cambridge University Press, 2005), pp. 172–88
Lijphart, A., *Democracies: Patterns of Majoritarian and Consensus Government in 21 Countries* (New Haven: Yale University Press, 1984)
Lokan, A., 'From Recognition to Reconciliation: The Functions of Aboriginal Rights Law' (1999) 23 *Melbourne University Law Review* 65–120
Lopez, A., 'For the Recovery and Protection of Traditional Indigenous Knowledge', Paper delivered in the International Workshop on Traditional Knowledge, Panama City, 21–23 September 2005, UN Doc. PFII/2005/WS.TK/6
Lowe, V. and Fitzmaurice, M. (eds.), *Fifty Years of the International Court of Justice, Essays in Honour of Sir Robert Jennings* (Cambridge: Grotius Publications, 1996)
Lowe, V. and Warbrick, C. (eds.), *The United Nations and the Principles of International Law, Essays in Memory of Michael Akehurst*, (London: Routledge, 1995)
Lucas, E., 'Towards an International Declaration on Land Rights' (1984) 33 *Review (International Commission of Jurists)* 61–8
Lumb, R. B., 'Aboriginal Land Rights: Judicial Approaches in Perspective' (1988) 62 ALJ 273–84
MacIntyre, A., 'Justice as a Virtue: Changing Concepts' in S. Avineri and A. de-Shalit (eds.), *Communitarianism and Individualism* (Oxford: Oxford University Press, 1992), pp. 51–64
After Virtue: A Study in Moral Theory (London: Duckworth, 1981)
Macklem, P. and Morgan, E., 'Indigenous Rights in the Inter-American System: The Amicus Brief of the Assembly of First Nations in Awas Tingni v. Republic of Nicaragua' (2000) 22 *Human Rights Quarterly* 569–602

Maclellan, N., 'Indigenous Peoples in the Pacific and the World Conference on Racism' at http://www.tebtebba.org

Makkonen, T., *Identity, Difference and Otherness: The Concepts of 'People', 'Indigenous People' and 'Minority' in International Law* (Helsinki: Helsinki University Press, 2000)

Mannens, W., 'A Structure called Culture' in Y. Donders, K. Henrard, A. Meijknecht and S. Tempelman (eds.), *Law and Cultural Diversity*, SIM Special No. 25 (Utrecht: SIM, 1999)

Mansell, M., 'Australians and Aborigines and the Mabo decision: Just who needs whom the most?' (1993) 15 *Sydney Law Review* 168–77

Manwaring, M., 'A Small Step or a Giant Leap? The Implications of Australia's First Judicial Recognition of Indigenous Land Rights: *Mabo and Others v. State of Queensland*, 107 *A. L.R.* 1 (1992) (Austl.)' (1993) 34 *Harvard International Law Journal* 177–91

May, S., Modood, T. and Squires, E. (eds.), *Ethnicity, Nationalism and Minority Rights*, (Cambridge: Cambridge University Press, 2004)

McCorquodale, R., 'An Inclusive International System' (2004) 17 *Leiden Journal of International Law* 477–504

McDonald, M., 'Should Communities have Rights? Reflections on Liberal Individualism' (1991) 4 *Canadian Journal of Law and Jurisprudence* 217–37

'Liberalism, Community and Culture' (1992) 42 *University of Toronto Law Journal* 113–31

McGoldrick, D., *The Human Rights Committee, its Role in the Development of the ICCPR* (Oxford: Clarendon Press, 1991)

McNeil, K., 'Aboriginal Title and Aboriginal Rights: What's the Connection?' 36 (1997) *Alberta Law Review* 117–48

Meijknecht, A., *Towards International Personality: The Position of Minorities and Indigenous Peoples in International Law* (Oxford: Intersentia, 2001)

Mitnick, E. J., 'Three Models of Group Differentiated Rights' 35 (2004) *Columbia Human Rights Law Review* 215–58

Moore, M., 'International Minorities and Indigenous Self-Determination' in A. Eisenberg and J. Spinner-Halev (eds.), *Minorities within Minorities, Equality, Rights and Diversity*, (Cambridge: Cambridge University Press, 2005), pp. 271–93

Morgan, R., 'Advancing Indigenous Rights at the United Nations: Strategic Framing and its Impact on the Normative Development of International Law' (2004) 13 *Social and Legal Studies* 481–500

Morris, G. T., 'In Support of the Right of Self-Determination for Indigenous Peoples under International Law' (1986) 29 *German Yearbook of International Law* 277–316

Moses, T., 'The Right of Self-Determination and Its Significance to the Survival of Indigenous Peoples' in P. Aikio and M. Scheinin (eds.), *Operationalizing the Right of Indigenous Peoples to Self-Determination* (Turku/ Åbo: Åbo Akademi University, 2000), pp. 155–77

Musgrave, T. D., *Self-Determination and National Minorities* (Oxford: Clarendon Press, 1997)

Myntti, K., 'National Minorities, Indigenous Peoples and Various Modes of Political Participation' in F. Horn (ed.), *Minorities and the Right to Political Participation* (Rovaniemi, Northern Institute for Environmental and Minority Law, 1996), pp. 1-26

'The Right to Self-Determination and Effective Participation' in P. Aikio and M. Scheinin (eds.), *Operationalizing the Right of Indigenous Peoples to Self-Determination* (Turku/ Åbo: Åbo Akademi University, 2000), pp. 85–130

Nettheim, G., 'Peoples and Populations: Indigenous Peoples and the Rights of Peoples' in J. Crawford (ed.), *The Rights of Peoples* (Oxford: Clarendon Press, 1988), pp. 107–26

Niec, H., *Cultural Rights and Wrongs* (Leicester: Institute of Art and Law and UNESCO, 1998)

Nino, C., *The Ethics of Human Rights* (Oxford: Oxford University Press, 1991)

Novellino, D., 'The Ominous Switch: From Indigenous Forest Management to Conservation - The case of the Batak on Palawan Island, the Philippines' in M. Colchester and C. Erni (eds.), *Indigenous Peoples and Protected Areas in South and Southeast Asia*, IWGIA Document No. 97, (Copenhagen: IWGIA, 1999) 250–97

Nwabueze, R. N., 'Ethnopharmacology, Patents and the Politics of Plants' Genetic Resources' (2003–4) 11 *Cardozo Journal of International and Comparative Law* 585–632

Nyamu, C. I., 'How Should Human Rights and Development Respond to Cultural Legitimization of Gender Hierarchy in Developing Countries' (2000) 41 *Harvard International Law Journal* 381–418

Oestreich, J. E., 'Liberal Theory and Minority Group Rights' (1999) 21 *Human Rights Quarterly* 108–33

Okafor, O. C., 'Entitlement, Process and Legitimacy in the Emergent Law of Secession' (2002) 9 *International Journal on Minority and Group Rights* 41–70

Okin, S., 'Is Multiculturalism Bad for Women' (1997) 22 *Boston Review* at http://www.bostonreview.net/BR22.5/toc.html

Okin, S. M., 'Multiculturalism and Feminism: No Simple Question, No Simple Answers' in A. Eisenberg and J. Spinner-Halev (eds.), *Minorities Within Minorities, Equality, Rights and Diversity* (Cambridge: Cambridge University Press, 2005), pp. 67–89

Ostergard, R. J., 'Intellectual Property: A Universal Human Right?' (1999) 21 *Human Rights Quarterly* 156–78

Palermo, F. and Woelk, J., 'Cross-border Cooperation as an Indicator for Institutional Evolution of Autonomy: The case of Trentino-South Tyrol' in Z. Skurbaty (ed.) *Beyond a One-Dimensional State: An Emerging Right to Autonomy?* (Leiden: Martinus Nijhoff Publishers, 2005), pp. 277–304

Parekh, B., 'A Varied Moral World' (1997) 22 *Boston Review* at http://bostonreview.net/BR22.5/parekh.html

Patel, J. (ed.), *Addressing Discrimination in the Vienna Declaration* (Tokyo: IMADR, 1995)

Pentassuglia, G., *Minorities in International Law* (Strasbourg: Council of Europe, 2002)

Pertney, W. F., *The Aboriginal Rights Provisions in the Constitution Act* (Saskatoon: Native Law Centre, 1987)

Phillips, A. and Rosas, A. (eds.), *Universal Minority Rights* (London and Åbo: Minority Rights Group and Åbo Akademi University, 1995)

Phung, C., 'Internally Displaced Persons and Refugees: Conceptual Differences and Similarities' (2000) 18 *Netherlands Quarterly of Human Rights* 215–29

Pritchard, S., *The United Nations Draft Declaration on the Rights of Indigenous Peoples: An Analysis* (New South Wales: Faculty of Law, University of New South Wales, 1996)

'Working Group on Indigenous Populations: Mandate, Standard-setting Activities and Future Perspectives' in S. Pritchard (ed.), *Indigenous Peoples, the United Nations and Human Rights*, London: Zed Books, 1998, 40–64

Prott, L. V. and O'Keefe, P. J., *Law and the Cultural Heritage*, Vol. I (London: Professional Books, 1984)

Quane, H., 'A Right to Self-Determination for the Kosovo Albanians?' (2000) 13 *Leiden Journal of International Law* 219–27

Raikka, J., 'Autonomy and Cultural Rights' in Z. Skurbaty (ed.), *Beyond a One-Dimensional State: An Emerging Right to Autonomy?* (Leiden: Martinus Nijhoff Publishers, 2005), pp. 211–75

Ramcharan, B. G., 'Individual, Collective and Group Rights: History, Theory, Practice and Contemporary Evolution' (1993) 1 *International Journal of Group Rights* 27–43

Rawls, J., *The Theory of Justice* (Cambridge, Mass.: Harvard University Press, 1971)

Raz, J., *The Morality of Freedom* (Oxford: Clarendon Press, 1986)

'Legal Principles and the Limits of Law' (1972) 81 *Yale Law Journal* 823–54

Rens, J., 'The Andean Indian Programme' (1961) 84 *International Labour Review* 423–61

'The Development of the Andean Programme and its Future' (1963) 88 *International Labour Review* 547–63

Rosas, A., 'The Right to Self-Determination' in A. Eide, C. Krause and A. Rosas (eds.), *Economic, Social and Cultural Rights, A Textbook* (Dordrecht: Martinus Nijhoff, 1995), pp. 79–86

Rotman, L. I., 'Defining Parameters: Aboriginal Rights, Treaty Rights, and the *Sparrow* Justificatory Test' (1997) 36 *Alberta Law Review* 149–79

Sandel, M., 'The Procedural Republic and the Unencumbered Self' in S. Avineri and A. de-Shalit (eds.), *Communitarianism and Individualism* (Oxford: Oxford University Press, 1992), pp. 12–28

Sautman, B., ' "Cultural Genocide" and Tibet' (2003) 38 *Texas International Law Journal* 173–95

Schachter, O., *International Law in Theory and Practice* (Martinus Nijhoff Publishers, 1991)

'Sovereignty – Then and Now' in R. St. J. Macdonald (ed.), *Essays in Honour of Wang Tieya* (Dordrecht: Martinus Nijhoff, 1993), pp. 671–88
Scheinin, M., 'What are Indigenous Peoples?' in N. Ghanea and A. Xanthaki (eds.), *Minorities, Peoples and Self-Determination* (Dordrecht: Martinus Nijhoff, 2005), pp. 3–14;
Schulte-Tenckhoff, M., 'The Right of Persons Belonging to Minorities to Enjoy their own Culture', Working paper submitted to the 1997 Working Group on Minorities, UN Doc. E/CN.4/Sub.2/ AC.5/1997/WP.7
Scott, C., 'Indigenous Self-Determination and Decolonisation of the International Imagination: A Plea' (1996) 18 *Human Rights Quarterly* 814–20
Scott, J., 'Indigenous Peoples and the Creation of an Inclusive International Legal System', Paper delivered at Carnegie Council on Ethics and International Affairs, New York, on 14 April 2004
Shaw, M. N., 'Re: Order in Council P.C. 1996–7 of 30 September 1996' in A. Bayevsky, *Self-Determination in International Law: Quebec and Lessons Learned* (Dordrecht: Kluwer Law International, 2000), pp. 125–50
Shaughnessy, M. F. and Sardoc M., 'An Interview with Michael Walzer' (2002) 21 *Studies in Philosophy and Education* 65–75
Shihata, I., *The World Bank Inspection Panel* (Oxford: Oxford University Press, 1994)
Shivji, G., *The Concept of Human Rights in Africa* (London: Codesria, 1989)
Shyllon, F., 'The Right to a Cultural Past: African Viewpoints' in H. Niec (ed.), *Cultural Rights and Wrongs* (Paris: UNESCO, 1998), pp. 103–19
Sicilianos, L.-A. and Gavouneli, M. (eds.), *Scientific and Technological Developments and Human Rights* (Athens: Ant. N. Sakoulas Publishers, 1996)
Skurbaty, Z. A. (ed.), *Beyond a One-Dimensional State: An Emerging Right to Autonomy?* (Leiden: Martinus Nijhoff, 2004)
Spiliopoulou Åkermark, A., *Justifications of Minority Protection in International Law* (The Hague: Kluwer International, 1996)
'The World Bank and Indigenous Peoples' in N. Ghanea and A. Xanthaki (eds.), *Minorities, Peoples and Self-Determination* (Dordrecht: Martinus Nijhoff, 2005), pp. 15–33
Spinner- Halev, J., 'Autonomy, Association and Pluralism' in A. Eisenberg and J. Spinner-Halev (eds.), *Minorities Within Minorities, Equality, Rights and Diversity* (Cambridge: Cambridge University Press, 2005), pp. 157–71
Spiry, E., 'From "Self-Determination" to a Right to "Self-Development" for Indigenous Groups' (1995) 38 *German Yearbook of International Law* 129–52
Stavenhagen, R., 'Cultural Rights: A Social Science Perspective' in H. Niec, *Cultural Rights and Wrongs* (Leicester: Institute of Art and Law and UNESCO, 1998), pp. 1–20
'Self-Determination: Right or Demon?' in D. Clark and R. Williamson, *Self-Determination: International Perspectives* (London: Macmillan Press, 1996), pp. 1–11
Steiner, H., 'Ideals and Counter-ideals in the Struggle over Autonomy Regimes for Minorities' 66 (1991) *Notre Dame Law Review* 1539–60

Steven, S. (ed.), *Conservation through Cultural Survival, Indigenous Peoples and Protected Areas* (Washington: Island Press, 1997)

Suksi, M. (ed.), *Autonomy: Applications and Implications* (The Hague: Kluwer Law International, 1998)

Sutherland, J., Craig, J., and Posey, D., 'Emerging New Legal Standards for Comprehensive Rights' (1997) 27 *Environmental Policy and Law* 13–30

Swepston, L., 'Indigenous and Tribal Populations: A Return to Centre Stage' (1987) 126 *International Labour Review* 447–55

'Economic, Social and Cultural Rights under the 1989 ILO Convention' in F. Horn (ed.), *Economic, Social and Cultural Rights of the Sámi, International and National Aspects* (Rovaniemi: Northern Institute for Environmental and Minority Law, 1988), pp. 38–46

Swepston, L. and Plant, R., 'International Standards and the Protection of the Land Rights of Indigenous and Tribal Populations' (1985) 124 *International Labour Review* 91–106

Tamir, Y., *Liberal Nationalism* (Princeton: Princeton University Press, 1993)

'Who do you trust?' (1997) 22 *Boston Review* at http://www.bostonreview.net/BR22.5/toc.html

Tarayia, G. N., 'The Legal Perspectives of the Maasai Culture, Customs, and Traditions' (2004) 21 *Arizona Journal of International and Comparative Law* 183–222

Taylor, C., 'Atomism' in S. Avineri and A. de-Shalit (eds.), *Communitarianism and Individualism* (Oxford: Oxford University Press, 1992), pp. 29–50

'The Politics of Recognition' in A. Gudmann, *Multiculturalism* (Princeton: Princeton University Press, 1994), pp. 25–73

Philosophical Arguments (Harvard: Harvard University Press, 1995)

Tennant, C., 'Indigenous Peoples, International Institutions, and the International Legal Literature 1945–1993' (1996) 16 *Human Rights Quarterly* 1–57

Tennant, C. C., and Turpel, M. E., 'A Case Study of Indigenous Peoples: Genocide, Ethnocide and Self-Determination' (1990) 59 *Nordic Journal of International Law* 287–319

Thornberry, P., 'Who is Indigenous?' in F. Horn (ed.), *Economic, Social and Cultural Rights of the Sámi, International and National Aspects* (Rovaniemi: Northern Institute for Environmental and Minority Law, 1988), pp. 1–37

'Self-Determination, Minorities, Human Rights: A Review of International Instruments' (1989) 38 *International and Comparative Law Quarterly* 867–89

International Law and the Rights of Minorities (Oxford: Clarendon Press, 1991)

'The Democratic or Internal Aspect of Self-Determination with Some Remarks on Federalism' in C. Tomuschat (ed.), *Modern Law of Self-Determination* (London: Martinus Nijhoff, 1993), pp. 101–38

'The UN Declaration on the Rights of Persons belonging to National or Ethnic, Religious and Linguistic Minorities: Background, Analysis, Observations and an Update' in A. Phillips and A. Rosas (eds.), *Universal Minority Rights*

(London and Abo: Minority Rights Group and Abo Akademi University, 1995), pp. 26–7

'The Principle of Self-Determination' in V. Lowe and C. Warbrick (eds.), *The United Nations and the Principles of International Law, Essays in Memory of Michael Akehurst*, (London: Routledge, 1995), pp. 175–203

'Images of Autonomy and Individual and Collective Rights in International Instruments on the Rights of Minorities' in M. Suksi (ed.), *Autonomy: Applications and Implications* (The Hague: Kluwer Law International, 1998), 97–124

'Ethnic Dimensions of International Human Rights' in A. Hegarty and S. Leonard (eds.), *Human Rights, An Agenda for the 21st Century* (London: Cavendish Publishers, 1999), pp. 355–77

'Self-Determination and Indigenous Peoples: Objections and Responses' in P. Aikio and M. Scheinin (eds.), *Operationalizing the Right of Indigenous Peoples to Self-Determination* (Turku/ Åbo: Åbo Akademi University, 2000), pp. 39–64

Indigenous Peoples and Human Rights (Manchester: Manchester University Press, 2002)

Tomei M., and Swepston L., *Indigenous and Tribal Peoples: A Guide to ILO Convention No. 169* (Geneva: International Labour Organisation, 1996)

Tomuschat, C. (ed), *Modern Law of Self-Determination* (London: Martinus Nijhoff, 1993)

Trifunovska, S., 'One Theme in Two Variations – Self-Determination for Minorities and Indigenous Peoples' (1997) 5 *International Journal on Minority and Group Rights* 175–97

Triggs, G., 'Australia's Indigenous Peoples and International Law: Validity of the *Native Title Amendment Act 1998* (Cth)' 23 (1999) *Melbourne University Law Review* 372–415

Turpel, M. E., 'Indigenous Peoples' Rights to Political Participation and Self-Determination' (1992) 25 *Cornell International Law Journal* 579–602

'Draft Declaration on the Rights of Indigenous Peoples – Commentary' [1994] 1 *Canadian Native Law Reporter* 50–2

Ülgen, Ö., 'The Labour Exploitation of Indigenous Peoples: The Interface between Labour Law and Human Rights Law' (PhD Thesis, University of Nottingham, 1999)

United Nations, Code of Conduct on Transnational Corporations, UN ESCOR, Organisational Session for 1998, UN Doc. E/1998/39/Add.1

United Nations, 'Internally Displaced Persons', Report of the Representative of the Secretary-General. Francis M. Deng, submitted pursuant to Commission on Human Rights Resolution 1995/57, Compilation and Analysis of Legal Norms, UN Doc. E/CN.4/1996/52/Add.2

United Nations, 'Legal Commentary on the Concept of Free, Prior and Informed Consent', Expanded Working Paper submitted by Antoinella-Iulia Motoc and the Tebtebba Foundation offering guidelines to govern the practice of implementation of the principle of free, prior and informed consent of indigenous peoples in relation to development affecting their lands and natural resources, UN Doc. E/CN.4/Sub.2/AC.4/2005/WP.1 of 14 July 2005

United Nations, Paper on 'Local and Indigenous Knowledge of the Natural World, An Overview of Programmes and Projects', Paper delivered by the Secretariat of UNESCO

United Nations, Paper on 'The Convention on Biological Diversity and Traditional Knowledge' by the Secretariat of the Convention on Biological Diversity, delivered at the International Workshop on Traditional Knowledge, Panama City, 21–23 September 2005, UN Doc. PFII/2005/WS.TK/1

United Nations, Preliminary Report of the Special Rapporteur, E.-I. Daes, submitted in conformity with Sub-Commission Resolution 1993/44 and Decision 1994/105 of the Commission on Human Rights, UN Doc. E/CN.4/Sub.2/1994/31

United Nations, 'Preliminary Report on the Relationship between the Enjoyment of Human Rights, in particular Economic, Social and Cultural Rights, and Income Distribution', prepared by J. José Bengoa, in conformity with Resolution 1994/40 of the Sub-commission and Decision 1995/105 of the Commission on Human Rights, UN Doc. E/CN.4/Sub.2/1995/14

United Nations, 'Strategies to Combat Racism and Racial Discrimination: Past Experiences and Present Perspectives', Background paper prepared by Theodor van Boven, UN Doc.E/CN.4/1999/WG.1/BP.7

United Nations, 'Study of the Problem of Discrimination against Indigenous Populations', by Jose R. Martinez Cobo, Special Rapporteur of the Sub-Commission on the Prevention on Discrimination and Protection of Minorities, Geneva: United Nations, 1986, UN Doc. E/CN.4/Sub.2/1983/21

United Nations, 'Study Concerning the Right to Restitution, Compensation and Rehabilitation for Victims of Gross Violations of Human Rights and Fundamental Freedoms', Final Report submitted by Theo van Boven, Special Rapporteur, UN Doc. E/CN.4/Sub.2/1993/8

United Nations, 'Study on the Protection of the Cultural and Intellectual Property of Indigenous Peoples', by Erica-Irene Daes, Special Rapporteur for the Sub-Commission on Prevention of Discrimination and Protection of Minorities and Chairperson of the Working Group on Indigenous Populations, UN Doc. E/CN.4/Sub.2/1993/28

United Nations, 'Study on the Rights of Persons Belonging to Ethnic, Religious and Linguistic Minorities', by the Special Rapporteur A. Capotorti for the UN Sub-Commission on Prevention of Discrimination and Protection of Minorities, UN Doc. E/CN4/Sub2/384/Add.1-7, Add. 2

United Nations, The Causes of, and Remedies for, Racial Discrimination, Background paper prepared by Michael Banton, UN Doc. E/CN.4/1999/WG.1/BP.6 (1999)

United Nations, Transnational Investments and Operations on the Lands of Indigenous Peoples, Report of the Centre on Transnational Corporation submitted pursuant to Sub-Commission resolution 1990/26 UN Doc. E/CN.4/Sub.2/1994/40

United Nations, Working paper on the question of the ownership and control of the cultural property of indigenous peoples prepared by Erica-Irene Daes, UN Doc. E/CN.4/Sub.2/1991/34

United Nations, Working paper prepared by R. Roldan, in Report of Expert Seminar on Practical Experiences Regarding Indigenous Land Rights and Claims, held at Whitehorse, Canada in March 1996, UN Doc. E/CN.4/Sub.2/AC.4/1996/6/Add.1

Vaddhanuphuti, C., 'The Present Situation of Indigenous Peoples in Thailand' in *'Vines that won't Blind', Proceedings of a Conference held at Chiang Mai, Thailand, 1995*, IWGIA Document 80, pp. 79–88

Van der Vlist, L. (ed.), *Voices of the Earth, Indigenous Peoples, New Partners and the Right to Self-Determination in Practice* (Ulterecht: The Netherlands Centre for Indigenous Peoples, 1994)

Van der Vyer, J. D., 'The Right of Self-Determination and its Enforcement' (2004) 10 *ILSA Journal of International and Comparative Law* 421–36

Van Dyke, V., 'Justice as Fairness: For Groups?' (1975) 69 *American Political Science Review* 607–14

'The Individual, the State and Ethnic Communities in Political Theory' (1977) 29 *World Politics* 343–69

'Human Rights and Rights of Groups' (1994) 18 *American Journal of Political Science* 725–41

Velin, J. A., 'Making the ILO Convention on Indigenous People Work, Sámi People Seek their Due' (1997) 21 *The World of Work, The Magazine of the ILO* 11–13

Vrdoljak, A. F., 'Minorities, Cultural Rights and the Protection of Intangible Cultural Heritage', Paper presented at the ESIL Research Forum on International Law, Conference on Contemporary Issues, Graduate Institute of International Studies, Geneva, 26–28 May 2005

Waldron, J., 'Minority Cultures and the Cosmopolitan Alternative' in W. Kymlicka (ed.), *The Rights of Minority Cultures* (Oxford: Oxford University Press, 1995), pp. 93–119

Wassendorf, K. (ed.), *Challenging Politics: Indigenous Peoples Experiences with Political Parties and Elections* (Copenhagen: IWGIA, 2001)

Wellman, C. H., 'Liberalism, Communitarianism and Group Rights' (1999) 18 *Law and Philosophy* 13–40

Wheatley, S., 'Deliberative Democracy and Minorities' (2003) 14 *European Journal of International Law* 507–27

Wiessner, S., 'Rights and Status of Indigenous Peoples: A Global Comparative and International Legal Analysis' (1999) 12 *Harvard Human Rights Journal* 57–128

'The Kurdish Issue and Beyond: Territorial Communities Rivaling the State' (2004) 98 *American Society of International Law Proceedings* 107–8

Williams, P. and Pecci, F., 'Earned Sovereignty: Bridging the Gap between Sovereignty and Self-Determination' (2004) 40 *Stanford Journal of International Law* 347–86

WIPO, 'Protection of Traditional Knowledge: A Global Intellectual Property Issue', Document prepared by the International Bureau of the WIPO in the *Roundtable on Intellectual Property and Traditional Knowledge*, organised by the World Intellectual Property Organisation, Geneva, November 1 and 2, 1999, WIPO Doc. WIPO/IPTK/RT/99/2

World Commission on Culture and Development, *Report: Our Creative Diversity* (Paris: UNESCO, 1995)

Xanthaki, A., 'Land Rights of Indigenous Peoples in Southeast Asia' (2003) 2 *Melbourne Journal of International Law* 467–96

'Indigenous Rights in the Russian Federation: The Case of Numerically Small Peoples of the Russian North, Siberia and Far East' (2004) 26 *Human Rights Quarterly* 74–105

'The Meaning of Self-Determination' in N. Ghanea and A. Xanthaki (eds.), *Minorities, Peoples and Self-Determination* (Dordrecht: Martinus Nijhoff, 2005), pp. 15–33

Young, I. M., 'Together in Difference: Transforming the Logic of Group Political Conflict' in W. Kymlicka (ed.), *The Rights of Minority Cultures* (Oxford: Oxford University Press, 1995), pp. 155–78

'Two Concepts of Self-Determination' in S. May, T. Modood and E. Squires (eds.), *Ethnicity, Nationalism and Minority Rights*, (Cambridge: Cambridge University Press, 2004), pp. 176–95

Index

CAMBRIDGE STUDIES IN INTERNATIONAL AND COMPARATIVE LAW

Books in the series

Indigenous Rights and United Nations Standards
Alexandra Xanthaki

International Refugee Law and Socio-Economic Rights
Michelle Foster

The Protection of Cultural Property in Armed Conflict
Roger O'Keefe

Interpretation and Revision of International Boundary Decisions
Kaiyan Kaikobad

Multinationals and Corporate Social Responsibility
Limitations and Opportunities in International Law
Jennifer A. Zerk

Judiciaries within Europe: A Comparative Review
John Bell

Law in Times of Crisis
Emergency Powers in Theory and Practice
Oren Gross and Fionnuala Ní Aoláin

Vessel-Source Marine Pollution
The Law and Politics of International Regulation
Alan Tan

Enforcing Obligations Erga Omnes *in International Law*
Christian J. Tams

Non-Governmental Organisations in International Law
Anna-Karin Lindblom

Democracy, Minorities and International Law
Steven Wheatley

Prosecuting International Crimes: Selectivity and the International Law Regime
Robert Cryer

Compensation for Personal Injury in English, German and Italian Law: A Comparative Outline
Basil Markesinis, Michael Coester, Guido Alpa, Augustus Ullstein

Dispute Settlement in the UN Convention on the Law of the Sea
Natalie Klein

The International Protection of Internally Displaced Persons
Catherine Phuong

Imperialism, Sovereignty and the Making of International Law
Antony Anghie

Necessity, Proportionality and the Use of Force by States
Judith Gardam

International Legal Argument in the Permanent Court of International Justice: The Rise of the International Judiciary
Ole Spiermann

Great Powers and Outlaw States: Unequal Sovereigns in the International Legal Order
Gerry Simpson

Local Remedies in International Law
C. F. Amerasinghe

Reading Humanitarian Intervention: Human Rights and the Use of Force in International Law
Anne Orford

Conflict of Norms in Public International Law: How WTO Law Relates to Other Rules of Law
Joost Pauwelyn

Transboundary Damage in International Law
Hanqin Xue

European Criminal Procedures
Edited by Mireille Delmas-Marty and John Spencer

The Accountability of Armed Opposition Groups in International Law
Liesbeth Zegveld

Sharing Transboundary Resources: International Law and Optimal Resource Use
Eyal Benvenisti

International Human Rights and Humanitarian Law
René Provost

Remedies Against International Organisations
Karel Wellens

Diversity and Self-Determination in International Law
Karen Knop

The Law of Internal Armed Conflict
Lindsay Moir

International Commercial Arbitration and African States: Practice, Participation and Institutional Development
Amazu A. Asouzu

The Enforceability of Promises in European Contract Law
James Gordley

International Law in Antiquity
David J. Bederman

Money Laundering: A New International Law Enforcement Model
Guy Stessens

Good Faith in European Contract Law
Reinhard Zimmermann and Simon Whittaker

On Civil Procedure
J. A. Jolowicz

Trusts: A Comparative Study
Maurizio Lupoi

The Right to Property in Commonwealth Constitutions
Tom Allen

International Organisations Before National Courts
August Reinisch

The Changing International Law of High Seas Fisheries
Francisco Orrego Vicuña

Trade and the Environment: A Comparative Study of EC and US Law
Damien Geradin

Unjust Enrichment: A Study of Private Law and Public Values
Hanoch Dagan

Religious Liberty and International Law in Europe
Malcolm D. Evans

Ethics and Authority in International Law
Alfred P. Rubin

Sovereignty Over Natural Resources: Balancing Rights and Duties
Nico Schrijver

The Polar Regions and the Development of International Law
Donald R. Rothwell

Fragmentation and the International Relations of Micro-States: Self-determination and Statehood
Jorri Duursma

Principles of the Institutional Law of International Organizations
C. F. Amerasinghe